An Introduction to Astrology
and
A Grammar of Astrology

An Introduction to Astrology
and
A Grammar of Astrology

WILLIAM LILLY
AND
ZADKIEL

Athens ‡ Manchester

An Introduction to Astrology and A Grammar of Astrology

Old Book Publishing Ltd

Book Cover Design: Old Book Publishing Ltd

Copyright © 2011 Old Book Publishing Ltd
All rights reserved.

Title of original: An Introduction to Astrology: by William Lilly with numerous emendations, adapted to the improved state of the science in the present day: A Grammar of Astrology, and Tables for calculating nativities.
Originally published in 1852 by H. G. Bohn

ISBN–10: 1-78107-042-3
ISBN–13: 978-1-78107-042-0

EDITOR'S NOTE

Old Book Publishing Ltd takes care in preserving the wording and images of the original books. For this reason we have invested in technology that enables us to enhance the quality of such reproduction. This investment helps overcome problems encountered when reproducing old books, such as stains, coloured paper, discolouration of ink, yellowed pages, see-through and onion skin type paper.

This reproduction book, produced from digital images of the original, may contain occasional defects such as missing pages or blemishes due to the original source content or were introduced by the scanning process.

These are scanned pages and the quality of print represents accurately the print quality of the original book, though we may have been able to enhance it.

As this book has been scanned and/or reformatted from the original we cannot guarantee that it is error-free or contains the full content of the original.

However, we believe that this work is culturally important, and despite its imperfections, have elected to bring it back into print as part of our commitment to the preservation of printed works.

Old Book Publishing

AN

INTRODUCTION TO ASTROLOGY:

BY

WILLIAM LILLY:

WITH

NUMEROUS EMENDATIONS, ADAPTED TO THE IMPROVED STATE
OF THE SCIENCE IN THE PRESENT DAY:

A

GRAMMAR OF ASTROLOGY,

AND

TABLES FOR CALCULATING NATIVITIES.

BY

ZADKIEL.

LONDON:
H. G. BOHN, YORK STREET, COVENT GARDEN.
MDCCCLII.

J. BILLING,
PRINTER AND STEREOTYPER,
WOKING, SURREY.

PREFACE.

AFTER a lapse of 205 years since the first publication, in 1647, of *Lilly's Introduction to Astrology*, there would be no necessity for an apology for its re-appearance, were it not for the prevailing fashion of the day, which is to rail at and vituperate that science, and all who dare to say a word, not in its favour, but in favour of examining into its merits, with a view to ascertain what were the grounds on which our honest ancestors believed, and strictly followed, that which we conceive only fit for ridicule. As I have long outlived the days when I, like many others, thought myself at liberty to laugh at, and condemn, what I did not understand; the world will forgive me if I be bold enough to advise those who value truth, to spend a few days (and but a few days will be necessary) in examining the principles laid down in this work, and applying them to their own individual cases, before they join the herd of learned and unlearned in pledging their words to a false assertion, viz. that Astrology is an unfounded science. If any man will take the trouble to examine for himself, and should find that the prejudices of his education against the science of foreseeing the future, and many other matters which it teaches, are in reality well-founded, and that it has no claims to truth, then will he have the proud satisfaction of knowing, that his opinions on a matter of some consequence are based on experiment, and are the result of his own conviction, not of another person's assertion. On the other hand, if he find truth flash with lightning force upon his mind, and convince him that Astrology, notwithstanding prejudice and abuse, is founded in nature, and is indeed a noble science, given by a benevolent Creator to enlighten man in his wanderings, and enable him to shun the vice and folly which his passions throw in his path; then will he, if a spark of piety exist within his breast, offer thanks to that Creator for the blessing he has discovered. In either case, he must admit that I do him a service in putting forth this plain and simple means of discovering the truth.

This is "the age of enquiry;" and yet prejudice continues to press down her leaden foot upon the neck of examination in this matter. I can only attribute the

PREFACE.

AFTER a lapse of 205 years since the first publication, in 1647, of *Lilly's Introduction to Astrology*, there would be no necessity for an apology for its re-appearance, were it not for the prevailing fashion of the day, which is to rail at and vituperate that science, and all who dare to say a word, not in its favour, but in favour of examining into its merits, with a view to ascertain what were the grounds on which our honest ancestors believed, and strictly followed, that which we conceive only fit for ridicule. As I have long outlived the days when I, like many others, thought myself at liberty to laugh at, and condemn, what I did not understand; the world will forgive me if I be bold enough to advise those who value truth, to spend a few days (and but a few days will be necessary) in examining the principles laid down in this work, and applying them to their own individual cases, before they join the herd of learned and unlearned in pledging their words to a false assertion, viz. that Astrology is an unfounded science. If any man will take the trouble to examine for himself, and should find that the prejudices of his education against the science of foreseeing the future, and many other matters which it teaches, are in reality well-founded, and that it has no claims to truth, then will he have the proud satisfaction of knowing, that his opinions on a matter of some consequence are based on experiment, and are the result of his own conviction, not of another person's assertion. On the other hand, if he find truth flash with lightning force upon his mind, and convince him that Astrology, notwithstanding prejudice and abuse, is founded in nature, and is indeed a noble science, given by a benevolent Creator to enlighten man in his wanderings, and enable him to shun the vice and folly which his passions throw in his path; then will he, if a spark of piety exist within his breast, offer thanks to that Creator for the blessing he has discovered. In either case, he must admit that I do him a service in putting forth this plain and simple means of discovering the truth.

This is "the age of enquiry;" and yet prejudice continues to press down her leaden foot upon the neck of examination in this matter. I can only attribute the pitiable fact to the circumstance of there being no recent publications on those parts of Astrology which are the most easily acquired. The art of *Nativities* requires many years of patient experimenting before it can be well understood, and practised with certainty and satisfaction. The art of *Atmospherical Astrology*, and also that of *Mundane Astrology*, alike demand much time to penetrate their arcana, and a good education to follow their practice. Hence we may account for their comparatively confined study: few have either the abilities or the opportunity to wrestle with their difficulties.

But *Horary Astrology*, the chief subject in this work, may be speedily learned by any person of even moderate abilities; and may, as far as regards its elementary difficulties, be mastered in a few days' study. It may be well understood, and reduced to constant practice in less than a quarter of a year, and no one will find himself at a loss for occasions to test its reality or its utility; for his own avocations, and the affairs of his friends, will offer these almost daily. If a proposition of *any nature* be made to any individual, about the result of which he is anxious, and therefore uncertain whether to accede to it or not, let him but note the hour and minute when it was *first* made, and erect a figure of the heavens, as herein taught, and his doubts will be instantly resolved. He may thus, in five minutes, learn infallibly whether the affair will succeed or not; and, consequently, whether it is prudent to adopt the offer made or not. If he examine the sign on the 1st house of the figure, the planet therein, or the planet ruling the sign, *will exactly describe the party making the offer*, both in person and character; and this may at once convince the inquirer for truth of the reality of the principles of the science.

Moreover, the descending sign, &c. will *describe his own person and character;* a farther proof of the truth of the science, if he require it. Here, then, is a ready test of the *truth* of Astrology. Will its adversaries dare to make its application? It would, methinks, be better than relaxing the broad muscles, which ever denote ignorance and surprise, the feelings which, combined, are the undoubted source of laughter; the only argument of the idiot, the ready resource of the ignorant.

In editing this work, my chief object has been to render it useful to the student in Astrology, and so, by forwarding the science, to promote the general interests of humanity.

With this view I have re-written those parts of the work which modern discoveries in Astronomy and Astrology have rendered obsolete. *Tables for calcu-*

lating Nativities and a *Grammar of Astrology* are adjoined, and every ingredient of the science given which the student is likely to require.

As regards the deviations I have made from the rules of the author, they are few, and founded on much experience. I have omitted his chapters on nativities, as in that part of the science he was less perfect than in any other; the reason being that he relied on essential dignities, which are, by my experience, of little, if any, avail. The rules for calculating arcs of direction will be found in the *Grammar*.

In conclusion, I have no desire to offend any class of men by putting forth this work: I do not know whether I should not respect even prejudice, for the sake of peace, were it not that I cannot conscientiously consent to abandon truth in the effort. I am callous to the puny efforts of critics who may desire to pour on me the waters of vituperation or ridicule, having already passed through a flood. After many years' experience, I have found the laws of Astrology unfailing; and as I can discover no prohibition of its practice in the Word of God, I am prepared to defend it against all the foolish attacks of those who falsely declare that it upholds fatality, or is opposed to the providence or the revelation of the Deity. And I am contented, with God's blessing, to give up the ghost in the firm persuasion, that, in maintaining what I believe is the truth in this respect, I shall meet, hereafter, through the goodness of God and the merits of my Saviour, with a merciful judgment.

I am, reader, your devoted friend and well-wisher in all science which may honour God and benefit mankind,

ZADKIEL.

TABLE OF CONTENTS

OF THE INTRODUCTION TO ASTROLOGY.

	Page
Life of William Lilly	1
Epistle to the Student in Astrology	10
Introduction to Astrology	13
Of the Planets	ib.
The Signs of the Zodiac	14
—— Northern Signs	ib.
—— Southern Signs	ib.
Diagram of the Sun's Motion in the Zodiac	15
Tropical Signs	16
Equinoctial Signs	ib.
Double-bodied Signs	ib.
Moveable ditto	ib.
Common ditto	ib.
Fixed ditto	ib.
Fiery ditto	ib.
Earthy ditto	ib.
Airy ditto	ib.
Watery ditto	ib.
Dragon's Head and Tail	16, 52
———— to find the place of	17
Figure of the Twelve Houses	20
Erecting Figure of the Heavens	21
Of the Aspects	24
—— Zodiacal ditto	ib.
Orbs of the Planets	25
—— Mundane Aspects	ib.
Of Parallels	ib.
Nature and Signification of the Twelve Houses	27
Of the First House	ib.
——— Second ditto	29
——— Third ditto	ib.

TABLE OF CONTENTS.

	Page
Of the Fourth House	30
———— Fifth ditto	ib.
———— Sixth ditto	31
———— Seventh ditto	31
———— Eighth ditto	32
———— Ninth ditto	ib.
———— Tenth ditto	33
———— Eleventh ditto	ib.
———— Twelfth ditto	34
Of Saturn and his Significations	35
— Jupiter and his Significations	38
— Mars and his Significations	40
— the Sun and his Significations	42
— Venus and her Significations	45
— Mercury and his Significations	47
— the Moon and her Significations	50
— Herschel	53
Colours of the Planets and Signs	57
Aries	ib.
Taurus	58
Gemini	59
Cancer	ib.
Leo	60
Virgo	61
Libra	62
Scorpio	63
Sagittary	64
Capricorn	ib.
Aquarius	65
Pisces	66
Use to be made of the Twelve Signs	67
Essential Dignities of the Planets	69
Table of ditto	72
Considerations before Judgment	74
Introduction to the Judgment of a Question	75
To know whether a Thing will be brought to perfection, yea or nay	77
Of the true time of erecting a Figure	80
Of the Planet which hinders or impedites the Thing demanded	81

TABLE OF CONTENTS.

	Page
QUESTIONS CONCERNING THE FIRST HOUSE. If the Querent be likely to live long?	83
To what part it is best the Querent should direct his affairs	86
What part of Life is likely to be best?	86
If one shall find the Party at Home he would speak with?	95
A thing suddenly happening, whether it signifies good or evil?	96
What Mark, Mole, or Scar, the Querent has on any part of his Body?	97
Parts of Man's Body ruled by the Twelve Signs	ib.
Whether one absent be dead or alive?	98
Measure of Time	100
Of a Ship, and her safety or destruction	105
Parts of a Ship ruled by the Signs	107
Example.—A Ship at Sea. If lost?	108
A Ship at Sea. In what condition?	111
JUDGMENTS CONCERNING THE SECOND HOUSE	112
Whether the Querent shall be rich? By what means attain it? &c.	ib.
Signs of Poverty, and its cause	115
If the Querent shall obtain the substance he hath lent, or which he demands?	116
If one shall acquire gain or profit from the Government, or any Nobleman or Person of high rank? &c.	117
Example.—If the Querent should be rich, or subsist himself without Marriage?	119
OF THE THIRD HOUSE, viz., of Brethren, Kindred, News, Short Journeys, &c.	122
— an absent Brother?	123
— Reports, News, Rumours, &c., whether true or false? &c.	126
— Counsel or Advice given by a Neighbour, &c.	127
— Short Journeys, whether good to go or not?	ib.
OF THE FOURTH HOUSE, viz., of Parents, Lands, Tenements, Cities, Towns, Farms, &c.	134
To find a Thing hidden or mislaid	ib.
Of Buying and Selling Lands, Houses, &c.	136
If it be good to take the House, Farm, &c.	138
Shall the Querent enjoy the estate of his Father?	140
Of removing from one House or Place to another	141, 221
— Treasure, Mines, &c. concealed in the Ground	142
Question of purchasing Houses	143

TABLE OF CONTENTS.

	Page
OF THE FIFTH HOUSE	147
If one shall have Children, yea or nay?	ib.
If a Woman ask whether she may have a Child?	ib.
Whether a Man shall have Children by his Wife, or his intended Wife?	148
Whether a Woman be with Child?	ib.
Is the Child male or female?	150
Shall the Child live or die?	ib.
Of the Time of the Birth?	151
— Messengers or Ambassadors	ib.
— a Message sent for Money	152
OF THE SIXTH HOUSE, viz. of Sickness, Servants, Small Cattle, &c.	158
What Part of the Body is afflicted?	159
The cause and nature of the Sickness	160
Diseases signified by the Houses	164
Signs of a short Disease	161
———— long Disease	162
Testimonies of Recovery	164
Arguments of Death	165
To know whether the Querent be really ill or not	166
Of the Crises, or of critical days	167
How long before Recovery?	168
Judgments from the Affliction of ☽ at the first Illness, &c.	169
Table, shewing what part of Man's Body each Planet signifies in the Twelve Signs	179
Diseases of ♄	180
———— of ♃	181
———— of ♂	182
———— of ☉	ib.
———— of ♀	183
———— of ☿	184
———— of ☽	185
THE SEVENTH HOUSE, &c.	186
Aphorisms and Considerations, for better judging any horary question	ib.
Whether a Man shall Marry?	190
———— a Woman shall Marry?	ib.
The Time of Marriage	ib.
Of Marriage with any particular Person	191
Testimonies that the Marriage shall be hindered	192

TABLE OF CONTENTS. xiii

	Page
What shall be the cause of the Marriage being prevented	192
To describe the person and qualities of the future Wife, &c.	194
Whether the future Wife, &c. shall be rich or not?	ib.
How the Parties shall agree?	195
From what part a person shall Marry?	197
Whether a Lady have a Lover? &c.	ib.
———— a Gentleman have a Lover? &c.	199
———— a Damsel be virtuous?	200
———— the Child conceived is the child of its reputed father?	ib.
———— a Woman living from her Husband shall return?	201
Of Runaways, Things lost, &c.	202
The Place where the Thing lost is	ib.
How the Thing was lost	203
Whether the Thing missing be stolen?	204
———— a Thing lost shall be found?	ib.
The kind of place a Thing lost is in?	205
Of a Fugitive, and whether he shall be found or returned	207
OF THEFTS	ib.
— the Age of the Thief	209
Whether the Thief be Male or Female?	210
———— one Thief or more?	ib.
In what part of a house Things lost or stolen may be	214
Whether the Goods shall be recovered or not?	216
Of the Thief's Person	217
— Battle, War, Duels, Prize Fights, &c.	219
— Partnership	221
— Removing from place to place	141, 221
Of Lawsuits	222
— Making Purchases or Sales	223
Whether the Querent have any Adversaries or open Enemies	227
OF THE EIGHTH HOUSE, AND ITS QUESTIONS	249
Whether an absent Person be dead or alive?	ib.
Of the Death of the Querent	250
Whether the Wife's Fortune will be great? &c.	251
———— the Querent shall suffer by a particular thing of which he is in fear?	252
OF THE NINTH HOUSE, &c.	254
— a Voyage, and its Issue	ib.

TABLE OF CONTENTS.

	Page
Of a long Journey, and its Issue	255
— the Return, &c. of a Person who is gone a long Journey	256
— Profit by any Science, &c.	257
— THE TENTH HOUSE, &c.	269
Whether a Person shall remain in the Office he holds?	270
———— a King expelled his Kingdom, &c., shall be restored	271
Of the Employment of which any one is capable	272
OF THE ELEVENTH HOUSE, &c.	276
Whether any one shall have the thing hoped for?	ib.
Of the Sincerity of Friends	277
OF THE TWELFTH HOUSE, &c.	278
To know who a private Enemy is	ib.
Whether a Person committed to Prison shall be discharged?	ib.
Whether a Prisoner of War shall escape, &c.	279
Figure of the time when King Charles the First set up his Standard at Nottingham	286
Figure of the exact time of the Death of King Charles the First	290
Fac-simile of the Hieroglyphic of the Great Plague	292
———— of the Astrological Hieroglyphic of the Great Fire in London	293
Aphorisms by Zadkiel	294
Appendix	295

LIFE OF WILLIAM LILLY.

In offering an abstract of the most valuable of this clever astrologer's works to the notice of the public, I consider myself called upon to make some mention of his personal history. And it fortunately happens that this is not made up of imaginary ideas, founded on a few known facts, and a multiplicity of suppositions; for what we know of this man of extraordinary talent rests on the best evidence. He undertook, in his sixty-sixth year, to write a history of his own life to his "worthy friend," Elias Ashmole, Esq., afterwards Sir Elias Ashmole, the founder of the celebrated museum which bears his name. Mr. Ashmole made marginal notes therein, which testify his high opinion of our Author; and, fortunately for the cause of Astrology, this gentleman verified the correctness of the Figures of Heaven, which are given in the subsequent pages; for we find the following note at the foot of page 131:—"*I devised the forms and fashions of the several schemes, E. A.*" This note was made after these observations of Lilly. "The desire I had to benefit posterity and my country, at last overcame all difficulties; so that what I could not do in one year, I perfected early the next year, 1647; and then in that year, viz. 1647, I finished the third book of nativities; during the composing whereof, for seven whole weeks, I was shut up of the plague, burying in that time two maid-servants thereof; yet, towards November that year, the Introduction, called by the name of *Christian Astrology*, was made publick."

The fact of this work having been chiefly composed under such awful circumstances, with a dreadful death immediately before his eyes, with the pestilence ravaging his own household, might, with unprejudiced men, have been taken as a proof that the writer was sincere in what he wrote; and really believed in the truth of that which he taught to others as truth under the solemn appeal to Almighty God, which is so beautifully worded in his introductory epistle. Modern critics, however, can see no force in this argument, but unhesitatingly condemn *William Lilly* "as an accomplished impostor, and a knavish fortune-teller."[*] Such, reader, is the force of prejudice. It will not allow men to examine before they condemn; for if it did, then would the literary world speedily acknowledge the reality of those doctrines which our Author has so ably set forth in the following pages.

William Lilly was born of an honest yeoman family, in the town of "Diseworth, seven miles south of the town of Derby, on the first day of May, 1602." At eleven years old he was sent to Ashby de la Zouch, to be instructed by one Mr. John Brindley. Here he says he learned the following authors, viz., *Sententiæ Pueriles, Cato, Corderius, Æsop's Fables, Tully's Offices, Ovid de Tristibus;* lastly, *Virgil,* then *Horace;* as also *Camden's Greek Grammar, Theognis,* and *Homer's Iliads;* and entered *Udall's Hebrew Grammar.* In the eighteenth year of his age his master "was enforced from keeping school, being persecuted by the Bishop's officers;" and our Author was "enforced to leave school." He then kept school himself for "one quarter of a year." On Monday, April 3rd, 1620, he left Diseworth and came to London, where he was compelled to accept the humble situation of a

[*] Retrospective Review, vol. ii. p. 51.

footboy, his father being then "in Leicester gaol for debt," and, of course, incapable of doing much for his son. He had only seven shillings and sixpence left when he arrived at London, having "footed it all along" with the carrier. In 1624 his mistress died, having given him "five pounds in old gold." After which he lived "most comfortably," his master having a great affection for him. In 1626 his master married again, having first settled on our Author twenty pounds a year, which he enjoyed all through life. In October, 1627, he was made free of the Salters' Company. And on the "eighth day of September, 1627," married his master's widow, this same lady; and they "lived very lovingly" until her death, October, 1633.

In the year 1632 he began to study Astrology, being instructed in the rudiments by one Evans, a Welshman, of indifferent abilities. Lilly tells us that he applied himself to these interesting studies "many times, twelve, or fifteen, or eighteen hours, day and night;" adding, "I was curious to discover whether there was any verity in the art or not." By this his first wife he acquired a fortune of "very near to one thousand pounds." In the year 1634 he purchased the moiety of thirteen houses in the Strand, for which he gave £530. The figure of the heavens, erected on this occasion, will be found in the following pages. November the 18th, 1634, he married again, and had £500 portion with that wife. "She was of the nature of Mars," and he lived not very lovingly with her, as seems by his observations at her death. He appears to have now practised horary astrology with success, and to have instructed numerous individuals in the art; among others he taught John Humphreys, in the year 1640, for which service he received forty pounds. He also wrote, in the year 1639, a Treatise on the Eclipse of the Sun, May 22d, 1639; and appears, about that period, to have turned his attention much to Mundane Astrology. He says,* "I did carefully, in 1642 and 1643, take notice of every grand action which happened betwixt king and parliament; and did first then incline to believe, that, as all sublunary affairs did depend upon superior causes, so there was a possibility of discovering them by the configurations of the superior bodies; in which way making some essays in those two years, I found encouragement to proceed further, which I did: I perused the writings of the ancients, but therein they were silent, or gave no satisfaction; at last, I framed unto myself that method which then and since I follow, which I hope, in time, may be more perfected by a more penetrating person than myself."

He appears to have dabbled a little in magic also, but he soon "grew weary of such employment," and burned his books. Lilly's better sense led him to perceive which of these studies was worthy of an honest and intelligent man's pursuit, and which not.

About April, 1644, he first published *Merlinus Anglicus Junior*. This work contained some of his most remarkable predictions, and was continued for many years. It attracted much attention, and was the means of adding greatly to the fame of our Author as an Astrologer. In that year he printed the *White King's Prophecy*, "of which were sold, in three days, eighteen hundred;" and some other works of like nature, the *Prophetical Merlin*, &c.

In 1645 he was twice had before a Committee of the Parliament, for some observations in his *Starry Messenger*; but he escaped, partly by means of his numerous friends, and partly by his own ingenuity.

In 1647, when he published the present work, he was introduced to General Fairfax, who paid him and his art some

* See p. 101 of Lilly's History of his Life and Times.

compliments. In this year he was consulted by King Charles I., as to a safe place to conceal his royal person; but the King, unfortunately for himself, neglected Lilly's advice, and was accordingly ruined. Again, in 1648, the King consulted Lilly; but though he promised to take the Astrologer's advice, and come up to London with the Commissioners, he did not, however, keep his word, and again lost a good opportunity of escaping from his evil destiny.

"In this year," says Lilly, "for very great considerations, the council of state gave me in money fifty pounds, and a pension of one hundred pounds *per annum*, which for two years I received, but no more." In January 1649 he was present at the trial of King Charles, "who spoke," says he, "excellently well."

In 1651 he published *Monarchy or No Monarchy*, which contained several hieroglyphics; among others those of the great plague and fire of London, which the reader will find a copy of in this work.

These celebrated predictions were made by means of the motions of the fixed stars, as is evident by the words of Lilly; who says, "the asterisms and signs and constellations give greatest light thereunto." The *Bull's North Horn*, a star which, Ptolemy says, is "like Mars," was, in the year 1666, when the fire occurred, in ♊ 17° 54′, which is the exact ascendant of London. It was, no doubt, by this means Lilly judged the city would suffer by fire; for in his Almanac for 1666 he states, that the 19th degree of ♊ is London's horoscope. Our Author was not very nice in his calculations; and it may be observed, that though it may be called the 19th degree, being within 6 minutes of it, yet, in reality, ♊ 17° 54′ is the true ascendant of London. It was that which ascended at the moment of *driving the first pile of the new London Bridge*.

The longitude of the *Bull's North Horn*, 1st January, 1834 . . . . Ⅱ 20° 15'
Longitude of London's ascendant . . . Ⅱ 17 54

Difference 2 21

This difference of 2° 21' is equal to 8460 seconds of longitude, which, divided by 50⅓" (the rate at which the fixed stars proceed yearly), gives 168.

From the year 1834
Take away 168

1666

it gives the year when that evil star was crossing the ascending sign of London. And as it is of the *fiery* nature of Mars, we need not be surprised that it produced such terrific results. The celebrated *Nostradamus* had predicted the same event in that year, about 111 years previously, as follows:—

> "Le sang du juste à Londres fera faute
> Bruslez par feu, de vingt et trois, les six."

The blood of the just, which has been spilt in London, requires it to be burned with fire in sixty-six. He states that he made this prediction by "Astronomical Affections."

In 1651 Lilly was again had before the Parliament, on account of his predictions, and was thirteen days in the custody of the Serjeant-at-Arms. But the prediction which gave offence, viz. that the "Parliament stood upon a tottering foundation, and that the commonalty and soldiery would join together against them," was amply fulfilled by the members being turned out of doors by Oliver Cromwell.

In February, 1654, his second wife died; and in October following he married a third, signified, in his nativity, "by *Jupiter in Libra;* and," says he, "she is so totally in her conditions, to my great comfort."

In 1655 he was indicted at Hicks's Hall by a half-witted young woman. The cause of the indictment was, that he had given judgment upon stolen goods, and received two shillings and sixpence; contrary to an act made in King James's time.

"I owned," says he, "the taking of half-a-crown for my judgment of the theft, but said, that I gave no other judgment but that the goods would not be recovered, being that was all which was required of me. I spoke for myself, and introduced my own *Introduction* into court, saying, that I had some years before emitted that book for the benefit of this and other nations; that it was allowed by authority, and had found good acceptance in both Universities; that the study of Astrology was lawful, and not contradicted by any scripture; that I neither had, or ever did, use any charms, sorceries, or enchantments, related in the bill of indictment, &c. The jury, who went not from the bar, brought in, No true Bill."

"In 1666 happened," says our Author, "that miraculous conflagration in the city of London, whereby, in four days, the most part thereof was consumed by fire." He then gives an account of his being brought before the House of Commons by the following summons:—

MONDAY, 22nd OCTOBER, 1666.

"At the Committee appointed to enquire after the causes of the late fires:—

"ORDERED,

"That Mr. Lilly do attend this Committee on Friday next, being the 25th of October, 1666, at two of the clock in the afternoon, in the Speaker's chamber, to answer such questions as shall be then and there asked him.

"ROBERT BROOKE."

In remarking on the circumstance, he says, "I conceive there was never more civility used unto any than unto myself; and you know there was no small number of parliament men appeared, when they heard I was to be there."

"Sir Robert Brooke spoke to this purpose:—

"'Mr. Lilly, this Committee thought fit to summon you to appear before them this day, to know, if you can say anything as to the cause of the late fire, or whether there might be any design therein. You are called the rather hither, because, in a book of your's long since printed, you hinted some such thing by one of your hieroglyphics.' Unto which I replied,

"May it please your honours,

"After the beheading of the late King, considering that in the three subsequent years the parliament acted nothing which concerned the settlement of the nation's peace, and seeing the generality of the people dissatisfied, the citizens of London discontented, the soldiery prone to mutiny, I was desirous, according to the best knowledge God had given me, to make enquiry by the art I studied, what might, from that time, happen unto the parliament and nation in general. At last, having satisfied myself as well as I could, and perfected my judgment therein, I thought it most convenient to signify my intentions and conceptions thereof in forms, shapes, types, hieroglyphicks, &c., without any commentary, that so my judgment might be concealed from the vulgar, and made manifest only unto the wise; I herein imitating the examples of many wise philosophers who had done the like. Having found, Sir, that the city of London should be sadly afflicted with a great plague, and not long after with an exhorbitant fire, I framed these two hieroglyphicks, as represented in the book, which, in effect, have proved very true."

"Did you foresee the year?" said one.—"I did not," said

I, "or was desirous; of that I made no scrutiny." "I proceeded:—'Now, Sir, whether there was any design of burning the city, or any employed to that purpose, I must deal ingenuously with you; that, since the fire, I have taken much pains in the search thereof, but cannot, or could not, give myself any the least satisfaction therein. I conclude that it was the finger of God only; but what instruments he used thereunto I am ignorant.'

"The Committee seemed well pleased with what I spoke, and dismissed me with great civility."

After this, nothing very remarkable happened to our Author. He left London, having acquired an independence, and settled at Hersham, in the year of the great plague, 1665. He then applied himself diligently to the study of physic, and on the 11th October, 1670, he received a licence to practise as a physician. He continued to practise with much success, no doubt by applying his astrological science thereto; and he gave his advice and prescriptions freely, without money. His skill and his charity gained him extraordinary credit and estimation.

He continued generally in good health till August, 1674; but his health and his eyesight remained very weak afterwards. He still continued to write his monthly observations and astrological judgments, though latterly by aid of an amanuensis (Mr. Henry Colley, who succeeded him as an astrologer), even until the year 1682.

In the beginning of 1681 he was seized with a flux, which he recovered from, but then became totally blind. The 30th of May of that year he was seized with a dead palsy; and, after some days of severe suffering, he died about three o'clock on the morning of the 9th of June, 1681, "without any shew of trouble or pangs."

He was buried in the chancel of Walton Church, his friend,

Sir Elias Ashmole, assisting at the laying him in his grave, which was "on the left side of the communion table."

A black marble stone was afterwards placed thereon by his friend, with the following inscription:—

Ne Oblivione Conteretur Urna
GULIELMI LILLII
ASTROLOGI PERITISSIMI
QUI FATIS CESSIT
Quinto Idus Junii Anno Christo Juliano
MDCLXXXI
Hoc Illi posuit amoris Monumentum
ELIAS ASHMOLE
ARMIGER.

"*An Epistle to the Student in Astrology.*

"My Friend, whoever thou art, that with so much ease shalt receive the benefit of my hard studies, and doest intend to proceed in this heavenly knowledge of the starres; In the first place, consider and admire thy Creator, be thankfull unto him, and be humble, and let no naturall knowledge, how profound or transcendant soever it be, elate thy mind to neglect that Divine Providence, by whose al-seeing order and appointment all things heavenly and earthly have their constant motion: the more thy knowledge is enlarged, the more doe thou magnify the power and wisdome of Almighty God: strive to preserve thyself in his favour; for the more holy thou art, and more neer to God, the purer judgment thou shalt give.

"Beware of pride and self-conceit: remember how that long agoe no irrationall creature durst offend man the Macrocosme, but did faithfully serve and obey him; so long as he was master of his own reason and passions, or until he subjected his will to the unreasonable part. But, alas! when iniquity abounded, and man gave the reins to his own affection, and deserted reason, then every beast, creature, and outward harmfull thing, became rebellious to his command. Stand fast (oh, man) to thy God: then consider thy own nobleness; how all created things, both present and to come, were for thy sake created; nay, for thy sake God became man: thou art that creature, who, being conversant with Christ, livest and reignest above the heavens, and sits above all power and authority. How many pre-eminences, privileges, advantages, hath God bestowed on thee: thou rangest above the heavens by contemplation, conceivest the motion and magnitude of the stars: thou talkest with angels, yea, with God himself: thou hast all creatures within thy dominion, and keepest the devils in subjection. Doe not, then, for shame deface thy nature, or make thyself unworthy of such gifts, or deprive thyself of that great power, glory, and blessednesse, God hath allotted thee, by casting from thee his favour for possession of a few imperfect pleasures.

"Having considered thy God, and what thyself art, during thy being God's servant, now receive instruction how in thy practice I would have thee carry thyself. As thou daily conversest with the heavens, so instruct and form thy mind according to the image of Divinity: learn all the ornaments of virtue, be sufficiently instructed therein: be humane, curtius, familiar to all, easie of accesse: afflict not the miserable with terrour of a harsh judgment; direct such to call on God to divert his judgments impending over them: be civil, sober, covet not an estate; give freely to the poor, both money and judgment: let no worldly wealth procure an erronious judgment from thee, or such as may dishonour the art. Be sparing in delivering judgment against the common-wealth thou livest in; avoyd law and controversie: in thy study be *totus in illus*, that thou mayest be *singulus in arte*. Be not extravagant, or desirous to learn every science; be not *aliquid in omnibus;* be faithfull, tenacious, betray no ones secrets. Instruct all men to live well: be a good example thyselfe; love thy own native country; be not dismaid if ill spoken of, *conscientia mille testes*. God suffers no sin unpunished, no lye unrevenged. Pray for the nobility, honour the gentry and yeomanry of England; stand firme to the commands of this parliament; have a reverent opinion of our worthy lawyers, for without their learned paines, and the mutual assistance of some true spirited gentlemen, we might yet be made slaves, but we will not; we now see light as well as many of the clergy. Pray, if it stand with God's will, that monarchy in this kingdom may continue, his Majesty and posterity reigne: forget not the Scottish nation, their mutual assistance in our necessity, their honourable departure. God preserve the illustrious *Fairfax*, and his whole armye, and let the famous city of London be ever blessed, and all her worthy citizens.*

"WILLIAM LILLY."

* I have retained the exact orthography of this epistle, which is a curious and interesting remnant of our author's day. It was penned in 1647.—ED.

AN

INTRODUCTION TO ASTROLOGY.

CHAPTER I.

THERE are in the heavens several bodies which appear to shed their light directly on this Earth; and also some others which, having no light of themselves, serve to reflect that of the Sun, and thereby become visible to our organs of sight. The former are termed *Fixed Stars*, because they appear to retain the same situation, or to be fixed in the same place; but the latter, being observed to wander, are termed Planets. The number and distance of the former are so extensive, that I shall take no further notice of them here, than to observe, that they are not much used in that portion of Astrology which is denominated *Horary*, and that those persons who desire to make use of them in nativities, will find their right ascensions and declinations given with great accuracy in the Nautical Almanack for each year. In the Appendix to this work, I shall give rules, to ascertain their latitude and longitude by trigonometry, for the benefit of such persons as may be curious to make experiments as to their influence; though I do not, in general, pay much attention to them when judging a nativity.

Of the Planets.

These are ♅ Herschel, ♄ Saturn, ♃ Jupiter, ♂ Mars,

⊙ Sol, the Sun,* ♀ Venus, ☿ Mercury, and ☽ Luna, the Moon. These characters have been always in use, and may, (with the exception of ♅,) be traced to the remotest antiquity, and their origin found among the hieroglyphics of Egypt. But as the object of this work is practical utility, no more need be said on the subject.

The Signs of the Zodiac.

They are twelve, each containing 30 degrees, thus making 360 degrees, into which every great circle is divided. The first six are,

Northern Signs.

♈ Aries, ♉ Taurus, ♊ Gemini, ♋ Cancer, ♌ Leo, ♍ Virgo.

Southern Signs.

♎ Libra, ♏ Scorpio, ♐ Sagittary, ♑ Capricorn, ♒ Aquarius, ♓ Pisces.

The first sign, ♈, commences the zodiac, its beginning being that spot in the heavens where the Sun is when crossing the equator in spring; and the latter sign, ♓, finishes the circle of the zodiac, the latter end of it being that spot in the heavens where the Sun is when he has gone his round, and is again about to enter ♈.

By referring to the annexed diagram, the student will perceive, that when the Sun enters ♈ (about the 21st of March) he proceeds northward, and *increases in declination* until he reaches the tropic of ♋ Cancer (about the 21st of June), when he speedily begins to return to the south; and when he reaches ♎, he again crosses the equator (about the 23d of September), where, having no declination, he causes equal

* The Sun and Moon are considered as planets in all astrological matters.

day and night all over the world. He then *declines away to the south;* shortening our days in the northern hemisphere, until he reaches the southern tropic ♑, Capricorn; at length he returns towards the equator, and crosses it by entering the sign ♈ (about the 21st of March), where again he has no declination, and gives equal days and nights.

Diagram of the Sun's Motion in the Zodiac.

EXPLANATION.—The space between the two outer circles may be considered as the line of the Sun's motion; and then the sign opposite the name of each month will shew where the Sun is about the 21st of each month. The globe in the centre may be taken for the Earth, the northern parts of which receive the greater portion of the Sun's light in summer, and the southern parts in winter.

These signs are divided into,

Northern Signs	♈, ♉, ♊, ♋, ♌, ♍.
Southern Signs	♎, ♏, ♐, ♑, ♒, ♓.
Tropical Signs	♋, and ♑.
Equinoctial Signs	♈, and ♎.
Double-bodied Signs	♊, ♍, ♐, ♓.

They are again divided into

Moveable	♈, ♋, ♎, ♑.
Common	♊, ♍, ♐, ♓.
Fixed	♉, ♌, ♏, ♒.

Also into

Fiery	♈, ♌, ♐.
Earthy	♉, ♍, ♑.
Airy	♊, ♎, ♒.
Watery	♋, ♏, ♓.

The student must become well acquainted with the above particulars; but especially so with the northern and southern signs, the former being *opposite* to the latter. By attending to this, he will readily come to understand the figure of the heavens, and the relative situations of the planets.

N.B. The moveable, common, and fixed signs are always in *square* aspect to each other, three signs apart; and the fiery, earthy, airy, and watery signs are always in *trine* aspect to each other, four signs apart.

THE DRAGON'S HEAD AND TAIL.

The Moon's north node is known by the character ☊,

INTRODUCTION TO ASTROLOGY. 17

termed the Dragon's Head; and her south node by this ☋, termed the Dragon's Tail. The former of these in horary questions denotes good, and is considered of the character of ♃, and increases the good qualities of a benefic, with which it may be found; and diminishes the evil of a malefic planet. The latter is of the nature of ♄, and does the reverse. In nativities these characters have no avail, and are not to be considered, except with regard to the Moon, who is found to produce good or evil when she reaches them by direction.*

THE PART OF FORTUNE.

This is that spot in the heavens which is equally distant from the degree ascending that the Moon is from the Sun. It is found by the following rule:—

To find the (⊕) Part of Fortune in a Nativity.

Add 90° to the right ascension of the meridian, and it will give the oblique ascension of the ascendant. From the oblique ascension of the ascendant subtract the oblique ascension of the Sun (having first added 360° to the former, if necessary); to the remainder add the right ascension of the Moon: the sum will be the right ascension of ⊕.

The ⊕ is always *under* the horizon *before* the full Moon, and *above* the horizon *after* the full Moon. Having found its right ascension, take it from that of the meridian above or below the earth, according as it may be situated; or, take that of the meridian from it, and the sum or difference will shew the distance of ⊕ from the cusp of the 10th or 4th house.

---

* These nodes are the points in the ecliptic where the Moon crosses from north into south latitude, or the reverse, which occurs twice each month.

18   INTRODUCTION TO ASTROLOGY.

Example :—A. R. of midheaven . . . 221° 5′
Add thereto 90 0
―――――
Oblique asc. of the ascendant . 311 5
Subtract oblique asc. of ☉ . . 17 34
―――――
293 31
Add right ascension of the ☽ . 345 34
―――――
639 5
Take away. 360 0
―――――
It leaves right ascension of ⊕ . 279 5

Then, as the birth took place after full Moon, and the ⊕ will be above the Earth, find the difference of right ascension between it and the meridian above the Earth.

Thus : Right ascension of ⊕ . . . . 279° 5′
Right ascension of the midheaven. 221 5
―――――
Distance of ⊕ from the 10th house 58 0

If the ⊕ be in the same hemisphere as the ☽; that is, if both be above or below the Earth, it will have the semi-arc of the ☽; but if otherwise, it will have the opposite semi-arc; which may be found by taking the ☽'s from 180°. In this nativity (which is that of the Duke of Wellington) the semi-arc of the Moon is 90° 57′, which taken from 180° leaves the semi-arc of ⊕ 89° 3′, two-thirds of which are 59° 22′; and it appears that ⊕ is just 1° 22′ outside the cusp of the 12th house.*

The ⊕ has no influence on the *health or life* of the native;

―――――

* This is found by taking its distance from the 10th 58° 0′ from ⅔ of its semi-arc 59° 22′.

but it influences the pecuniary affairs very powerfully, and also, in some degree, the profession or employment.*

To find the Place of ⊕ in the Figure of a Horary Question.

In horary astrology ⊕ is merely a symbol, and has much to do with all questions regarding property, loss or gain, &c. In this case it is found by a more simple rule, as follows :—

Add together the longitude of the ascendant and longitude of the ☽, from which subtract the longitude of the ☉: the remainder will be the longitude of ⊕.

Example :—Where was the ⊕ at 3h. 20m. P.M. 28th of December, 1644 ?†

	Signs	deg.	min.
The Ascendant was ♋ 11° 33', or	3	11	33
The ☽ was in ♉, 16° 49', or . .	1	16	49
	4	28	22
For subtraction add	12	0	0
	16	28	22
The ☉ in ♑, 17° 54', or . . .	9	17	54
Place of ⊕ in the figure . . .	7	10	28
or ♏ 10° 28'.			

* In proof of this, it is evident that in the Duke's nativity ☽ came to ☌ of ⊕ in November 1834, when he was appointed to the ministry. Thus ⊕ is 58° from the meridian, and ☽ 124° 29', ; the difference is 66° 29'; which arc of direction, added to the right ascension of ☉ at his birth 39° 21', gives 105° 50', the right asc. of ♋ 14° 34'. The ☉ arrived at this point at 1 P.M. 6th July 1769, or 65 days 13 hours after birth, which, by the Placidian measure of a year for a day, gives 65 years 6½ months, the Duke's age when the event occurred.—N.B. The ascendant came to ☌ of ☉ at the same time, which, by referring to our author's rules for the effects of directions, will be seen to cause such eminent preferment. The semi-arc of ☉ is 68° 13', ☉ dist. from 4th house 1° 44'; the difference is 66° 29', the arc of direction.

† See the figure—Question, " A ship at sea, if lost ?"

c 2

CHAPTER II.

Fig. 1.

EXPLANATION.—In the above figure the ANGLES and the succeedent and cadent houses appear at one view. The 1st house embraces 24° of longitude in the zodiac, viz. from ♎ 0° 0′ to ♎ 24°; the 2nd house contains 30°, viz. from ♎ 24° to ♏ 24°; the 3d house contains 36°, viz. from ♏ 24° to

INTRODUCTION TO ASTROLOGY. 21

♑ 0° 0′, being 6° of ♏ and the whole of ♐; the 4th house contains 36°, viz. the whole of ♑ and 6° of ♒; the 5th house contains 30°, viz. from ♒ 6° to ♓ 6°; and the 6th house contains 24°, viz. from ♓ 6° to the end of that sign, or ♈ 0° 0′.—N.B. The other *six* houses will be found to embrace exactly the same number of degrees of the opposite signs of the zodiac ; the 7th being opposite to the 1st, the 8th to the 2d, &c. If the student look for ♋ 0° 0′ on the 10th house in the table of houses for London, he will find the longitude of the six *eastern* houses, as here noted; and, of course, the six opposite or *western* houses have the same degrees of the opposite signs on their cusps.

OF ERECTING A FIGURE OF THE HEAVENS.

THIS is merely a map to represent the heavens at any particular moment, such as when a child is born, or a question asked, &c. In the first place, draw three circles, as in *figure* 1; and then draw lines to represent the horizon, and others, at right angles with them, to represent the meridian : thus will be shewn, the natural divisions formed by the rising and setting of the Sun, and by his passing the meridian at noon and midnight. Each of these quarters or quadrants is to be again divided into three equal parts, forming

The Twelve Houses.

These are marked from No. 1 to No. 12 ; and it will be observed, that the double lines 1 and 7, which represent the eastern and western horizons, and those marked 4 and 10, which represent the meridians below and above the Earth, are the cusps or commencement of the *angles*. Those lines numbered 2, 5, 8, and 11, are the cusps of the *succeedents*, so called because they follow or *succeed* to the angles. These houses are next in power to the angles. Those lines marked 3, 6, 9, and 12, are the cusps or beginnings of the *cadent* houses; so called because they are *cadent*, that is, *falling from the angles*: these are the weakest of all the houses.

Thus the student will perceive, that if a planet, &c. be in one of the *angles*, it is powerful; if in a *succeedent* house, it is less powerful; and if in a *cadent* house, it is weak and incapable of effecting much either good or evil.

Rule to erect the Figure of the Heavens at any Time.

1. Learn in an ephemeris* for the year what was the right ascension of ☉ at the noon previous to the required time, in hours, minutes, and seconds. To this right ascension add the number of hours and minutes which have elapsed since that noon:† the sum will be the right ascension in time of the meridian above the Earth (the mid-heaven) at the required time.

2. Find the longitude answering to this right ascension, in the column marked 10th house in the Table of Houses, which longitude is to be marked over the line which denotes the mid-heaven or 10th house.

3. In a line with this will be found the longitude on the cusps of the 11th, 12th, 1st, 2d, and 3d houses; which copy out from the table, and enter over the lines which denote those respective houses.

4. Having thus completed the *six eastern* houses, find the signs and degrees exactly opposite to each of them, and enter it over the cusps of the opposite or western houses, in the following order:—

10th house	opposite	4th house
11th	do.	5th

* Ephemeris signifies a journal or Almanac, in which the places of the planets, &c. for each day are registered. For all years before 1834, *White's* is the best.

† This time must first be corrected for the error of the clock, by adding what the clock is too slow, or subtracting what it is too fast.

INTRODUCTION TO ASTROLOGY.   23

12th	opposite	6th house
1st or ascendant	do.	7th
2d	do.	8th
3d	do.	9th

5. Having thus completed the figure, as far as regards the signs of the zodiac, it now remains to place in the planets as they may be situated. The most distant from the ☉ is ♅, whose longitude is generally given in the ephemeris for each ten days, and if the time of the figure fall between it, it must be found by proportion. When his longitude is found, write it in the figure, thus, ♅ 13° 19′, just by the cusp of the house, which falls in the same sign in which ♅ is found. If the cusp be farther on than the planet in the sign, place the planet *outside* the cusp; but if the planet be the farthest advanced in the sign, place it *inside* the cusp. After having entered ♅, enter in the same way ♄, then ♃, ♂, ☉, ♀ ☿ and the ☽. To find the exact longitude of these seven, which is usually given for the noon of each day, find the distance they travel in longitude between the two noons preceding and succeeding the time of erecting the figure; and then take the proportional part for the time after the previous noon, and add it to, (or if the planet be retrograde subtract it from), the planet's longitude for the previous noon.

6. Find the longitude of ☊ in the same manner, and enter it accordingly, and place ☋ in the sign and degree and minute exactly opposite thereto.

7. If it be a horary question, calculate the place of ⊕, and enter it accordingly; when the figure of heaven will be complete. But if it be a nativity, you must calculate the ⊕ according to the rule given, first having prepared a Speculum, or Table of Data, as taught in *Chap.* 9 of the *Grammar of Astrology*.

CHAPTER III.

OF THE ASPECTS.

THE figure of the heavens being erected, it now remains to observe how the planets are situated as regards each other; or, in other words, how they are aspected. And, first,

Of Zodiacal Aspects.

These are as follow:—
    Semi ✶, a Semi-sextile, or 30 degrees.
    Semi ☐, a Semi-square, or 45 degrees.
    ✶, a Sextile, or 60 degrees.
    A Quintile, or distance of 72 degrees.
    ☐, a Square, or quartile, 90 degrees.
    △, a Trine, or distance of 120 degrees.
    A Sesquiquadrate, or square and a half, 135 degrees.
    A Biquintile, or double quintile, 144 degrees.
    ☍ an Opposition, 180 degrees.

Good aspects are the semi-sextile, sextile, quintile, trine, and biquintile.

Evil aspects are the semi-square, square, sesquiquadrate, and opposition.—N.B. The conjunction, marked thus ☌, is when two planets are in the same degree and minute of the zodiac: when it is exact, it is very powerful, and is called a *partile* ☌; but if within the planets' orbs, it is called a *platic* conjunction, and is less powerful. To know whether it should be considered at all, the orbs of the two planets should be added together, and one-half the sum taken; if the planets be beyond that distance, they are not even in platic ☌. The same holds good with regard to other aspects.

The orbs of the cusps of the houses are 5°, so that if a

planet be one-half its orb and 5° more distant from a house, it is not in aspect to that house; the same if the *aspect* of the planet fall beyond that distance from the cusp of any other house.

Orbs of the Planets.

♄, 9°; ♃, 9°; ♂, 7°; ☉, 15°; ♀, 7°; ☿, 7°; ☽, 12°.—N.B. ♅ has had no orb of operation discovered; but I think it may safely be considered as 7° in all horary figures, &c.

Of Mundane Aspects.

These are formed by the houses in horary astrology, and by the semi-arcs of the planets in nativities. Thus, a semi ✶ is 1 house; a semi □, 1½; a ✶, 2 houses; a □, 3 houses; a △, 4 houses; a sesqui □, 4½ houses; and an ☍, 6 houses.

The ¼ of a semi arc is a semi ✶; the ½ of a semi-arc is a semi □; the ⅔ of a semi-arc is a ✶; the whole semi-arc is a □; and 1-5th less than the semi-arc is a quintile; the whole semi-arc and ⅓ more is a △; the whole semi-arc and ½ more is a sesqui □; the one-tenth part of a semi-arc added to a sesqui □, is a biquintile.—N.B. The entire arc of a planet, or double the semi-arc, will not give the measure of its distance from the opposite point of its place; but if the two semi-arcs of a planet, both diurnal and nocturnal, be added together, they make 180°, an opposition aspect.

Of Parallels.

The Zodiacal Parallel is when two planets have the same amount of declination from the equator. It is the most powerful of all aspects, but is not generally used in horary astrology.

The Mundane Parallel is an equal distance from the meridian. It is used by some horary astrologers. When any of the above aspects are formed between the planets, they are found to have a mutual influence or action on each other, according to the nature of the aspect. For example: if the ☉ be 60 degrees (a ✶) from ♃ in any figure, it *denotes* that the person signified by the Sun is under the benefic influence of the benevolent ♃; and *shews* success according to the nature of the question. In nativities it *causes* good health and good fortune in life. But if ☉ be 90 degrees (a □) from ♄, it *shews* discredit, a failure of hopes, &c. in a question; and in a nativity it produces much sickness to the native, and also misfortunes to his father. This was verified in the nativity of Napoleon Bonaparte's son, who was born at 9h. 15m. A.M. 20th March, 1811, when ☉ was in 28° 53' of ♓, and ♄ was in 26° 28' of ♐; just 92° 25' distant from each other. This very close □ aspect of ☉ and ♄ caused great trouble to the native, through his father's misfortunes; and, as ☉ was the hyleg, produced a consumptive disease, and early death. It is remarkable, that his father's troubles began immediately after his birth; and it will always be found in the nativity of a child, that the fortune of its parents may be ascertained thereby until the birth of another child. If, for example, the child have evil planets in the fourth house, its father will be more or less unfortunate until the birth of another child; when, if that other have ♃ and ♀ in the fourth house, the father's affairs will become more fortunate: so very beautifully do the nativities of parents and their children sympathise together.

CHAPTER IV.

OF THE TWELVE HOUSES, THEIR NATURE AND SIGNIFICATION.

As before we have said there are twelve signs, and also twelve houses of heaven; so now we are come to relate the nature of these twelve houses, the exact knowledge of which is so requisite, that he who learns the nature of the planets and signs without exact judgment of the houses, is like an improvident man, that furnishes himself with a variety of household stuff, having no place wherein to bestow them. There is nothing appertaining to the life of man in this world which, in one way or other, hath no relation to one of the twelve houses of heaven; and as the twelve signs are appropriate to the particular members of man's body, so also do the twelve houses represent, not only the several parts of man, but his actions, quality of life, and living. And the curiosity and judgment of our forefathers in astrology was such, that they have allotted to every house a particular signification; and so distinguished human accidents* throughout the whole twelve houses. He that understands the questions appertaining to each of them, shall not want sufficient grounds whereon to judge or give a rational answer upon any contingent accident, and success thereof.

Of the FIRST *House, and its Signification.*†

The first house contains all that part of heaven from the line where the figure 1 stands unto the figure 2, where the second house begins: it is *one-third* of the distance between the horizon and meridian below the earth. It has significa-

* The term *accidents* here signifies the events of life generally.
† See *Fig* 1.

tion of the *life* of man, of the stature, colour, complexion, form, and shape of him that propounds the question, or is born; in eclipses and great conjunctions, and upon the Sun his annual ingress into ♈; it signifies the common people, or general state of that kingdom where the figure is erected. And as it is the first house, it represents the head and face of man; so that if either ♄ or ♂ be in this house, either at the time of a question or at the time of birth, you may observe some blemish in the face,* or in that member appropriated to the sign that is then upon the cusp of the house; as, if ♈ be in the ascendant, the mark, mole, or scar is, without fail, in the head or face; and if few degrees of the sign ascend, the mark is in the upper part of the head; if the middle of the sign be on the cusp, the mole, mark, or scar is in the middle of the face, or near it; if the latter degrees ascend, the face is blemished near the chin, towards the neck; this I have found true in hundreds of examples. Of colours, it hath the white; that is, if a planet be in this house that has signification of white, the complexion of the party is more pale or wan; or, if you inquire after the colour of the clothes of any man, if his significator be in the first house, and in a sign corresponding, the party's apparel is white or grey, or somewhat near that colour: so also if the question be regarding cattle, when their significators are found in this house, it denotes them to be of that colour, or near it: the house is masculine. The consignificators of this house are ♈ and ♄: for as this house is the first house, so is ♈ the first sign, and ♄ the first of the planets; and therefore, when ♄ is but moderately well fortified in this house, and in any benevolent aspect of ♃, ♀, ☉, or ☽, it promises a good sober constitution of body, and usually long life; ☿ doth also joy in this

---

* This is verified in the nativity of Lord Brougham, who was born with ♄ ascending in ♏: he has a very great natural defect in the face, a nervous catching of the muscles of the mouth, &c.

house, because it represents the head, and he the tongue, fancy, and memory; when he is well dignified and posited in this house, he produces good orators;* it is called the Ascendant, because when the ☉ and planets come to the cusp of this house, they *ascend*, or then arise, and are visible in our horizon.

Questions concerning the SECOND *House.*

From this house is required judgment concerning the estate or fortune of him that asks the question, of his wealth of property, of all moveable goods, money lent, of profit or gain, loss or damage; in suits of law, it signifies a man's friends or assistants; in private duels, the querent's second; in an eclipse or great conjunction, the poverty or wealth of the people: in the Sun his entrance into ♈, it represents the ammunition, allies, and support the commonwealth shall have; it imports their magazines. It represents, in man, the neck and hinder part of it towards the shoulders; of colours, the green. It is a feminine house, and succeedent.

It has consignificators, ♃ and ♉; for if ♃ be placed in this house, or be lord hereof, it is an argument of an estate or fortune; ☉ and ♂ are never well placed in this house: either of them shew dispersion of substance, according to the capacity and quality of him that is either born or asks the question.†

The THIRD *House*

Has signification of brethren, sisters, cousins, or kindred, neighbours, small journeys, or inland journeys, often removing from one place to another; epistles, letters, rumours, messengers: it rules the shoulders, arms, hands, and fingers.

* Lord Brougham, who is one of the best orators of the age, was born with ☿ just rising.

† ☽ in this house, if in good aspect to ♃, gives the native wealth. The Duke of Wellington had ☽ in this house in △ to ♃ in the 10th.

Of colours, it governs the red and yellow, or sorrel colour; it has consignificators, ♊ and ♂, which is one reason why ♂ in this house, unless joined with ♄, is not very unfortunate: it is a cadent house, and is the joy of the ☽; for if she be posited therein, especially in a moveable sign, it is an argument of much travel, trotting, and trudging, or of being seldom quiet: the house is masculine.

The FOURTH *House*

Gives judgment of fathers in general, or ever of his father that inquires, or that is born; of lands, houses, tenements, inheritance, tillage of the earth, treasures hidden; the determination or *end* of any thing; towns, cities, or castles besieged or not besieged; all ancient dwellings, gardens, fields, pastures, orchards; the quality and nature of the grounds one purchases, whether vineyards, cornfields, &c., and shews whether the ground be woody, stony, or barren.

The sign of the fourth denotes the town, the lord thereof, the governor;* it rules the breast and lungs; and of colours, the red: its consignificators are ♋ and the ☉: we call it the angle of the Earth, or *Imum Cœli:* it is feminine, and the north angle. In nativities or questions this fourth house represents fathers; so does the ☉ by day, and ♄ by night; yet if the ☉ be here placed, he is not ill, but rather shows the father to be of a noble disposition, &c.

The FIFTH *House.*

By this house we judge of children, of ambassadors, of the state of a woman with child, of banquets, of ale-houses, taverns, plays, messengers or agents for republics, of the wealth of the father, the ammunition of a town besieged; if

---

* This alludes to questions of sieges, which were too frequent in the land in the author's time.

the woman with child shall bring forth male or female; of
the health or sickness of his son or daughter that asks the
question. It rules the stomach, liver, heart, sides, and back,
and is masculine. Of colours, black and white, or honey
colour; and is a succeedent house; its consignificators are
☊ and ♀, who does joy in this house, in regard it is the house
of pleasure, delight and merriment; it is wholly unfortunate
by ♂ or ♄, and they therein shew disobedient children, and
untoward.

The SIXTH House.

It concerns men and maid servants, galley slaves, hogs,
sheep, goats, hares, conies, all manner of lesser cattle, and
profit or loss got thereby; *sickness*, its quality and cause; the
principal humour offending, curable or not curable; whether
the disease be short or long; day-labourers, tenants, farmers,
shepherds, hogherds, neatherds, warreners, and it signifies
uncles, or the father's brothers and sisters. It rules the inferior part of the belly and intestines, even to the *rectum*.
The house is a feminine and cadent house, unfortunate as
having no aspect to the ascendant. Of colours, *black*; ♂
rejoices in this house, but its consignificators are the sign ♍
and planet ☿: we usually find that ♂ and ♀ in conjunction
in this house are arguments of a good physician.*

The SEVENTH House.

It gives judgment of marriage; and describes the person
inquired after, whether it be a man or woman; all manner of
love questions; or public enemies, the defendant in a lawsuit,
in war, the opposing party; all quarrels, duels, lawsuits; in
astrology, the artist himself; in physic, the physician; thieves
and thefts, the person stealing, whether man or woman; wives,

---

* This alludes to questions regarding sickness, and by no means to
nativities.

sweethearts, their shape, description, condition, nobly or ignobly born; in an annual ingress, whether war or peace may be expected; of victory, who overcomes and who is worsted; fugitives or runaways, banished or outlawed men. It has consignificators ♎ and ☽; ♄ or ♂ unfortunate herein, shew ill in marriage.* Of colour, a dark black. It rules the haunches, and the navel, to the buttocks, is called the angle of the west, and is masculine.

The EIGHTH *House.*

The estate of men deceased; death, its quality and nature; the wills, legacies, and testaments of men deceased; dowry of the wife, portion of the maid, whether much or little, easy to be obtained or with difficulty. In duels, it represents the adversary's second; in lawsuits, the defendant's friends; what kind of death a man shall die; it signifies fear and anguish of mind;† also who shall be heir to the deceased. It rules the privy parts. Of colours, the green and black. Of signs, it has ♏ for consignificator and ♄. The hemorrhoids, the stone, stranguary, and bladder, are ruled by this house, also poisons; it is a succedent house, and feminine.

The NINTH *House.*

By this house we give judgment of voyages or long journies beyond seas, of religious men, or clergy of any kind, whether bishops or inferior ministers; dreams, visions, foreign countries, books, learning, church livings or benefices, and of the kindred of one's wife or husband. Of colours, it has the

* We always find that ♄, ♂, or ♅, in this house are *causes* of ill-fortune in marriage, or the married state, in nativities, let them be aspected how they will; and in questions, we have no opinion of them, though ever so strongly dignified. The Duke of Wellington had both ♄ and ♂ in the 7th, and was unfortunate in marriage.

† This alludes to the significator of the querent being placed in the 8th house.

green and white; of man's body, it rules the fundament, the hips, and thighs; ♃ and ♂ are consignificators of this house; for if ♃ be herein placed, it naturally signifies a devout man in his religion, or one modestly given. I have often observed when the Dragon's tail, ♄, or ♂ have been unfortunately placed in this house, the querent has either been little better than an atheist or a desperate sectarian.* ☉ rejoices to be in this house, which is masculine and cadent.

The Tenth *House.*

Commonly it personates kings, princes, dukes, earls, judges, prime officers, commanders-in-chief, whether in armies or towns; all sorts of magistracy and officers in authority, also mothers; honour, preferment, dignity, office, lawyers, professions or trade; it also signifies kingdoms, empires, dukedoms, counties; it has of colours red or white, and rules the knees and thighs. It is called the *medium cœli*, or midheaven, and is feminine. Its consignificators are ♑ and ♂. Either ♃ or the ☉ are very fortunate in this house, especially when they are placed together; ♄ or ☋ usually deny honour as to persons of quality, and to the vulgar little prosperity in profession or trade.

---

* This merely alludes to horary questions, and can have no kind of *influence* this way, these things being at the most *symbols* of a good or bad man; for in nativities the mind is influenced by the Moon and Mercury only. The error of confounding these two branches of the science, nativities, in which the planets are *causes* (under God) of events, and horary questions, in which they are only *signs* of the events, has been the chief means of bringing this sublime science into disrepute. This error appears to have arisen from the low state and condition of astronomy in the middle ages, when, even as late as the days of Charles II., Dr. Goad, his physician, assures us that the astronomers could not calculate an opposition of the planets ♃ and ♄ nearer than a week. How, then, can it be expected that the judgments of astrologers should have always been correct, when the very data on which they depended were often erroneous?

The Eleventh *House.*

It does naturally represent friends and friendship, hope, trust, confidence, the praise or dispraise of any one; the fidelity or falseness of friends. As to kings, it personates their favourites, counsellors, servants, their associates or allies; their money, exchequer or treasure; in war, ammunition and soldiery, it represents courtiers, &c. In a commonwealth, governed by a few of the nobles and commons, it personates their assistance in council; as, in London, the tenth house represents the lord mayor; the eleventh, the common council, the ascendant the generality of the commoners of the said city. Of members, it rules the legs to the ancles; of colours, saffron or yellow. It has ☉ and ♒ for consignificators: ♃ especially rejoices in this house. It is a succeedent house, and masculine, and in virtue is nearly equivalent either to the seventh or fourth house.

The Twelfth *House.*

It has signification of private enemies, great cattle, or horses, oxen, elephants, &c.; sorrow, tribulation, imprisonment, all manner of affliction, self-undoing, &c.; and of such men as maliciously undermine their neighbours, or inform secretly against them. It has consignificators ♓ and ♀. Saturn does much delight in that house, for he is naturally the author of mischief. It rules, in man's body, the feet. In colour it represents the green. It is a cadent house, and feminine.

This is the true character of the several houses, according to the Ptolomeian doctrine, and the experience I have had myself for many years. I must confess the Arabians have made several other divisions of the houses; but I could never, in my practice, find any verity in them; therefore I will say nothing of them.

CHAPTER V.

OF SATURN, AND HIS SIGNIFICATION.

HE is the supremest or highest of all the planets,* and is placed between Jupiter and the firmament; he is not very bright or glorious, nor does he twinkle or sparkle, but is of a pale or wan ashy colour; slow in motion, finishing his course through the twelve signs of the zodiac in 29 years, 167 days, and 5 hours, or thereabouts. His mean motion is two minutes and one second; his diurnal motion sometimes is three, four, five, or six minutes, seldom more; his greatest north latitude from the ecliptic is 2 degrees 48 minutes; his greatest south latitude is 2 degrees 49 minutes.

In the zodiac he has two of the twelve signs for his houses; viz. Capricorn ♑, his night house; Aquarius ♒, his day house. He is exalted in ♎, receives his fall in ♈, and rejoices in the sign Aquarius, ♒. He governs the airy triplicity by day, which is composed of ♊, ♎, ♒.

If in any question he be in any degree wherein he has a term, he cannot be said to be peregrine, or void of essential dignities; or if he be in any of those degrees allotted him for his face or decanate, he cannot then be said to be peregrine: understand this in all the other planets.†

He continues retrograde 140 days; is five days in his first stage before retrogradation, and so many in his second station before becoming direct. He is cold and dry (being far removed from the Sun); melancholy, earthy, masculine; and the greater infortune, author of solitariness, malevolent, &c.

When well dignified, he is profound in imagination, in his

---

* This was true, as far as the author knew; the planet Herschel not having been then discovered.

† For the terms, &c., see the table of Essential Dignities.

acts severe, in words reserved, in speaking and giving very spare; in labour patient, in arguing or disputing grave, in obtaining the goods of this life studious and solicitous, in all manner of actions austere.*

When ill dignified, he is envious, covetous, jealous, and mistrustful; timorous, sordid, outwardly dissembling, sluggish, suspicious, stubborn; a contemner of women, a liar, malicious, murmuring; never contented, and ever repining.

Corporature.—Most part of his body cold and dry; of a middle stature, his complexion pale, swarthy or muddy; his eyes little and black, looking downward; a broad forehead, black or sad hair, and it hard or rugged; great ears, hanging, lowering eyebrows, thick lips and nose; a rare or thin beard, a lumpish, unpleasant countenance, either holding his head forward or stooping; his shoulders broad and large, and many times crooked; his belly somewhat short and lank; his thighs spare, lean, and not long; his knees and feet ill made; and frequently striking against each other, with a shuffling gait.

Saturn *Oriental.*—You must observe, if Saturn be oriental of the Sun, the stature is more short, but decent and well composed.

Saturn *Occidental.*—The man is more black and lean, and fewer hairs; and again, if he wants latitude, the body is more lean; if he have great latitude, the body is more fat or fleshy; if the latitude be south, more fleshy, but quick in motion. If north, hairy and much flesh.

♄ in his first station, a little fat; in his second station, fat, ill-favoured bodies, and weak; and this observe constantly in all the other planets.

Quality of Men.—In general ♄ signifies husbandmen,

* By these descriptions is meant, that persons signified in horary questions by this planet are of such a character; and if he influence the native by being in the ascendant at the time of birth, it applies also in nativities.

clowns, beggars, day labourers, old men, fathers, grandfather, monks, jesuits, sectarians.

Employment. — Curriers, night-farmers, miners under ground, tinners, potters, broom men, plumbers, brickmakers, maltsters, chimney-sweepers, sextons of churches, bearers of corpses, scavengers, hostlers, colliers, carters, gardeners, ditchers, chandlers, dyers of black cloth, and herdsmen, shepherds, or cow-keepers.

Sicknesses.—All impediments in the right ear, or teeth; all quartan agues proceeding from cold, dry and melancholy distempers, leprosies, consumptions, black jaundice, palsies, tremblings, vain fears, fantasies, dropsy, the hand and foot gout, apoplexies, too much flux of the hemorrhoids; and *ruptures*, if in Scorpio or Leo, in any ill aspect with Venus.

Orb.—His orb is nine degrees before and after; that is, his influence begins to work when either he applies or any planet applies to him, and is within the half of nine degrees added to the half of that planet's orb, and continues in force until he is separate an equal distance.

Years.—The greatest years he signifies is 465. His greater 57; his medium years $43\frac{1}{2}$; his least 30. The meaning whereof is this: admit we frame a new building, erect a town or city, or a family, or principality is begun when Saturn is essentially and occidentally strong, the astrologer may probably conjecture the family, principality, &c. may continue 465 years in honour, &c. without any sensible alteration. As to age, he relates to decrepit old men, fathers, grandfathers; the like in plants, trees, and all living creatures.

Places.—He delights in deserts, woods, obscure vallies, caves, dens, holes, mountains, or where men have been buried, churchyards, &c.; ruinous buildings, coal-mines, sinks, dirty and stinking places, houses of office, &c.

Countries.—Late authors say he rules over Bavaria, Saxony, Stiria, Romandiola, Ravenna, Constantia, Ingoldstadt.

CHAPTER VI.

OF THE PLANET JUPITER, AND HIS SIGNIFICATION.

JUPITER is placed next to Saturn. He is the greatest in appearance to our eyes, of all the planets (the ☉, ☽, and ♀ excepted): in his colour he is bright, clear, and of an azure hue. In his motion he exceeds Saturn, finishing his course through the twelve signs, in 14 years, 314 days, and 12 hours; his middle motion is 4 minutes 52 seconds. His greatest north latitude is 1° 38′. His greatest south latitude is 1° 40′. He is retrograde about 120 days, is five days in his first station before retrogradation, and four days stationary before direction.

Nature.—He is a masculine planet, temperately hot and moist, and the *greater fortune;* author of temperance, modesty, sobriety, justice.

Manners and Actions when well placed.—Then he is magnanimous, faithful, bashful, aspiring in an honourable way at high matters; in all his actions a lover of fair dealing, desiring to benefit all men; doing glorious actions; honourable and religious, of sweet and affable conversation, wonderfully indulgent to his wife and children, reverencing aged men, a great reliever of the poor, full of charity and godliness; liberal, hating all sordid actions; just, wise, prudent, grateful and virtuous; so that when you find ♃ the significator of any man in question, and well dignified, you may judge him well qualified as aforesaid.

When ill dignified.—When ♃ is unfortunate, then he wastes his patrimony, suffers every one to cozen him, is hypocritically religious, tenacious, and obstinate in maintaining false tenets in religion; he is ignorant, careless, nothing caring for the love of his friends; of a gross, dull capacity;

systematical, abasing himself in all companies, insinuating and stooping where no necessity is.

Corporature.—He signifies an upright, straight, and tall stature; brown, ruddy, and lovely complexion; of an oval or long visage, and full or fleshy; high forehead; large grey eyes; hair soft, and a kind of auburn brown; much beard; a large deep belly; strong proportioned thighs and legs, his feet long, being the most uncomely parts of his body; in his speech he is sober, and of grave discourse.

Oriental.—The skin more clear, his complexion honey colour, or between a white and red, sanguine, ruddy colour; great eyes, the body more fleshy; generally some mole or scar on the right foot.

Occidental.—A pure and lovely complexion, the stature more short, the hair a light brown, or near a dark flaxen, and smooth; bald about the temple or forehead.

Quality in general.—He signifies judges, senators, counsellors, ecclesiastical men, bishops, priests, ministers, cardinals, chancellors, doctors of the civil law, young scholars and students in an university or college, lawyers, clothiers, woollen drapers.

Diseases.—Pleurisies, all infirmities in the liver, apoplexies, inflammation of the lungs, palpitation and trembling of the heart, cramps, pain in the back bone, all diseases lying in the veins or ribs, and proceeding from corruption of blood; quinzies, flatulence; all putrefaction in the blood, or fevers proceeding from too great abundance thereof.

Places.—He delights in being near altars of churches, in public conventions, synods, convocations; in places neat and sweet; in wardrobes, courts of justice, and oratories.* His greatest years are 428; his greater, 79; his mean, 45; least, 12.

* This implies, that the person inquired about in a horary question, if signified by ♃, frequents such places.

Men of middle age, or of a full judgment and discretion, are described by him. Babylon, Persia, Hungaria, Spain, Cullen, are ruled by him.*

CHAPTER VII.

OF THE PLANET MARS, AND HIS SEVERAL SIGNIFICATIONS.

MARS does in order succeed Jupiter, is less in body, and appears to our sight of a shining, fiery, sparkling colour: he finishes his course in the zodiac in 1 year, 321 days, and 22 hours: his greatest latitude north is about 4° 31'; his south, 6° 47'; and is retrograde 80 days; stationary two or three. He governs wholly the watery triplicity, viz. ♋, ♏, and ♓.

Nature.—He is a masculine, nocturnal planet, in nature hot and dry, choleric and fiery; the lesser infortune, author of quarrels, strifes, and contentions.

Manners when well dignified.—In feats of war and courage invincible, scorning that any should exceed him; subject to no reason, bold, confident, immoveable, contentious, challenging all honour to themselves; valiant, lovers of war and things pertaining thereto, hazarding himself in all perils, unwilling to obey or submit to anybody; a boaster of his own acts; one that slights all things in comparison of victory, and yet of prudent behaviour in his own affairs.

When ill dignified.—Then he is a prattler, without modesty or honesty; a lover of slaughter and quarrels, murder, thievery, a promoter of sedition, frays, and commotions; an highway thief, as wavering as the wind, a traitor, of turbulent spirit, perjured, obscene, rash, inhuman, neither fearing God nor

* We have no opinion of the rule of the planets over different countries: but in mundane astrology the signs which rule them must be observed.

caring for man; unthankful, treacherous; oppressors, ravenous, cheaters, furious, and violent.*

Corporature.—Generally martialists have this form; they are but of middle stature, their bodies strong, and their bones large, rather lean than fat; their complexion of a brown, ruddy colour, their visage round, their hair red or sandy, and many times crisping or curling; sharp, hazel, piercing eyes; a bold confident countenance; and they are active and fearless.

Oriental.—He signifies valiant men; some white mixed with their redness, inclined to be tall, and of a hairy body.

Occidental.—Very ruddy complexion, but low stature, little head, smooth body, and not hairy; yellow hair, stiff, and the natural humours generally more dry.

Qualities of Men and their Professions.— Generals of armies, colonels, captains, or any soldiers having command in armies; all manner of soldiers, physicians, apothecaries, surgeons, chemists, gunners, butchers, marshals, sergeants, bailiffs, hangmen, thieves, smiths, bakers, armourers, watch-makers, tailors, cutlers of swords and knives, barbers, dyers, cooks, carpenters, gamesters, bear-wards, tanners, and curriers, according as ♂ may be strong or weak.

Diseases.—The gall, tertian fevers, pestilent burning fevers, meagrims in the head, carbuncles, the plague, and all plague sores, burnings, ringworms, blisters, phrensies, mad sudden distempers in the head, yellow jaundice, bloody flux, fistulas; all wounds and diseases in men's genitals, the stone both in the reins and bladder, scars or smallpox in the face.†

---

* These extremely evil qualities obtain only when the ☽ and ☿ are also very much afflicted.

† ♂ coming to ill aspect of the ascendant by direction early in nativities generally causes either smallpox, measles, or scarlet fever; but if the nativity denote it, he may give hurts, wounds, fevers, &c.

Mars causes all hurts by iron, the shingles, and such other diseases as arise by too much choler, anger, or passion.

Places.—Smiths' shops, furnaces, slaughter-houses, places where bricks or charcoal are burned, or have been burned; chimneys, and forges.*

His orb is only seven degrees.

Years.—In man he governs the flourishing time of youth, and from 41 to 56; his greatest year is 264; greater 66, lower 40, and least 15.

Countries.—Saromatia, Lombardy, Batavia, Ferraria, Gothland.

CHAPTER VIII.

OF THE SUN, HIS GENERAL AND PARTICULAR SIGNIFICATIONS.

THE Sun is placed in the middle of all the planets, continually visible to all mortal men. He passes through all the twelve signs of the zodiac in one year: his mean motion is 59 minutes 8 seconds, yet his diurnal motion is sometimes 57 minutes 16 seconds, sometimes more, but never exceeding 61 minutes and 6 seconds. He always moves in the ecliptic, and is ever void of latitude. He has only the sign ♌ for his house, and ♒ for his detriment. He is exalted in the 19th degree of ♈, and receives his fall in 19° ♎.

The Sun governs the fiery triplicity, viz. ♈, ♌, ♐, by day. He is always direct, and never can be considered retrograde.

In nature.—He is naturally hot and dry, but more tem-

---

* To this may be added, cutlers' shops, and places where iron is manufactured in any manner, armouries, &c.

perate than ♂; is a masculine, diurnal planet, and equivalent if well dignified to a fortune.

Manners when well dignified.—Very faithful, keeping their promises with the greatest punctuality; a kind of itching desire to rule and sway wherever he comes. Prudent, and of incomparable judgment; of great majesty and stateliness, industrious to acquire honour and a large patrimony, yet as willing to spend it again. The solar man usually speaks with gravity, but not many words, and these with great confidence and command of his own feelings; full of thought, secret, trusty, speaks deliberately, and, notwithstanding his great heart, he is affable, tractable, and very humane to all people; one loving sumptuousness and magnificence, and whatever is honourable; no sordid thoughts can enter his heart.

When ill dignified.—Then the solar man is arrogant and proud, disdaining all men, boasting of his pedigree; he is purblind in sight and judgment, restless, troublesome, domineering, a mere vapour, expensive, foolish, endowed with no gravity in words, or soberness in actions; a spendthrift, wasting his patrimony, and hanging on other men's charity; yet he thinks all men are bound to him, because a gentleman born.

Corporature.—Usually the ☉ presents a man of a good, large, and strong corporature, a yellow, saffron complexion, a round large forehead, large goggle eyes, sharp and piercing; a body strong and well composed, not so beautiful as lovely; full of heat, with hair yellowish, and therefore quickly bald; much hair on their beard, and usually an high ruddy complexion; their bodies fleshy; in disposition they are very bountiful, honest, sincere, well-minded, of good heart; healthful constitution; very humane, yet sufficiently spirited, and not loquacious.

Oriental.—We can only say the ☉ is oriental in the figure,

or in an oriental quarter of the figure, or occidental, &c.*
The planets are oriental when they rise, or appear before him
in the morning, and occidental when they set after him.

Quality of Men, and their Professions.—He signifies, kings,
princes, emperors, &c. dukes, marquisses, earls, barons, lieutenants, deputy lieutenants of counties, magistrates, gentlemen in general, courtiers, desirers of honour and preferment.
Justices of peace, mayors, high sheriffs, high constables,
stewards of noblemen's houses, the principal magistrate of
any city, town, castle, or country village; yea, even a petty
constable, where no better is; goldsmiths, braziers, pewterers,
coppersmiths, and minters of money.

Sicknesses.—Pimples in the face, palpitation or trembling,
diseases of the brain and heart, infirmities of the eyes, cramps,
sudden swoonings, diseases of the mouth and impure breath,
catarrhs, putrid fevers. Principally in man he governs the
heart and the brain; in women, the vital spirit, and denotes
hysterics.

Places.—Houses or courts of princes, palaces, theatres,
all magnificent structures, being clean and decent; halls, and
dining rooms.

Orb.—Is 15 degrees.

Years.— In age he rules youth, or when one is at the
strongest; his greatest years are 1460,† greater 120, lesser
69, and least 19.

Countries.—Italy, Sicily, Bohemia, Phenicia, and Chaldea.

* In nativities the ☉ and ☽ are oriental between the 1st and 10th
houses, and in the opposite quarter of the figure; they are occidental between the 10th and 7th houses, and in the opposite quarter: but in horary
questions they are oriental between the 4th and 10th, and occidental after
leaving the 10th, until they reach the 4th; oriental when rising, and
occidental when setting.

† It is a very remarkable fact, that this period is the *sothic* or *canicular*
year of the Egyptians; whence it is pretty evident that these astrological
doctrines came originally from that people, and are, in fact, of the very
highest antiquity.

CHAPTER IX.

OF THE PLANET VENUS, AND HER SEVERAL SIGNIFICATIONS AND NATURE.

Name.—After the Sun succeedeth Venus.

Colour in the Element.—She is of a bright, shining colour, and is well known by the name of the evening star, or Hesperus; and that is when she appears after the Sun is set; she is commonly called the morning star, but by the learned Lucifer, when she is seen long before the rising of the Sun. Her mean motion is 59 minutes and 8 seconds; her diurnal motion is sometimes 62 minutes a-day, and 82 minutes she never exceeds. Her greatest latitude is 9° 2'. She is retrograde 42 days, and stationary 2. Her year is 224 days and 7 hours.

Element.—She is a feminine planet, temperately cold and moist; nocturnal, the lesser fortune, author of mirth and cheerfulness.

Manners and Quality when well dignified.—She signifies a quiet man, not given to law, quarrel, or wrangling; not vicious; pleasant, neat and spruce, loving mirth in his words and actions, cleanly in apparel, rather drinking much than gluttonous; prone to venery, often entangled in love matters, zealous in their affections, musical, delighting in baths and all honest merry meetings, or amusements and theatricals; easy of belief, and not given to labour, or take any pains; a company keeper, cheerful, nothing mistrustful, a right virtuous man or woman, often jealous, yet without cause.

When ill dignified.—Then he is riotous, expensive, wholly given to dissipation and lewd companies of women, nothing regarding his reputation, coveting unlawful beds, incestuous, an adulterer, fantastical, a mere skip-jack, of no faith, no repute, no credit, spending his means in ale-houses, taverns, and among scandalous loose people; a mere lazy companion, nothing careful of the things of this life, or any thing religious.

Corporature.—A man of fair but not tall stature, his complexion being white, tending to a little darkness* which makes him more lovely, very fair, lovely eyes, and sometimes black; a round face and not large, fair hair, smooth and plenty of it, and it is usually of a light brown colour; a lovely mouth and cherry lips, the face pretty fleshy, a rolling wandering eye, a body very delightful, lovely, and exceedingly well shaped; one desirous of trimming and making himself neat and complete both in clothes and body, a love dimple in his cheeks,† a stedfast eye, and full of amorous enticements.

Oriental.—When oriental, the body inclines to tallness or a kind of upright straightness in person; not corpulent or very tall, but neatly composed; a right Venus person is a pretty, complete, handsome man or woman.

Occidental.—When she is occidental, the man is more short in stature, yet very decent and comely in shape and form, well liked of all.

Quality of Persons, and Employments.—Musicians, gamesters, silkmen, mercers, linen-drapers, painters, jewellers, players, lapidaries, embroiderers, woman-tailors, wives, mothers, virgins, choristers, fiddlers, pipers: when joined with the ☽, ballad-singers, perfumers, seamstresses, picture-drawers, engravers, upholsterers, limners, glovers, and such as sell those

---

* This signifies a pale or wan complexion, yet with a dark hue.

† Those who have Venus strong, either in their nativities, or as their significators in questions, invariably have dimples either in the cheek or chin.

commodities which adorn women, either in body (as clothes) or in face (as complexion waters).

Sicknesses.—Diseases by her signified are principally in the matrix and members of generation; in the reins, belly, back, navel, and those parts; the gonorrhœa or running of the reins, lues venerea or any disease arising from inordinate lust, priapism, impotency in generation, hernias, &c., the diabetes, or an involuntary discharge of urine.

Orb.—Her orb is 7 degrees.

Years.—Her greatest years are 151; her greater 82, her mean 45, her least 8. In man she governs youth from 14 to 28.

Countries.—Arabia, Austria, Campania, Vienna, Polonia the Greater, Turin, Parthia, Media, Cyprus.*

CHAPTER X.

OF MERCURY, AND HIS SIGNIFICATION, NATURE, AND PROPERTY.

MERCURY is the least of all the planets, never distant from the Sun above 28 degrees; by which reason he is seldom visible to our sight.

Colour and Motion.—He is of a dusky silver colour; his mean motion is 59 minutes and 8 seconds, but he is sometimes so swift, that he moves above 1 degree and 40 minutes in one day. He is stationary one day, retrograde twenty-four days. His year is 87 days and 23 hours.

---

* These observations are retained from respect to our author; but we must repeat, that it is ♉ and ♎, the houses of ♀, which govern these countries.

Latitude. — His greatest south latitude is 3 degrees 35 minutes, greatest north latitude 3 degrees 33 minutes.

Nature.—We may not call him either masculine or feminine, for he is either the one or the other as joined to any planet; for if in ♂ with a masculine planet, he becomes masculine:* if with a feminine, then feminine; but of his own nature he is cold and dry, and therefore melancholy: with the good he is good, with the evil planets, ill; he is author of subtlety, tricks, devices, perjury, &c.

Manners when well dignified.—Being well dignified, he represents a man of a subtle and political brain and intellect, an excellent disputant or logician, arguing with learning and discretion, and using much eloquence in his speech; a searcher into all kinds of mysteries and learning, sharp and witty, learning almost any thing without a teacher; ambitious of being exquisite in every science, desirous naturally to travel and see foreign parts; a man of an unwearied fancy, curious in the search of any occult knowledge, able by his own genius to produce wonders, given to divination and the more secret knowledge. If he turn merchant, no man exceeds him in way of trade, or invention of new ways whereby to obtain wealth.

Manners when ill dignified.—A troublesome wit, a kind of phrenetic man, his tongue and pen against every man; wholly bent to fool his estate and time in loquacity and trying nice conclusions to no purpose, a great liar, boaster, prattler, busybody; false; a tale-carrier, addicted to wicked arts, as necromancy, and such like ungodly knowledges; easy of belief, an ass or very idiot, constant in no place or opinion, cheating and thieving everywhere; a newsmonger, pretending all manner of knowledge, but void of true or solid learning;

---

* This applies to aspects also; but, of course, only in horary questions.

a trifler, a mere frantic fellow; if he prove a divine, then a mere verbal fellow, frothy, of no judgment, easily perverted, constant in nothing but idle words and bragging.

Corporature.—Generally he denotes one of an high stature, and straight, thin, spare body; a high forehead, and somewhat narrow long face, long nose, fair eyes, neither perfectly black nor grey, thin lips and nose, little hair on the chin, but much on his head, and of a sad brown inclining to blackness; long arms, fingers, and hands; his complexion like an olive or chesnut colour. You must observe ☿ more than all the planets; for having any aspect to a planet, he partakes more of the influence of that planet than any other does; if with ♄, then heavy; with ♃, more temperate; with ♂, more rash; with ☉, more genteel; with ♀, more jesting; with ☽, more changeable.

Oriental.—When he is oriental, his complexion is honey-colour, or like one sunburnt; in the stature of his body not very high, but well jointed; small eyes, not much hair; in very truth, according to the height of body, very well composed, but still a defect in the complexion, swarthy brown, and in the tongue all for his own interest.

Occidental.—When occidental, a tawny visage, lank body, small slender limbs, hollow eyes, either sparkling, red or fiery; the whole frame of body inclining to dryness.

Quality of Men and Professions.—He generally signifies all literary men, philosophers, mathematicians, astrologians,* merchants, secretaries, writers, sculptors, poets, orators, advocates, schoolmasters, stationers, printers, exchangers of money, attorneys, ambassadors, commissioners, clerks, artificers, generally accomptants, solicitors; sometimes thieves, prattling ministers, busy secretaries, and they unlearned; grammarians, tailors, carriers, messengers, footmen, usurers.

* This more especially if with or in good aspect to *Herschel.*

Sickness.—All vertigos, lethargies, or giddiness in the head; madness, either lightness or any disease of the brain; phthisic; all stammering and imperfection in the tongue, vain and fond imaginations, all defects in the memory, hoarseness, dry coughs, too great abundance of spittle, all snaffling and snuffling in the head or nose; the hand and feet gout, dumbness, foul or diseased tongue; all evils in the fancy and intellectual parts.

Orb.—His orb is 7 degrees.

Years.—His greatest years are 450, his greater 76, his mean 48, his little or least 20.

Countries.—He has Grecia, Flanders, Egypt. Of towns, Paris.

CHAPTER XI.

OF THE MOON, HER PROPERTIES AND SIGNIFICATIONS.

Name.—The Moon we find called by the ancients Lucina, Cynthia, Diana, Phœbe, Latona, Noctiluca, Proserpina;* she is nearest to the earth of all the planets.

Motion.—She terminates her course through the whole twelve signs in 27 days, 7 hours, 43 minutes, 5 seconds; her mean motion is 13 degrees, 10 minutes, and 36 seconds; but she moves sometimes less and sometimes more, never exceeding 15 degrees and 12 minutes in 24 hours' time.

Latitude.—Her greatest north latitude is 5 degrees and 17 minutes. Her greatest south latitude 5 degrees and 12 minutes. She is never retrograde; but when she is slow in motion, and goes less in 24 hours than 13 degrees and 11 minutes; she is then equivalent to a retrograde planet.

* These names prove the various mythological fables to have had their origin in the ancient astrology of the Egyptians.

Nature.—She is a feminine, nocturnal planet; cold, moist, and phlegmatic.

Manners when well placed or dignified.—She signifies one of composed manners, a soft tender creature, a lover of all honest and ingenious sciences, a searcher of and delighter in novelties, naturally inclined to flit and shift his habitation; unsteadfast, wholly caring for the present times; timorous prodigal, and easily frightened; loving peace, however, and to live free from the cares of this life. If a mechanic, the man learns many occupations, and frequently will be tampering with many ways to trade in.

When ill.—A mere vagabond, idle person, hating labour; a drunkard, a sot, one of no spirit or forecast, delighting to live beggarly and carelessly; one content in no condition of life, either good or ill.

Corporature.—She generally presents a man of fair stature, whitely coloured; the face round, grey eyes, and a little lowering; much hair both on the head, face, and other parts; usually one eye a little larger than the other; short hands and fleshy; the whole body inclining to be fleshy, plump, corpulent, and phlegmatic. If she be impedited of the ☉ in a nativity or question, she usually signifies some blemish in or near the eye; a blemish near the eye, if she be impedited in succeedent houses; in the sight, if she be unfortunate in angles, and with fixed stars called nebulæ.

Qualities of Men and Women.—She signifies queens, countesses, ladies, all manner of women, as also the common people, travellers, pilgrims, sailors, fishermen, fishmongers, brewers, tapsters, publicans, letter carriers, coachmen, huntsmen, messengers, mariners, millers, maltsters, drunkards, oysterwives, fishwomen, charwomen, tripewomen, and generally such women as carry commodities in the streets; as also midwives, nurses, &c.; hackneymen, watermen, water-bearers.*

Sickness.—Apoplexies, palsy, the cholic, the stomach-ache, diseases in the left side, the bladder and members of generation; the menstrues and liver in women, dropsies, fluxes of the belly, all cold rheumatic diseases, cold stomach, the gout in the wrists and feet; sciatica, worms, hurts in the eyes, surfeits, rotten coughs, convulsive fits, the falling sickness, king's evil, abscess, smallpox, and measles.

Orb.—Is 12 degrees.

Years.—Her greatest years are 320, greater 108, mean 66, least 25.

Countries.—Holland, Zealand, Denmark, Nuremberg, Flanders.

CHAPTER XII.

The Head of the Dragon.—THE head of the Dragon is masculine, of the nature of ♃ and ♀, and of himself a fortune.†

The Tail of the Dragon.—The Tail of the Dragon by nature is quite contrary to the Head, for he is evil. I ever found the ☊ equivalent to either of the fortunes, and, when joined with the evil planets, to lessen their malevolent signification; when joined with the good, to increase the good promised by them. The Tail of the Dragon I always, in my practice, found, when he was joined by the evil planets, their malice or the evil intended thereby was doubled and trebled, or ex-

---

* Generally, all persons who are connected with liquids in their occupation.

† These points are of no consequence in nativities, except as regards the Moon, who brings benefits when she reaches the ☊ in the zodiac by directional motion, and evil when she reaches the ☋.

tremely augmented, &c.; and when he chanced to be in conjunction with any of the fortunes who were significators in the question, though the matter by the principal significator was fairly promised and likely to be perfected in a small time, yet did there ever fall out many rubs and disturbances, much wrangling and controversy, that the business was many times given over for desperate before a perfect conclusion could be had; and unless the principal significators were angular, and well fortified with essential dignities, many times unexpectedly the whole matter came to nothing.

CHAPTER XIII.

ANOTHER BRIEF DESCRIPTION OF THE SHAPES AND FORMS OF THE PLANETS.

Herschel.—THIS is the most distant planet from the Sun; his motion is very slow, as he takes 83 years 151 days to go through the twelve signs. The nature of ♅ is extremely evil. If he ascend or be with the chief significator in any figure, he denotes an eccentric person, far from fortunate, always abrupt, and often violent in his manners. If well aspected, he gives sudden and unexpected benefits; and if afflicted, he will cause remarkable and unlooked-for losses and misfortunes. He is not so powerful as Saturn or Mars, yet can do much evil. Persons under his influence are partial to antiquity, astrology, &c., and all uncommon studies, especially if Mercury and the Moon be in aspect to him. They are likely to strike out novelties, and to be remarkable for an inventive faculty. They are generally unfortunate in marriage, especially if he afflict ♀, the ☽, or the seventh house, either in nativities or questions.

INTRODUCTION TO ASTROLOGY.

Saturn—Signifies one of a swarthy colour, palish like lead, or of a black earthly brown; one of rough skin, thick and very hairy on the body, small eyes; many times his complexion is between black and yellow, or as if he had an affection of the black or yellow jaundice; he is lean, crooked, or beetle-browed; a thin weak beard; great lips, like negroes; he looks to the ground,* is slow in motion, either is bow-legged or hits one leg or knee against another; most part a disagreeable breath, seldom free from a cough; he is crafty for his own interest, seducing people to his opinion; full of revenge and malice, little caring for religion; is a foul, nasty, slovenly knave, or a harlot, a great eater and glutton, a brawling fellow; has broad, great shoulders; is covetous, and yet seldom rich, &c.†

Jupiter.—We must describe ♃ and a jovialist to be one of a comely stature, full-faced, full-eyed, a sanguine complexion, or mixture of white and red; a large space between his eyebrows; usually his beard is of a flaxen or sandy-flaxen colour; sometimes also, when ♃ is combust, very sad or black; his hair thick, his eyes not black; good broad, well-set teeth, but usually some mark of difference in the two fore teeth, either by their standing awry, or some blackness or imperfection in them; his hair gently curls (if he be in a fiery sign); a man well spoken, religious, or at least a good moral honest man; a person comely, and somewhat fat (if ♃ be in moist signs), fleshy; if in airy signs, large and strong; if in earthly signs, a man usually well descended; but if he be significator, if an ordinary clown, as sometimes he may be, then is he of more humanity than usual in such kind of men.

---

* This downward look, keeping the eyes on the earth, is one of the most remarkable circumstances in the character of the persons described by Saturn, or who have him in the ascendant at birth.

† These evil qualities when Saturn is weak and afflicted.

Mars.—A martial man is many times full-faced, with a lively, high colour, like sun-burnt, or like raw tanned leather; a fierce countenance, his eyes being sparkling or sharp and darting, and of yellow colour; his hair, both of head and beard, being reddish (but herein you must vary according to the sign). In fiery signs, and airy, where ♂ falls to be with fixed stars of his own nature, there shews a deep sandy red colour; but in watery signs, being with fixed stars of his own nature, he is of a flaxen or whitish bright hair; if in earthy signs, the hair is like a sad brown, or of a chesnut colour. He has a mark or scar on his face; is broad-shouldered, a sturdy, strong body, being bold and proud, given to mockery and scorn, to quarrel, drink, game, and wench; which you may easily know by the sign he is in: if in the house of ♀, he wenches; in that of ☿, he steals; but if he be in his own house, he quarrels; in that of ♄, is dogged; in the ☉'s, is lordly; in the ☽'s, is a drunkard.

The Sun.—The Sun generally denotes one of an obscure white colour, mixed with red; a round face, and short chin, a fair stature, and one of a comely body; his colour sometimes between yellow and black, but for the most part more sanguine than otherwise; a bold man, and resolute; his hair curling; he has a white and tender skin; one desirous of praise, fame, and estimation among men; he has a clear voice, and great head; his teeth somewhat distorted or obliquely set; of slow speech, but of a composed judgment; using outwardly a great decorum in his actions, but privately he is lascivious and prone to many vices.

Venus.—Whoever is signified by Venus, whether man or woman, has a good and fair round visage, a full eye, usually we say goggle-eyed: red ruddy lips, the nether more thick or longer than the upper; the eyelids black, yet lovely and graceful; the hair of lovely colour, (but most part according to the sign as before repeated); in some it is coal black, in others a light brown; a soft smooth hair; and the body extremely well shaped, even rather inclining to shortness than tallness.*

Mercury.—We describe Mercury to be a man neither black nor white, but between both, of a sad brown or dark yellow colour; long visaged, high forehead, black or grey eyes, a thin, long, sharp nose; thin spare beard, (many times none at all) of an auburn sad colour, next to black; slender of body, small legs; a prattling, busy fellow; and in walking he goes nimbly, and always would be thought to be full of action.

The Moon.—She, by reason of her swiftness, varies her shape very often, but, in general, she personates one having a round visage and full face, in whose complexion you may perceive a mixture of white and red, but paleness overcomes: if she be in fiery signs, the man or woman speaks hastily; in watery signs, he or she has some freckles in his or her face, or is blub-cheeked, not a handsome body, but a muddling creature; and unless very well dignified, she ever signifies an ordinary vulgar person.†

* We have always observed that Venus causes *dimples* and a smiling face.

† We have given these descriptions in addition to the former, as it is most material for the student to be able to describe the person inquired of well; as, by that means, the character being known, his conduct may be more accurately foreseen.

CHAPTER XIV.

THE COLOURS OF THE PLANETS AND SIGNS.

♄ Gives black colour; ♃ a colour mixed with red and green; ♂ red, or iron colour; ☉ yellow or yellow purple; ♀ white or purple colour; ☿ sky colour, or blueish: ☽ a colour spotted with white, and other mixed colours.

♈ White mixed with red; ♉ white mixed with lemon; ♊ white mixed with red; ♋ green or russet; ♌ red or green; ♍ black speckled with blue; ♎ black or dark crimson, or tawny colour; ♏ brown; ♐ yellow, or a green sanguine; ♑ black or russet, or a swarthy brown; ♒ a sky colour with blue; ♓ white, glistening colour.*

CHAPTER XV.

THE NATURE, PLACE, COUNTRIES, GENERAL DESCRIPTION, AND DISEASES SIGNIFIED BY THE TWELVE SIGNS.

ARIES

Is a masculine, diurnal sign, moveable, cardinal, equinoctial; in nature fiery, hot and dry, choleric, bestial, luxurious, intemperate, and violent; the diurnal house of ♂; of the fiery triplicity, and of the east.

Diseases.— All gumboils, swellings, pimples in the face, smallpox, hair lips, polypus, ringworms, falling sickness, apoplexies, megrims, tooth-ache, head-ache, and baldness.

Places ♈ *signifies.*—Where sheep and cattle do feed, sandy or hilly grounds; a place of refuge for thieves, (as unfrequented places); in houses, the covering, ceiling, or plaster-

---

* Like a fish just taken out of the water.

ing; a stable for small beasts; lands newly taken in or recently ploughed, or where bricks or lime has been burnt.

Description of the Body or Shape ♈ represents. — A dry body, not exceeding in height; lean or spare, but lusty bones, and his limbs strong; the visage long, black eye-brows, a long scraggy neck, thick shoulders; the complexion dusky, brown or swarthy.

Countries ruled by ♈. — England, Germany, Denmark, Lesser Poland, Palestine, Syria, Naples. — *Towns:* Florence, Verona, Padua, Marseilles, Burgundy, Saragossa, Bergamo.

TAURUS.

Qualities of the Sign ♉. — It is an earthy, cold, dry, melancholy, feminine, nocturnal, fixed, bestial sign; of the earthy triplicity, and south; the night house of Venus.

Diseases. — The king's evil, sore throats, wens, fluxes of rheums falling into the throat, quinzies, abscesses in those parts.

Places. — Stables where horses are, low houses, houses where the implements of cattle are laid up; pasture or feeding grounds, where no houses are near; plain grounds, or where bushes have lately been eradicated, and wherein wheat and corn are substituted; some little trees not far off; in houses, cellars, low rooms.

Shape and Description. — It represents one of a short, but full, strong and well-set stature; a broad forehead; great eyes, large swarthy face, and broad strong shoulders; great mouth, and thick lips; gross hands; black, rugged hair.

Countries ruled by ♉. — Ireland, Persia, Great Poland, Asia Minor, the Archipelago, and the southern parts of Russia. — *Towns:* Dublin, Mantua, Leipsic, Parma, Franconia, Lorraine: also the islands of Cyprus and Samos, and the port and vicinity of Navarino.

GEMINI.

Quality and Property of ♊.—It is an aerial, hot, moist, sanguine, diurnal, common or double-bodied human sign; the diurnal house of ☿; of the airy triplicity, western, masculine.

Diseases.—It signifies all diseases, accidents, or infirmities in the arms, shoulders, or hands; corrupted blood, windiness in the veins, distempered fancies, and nervous diseases.

Places.—Wainscot of rooms, plaistering, and walls of houses; the halls, or where play is used; hills and mountains, barns, storehouses for corn, coffers, chests and high places.

Countries ruled by ♊.—North America, Lower Egypt, Lombardy, Sardinia, Brabant, Belgium, West of England.— *Towns:* London (especially ♊ 17° 54′), Versailles, Mentz, Bruges, Louvaine, Cordova, New York, and Nuremberg.

Description.—An upright, tall, straight body, either in man or woman; the complexion sanguine, not clear, but obscure and dark; long arms, yet many times the hands and feet short, and very fleshy; a dark hair,* almost black; a strong, active body, a good piercing hazel eye, and wanton, and of perfect and quick sight; of excellent understanding, and judicious in worldly affairs.

CANCER.

Quality and Property of ♋.—It is the only house of the Moon, and is the first sign of the watery triplicity; is a watery, cold, moist, phlegmatic, feminine, nocturnal, moveable sign; mute, and slow of voice; fruitful, northern.

---

* In all cases, I think the hair will be found to be of the colour given by the planet near to or aspecting closely the degree ascending, or on the cusp of the house which signifies the party. I find that ♊ more frequently gives brown hair in questions.—ZAD.

Diseases. — It signifies imperfections all over, or in the breast, stomach, and paps; weak digestion, cold stomach, phthisic, salt phlegms, rotten coughs, dropsical humours, imposthumations in the stomach, cancers,* which are mostly in the breast.

Places.—The sea, great rivers, navigable rivers; but in inland countries it denotes places near rivers, brooks, springs, wells, cellars in houses, wash-houses, marsh-grounds, ditches with rushes, sedges, sea banks, trenches, cisterns.

Shape and Description.—Generally a low and small stature, the upper parts larger than the lower; a round visage; sickly, pale, and white complexion; the hair a sad brown; little eyes; prone to have many children, if a woman.

Countries ruled by ♋.—Holland, Scotland, Zealand, Georgia, and all Africa.—*Towns:* Constantinople, Tunis, Algiers, Amsterdam, Cadiz, Venice, Genoa, York, St. Andrews, Manchester, New York, Bern, Lubeck, Milan, and Vicentia.

LEO.

Quality and Property of ♌.—It is the only house of the Sun; by nature, fiery, hot, dry, choleric; diurnal, commanding, bestial,† barren; of the east, and fiery triplicity; masculine.

Diseases.—All sicknesses in the ribs and sides, as pleuri-

---

* There is little doubt that this disease took its name from the astrological fact, that the sign ♋ rules the breast, in which it generally occurs. Persons born with this sign ascending have always some defect, scar, mark, or disease in the breast.—ZAD.

† This term signifies, that if a person be born under or signified by this sign, or if they have ☽ therein, and at all afflicted by the malefics, they will have less of humane feelings than when under any other sign, except the last half of ♐. They do not sympathize with other persons' sufferings, or feel compassion.

sies, convulsions, pains in the back, trembling or passion of the heart, violent burning fevers; all weakness or diseases in the heart, sore eyes, the plague, the pestilence, the yellow jaundice.

Places. — A place where wild beasts frequent; woods, forests, desert, steep, rocky, and inaccessible places; king's palaces, castles, forts, parks; in houses where fire is kept, near a chimney.

Shape and Form.—Great round head; large prominent eyes, as if staring out, or goggle eyes, quick sighted; a full and large body, and more than of middle stature; broad shoulders, narrow sides, yellow or dark flaxen hair, and it curling or turning up; a fierce countenance, but ruddy high sanguine complexion; strong, valiant, and active; step firm, and mind courteous.

Countries ruled by ♌. — France, Italy, Bohemia, Sicily, Rome.— *Towns:* Rome, Bath, Bristol, Taunton, Cremona, Prague, Apulia, Ravenna, and Philadelphia; also the Alps and the ancient Chaldea, as far as Bussorah.

VIRGO.

Property and Quality of ♍.—It is an earthy, cold, melancholy, barren, feminine, nocturnal, southern sign; the house and exaltation of ☿; of the earthy triplicity.

Places.—It signifies a study, where books are kept; a closet, a dairy-house, corn-fields, granaries, malt-houses, hay, barley, wheat or peas ricks, &c.; or a place where cheese and butter is preserved and stored up.

Diseases.—The worms, wind, cholic; all obstructions and croaking of the bowels, infirmities in the testicles, any disease in the belly.

Countries ruled by ♍.—Turkey in Europe and Asia, Switzerland, Mesopotamia, or Diarbed; all the country between the Tigris and the Euphrates, the land of the Turcomans, &c., and the West Indies.—*Towns :* Paris, Lyons, Toulouse, St. Etienne, Basil, Heidelburg, Reading ; also Jerusalem, Candia, Lower Silesia, Croatia or Liburnia, Babylon or Bagdat, Thessaly, Corinth, and the Morea. Also the trade and government of Liverpool, which are ruled especially by the 9th degree.

Shape and Form.—A slender body, rather tall, but well composed; a ruddy, brown complexion ; black hair,* well favoured or lovely, but not a beautiful creature ; a small, shrill voice, all members inclining to brevity;† a witty, discreet soul, judicious, and exceedingly well spoken ; studious, and given to history, whether man or woman. It produces a rare understanding, if ☿ be in this sign, and ☽ in ♋ ; but somewhat unstable.

LIBRA.

Nature and Property of ♎.—This sign is hot and moist, sanguine, masculine, moveable, equinoctial, cardinal, humane, diurnal : of the airy triplicity, and western ; the chief house of ♀.

Diseases.—All diseases, (or the stone and gravel) in the reins of the back and kidneys ; heats and diseases in the loins or haunches; imposthumes or ulcers in the reins, kidneys, or bladder ; weakness in the back, corruption of blood.

Places.—In the fields it represents ground near windmills, or some straggling barn or outhouse, or sawpits, or where coopers work, or wood is cut, sides of hills, tops of mountains, trees, grounds where hawking and hunting is used ; sandy and gravel fields ; pure clear air, and sharp ; the upper

---

* The early part of the sign gives brown hair.
† If ♅ ascend therein, the limbs will be long and the body taller.

rooms in houses, chambers, garrets, one chamber within another; tops of chests of drawers, wardrobes, &c.

Shape and Form. — It personates a well-framed body, straight, tall, and more subtle or slender than gross; a round, lovely, and beautiful visage; a pure sanguine colour; in youth, no abundance or excess in either red or white; but in age, pimples, or a very high colour; the hair yellowish, smooth, and long, eyes generally blue, and temper even.

Countries ruled by ♎. — China, Japan, parts of India near them; Austria, Usbeck in Persia, towards India; Upper Egypt, Livonia, the vicinity of the Caspian Sea.—*Towns* : Lisbon, Vienna, Antwerp, Francfort, Spires, Fribourg, Charlestown in America, and its vicinity.

SCORPIO.

Nature and Property of ♏. — It is a cold, watery, nocturnal, phlegmatic, northern, feminine sign; of the watery triplicity; the house and joy of Mars; usually it represents subtle, deceitful men.

Diseases.—Gravel, the stone in the secret parts or bladder; ruptures, fistulas, or the piles; priapisms, all afflictions in the private parts, either of men or women; defects in the matrix, and its diseases; injuries, &c. to the spermatic cord, the groin, &c.

Places.—Places where all kinds of creeping beasts use, as beetles, &c.; or such as be without wings and are poisonous; gardens, vineyards, orchards, ruinous houses near waters; muddy, moorish grounds; stagnant lakes, quagmires, ponds, sinks, the kitchen or larder, washhouse, &c.

Form and Description.—A corpulent, strong, able body, somewhat a broad or square face; a dusky, muddy complexion, and sad dark hair, much and crisping; a hairy body, somewhat bow-legged, short-necked; a squat, well-trussed fellow.

Countries ruled by ♏.—Barbary, Morocco, Norway, Valentia, Catalonia, Bavaria, and the ancient Cappadocia. — *Towns:* Francfort on the Oder, Messina, Ghent, Liverpool, which is especially ruled by the 19th degree.

SAGITTARY.

Quality and Nature of ♐.—It is of the fiery triplicity, east; in nature hot, dry, masculine, choleric; diurnal, common, bicorporal or double body, the house and joy of ♃.

Diseases.—It rules the thighs and buttocks, and all fistulous tumours or hurts falling in those members; and generally denotes heated blood, fevers, pestilence, falls from horses, or hurts from them or four-footed beasts; also prejudice by fire, heat, and intemperateness in sports.

Places.—A stable for war-horses, or a house where great four-footed beasts are usually kept; it represents in the fields, hills, and the highest land; also grounds that rise a little above the rest. In houses, upper rooms and places near the fire.

Shape and Form of Body.—It represents a well-favoured countenance, somewhat long visage, but full and ruddy, or almost like sunburnt, the hair light chestnut colour, the stature somewhat above the middle size, a conformity in the members, and a strong, able body; inclined to baldness, and one fond of horses.

Countries ruled by ♐. — Arabia Felix, Spain, Hungary, parts of France near Cape Finisterre, Dalmatia, Istria, Tuscany, Moravia, Sclavonia.—*Towns:* Cologne, Buda, Avignon, Narbonne, Toledo.

CAPRICORN.

Quality and Nature of ♑.—It is the house of Saturn, and is nocturnal, cold, dry, melancholy, earthy, feminine, cardinal, moveable, four-footed, southern; the exaltation of ♂.

Diseases.—It has government of the knees, and all diseases incident to those places, either by strains or fractures; it denotes leprosy, itch, and cutaneous complaints.

Places.—It shows an ox-house or cow-house, or where calves are kept, or tools for husbandry, or old wood is laid up, or where sails for ships and such materials are stored; also sheep-pens, and grounds where sheep feed; fallow grounds, barren fields, bushy and thorny; dunghills in fields, or where soil is laid in low houses; dark places, near the ground or threshold.

Corporature.—Usually dry bodies, not high of stature, long, lean, and slender visage; thin beard, and black hair, a narrow chin, long small neck, and narrow chest. I have found many times, ♑ ascending, the party to have white hair, but in the seventh ever black.*

Countries ruled by ♑.—India, Greece, parts of Persia about Circan, Macran, and Chorassan; Lithuania, Saxony, Albania, Bulgaria, Stiria, Mexico, and parts about the Isthmus of Darien, Santa Martha, Popayan, Pasta, &c.—*Towns:* Mecklenburgh, Hesse, Oxford; and also the Orkney Islands.

AQUARIUS.

Nature and Property of ♒.—This is an airy, hot, and moist sign; diurnal, sanguine, fixed, humane, masculine, the principal house of ♄; western.

Sickness.—It governs the legs, ancles, and all manner of infirmities incident to those members; spasmodic and nervous diseases, cramps, wind, &c.

---

* This remark of the author confirms our previous opinion, that the colour of the hair in questions depends on the ruler of the term ascending; in nativities, on the planets aspecting the ascendant, as well as the sign ascending.

Places.—Hilly and uneven places; spots newly dug or ploughed, or where quarries of stone are, or any minerals have been dug up; in houses, the roofs, eaves or upper parts; vineyards, or near some little spring or conduit head.

Shape and form.—It represents a squat, thick corporature, or one of a strong, plump, well-composed body, not tall: a long visage, sanguine complexion; if ♄, who is lord of this house, be in ♑ or ♒, the party is black in hair, and in complexion sanguine, with prominent teeth; otherwise I have observed the party is of clear, white, or fair complexion, and of sandy-coloured hair, or very flaxen, and a very pure skin.*

Countries ruled by ♒.—Arabia the stony, Russia, Tartary, Prussia, parts of Poland, Lithuania and Muscovy, Lower Sweden, Westphalia.—*Towns:* Hamburgh, Bremen, Piedmont; also Affghaunistan, and other parts of Asia bordering on Persia; and this sign has rule over the affairs of state in England, especially the 13th degree.†

PISCES.

Property and Quality of ♓.—This is a northern, cold sign, fruitful, phlegmatic, feminine, watery; the house of ♃ and exaltation of ♀; a bicorporeal, common or double-bodied sign; an idle, effeminate, sickly sign, or representing a party of no action.

Sickness.—All diseases in the feet, as the gout; and all lameness and pains incident to those members, mucous discharges, itch, blotches, breakings out; boils and ulcers pro-

* The Princess Charlotte of Wales was born with this sign ascending; it gives more beauty than any other sign except ♎.

† Eclipses in ♒ cause great innovations in the state in England: comets plunge the nation into war. The greatest changes have occurred in the laws while ♅ has been in ♒.

ceeding from corrupt blood; colds and moist diseases, and bowel complaints caused by wet feet.

Places.— It represents grounds full of water, or where many springs and many fowl are: also fish-ponds, or rivers full of fish; places where hermitages have been, moats about houses, water-mills. In houses, places near the water, as some well or pump, or where water stands.*

Corporature.—A short stature, not very well made; a good large face, pale complexion, the body fleshy or swelling, not very straight, but incurvating, or stooping somewhat with the head.†

Countries ruled by ♓. — Portugal, Calabria, Normandy, Galicia in Spain, Cilicia.—*Towns:* Alexandria, Ratisbon, Worms, Seville, Compostella, Tiverton.

CHAPTER XVI.

TEACHING WHAT USE MAY BE MADE OF THE FORMER DISCOURSE OF THE TWELVE SIGNS.

IF one demand of the artist, what condition, quality, or stature the person inquired of is, then observe the sign of that house whereby he is signified, and the planet in it, the sign wherein the lord of that house is, and wherein the Moon is; mix one with another, and by the greater testimonies judge; for if the sign be humane, viz. ♊, ♍, ♒, or the first half of ♐ that ascends, and the lord of that sign, or the ☽ in any sign of the same nature, you may judge the body to be handsome, and the conditions of the party to be sociable, or very courteous,

---

* This sign denotes standing water, as ♋ does running water.
† I have generally found persons born under this sign have a very delicate skin, and often a white chalky appearance, and flabby.—ZAD.

&c. If the query be concerning a disease, and ♈ be either on the cusp of the ascendant or descending in the sixth house, you may judge he has something in his disease of the nature of ♈, but what it is, you must know by the concurrence of the other significators.

If a person has lost or missed any cattle, or any material thing, let him observe what sign the significator of the thing is in; if in ♈, and it be a beast strayed, or the like, let him see what manner of places that sign directs into, and let him repair thither to search, considering the quarter of heaven the sign signifies; if it be a piece of goods that without hands cannot be removed, then let him look into such parts of or about his house, as ♈ signifies.

If one asks concerning travel, whether such a country, city, or kingdom will be healthful or prosperous unto him, see in the figure what sign the lord of the ascendant is in: if the significator be fortunate in ♈, or if ♃ or ♀ be therein, he may safely travel or sojourn in such cities or countries as the sign ♈ represents; which you may easily perceive in the above-named catalogue. Those countries subject to the sign wherein the infortunes are posited, unless they themselves be significators, are ever unfortunate. Remember, that a gentleman inquires, usually, if he shall have his health and live jocundly in such or such a country or city; the merchant wholly aims at trade, and the increase of his stock; therefore, in the merchant's figure, you must consider the country or city subject to the sign of the second house, or where the part of fortune, or lord of the second house is, and which is most fortified, and thither let him trade.*

---

* This implies, that you must judge by the sign on the house which rules the particular subject of inquiry; as if it be, where he may gain a good wife, look to the seventh house.

CHAPTER XVII.

OF THE ESSENTIAL DIGNITIES OF THE PLANETS.

THE exact way of judicature in astrology is, first, by being perfect in the nature of the planets and signs; secondly, by knowing the strength, fortitude, or debility of the significators, and well poising of them, and their aspects and several mixtures, in your judgment; thirdly, by rightly applying the influence of the figure of heaven erected, and the planets' aspects to one another at the time of the question, according to natural and not enforced maxims of art; for by how much you endeavour to strain a judgment beyond nature, by so much the more you augment your error. A planet is then said to be really strong when he has many essential dignities,* which are known by his being either in his house, exaltation, triplicity, term, or face, at the time of erecting the figure. As, for example, in any scheme of heaven, if you find a planet in any of those signs we call his house, he is then essentially strong; as ♄ in ♑, or ♃ in ♐, &c.

Essential Dignity by House.—In judgment, when a planet or significator is in his own *house*, it represents a man in such a condition, as that he is lord of his own house, estate, and fortune; or a man wanting very little of the goods of this world; or it tells you the man is in a very happy state or condition: this will be true, unless the significator be retrograde, or combust, or afflicted by any other malevolent planet or aspect.

Exaltation.—If he be in that sign wherein he is *exalted*, you may consider him essentially strong; whether he be

* These apply not to nativities where the angular position and good aspects received by a planet constitute its strength.—ZAD.

near the very degree of his exaltation, or not; as ♂ in ♑, or ♃ in ♋.

If the significator be in his exaltation, and no ways impedited, but angular, it represents a person of haughty condition, arrogant, assuming more to himself than his due; for it is observed, the planets in some part of the zodiac do more evidently declare their effects than in others.

Triplicity.—If he be in any of those signs which are allotted him for his *triplicity*, he is also strong, but in a less degree.

A planet in his *triplicity* shews a man modestly endued with the goods and fortune of this world; one well descended, and the condition of his life, at present time of the question, to be good; but not so much so as if in either of the two former dignities.

Term.—If any planet be in those degrees we assign for his *terms*, we allow him to be slightly dignified.

A planet fortified, only as being in his own *terms*, rather shews a man more of the corporature and temper of the planet, than any extraordinary abundance in fortune, or eminence in the commonwealth.

Face.—If any planet be in his decanate, or face, he has the least possible essential dignity; but being in his own decanate or face, he cannot then be called peregrine.

A planet being in his decanate or *face*, describes a man ready to be turned out of doors, having much to do to maintain himself in credit and reputation; and in genealogies it represents a family at the last gasp, even as good as quite decayed, hardly able to support itself.

The planets may be strong in another way; viz. accidentally; as when direct, swift in motion, angular, in △ or ✶ aspect with ♃ or ♀, &c., or in ☌ with certain notable fixed stars, as shall hereafter be related. Here follows a table of essential dignities: by only casting your eye thereon, you may perceive what essential dignity or imbecility any planet has.

There has been much difference between the Greeks, Arabians, and Indians, concerning the essential dignities of the planets: I mean, how to dispose the several degrees of the signs suitably to any planet. After many ages had passed, and until the time of Ptolemy, the astrologians were not resolved hereof; but since Ptolemy's time, the Grecians unanimously followed the method he left, which the other Christians of Europe to this day since retain as most rational: but the Moors of Barbary at present, and those astrologians of their nation who lived in Spain, do somewhat vary from us to this very day: however, I present thee with a table according to Ptolemy.

CHAPTER XVIII.

TABLE OF THE ESSENTIAL DIGNITIES OF THE PLANETS, &c.

Signs	Houses	Exaltations	Triplicity Day	Triplicity Night	Terms					Faces			Detriment	Fall
♈	♂ D.	☉ 19	☉	♃	♃ 6	♀ 14	☿ 21	♂ 26	♄ 30	♂ 10	☉ 20	♀ 30	♀	♄
♉	♀ N.	☽ 3	♀	☽	♀ 8	☿ 15	♃ 22	♄ 26	♂ 30	☿ 10	☽ 20	♄ 30	♂	
♊	☿ D.	☊ 3	♄	☿	☿ 7	♃ 14	♀ 21	♄ 25	♂ 30	♃ 10	♂ 20	☉ 30	♃	
♋	☽ D.	♃ 15	♂	♂	♂ 6	♃ 13	☿ 20	♀ 27	♄ 30	♀ 10	☿ 20	☽ 30	♄	♂
♌	☉ D.		☉	♃	♄ 6	☿ 13	♀ 19	♃ 25	♂ 30	♄ 10	♃ 20	♂ 30	♄	
♍	☿ N.	☿ 15	♀	☽	☿ 7	♀ 13	♃ 18	♄ 24	♂ 30	☉ 10	♀ 20	☿ 30	♃	♀
♎	♀ D.	♄ 21	♄	☿	♄ 6	♀ 11	♃ 19	☿ 24	♂ 30	☽ 10	♄ 20	♃ 30	♂	☉
♏	♂ N.		♂	♂	♂ 6	♃ 14	♀ 21	☿ 27	♄ 30	♂ 10	☉ 20	♀ 30	♀	☽
♐	♃ D.	☊ 3	☉	♃	♃ 8	♀ 14	☿ 19	♄ 25	♂ 30	☿ 10	☽ 20	♄ 30	☿	
♑	♄ N.	♂ 28	♀	☽	♀ 6	☿ 12	♃ 19	♂ 25	♄ 30	♃ 10	♂ 20	☉ 30	☽	♃
♒	♄ D.		♄	☿	♄ 6	☿ 12	♀ 20	♃ 25	♂ 30	♀ 10	☿ 20	☽ 30	☉	
♓	♃ N.	♀ 27	♂	♂	♀ 8	♃ 14	☿ 20	♂ 26	♄ 30	♄ 10	♃ 20	♂ 30	☿	☿

EXPLANATION OF THE TABLE.

Every planet has two signs for his HOUSES, except Sol and Luna; they but one each. ♄ has ♑ and ♒; and ♃ has ♐ and ♓; ♂ has ♈ and ♏; ♀ has ♉ and ♎; ☿ has ♊ and ♍. One of these houses is called diurnal, noted in the second column by the letter D; the other is nocturnal, noted by the letter N. The planets have their EXALTATIONS, as the third column points out: thus ☉ in 19 ♈; ☽ in 3 ♉; ☊ in 3 degrees ♊, &c. are exalted. These twelve signs are divided into FOUR TRIPLICITIES. The fourth column tells you which planet or planets, both night and day, governs each triplicity; as over against ♋, ♏, ♓, you find ♂, who governs by day and night in that triplicity; and over against ♈, ♌, ♐, you find ☉ and ♃, viz. that ☉ has domination by day, and ♃ by night, in that triplicity: the first six degrees of ♈ are the TERMS of ♃, from six to fourteen, the TERMS of ♀, &c. &c. Over against ♈, in the tenth, eleventh, and twelfth columns, you find ♂ 10, ☉ 20, ♀ 30; viz. the first ten degrees of ♈ are the FACE of ♂; from ten to twenty, the FACE of ☉; from twenty to thirty, the FACE of ♀, &c.

In the thirteenth column, over against ♈, you find ♀ DETRIMENT, viz. ♀ being in ♈, is in a sign opposite to one of her own houses, and so is said to be in her DETRIMENT. In the 14th column, over against ♈, you find ♄, over his head FALL, that is, ♄ when he is in ♈ is opposite to his exaltation, and so is unfortunate, &c. Though these things are expressed in the nature of the planets already, yet this table makes it appear more evident to the eye, and is useful for reference.

CHAPTER XIX.

CONSIDERATIONS BEFORE JUDGMENT.

ALL the ancients that have written of questions do give warning to the astrologer, that before he delivers judgment he well consider whether the figure is radical* and capable of judgment: the question then shall not be taken for radical: 1st, when either the first or second degrees of a sign ascend, (especially in signs of short ascensions, viz. ♑, ♒, ♓, ♈, ♉, ♊). You may not then adventure judgment, unless the querent be very young, and his corporature, complexion, and moles or scars of his body, agree with the quality of the signs ascending. 2d. If 27 or more degrees of any sign ascend, it is not safe to give judgment, except the querent be in years corresponding to the number of degrees ascending, or unless the figure be set upon a time certain, viz. any event happening, such as a man went away or fled at such a time precisely; to learn the result: here you may judge, because it is no propounded question. 3d. It is not safe to judge when the ☽ is in the later degrees of a sign, especially in ♊, ♏, or ♑; or, as some say, when she is in *via combusta*, which is, when she is in the last 15 degrees of ♎, or the first 15 degrees of ♏.

All manner of matters go hardly on (except the principal significators be very strong) when the ☽ is void of course; yet sometimes she performs it void of course, if in ♉, ♋, ♐, or ♓. You must also be wary, when in any *question* propounded you find the cusp of the seventh house afflicted, or

---

* This term signifies, like the *radix* or root, the figure of birth; for when a person asks his first question of an astrologer, it will generally be found that the same sign, and often the same degree, will ascend that ascended at his birth.

the lord of the house retrograde or impedited, and the matter at that time not concerning the seventh house, but belonging to any other house: it is an argument that the judgment of the astrologer will give little content, or nothing please the querent, for the seventh house generally has signification of the artist. The Arabians, as Alkindus and others, do deliver the following rules, as very fit to be considered before a question be judged:— viz. if ♄ be in the ascendant, especially retrograde, the matter of that question seldom or never comes to good: ♄ in the seventh either corrupts the judgment of the astrologer, or is a sign the matter propounded will come from one misfortune to another. If the lord of the ascendant be combust, neither question propounded will take, nor the querent be regulated. The lord of the seventh unfortunate, or in his fall, or terms of the infortunes, the artist shall scarce give a solid judgment.

When the testimonies of fortunes and infortunes are equal, defer judgment: it is not possible to know which way the balance will turn; however, defer your opinion till another question better inform you.

CHAPTER XX.

WHAT SIGNIFICATOR, QUERENT, AND QUESITED, ARE; AND AN INTRODUCTION TO THE JUDGMENT OF A QUESTION.

THE querent is he or she that propounds the question and desires resolution; the quesited is he or she, or the thing sought and inquired after.

The significator is no more than that planet which rules the house that signifies the person or thing demanded; as if ♈

is ascending, ♂ being lord of ♈, shall be significator of the querent, viz. the sign ascending shall in part signify his corporature, body, or stature: the lord of the ascendant, according to the sign he is in, the ☽ and planet in the ascendant, equally mixed together, shall shew his quality or conditions; so that let any sign ascend, what planet is lord of that sign shall be called lord of the house, or significator of the person inquiring, &c.

So that, in the first place, when any question is propounded, the sign ascending and his lord are always given unto him or her that asks the question.

Secondly: You must then consider the matter propounded, and see to which of the twelve houses it does properly belong: when you have found the house, consider the sign and lord of that sign, how, and in what sign and what part of heaven he is placed, how dignified, what aspect he has to the lord of the ascendant, who impedites your significator, who is a friend unto him, viz. what planet it is, and what house he is lord of, or in what house posited; from such a man or woman signified by that planet shall you be aided or hindered, or by one of such relation unto you as that planet signifies; if lord of such a house, such an enemy; if lord of a house that signifies enemies, then an enemy verily; if of a friendly house, a friend.

The whole natural key of astrology rests in the words preceding, rightly understood. By the examples following, I shall make all things more plain; for I do not desire or will reserve any thing whereby the learner may be kept in suspense of understanding what is useful for him, and most fit to be known. In every question we do give the ☽ as a consignificator with the querent or lord of the ascendant. Having well considered the several applications and separation of the lords of those houses signifying your questions, as also the ☽, her situation and quality of the aspects she has, and each significator has to each, you may begin to judge and consider whether the thing demanded will come to pass, yea or nay; by what or whose means, the time when, and whether it will be good for the querent to proceed further in his demands, yea or nay.

CHAPTER XXI.

TO KNOW WHETHER A THING DEMANDED WILL BE BROUGHT TO PERFECTION, YEA OR NAY.

THE ancients have delivered unto us, that there are four ways or means which discover whether a person's question demanded shall be accomplished, yea or nay.

Conjunction.—First, by conjunction: when therefore you find the lord of the ascendant, and the lord of that house which signifies the thing demanded, hastening to a ☌, and in the first house, or in any *angle*, and the significators meet with no prohibition or refranation, before they come to perfect ☌, you may then judge that the thing sought after shall be brought to pass without any manner of let or impediment; the sooner, if the significators be swift in motion, and essentially or accidentally strong; but if this ☌ of the significators be in a *succeedent* house, it will be perfected, but not so soon; if in *cadent* houses, with infinite loss of time, some difficulty, and much struggling.

Aspects of ✶ or △.—Things are also effected, when the principal signifiers apply by ✶ or △ aspect out of good houses and places where they are essentially well dignified, and meet with no malevolent aspect to intervene ere they come to be in perfect ✶ or △.

Aspects of □ *and* ☍.—Things are also produced to perfection when the significators apply by □ aspect, provided each planet have dignity in the degrees wherein they are, and apply out of proper and good houses; otherwise not. Sometimes it happens that a matter is effected when the significators apply by ☍, but it is when there is mutual *reception* by *house*, and out of friendly houses, and the ☽ separating from the significator of the thing demanded, and applying presently to the lord of the ascendant. I have seldom seen any thing brought to perfection by this way of opposition, but the querent had been better the thing had been undone; for, if the question was concerning marriage, the parties seldom agreed, but were ever wrangling and disputing, each party repining at his evil choice, laying the blame upon their covetous parents, as having no mind to it themselves; and if the question was about portion or monies, the querent did, it is true, recover his money or portion promised, but it cost him more to procure it in suit of law than the debt was worth; and so have I seen it happen in many other things, &c.

Translation.—Things are brought to perfection by *translation* of light and nature, in this manner:—When the significators both of querent and quesited are separating from ☌, or ✶, or △ aspects of each other, and some other planet separates himself from one of the significators, of whom he is received, either by house, triplicity, or term,* and then this planet applies to the other significator by ☌ or aspect, before he meets with the ☌ or aspect of any other planets; he thus translates the force, influence, and virtue of the first significator to the other, and then this intervening planet, (or such a man or woman as is signified by that planet,) shall bring the matter in hand to perfection.

Consider what house the planet interposing or translating

* This means being in these dignities of that significator.

the nature and light of the two planets is lord of, and describe him or her; and say to the querent, that such a party shall do good in the business of, &c.; viz. if lord of the second, a good purse effects the matter; if lord of the third, a kinsman or neighbour; and so of all the rest of the houses; of which more hereafter.

Collection.—Matters are also brought to perfection, when the two principal significators do not behold one another, but both cast their several aspects to a more weighty planet than themselves, and they both receive him in some of their essential dignities; then shall that planet, who thus *collects* both their lights, bring the thing demanded to perfection; which signifies that a person somewhat interested in both parties, and described and signified by that planet, shall perform the thing which otherwise could not be perfected; as many times you see two fall at variance, and of themselves cannot think of any way of accommodation, when suddenly a neighbour or friend accidentally reconciles all differences, to the content of both parties; and this is called a collection.

In all questions, you are generally to observe this method following:—The ascendant represents the person of the querent, and the second his estate, the third his kindred, the fourth his father, the fifth his children, the sixth his servant or sickness, the seventh his wife, the eighth the manner of his death, the ninth his religion or journeys, the tenth his estimation or honour, mother, trade, &c.; the eleventh his friends, the twelfth his secret enemies: also understand, that when one asks concerning a woman, or any party signified by the seventh house and the lord thereof, that then the seventh house shall be her ascendant, and signify her person; the eighth house shall signify her estate, and be her second; the ninth house shall signify her brethren and kindred; the tenth shall represent her father; the eleventh her children, or whether apt to have children; the twelfth her sickness and servants; the first house her sweetheart; the second house her death; the third her journey; the fourth her mother, or trade, &c.; the fifth her friends; the sixth her sorrow, care, and private enemies. Let the question be of or concerning a churchman, minister, or the brother of the wife or sweetheart, the ninth house shall represent each of these; but the tenth house shall be significator of *his* substance; the eleventh house of his brethren; and so in order: and so in all manner of questions, the house signifying the party quesited shall be his ascendant or first house, the next his second house, and so continuing round about the whole heavens of twelve houses. If a question be made of a king or nobleman, the tenth is his first house, the eleventh his second, &c.; but in nativities, the ascendant always influences the party born, whether king or beggar. These things preceding being well understood, you may proceed to judgment; not that it is necessary you have all that is written in your memory exactly, but, that you be able to know when you are in error, when not; when to judge a question, when not.

Of the true Time of erecting a Figure.

The proper time is that when you feel most anxious about any matter, and first form the resolution to erect a figure on the subject: if you find the figure radical, and lay aside all self-love and prejudice, you may safely judge a figure erected for that instant of time.

If a person apply to an astrologer, the figure must be taken for the exact time he first speaks on the subject; or, if it be by letter, when it is first read and understood by the artist. If it be not a question, but an event suddenly happening, then the moment of its commencement will shew, by a figure, its result, &c.; as the first setting off on a journey, beginning a letter, or any business, &c.; or when you first discover the loss of any article, or hear of any event happening: in all these cases, the first impression on your mind is the true moment for the figure.

Of the Planet or Planets which hinder or impedite the Thing demanded in any Question.

In all questions consider carefully what planet it is which obstructs or hinders the perfection of the thing desired. We receive judgment herein from that planet with whom the lord of the ascendant be joined, (whether by bodily ☌ or by aspect), or the significator of the thing inquired after, whether it be the ☽ herself, or that she be partaker with the lord of the ascendant or not, or signify the thing demanded.

Carefully observe the planet to which the querent's significator is joined, or the ☽; and observe how that planet is disposed, and unto whom *he* is joined; for if the lord of the ascendant, ☽, or significator of the thing propounded, be joined to an evil planet, evilly disposed, without reception, or if he be not evilly disposed, but be joined to an infortune, and that infortune receive him not, it denotes the destruction of the thing demanded.

A planet is ill-disposed when he is *peregrine, retrograde, combust;* also if *cadent* and behold not the lord of the house or the cusp of the house of the thing demanded. The aspect to the cusp is better than to the lord of the house.

If the significator, as above, be joined to an unfortunate planet, viz. one retrograde, combust, or cadent; then observe whether mutual reception intervene; which shews the perfection of the matter, though with much labour and solicitation. If there be no reception, the affair will come to nothing, though there may have been much probability of its performance.

If the lord of the ascendant, the ☽, or lord of the thing demanded, or the planet who receives any of them, be free from affliction, though without mutual reception, it perfects the matter with facility.

If any one of them be free from the infortunes, and joined with any benevolent planet, who is himself aspected by a malevolent, without mutual reception, the matter will be brought to a good conclusion.

Consider carefully whether planets in aspect be without reception, for when they are in reception, things are ever brought to pass; though, if the aspect be evil, with degree of trouble, delay, &c.

Consider also, whether any other planet *prohibit* before the significators join in perfect ☌ with an evil planet; if so, it hinders the thing from happening: but if no such prohibition or cutting off the light of the *infortune* occur, by which its malevolence may be taken off, the thing will be effected.

If an infortune *collect* the light of other planets, or if light be translated to an infortune, the matter will not be effected unless there be reception; viz. that the infortune be received by, or disposed of, or ruled by, (which is all one thing), the significators.

THE RESOLUTION OF ALL MANNER OF QUESTIONS AND DEMANDS.

CHAPTER XXII.

QUESTIONS CONCERNING THE FIRST HOUSE. IF THE QUERENT BE LIKELY TO LIVE LONG—YEA OR NOT?

Signs of Health and long Life.

CONSIDER whether the sign ascending, the lord thereof, and ☽, be free from affliction; viz. combustion or ☌, ☐ or ☍ of the lords of the 8th, 12th, 6th, or 4th houses; whether they be direct, strong in dignities, swift in motion, angular, especially in the 1st, or 10th houses; or if in the 11th or 9th, and in good aspect with ♃, ♀, or ☉, or in the terms of ♃ or ♀: these are arguments of health and long life; and the contrary, viz. the asc. ☽, or lord of the 1st, in bad houses, and afflicted, shew mischief at hand.

If the lord of the ascendant be under the Sun's beams, or going to combustion, which is worse than when he is leaving ☉; or ☽ cadent and unfortunate, by being afflicted by those planets having rule in the 8th, or 6th; or ♄, ♂ or ☋ in the ascendant or 7th house peregrine, or in their detriments or retrograde, judge that the querent will not be long lived, but is near some danger or misfortune, according to the quality of the significators, and of the houses those planets are lords of, which afflict the ☽, &c.

The Time when any of those Accidents shall happen.

If the lord of the ascendant be going to ☌, &c. of ☉, or lords of the 8th, or 4th, see how many degrees he is distant, and in what sign either of them are; and for each degree allow one week in a moveable sign, one month in a common sign, and one year in a fixed sign; this is only for example; for the measure of time must be limited according to the other significators concurring in judgment herein.

Secondly.—Consider also how many degrees ☽ is from any infortune, or the lords of the 6th or 8th, according to the signs and houses in which they are found, and their nature and quality.

Thirdly.—If there be an infortune in the ascendant, see how many degrees the cusp of the 1st house wants of the place of the evil planet; or, if he be in the 7th house, how far it is from the cusp of that house, and compute the time of death, sickness, or misfortune, by the degrees, as they may be in fixed, common, or moveable signs.

If the lord of the ascendant be most afflicted by the lord of the 6th, and in the 6th, or come to combustion in the 6th, the querent will have very many and tedious sicknesses, which will scarce leave him till his death. This will be more certain if the lords of the ascendant, 8th house, and ☽, be all placed in the 6th.

If the ☽, lord of the ascendant, or sign ascending, be most afflicted by the lord of the 8th, or by a planet situated in the 8th, judge that the sickness which now afflicts him, or shortly will, will end fatally, and that death is approaching. But if the ☽ and other significators are chiefly afflicted by the lords of other houses, judge the misfortune from the nature of the house or houses of which the afflicting planets are lords; and the first origin thereof from some person or thing belonging to that house, wherein you find the afflicting planet posited. Judge thereby a misfortune, but not death.

If there be any fixed star, of much power, near the ☽, lord of the ascendant or the degree ascending, or with the planet which afflicts any of these, you may judge evil thereby, according to the nature of that star; for which, see the chapter on Fixed Stars.

Caution.

Avoid rash judgments; especially of death. This should never be judged by one single testimony, however strong. And though the lord of the ascendant be going to combustion in the house of death, observe whether the ☽, ♃, or ♀ (or ☿ if well aspected and strong), throw any good aspect to the lord of the ascendant, before he come to perfect ☌ with ☉; for then either medicine or natural strength will contradict that malignant influence, or take off part of that misfortune. When two or more of the rules aforesaid occur, you may be more bold; yet concerning the absolute time of death, I have found it best to be wary. Though you may safely judge that the querent will not be long-lived, or else subject to many calamities; and this I know by many verified examples. This knowledge will be useful to those who will use their reason to avoid those casualties their nature or inclinations would run them into.*

---

* The student will perceive, by this observation of the author, how false is the assertion, that astrology teaches or upholds fatality. On the contrary, it expressly teaches that the worst influence may be overcome by the use of reason, which, of course, implies by the assistance also of God's blessing, which both reason and revelation inform us we should pray for when we perceive any impending evil.—ZADKIEL.

To what Part is it best the Querent should direct his Affairs, or where may he live most happily?

The 12 houses are divided into the four quarters of heaven, east, west, north and south. From the cusp of the 1st, where the ☉ and planets rise, to the cusp of the 10th, is the south-east quarter. The 1st, is due east; the 12th, is about two points south of east; the middle of the 11th, is south east; the cusp of the 11th, is about two points east of south; and the 10th, is due south. In like manner, from the 10th to the 7th house is the south-west quarter; and from the 7th to the 4th is the north-west quarter; and, lastly, from the 4th to the ascendant is the north-east quarter. In that quarter wherein you find ♃, ♀, ☽, or ⊕, or most of them, direct the querent to proceed in that direction, especially if ⊕ and ☽ be free from combustion and be strong. If ♃ or ♀ be lords of the 8th, 12th, or 6th houses, you must avoid them; and avoid that quarter wherein the evil planets are, unless they be essentially strong, and lords of the 1st, 2d, 10th, or 11th houses, when they may prove friendly.*

If the querent desire to live where he may most enjoy *health*, look to the quarter of the lord of the ascendant, or ☽; and whichever is strongest, or casts the best aspect to the degree ascending, to that quarter repair for health. If an increase of *wealth* be considered, see where the lord of the 2d, the ⊕, and its dispositor, or any two of them, be, and thither repair for that end. Of this I shall speak in other judgments.

What Part of LIFE *is like to be best?*

See in what angle or quarter of heaven the fortunate and

---

* I should not myself choose the directions of the infortunes in any case.—ZADKIEL.

promising planets are; for in this way of judging we usually give to every house five years, more or less, as the significators promise life or death. Begin with the 12th, then the 11th, then the 10th, &c., and so round to the ascendant. If ♃ or ♀ be in the 11th or 10th, judge the querent to have lived happily from the 5th to the 15th year of age: if they be in the 8th or 7th, he will or hath lived contented from fifteen to thirty; if ♃, &c. be in the 6th, 5th, or 4th, house, say that after his middle age, from 30 to 45, he may do well; but if the benefics be in the last quarter, his greatest happiness will be in his last days, or after 45. If you find the significators very strong, you may add a year to each house. Lastly, the aspects the ☽ and lord of the ascendant are separated from shew what and what manner of accidents have preceded the question; their next application what may be next expected. If you consider the house or houses the planets they separated from are lords of, it acquaints you with the matter, nature, person, and quality of the things already happened—evil if the aspects were evil, and good if they were good. Also if you note the quality of the next aspect by application, and the well or ill-being and position of the planets applied to, it shews the character of the next succeeding accidents and events, their nature, proportion, &c., and the time when they will happen.

Fig. 2.

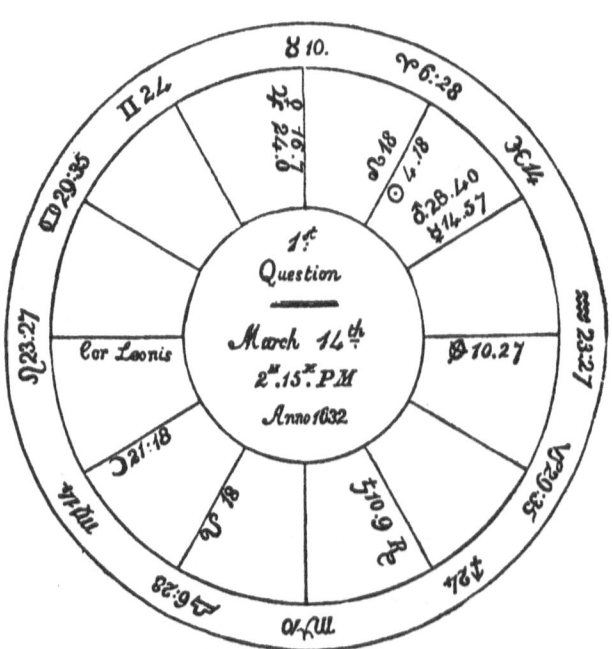

An ASTROLOGICAL JUDGMENT *concerning these Demands by the Querent.*

1. If he were likely to live long, yea or not?
2. To what part of the world he were best direct his course?
3. What part of life was likely to be most fortunate?
4. He desired I would relate some of the general accidents which had happened to him already?
5. What accidents in future he might expect?
6. The time when?

The stature of the querent is shewn by ♌, the sign ascending; a fixed star of the 1st magnitude, of the nature of ♂ and ♃, called *Cor* ♌, the lion's heart, is near the cusp of the 1st house, in ♌ 24° 34';* both the cusp of the 1st house and the degree wherein ☉ lord of the ascendant is, are the terms of ♃; the ☽ is in △ aspect to both ♃ and ♀, and they in the 10th house; so that the form and stature of the querent were decent. He was of middle stature, strongly compacted, neither fat nor fleshy, but comely and graceful, a fair visage, reddish hair, clear skin, some cuts on his right cheek (he was a soldier), and certainly the presence of the fixed star in the ascendant, which represents the face, occasioned those hurts or scars.†

As the sign ascending, and its lord, were in the *fiery* triplicity, and by nature hot and dry, so was this gentleman's temper and condition, being exceedingly valiant, choleric, high-minded, and of great spirit: for ☉ is in his exaltation; yet ☽ being in △ to the two fortunes, he was sober, modest, and excellently educated, thereby having great command of his passion; but as ☽ was in ☍ to ☿, he had his times of anger and folly, whereby he much prejudiced his affairs.‡

1st QUERY.—*If live long, &c. ?*

The ascendant not vitiated by the lords of the 6th or 8th; the lord of the ascendant in his exaltation no way impeded, pretty quick in motion, in the 9th house, and in terms of ♃;

* This star has now advanced to about 27° 30' of the sign Leo.

† I differ from the author on this point, and believe that the lord of the ascendant being in ♈, which rules the head, shewed them; it being a *masculine* sign, caused them to be on the right side ; and, being *above the earth*, they were in front of the head, or in the face. The ☉ being afflicted by the ☌ of ♂, caused them to be scars or wounds: if he had been alone, they would have been merely *moles*.—ZADKIEL.

‡ The ☉ in ☌ with ♂ would render him very fiery, and at the same time very brave and fortunate, as a soldier.

☽ separating from △ of ♀ applying to △ of ♃, he strong in the midheaven, and the malice of ♂ restrained by the ✶ of ♃ ; ☉ above the earth, the fortunes angular and more potent than the infortunes; I concluded that, according to natural causes, he might live many years; that nature was strong, and he subject to few diseases. This has hitherto proved true; he being yet alive this present March, 1646.

2d QUERY.—*To what part of the world he were best direct his course?*

☉ lord of the ascendant near the cusp of the 9th, (and the sign thereof moveable), the house of long journeys; I intimated that he was resolving suddenly upon a *journey* southeast: south, because the quarter of heaven wherein the lord of the ascendant is, is south; east, because the *sign* where ☉ is, is east, (*this he confessed*); and as ☉ was but 2° 10′ distant from the cusp of the 9th, he went away within two months.

I judged those countries subject to ♈ might be propitious. Had his resolution been to stay in England, it might have been good for him, for England is subject to ♈ : I would have advised him to steer towards Kent, Essex, Sussex or Suffolk; for they lie south-east from London. But if sometimes you find a city, town or kingdom, subject to the *sign* which promises good, stands not in the direction the sign or quarter of heaven points out as above, observe this rule—that if enforced to live in that country, city, &c., then direct your actions or employment *to those parts* of that country, &c., which lie east, west, &c., as in the figure is directed.

As the ☽ applied strongly to the △ of ♃, and he and ♀ were in ♉, which rules *Ireland*, I advised him that *Ireland* would agree with his constitution, and that he might get *honour* there, as the planet to whom ☽ applies is in the house of *honour*. And the querent did go into Ireland, and there performed good service, and obtained a notable victory against the rebels.

3d Query.—*What part of his* LIFE *would be best?*

Considering the two fortunes were placed in the 10th, and ☋ and ☉ in the 9th, I judged his younger years would be the most pleasant; and ♂ being in the 8th, which comes to about the 24th, 25th, or 26th years of his age, I judged about that time many crosses, and that his afflictions first began. And seeing no fortunate planet either in the 7th, 6th, 5th, 4th, or 3d houses, I said the remainder of his life, for many years, would be little comfortable, and full of labour and trouble. Yet I judged those calamities should not suddenly come upon him, because ☽ applied to △ of ♃, and wanted almost 3° of coming to a perfect aspect. Therefore I conceived by means of some person in authority represented by ♃, he should be supported or assisted in his affairs for almost three years after the question. Had ♃ been essentially dignified, I should have judged him a more durable fortune.

4th Query. — *What general* ACCIDENTS *had happened already?*

Although it is not usual to be so inquisitive, yet, seeing the figure so radical, I considered from what planets ☉, lord of the ascendant, had last separated. The ☉ had lately been in ☌ ♂, then □ ♄, then ✶ ♃. Now as ♂ is lord of the 4th house, signifying lands, &c., and was now in the 8th, which signifies the *substance of women*, I judged he had been molested of late concerning some lands, or the jointure or portion of his wife, or a woman; wherein I was confirmed the more, as ☽ applies to ☍ ♂ in the 8th house; she being in the querent's house of property, which shewed that the quarrel or strife should be concerning money or things signified by that house. (*All this was very true.*)

As ☉ had lately been in □ ♄, significator of the querent's wife, I told him that his wife and he had been at great variance; and because her significator ♄ did dispose of his ⊕, I judged that she had no mind that he should have any of her estate or manage it, but kept it to her own use. For ♄ is retrograde in a fiery sign, and the sign of the 7th fixed, all which shews her to be a woman not willing to be curbed or to submit. (*This was confessed.*)

Lastly, as ☉ was lately in ⚹ to ♃, and ♃ in the 10th, I told him that some great lawyer or courtier* had endeavoured to reconcile the differences between them; and as ☉ and ♄ did now apply to △ aspect, there seemed, at present, a willingness in both parties to be reconciled. Nor did I see any obstruction in the matter, except ☿, who is in □ aspect to ♄, did impedite it. I judged ☿, in general, to signify some lawyer, attorney, or writings; but, as he was lord of the querent's 2d, it might be because the querent would not consent to allow her such a sum of money as might be asked; or that, his purse being weak, he had not wherewithal to solicit his cause; or ☿ being lord of the 11th, some pretended friend would advise the contrary, or some of her lawyers; or, as the 11th is the 5th from the 7th, a *child* of the querent's wife might be the occasion of continuing the breach. (*I believe every particular herein proved true; however, this was the way to find the thing which disturbed their unity.*)

Observe, that as ♀, lady of the 10th, doth dispose of ♃, lord of the 8th, viz. the wife's fortune, so she had entrusted her estate to a great nobleman.

5th QUERY.—*What* ACCIDENTS, *in future, he might expect?*

In this query, I first considered ☉, lord of the ascendant, no ways unfortunate or in ill aspect with any planet; but, on the contrary, excellently fortified: I judged he had the wide world to ramble in, (for a planet strong, and in no aspect with others, shews a man at liberty to do what he will); and, for many years he might (*quoad capax*) live in a prosperous con-

* It was the *Lord Coventry*.

dition, and traverse much ground, or see many countries. For ♈, the sign which ☉ is in, is moveable and on the cusp of the 9th, the house of long journeys; which denoted many changes and variety of action in sundry parts.

2dly: I observed ☽ in his house of substance, applying to ♃ in the 10th, and ♃ lord of the 5th and 8th; the former the house of children; the latter that of the wife's substance. Hence I gathered, that the querent was desirous to treat with some nobleman (♃ being in the 10th) about the education of his children; and that there might be a salary payable out of the wife's jointure. (*Such a thing he did settle before he left England.*)

3dly: I found ☽ in ♍ *peregrine*.

4thly: ☿ lord of his 2d, signifying his estate in ♓, his *detriment*; yet, in his own terms, afflicted by ♂, and having lately had the ☍ of ☽. Hence I judged that he had been in great want of money a little before the question was asked. And if we note the distance between the ☍ of ☽ and ☿, we find 6° 21', shewing that he had been in want of money about six months and somewhat more, previously to asking the question. (*This was confessed.*)

5thly: Seeing ☽ was applying to △ of ♃, and then, before she got out of the sign ♍, did occur the ☍ of ♂, I acquainted the querent that, after some years of pleasure, he would be in great danger of losing his life, goods, lands, and fortune. His *life*, because ♂ is in the 8th: his *estate*, because ☽ is in the 2d; and his *lands* or *inheritance*, because ♂ is lord of the 4th and situated in the 8th house; for the 4th house denotes *lands*, &c.

6th QUERY.—*The time when?*

In this query, I considered the application of ☽ to △ ♃; which wanting about 3 degrees, I judged that he might live pleasantly for about three years to come.

94 INTRODUCTION TO ASTROLOGY.

2dly: Seeing that ☉ lord of the ascendant, during his motion through ♈, did not meet any malevolent aspect, and had got 26 degrees to run through the sign, I gave this nature of judgment: I told him that for about 26 months, or until over two years to come, I judged he should live in a free condition, in those parts in which he intended his journey, &c.

Lastly: I considered how many degrees ☽ wanted of the ☍ of ☽.

Longitude of ♂	28° 40′
Longitude of ☽	21 18
Difference	7 22

This difference, if in proportion unto time, and neither give years, because the *significators* are in common signs and not in fixed; nor months, because the signs signify somewhat more; but proportion a *mean* between both: the time limited in this way will amount to about three years and three quarters ere the ☍ of ♂ to ☽ should take effect. But as this query was general, I might have allowed for every degree one year.* After, or about which time, he was in several actions, both dangerous to his person and fortune; and since that time till the present, he has had his intervals of good and ill, but is now under the frown of fortune, &c.

As the ☉ at the time of the question was strong, he did overcome all manner of difficulties for many years, and has, in our unlucky differences, had honourable employment on his Majesty's part. But as ☽ † is in ☍ to ♂, so it was not without the general outcry and exclamations of the people; nor was it his fortune, though in great command, ever to do his Majesty any notable piece of service. And he is now for

* I should certainly always do so.—ZAD.

† In all questions ☽ signifies the people, where they are at all concerned.

ever, by just sentence of the Parliament, deprived of the happiness of ending his days in England; which might, in some measure, have been foreseen by the ☍ of ☽ to ♂, he being lord of the 4th, the end of all things.*

N.B. All young beginners should at first write down their judgments on each figure at full length, and afterwards contract their opinions into a narrow compass; by this means they will soon acquire experience. It is well to enter every figure in a book for farther reference, and to remark and register such things as have occurred according to their predictions or otherwise; by which they will be able to correct their future judgments.

CHAPTER XXIII.

If one shall find the Party at Home he would speak with?

THE ascendant and its lord are for the querent, the 7th and its lord for him you would speak with; but if it be with any relation, take the house signifying that relation and its lord; as, for the father the 4th, for a child the 5th, and for an intimate friend the 11th; if the lord of the 7th, or quesited's significator, be in any of the four angles, the party is at home; but if he be in a succeedent house, he is not far from home; but if in a cadent house, then he is far from home.

If you find the lord of the ascendant apply to the quesited's perfect aspect the same day you intend to visit him, you may be assured either to meet him going to his house, or hear of him by the way; or, if any planet separate from the lord of the quesited's house, and transfer his light to the lord of the ascendant, you will learn where he is by a person signified by

* I should say also, by ♄ being in the 4th house and retrograde, for such a position ever denotes a final catastrophe

that planet. Describe the planet, and it personates the individual; and the nature of the planet, sign, and quarter of heaven it is in, will, by the plurality of testimonies, shew whether it be male or female.

Of a thing suddenly happening, whether it signifies Good or Evil?

Erect your figure of heaven at the exact time of any event happening, or when you first heard of it: then consider who is lord of the ascendant, and which planet disposes of ☉ and ☽; and see if either of these be in the ascendant, and, if more than one, take the most powerful; and let his position be well considered. If he be in good aspect with ☉, ♃, or ♀, there will no evil arise from the accident, rumour, or whatever the event may be; but if you find that planet weak in the scheme, combust, or in evil aspect to ♅, ♄, ♂, or ☿, there will be some evil occur. If you consider the afflicting planet and his nature and position, you may learn the nature of the misfortune. If it be the lord of the 3d, it will come through some kinsman or neighbour, or by some short journey; if the lord of the 2d cast the ray, or the evil planet be in the 2d, it denotes loss of money;* if the lord of the 4th, trouble about houses, &c., or by means of a father or wife's mother; if the 5th, by intemperance, or by children, &c., and so of the rest.†

* the same if ⊕ receive evil rays approaching.

† The nature of the planet casting the ray, also may be expected to shew the nature of the evil; ♂ shews robbers, &c., ♄ elderly persons, ☿ young persons and lawyers, ♅ unlooked-for and uncommon events, ♀ females, ☉ men in power, ♃ clergymen and magistrates, ☽ sailors, low people, mobs, &c. But note, that unless the benefic planets be lords of evil houses, their ill aspects do not import much evil. And if they be lords of good houses, or placed in good houses and strong, their good aspects denote benefits in the same manner; and in all cases ⊕ shews gain or loss, as it may be aspected; and ☊, with the chief significator, imports benefits, and ☋ the reverse.

QUERY.—*What Mark, Mole, or Scar has the Querent on any Part of his Body? This is useful to prove that a question is radical, and to satisfy sceptics of the truth of the science.*

When you have, upon any demand, erected the querent's figure, observe what member of man's body the ascending sign represents; for upon that part of his body will the querent have a mole, mark, or scar; as, if the ascendant be ♈, the same will be on the head; if ♉, it will be on the neck; if ♊, on the arms or shoulders, &c.* And also in the part ruled by the sign in which the lord of the ascendant is, will there be another mark.

The signs on the cusp of the 6th house, and that in which the lord of the 6th is, will give other marks on the parts they rule. Also the sign in which ☽ is found will give a mark in that part it governs.

If ♄ give the mark, it is dark, obscure, or black; ♂ usually gives a red mole; but if he be in a fiery sign, it is generally a cut or scar.

If the sign or planet signifying the mark or mole be much afflicted, the mark, &c. will be more obvious and eminent.

If the sign or planet be masculine, the mark is on the *right* side of the body; but if they be feminine, on the *left* side. And if the significator of the mole, &c. be *above* the horizon, the mark or mole will be on the *fore part*, or visible to the eye, or on the outside of the member, &c.; but if the planet be *below* the earth, it will be found on the inside, or

---

* PARTS *of* MAN'S BODY *ruled by the* TWELVE SIGNS.

♈ *Head and face.*	♎ *Reins and loins.*
♉ *Neck and throat.*	♏ *Secret members.*
♊ *Arms and shoulders.*	♐ *Hips and thighs.*
♋ *Breast and stomach.*	♑ *Knees and hams.*
♌ *Heart and back.*	♒ *Legs and ancles.*
♍ *Bowels and belly.*	♓ *Feet and toes.*

hinder part, or not visible. If few degrees are on the cusp of the house, or the planet signifying the mole, &c. be in few degrees of the sign, the mark, mole, &c., will be in the upper part of the member. If they be in the middle of the sign, it will be in the middle of the member or part ruled by the sign. But if the latter degrees ascend, or are on the 6th, or their lords, or ☽ be in the latter degrees of a sign, then will the mark, mole, or scar be near the lower part of the member. If your question be radical, and the time rightly taken, the above rules will always exactly hold good. And so will they (*mutatis mutandis*) upon the body of the quesited; for if a person inquire concerning his wife, then the sign on the 7th and its lord will shew the woman's marks; and the sign on the 12th, (the 6th from the 7th), and its lord will shew two other marks.

Many times if the ☽ be in ☌ or ☍ ☉, the querent has some blemish in or near his eyes: and this is ever true, if the ☌ or ☍ be in angles, and ☽ or ☉ be afflicted by Mars.*

Whether one absent be dead or alive?

If the quesited have no relation to the querent, then the

---

* If ♃ give the mark, it will be bluish or purple; ♀ gives it yellow; ☿ a pale lead colour; ☉ olive or chesnut; and ☽ a whitish hue, or partly of the colour of the planets she aspects. The infortunes ♄ and ♂, especially when together, or in exact aspect, mark according to their position. If they be in the ascendant, a mole, &c. will be in the face; if in the 2d, on the neck; in the 3d, on the arms, &c.

And all these rules apply to the figure of birth, as well as horary figures; but *defects*, such as protrusion of the breast bone, or a humped back, &c. (to persons born with ♋ or ♌ rising), may sometimes be found in lieu of moles or scars. For example, her present majesty, having ♄ in ♓, which rules the feet, and situated near the cusp of the 12th *house*, at her birth, she has a *weakness* in her feet. Had *one* testimony only existed, and ♄ been in ♓ elsewhere, she would have merely had a mole on her foot.

ascendant, its lord, and ☽ shall signify the absent person.*
But if the party inquired after be a relation, then take the
house and its lord which signifies that relation; as the 3d for
a brother or sister, the 4th for a father, the 6th for a paternal
uncle or aunt, the 10th for a mother, &c.

In judging this question, see whether the quesited's lord of
the 1st and 8th be joined corporally together in the 8th, or be
in ☍ from the 6th or 8th. These are tokens of his being
sick or near to death. See if there be any translation of light
between the lord of his ascendant and the 8th, or if the lord
of the 8th being in his ascendant, the lord of his ascendant
be also in the 8th; or the lord of the 8th in the 4th, and the
lord of the 4th in the 8th; these are all tokens that the party
is dead; especially if his significator be much afflicted by ill
aspects, and the evil planets be angular, and the good ones
cadent.

If the lord of his ascendant be separating from ill aspect
of the lord of the 6th, the absent party has been lately sick;
if from the lord of the 8th, he has been near death, but is not
dead, without other striking testimonies, as above, concur. If
from the lord of the 12th, he has been troubled with anxiety
about arrests or fear of imprisonment; and if his significator
be in the 12th, he is in much trouble by means of a private
enemy; and if in a fixed sign, and other testimonies of trouble agree, he is in prison. If he separate from the lord of
the 2d by ill aspect, he is now suffering by want of money.
If from the lord of the 7th, he has had some quarrel or contention. If the 9th, trouble on journeys or by law, &c.;
and so of the other houses. I have ever found that if the
lord of his ascendant be in the 9th, 10th, or 11th, though re-

* We should always take the ascendant, &c. for the querent, and the
7th and its lord for the quesited. But if the figure be erected by an artist
at his own suggestion, let the ascendant, &c. shew the absent person.

ported dead, he was alive. If you find him alive, and would know when you will hear from or see him, observe in the Ephemeris when the lord of the querent's 11th and the quesited's ascendant come to ✶ or △ aspect: about that time news of him will arrive. If the ☽ apply to ✶ or △ of his significator, then allow a day, week, or month, for each degree she be distant, according as the significators may be placed in angles, succeedent or cadent houses, and the signs be moveable, common, or fixed.*

---

* The most difficult thing in all questions is to judge of *time* with accuracy. I should advise the young student to be cautious of giving any judgment on this head, unless where it is the chief point desired to be known. In this case, and if the figure be very radical, and if *the planet which is applying* to the other be taken, the following rule will hold good:—

Each Degree gives

IN MOVEABLE SIGNS AND ANGLES..........DAYS.
IN COMMON SIGNS AND ANGLES............WEEKS.
IN FIXED SIGNS AND ANGLES.............MONTHS.

Succeedent houses give *weeks, months*, and *years*, as the sign is *moveable, common*, or *fixed;* and *cadent houses* give *months* in *moveable signs, years* in *common*, and an indefinite time in *fixed* signs.—ZAD.

Fig. 3.

THE ABOVE FIGURE WAS FOR RESOLUTION OF THE FOLLOWING QUERIES.

1st. *If a Party might be found at Home?*
2d. *A Thing suddenly happening, whether Good or Ill is about to follow?*
3d. *What Moles or Marks the Querent has?*
4th. *If one absent be dead or alive?*

1st QUERY.—*A Woman demanded whether her Son was with his Master at her own House?*

In this figure, ♀ lady of the ascendant denotes the querent. The 5th house is that of children, and describes the matter inquired of. I found ♃, lord of the 5th, youth's significator, in the east angle; one argument that the party was at home at his mother's house. The ☽ was applying to ⚹ of ♄ lord of the 4th, the significator of the querent's dwelling: I judged that she would find him there at her coming home: which she did. Now, had I found ♃, lord of the 5th, in the 10th, which house signifies the master; or had ☽ separated from ♃, the youth's significator, and then applied to ☉, the ☽ being in an angle, I would have judged him at his master's house. I considered further, that the 25th of July following at 2 P.M., the significators of the mother and son (♃ and ♀) came to △ aspect; and therefore I judged that she should see him at that time: which she did. For usually about that day when the *significators* come to ⚹ or △ aspect (which may be seen in the *Ephemeris*), it is very probable that news of, or a letter from, the quesited will arrive, if the distance will permit. But if the querent and quesited be not far asunder, without question they meet on that very day.

Had the party inquired for been a stranger, he would have been denoted by ♂ lord of the 7th; and being in the 2d, a *succeedent* house, I should have said he is not at home, but yet not far from home. And as the sign ♐ is eastern, and the 2d house is north east, I should judge him in that direction; and as ♐ governs fields, hills, or high grounds, I should direct a messenger, if sent for him, to go in that direction, and look for him in such places; but if it were in a town, as ♐ governs stables, fire-places, &c., I should cause him to be sought near a stable, smith's or butcher's shop, &c., as ♂ delights in such places.

2d QUERY.—*A Thing suddenly happening, whether Good or Ill is about to follow?*

The ☉ is here lord of the sign he is in; ♃ is lord of ♓, where ☽ is; ♀ is lady of the ascendant, and is casting a △ to the ascendant, and is in △ to ♃, and he in the ascendant; from all which we might safely have judged, had this been the time of a sudden accident, or thing done, that it could not have redounded to the querent's injury. But had ♀ been nearer to ☍ of ♂, he being in the 2d, I should have judged that the querent would have received some loss of money shortly, and so of the rest.*

3d QUERY.—*What Moles or Marks the Querent has?*

I find 25° of ♎ ascending and ♃ in the ascendant, which signifies the face. This querent had a wart or mole on the right side of her face, near her mouth; for ♃ and ♎ are *masculine*. And as the latter degrees of ♎ ascend, so the querent confessed a mole on the lower part of her reins towards the haunches. ♈ being the sign of the 6th, shewed she had one on the forehead, near the hair, for the cusp of the house is but 4 degrees. ♂ lord of the 6th, being in ♐ a masculine sign and under the earth, shewed a mole on the right thigh, towards the middle of it, on the back part, or

---

* We consider that our author has been rather brief on this point, for numerous occasions occur where the mind is desirous of knowing the result when events happen. If ♀ had been within orbs of ♂ opposition, that is, *half the distance of their united orbs*, or 7°; we should have judged loss of money by a party shewn by ♀, and her situation considered with the houses she governs. As, for example, ♀ ruling the 12th, some private female enemy, among the relations of the wife or husband; because ♀ is in the 3d from the 7th house. And as ♂ is ☍ to ⊕, we should predict a loss by a servant (since ♂ rules the 6th); and as ⊕ is in the 8th, it might be by one who comes to char or go messages; if ⊕ had been in a watery sign, a washerwoman. But the general testimonies being good, we should say the evil will be but trifling. Experience will teach the student these points.

that part which is not visible. The ☾ in 27th degree of ♓,
a feminine sign, under the earth, I told her she had one mole
under and towards the extremity of her left foot.

The quesited being her son, had ♓ for his ascendant, which
denoted a mole on the left side of his cheek; and as ♓ signifies the foot, so he had one on the left foot a little below the
ancle, as few degrees ascend. The 6th from the 5th is the
10th in the figure, which having 4° ♌, shewed that near his
right side, below his breast, he had some scar, mole, or mark.

In this way follow the directions of the rule.

4th QUERY.—*Whether one absent be dead or alive?*

In the aforesaid figure, the ascendant ♃ therein and ♀
its ruler, as also ☾, are the significators of the party absent.
The ascending sign and ♃ therein describe his person;* and
☾ and ♀ shew his condition.

The ☾ and ♀ are free from any evil aspect of the lord of
the 8th, and a benefic is in the ascendant, and ♀ in the 9th;
I should therefore pronounce the absent in health. But ♀
having been recently in ☍ to ♂, lord of the 2d and 6th, he
had been lately in trouble about money, and also inclined to a
feverish state. But by ♃ in the ascendant, and in △ to ♀,
I should say that medicine, or such a person as is described
by ♃, had relieved him. And as ☿ lord of the 11th applies
to a □ of ♃, (both of them in signs of long ascension, which
is equivalent to a △,)† I should judge the querent to have
news of the absent about ten weeks from the time of the

---

* If no planet be in the ascendant of the party, look to the lord of the
ascendant for a description of his person, according to the sign it is in,
and judge by that and the sign ascending; but if the lord of the ascendant
be much *afflicted*, the ☾, according to the sign she is in, must be taken.

† This doctrine of the signs of long ascension, causing a ✶ to be equal
to a □, and a □ to a △, and the reverse in signs of short ascension, can
only be received in horary and mundane astrology; and not in nativities.

question, because ☿ wants ten degrees of the □ of ♃. If the absent be known to be at a short distance from the quesited, I should have judged that in ten days they should hear of him, because the signs are moveable.*

CHAPTER XXIV.

OF A SHIP, AND HER SAFETY OR DESTRUCTION.

The ascendant and the ☽ signify the ship and cargo; the lord of the ascendant, those that sail in her. If you find a malevolent, having dignities in the 8th, placed in the ascendant, or the lord of the ascendant in the 8th in ill configuration with the lords of the 8th, 12th, 4th, or 6th, or if the ☽ be combust, and under the earth, you may judge that the ship is lost, and the men drowned. But if you find reception between the significators at the same time, the ship was wrecked, but some of the crew escaped: if all the preceding significators be free from affliction, then both ship and cargo are safe; and if there be reception, the more so. If the ascendant and ☽ be unfortunate, and the lord of the ascendant fortunate, the ship is lost, but the men saved.

But when the querent demand, of any ship setting forth, and the state of the ship ere she return, and what may be hoped of the voyage; then, behold the *angles* of the figure, and see if the fortunes are therein, and the infortunes remote from angles, cadent, combust, or under the ☉ beams, then you may judge the ship will go safe with all her lading. But if you find the infortunes in angles, or succeeding houses,

---

* We should, in this latter case, prefer looking to the Ephemeris for the day when ☿ formed a △ of ♃ for hearing news, and when ♀ and ☿ came to ☌ for his return.

there will chance some hinderance unto the ship. If the infortune be ♄, the vessel will strike ground. If ♂, and he be in an earthy sign, he will signify the same, or very great danger and damage. But if the fortunes cast their benevolent rays to the place of ♄ or ♂, and the lords of the angles and of the dispositor of the ☽ be free, then the ship shall labour hard, and suffer damage, yet the greater part of the crew and cargo shall be preserved. If ♂ afflict the lords of the angles, and dispositor of ☽, the crew will be in danger by enemies or pirates; and if there be any additional evil configurations among these significators, there will be quarrels on board, thieving, and purloining, &c., with bloodshed: ♄ causes thefts only, if so situated, but no bloodshed.

If the signs afflicted by ♄, ♂, ☋ (and ♅, if he be ill aspected), be those that signify the vessel's bottom, or parts under water, she springs a leak; if the signs be unfortunate in the midheaven, fiery signs, and ♂ therein, there is danger of lightning or fire; if airy signs and ☿ afflict, damage by high winds. If ♂ be in the 4th, and afflicted, it denotes fire beneath; and if ♅ be with him, spontaneous combustion. If the sign be ♊, ♎, or ♒, she may be set on fire by an enemy.

If ♄ be in the midheaven, and shew damage, it will be by rotten sails or gear, and bad weather, foul winds, &c. An infortune in the ascendant shews damage to the fore part of the vessel; and if the lord of the ascendant be retrograde, it denotes that she will put into some harbour; and if he be in a moveable sign, she returns to the very port she sailed from. If the lord of the 8th afflict the lord of the 1st, and he in the 8th, the ship will be injured according to the nature of the planet afflicting. If he impedite the ☽'s dispositor, the lord of the ascendant and ☽, it shews the death of the master, and probably of his mate. If it be ⊕ which is afflicted, it foreshews evil to the cargo or a bad market; but if ♃, ♀, or ☊ be in the second, or assist its lord, or the lord of ⊕, it shews good profit, which will be according to their strength.

If the lords of the ascendant, of the ☽ and their dispositors be slow in motion, the voyage will be long; if they be swift, the ship will return quickly. If there be ill aspects between the lord of the 1st and the dispositor of ☽ without reception, there will be discord among the seamen, and with them and the owner. If the lord of the ascendant be strongest, the seamen will prevail; but if the lord of the house where ☽ is, then the owner. If the dispositor of ⊕ be not with it, or the lord of the 2d be weak, there will be scarcity of provisions, and, if they be in watery signs, of fresh water.

PARTS *of a* SHIP *ruled by the* SIGNS.

♈ The breast, or bows of the ship.
♉ The cutwater, and parts beneath.
♊ The rudder, or stem.
♋ The bottom, or floor.
♌ The upper works.
♍ The hold.
♎ The parts about the water's edge.
♏ The seamen's berths, or cabin.
♐ The seamen themselves.
♑ The ends of the vessel.
♒ The master, or captain.
♓ The oars, in galleys; the wheels, in steam-vessels; and the sails in others.

Fig. 4.

AN EXAMPLE OF A SHIP AT SEA.

In December 1644, a merchant, in London, having sent a ship to the coast of Spain to trade, had several times news that his ship was wrecked. He would have given £60 per cent. to insure her, but no insurance company would meddle, no, not upon any terms. A friend of the merchant asked, *What I thought of the ship, if sunk or living?* I gave my opinion, *that the ship was not lost, but did live, and though of late in some danger, yet was now recovered.* My judgment was founded on the considerations in *act* following:—

In the first place, the ascending degrees of Cancer shewed the bulk or body of the ship. I find ♄ casts his □ from a cardinal sign, out of the 11th house, very near to the ascendant. After his □ I find ☽ in her exaltation, casting a ✶ to the ascendant, interposing her ✶ between the ☍ aspects of ☿ and ☉ in the 7th, which otherwise had been dangerous, for all ☍ aspects to the ascendant in this judgment are dangerous. From the ascendant afflicted by □ of ♄, and presence of fixed stars of his nature, I judged the ship was of ♄'s nature, sluggish, heavy, and not very sound. And ♋ being a weakly sign, made me judge the ship was of such nature; (*and it was so confessed*). From hence, and ♉ in the 9th, I judged that the ship had been in some distress in her voyage, occasioned by such casualties as ♄ signifies, viz. some leak or damage in or near her breast, as ♈, the sign ♄ is in, represents that part.

But as ☽, lady of the ascendant, is in the 11th in her exaltation, in no way impeded, and by a benevolent △ aspect applying to ☉ and ☿, and is so near the body of ♃, and as all the significators are above the earth, and no infortunes in angles; I judged the ship, sailors, and officers, were safe, and in good condition. The next QUERY was—

Where the Ship was, upon what Coast, and when any News would come of her?

Herein I considered the ☽ was fixed, and in the 11th house; ♉ is a southern sign, but in an east quarter of heaven, verging to the south; her application is to △ of ☿, and he in ♑ a south sign and west angle; all this made me judge that the ship was *south-west* from London, and upon our own coasts, or near those which lie between Ireland and Wales. I judged her at that time to be in some harbour, because ♉, where ☽ is, is fixed, and in the 11th, or house of comfort and relief, and that she was put in to repair. (*It proved that she was in a harbour in the west.*)

Because ☽ applied to △ of ☿ and ☉, and they in an angle, and all three very swift in motion, and did want but a few minutes of a perfect △, I judged there would be news, or a certain discovery of the ship in a very short time. The significators being so near a perfect aspect, I said, either that night, or within two days, the news would arrive. (*And so it proved.*) And, observe, that it gave me good encouragement when I saw ⊕ disposed of by ♂, and that ☿, to whom ☽ applied, was in reception with ♂; also, that ☽ did so well apply to ☉, lord of the 2d, or house of *substance:* a sign that the merchant should gain by that adventure.

Besides, usually when ☽ applies to a good aspect of a *retrograde* planet, it brings the matter to an issue one way or other speedily, and when least expected; and it is a general maxim, that if ☽ apply to the fortunes, or by good aspect to any planet or planets in angles, it is reason that we hope well, &c.

Fig. 5.

EXAMPLE *of another* SHIP *at* SEA.

Here the ascendant and ☽ are significators of the ship, and those who sail in her. The ☽ lately separated from a ☐ of ♄, lord of the 8th and 9th, and afterwards applied to △ of ♄, then to ☍ of ☿, lord of the 12th and 4th houses. This shewed that the ship had lately been in danger of shipwreck: and as the ☽ had been void of course, so had no news been heard of her; for, after being in ☐ of ♄ in fixed signs, and at the time in a cadent house, and then not next applying to the good aspect of any benefic planet, but being void of course, and then again continuing her application out of the 4th to ♄, who is still lord of the 8th, though it was by good aspect; and then to ☍ of ☿, her dispositor, who is in his detriment and entering combustion; and ♃, dispositor of ☿, subterranean, and ☌ with ♂ and in term of an infortune; and, moreover, as ♂ is in his fall near the cusp of the 2d, I judged, by all this, loss to the merchant. Besides ⊕, is in the 6th disposed by ♃, he retrograde and afflicted in the 2d in no aspect to ⊕, the ☽ also in □ to it, as also ☿. There being so many ill testimonies, I judged he would lose much, if not all, in this ship; and so consequently that she was cast away. (*And so it proved.*) The principal significator in the 4th and afflicted, was a sure sign of the ship sinking.

CHAPTER XXV.

JUDGMENTS CONCERNING THE SECOND HOUSE.

WHETHER *the Querent shall be rich? or have a competent Fortune? By what Means attain it? The time when? and if it shall continue?*

Whoever interrogates, the lord of the ascendant and the ☽ are invariably his significators.

Consider the sign on the 2d, its lord, and the planets therein, or aspecting the cusp or its lord; also the ⊕.

If you find the planets all angular or even succeedent, if direct and swift in motion, it is a good sign. If in good houses, direct, and moderately well dignified, it is also a good sign. Those two rules are general.

If the lord of the 1st, the ☽, and lord of the 2d, be joined together, or if they have good aspect to the lord of the 2d, or if ♃ or ♀ cast a good aspect to ⊕, or if the lord of the 2d or ☽ be in the ascendant, or lord of the 1st in the 2d, or benefics do ascend or be found unafflicted in the 2d, or ☊ be there, all these are testimonies that the querent need fear no poverty. As the significators may be strong, and the testimonies numerous, the querent shall be in proportion rich. Always remember to judge according to his condition in life; for, *quoad capax*, it shall happen to the interrogator.

By what Means attain it?

If the lord of the 2d be in the ascendant, he may gain a fortune unexpectedly, (especially if well aspected by ♅, and this planet be strong), or gain it without much labour. If the lord of the 2d or the Moon promise substance by any mutual aspect, observe from what house the aspect is, or what house ☽ rules; if neither of these promise substance, see what house ⊕ and its dispositor be in.

If the planet assisting be in the ascendant, the querent will gain by his own industry, and, if he be a mechanic, by his own labour, care, or invention. But if the assisting planet be not lord of the 2d, he will gain by well managing his own affairs, estate, &c.; or by such things as are of the nature of that planet, the sign he is in being also considered.

If the lord of the 2d be in the 2d, he shall profit by his own industry. If the lord of the 3d benefit the lord of the 2d, ⊕, or other significators of wealth, he will be assisted by his neighbours, brethren, or kindred; or by removing to that quarter from whence the lord of the 3d throws the aspect.

The lord of the 4th gives wealth by means of his father, or some aged person; or by taking lands, or purchasing houses, &c.; or by well managing money lent him by his kindred or neighbours; or property left him by his ancestors.

The lord of the 5th promises gain by cards or other gambling; or stock-jobbing; or by holding office as an ambassador or messenger. If a man of low quality ask, by keeping an inn, &c., or being porter to some institution, or connected with theatres, &c., and such things as the 5th house denotes. It may be by well managing his father's estate, or receiving something thereout.

The lord of the 6th gives gain by servants, dealing in small cattle, &c., or by turning surgeon, &c., if capable.

The lord of the 7th gives gain by means of a wife, by the sword or warfare, by contracting bargains in his way of business, or by gaining some lawsuit, &c.

The lord of the 8th or planet therein denotes legacies, or a wife's portion, which may be unexpected at the time, (especially if ♅ assist), or he may suddenly go and settle in some country wherein he shall thrive and grow rich.

The lord of the 9th, &c., gives property by the wife's relations, or some neighbour of her's when he did marry; or some clergyman or lawyer shall befriend him; or if ♋ or ♓ be in the 9th, he may thrive by a distant sea voyage. But if an earthy sign be there, he may gain by removing to the part signified by that sign, and by dealing in the commodities belonging to that country, &c.

The lord of the 10th, &c. promises gain by the service of the king or some great man, holding office, &c. If the querent be young and of small fortune, let him learn some trade or business that may be shewn by the sign and planet in the 10th.

The 11th and its lord denote unexpected benefit by friends, or the employment of some king, nobleman or other great person.

If the fortunate aspect be cast from the 12th or by its lord, the querent will advance his fortune by great cattle or

INTRODUCTION TO ASTROLOGY.   115

horse-races; or if the sign be human, that is, ♊ or ♒, by means of prisons, &c., such as being governor or turnkey of a jail, a sheriff's officer, &c. If the sign be ♈, ♉, or ♑, by cattle; if ♍, by corn. Herein mix your judgment with reason.

The most assured testimonies of riches are if the lords of the 1st, 2d, and ♃ be joined in the 2d, 1st, 10th, 7th, 4th, or 11th houses; or if not in ☌, if they apply by ✶ or △ and be in mutual reception. If they apply by □ or ☍, yet have reception, the querent will gain wealth, though with much labour and pains.

Signs of Poverty, and its Cause.

If you find that the querent will *not* be rich, and he desire to know *why*, that he may the better order his affairs and be wary of such difficulties as may threaten, then carefully observe as follows. The planet afflicting most the lords of the 2d and 1st, the ☽, ⊕, or their dispositors, or the cusp of the 2d or planet therein, shews the cause. If the lord of the 1st, then the querent himself is the cause, and the house in which he is found may shew how. The lord of the 2d shews want of money or sufficient capital to set up with. The lord of the 3d shews that his kindred or neighbours will oppose him much, or undersell him, &c. And in this way you may go through the twelve houses, judging the reverse of what you were instructed when the aspects, &c. were good.

Caution.—If the lord of the 2d or the dispositor of ⊕ be infortunes, yet be strong and well aspected, they may denote gain as well as ♃ or ♀, though with less satisfaction and more painstaking. Also ♃ or ♀ being afflicted, may obstruct as well as any other; for every planet must do the work for which he is by Providence assigned. Again, wherever ☋ may be found, he denotes evil by that house, as if in the 6th, by

If the querent shall obtain the Substance he hath lent, or which he demands?

The lord of the ascendant and ☽ are the querent's significators, the lord of the 2d denotes his substance.*

The 7th and its lord denote the person of whom he means to ask the money, and the 8th and its lord, &c., his property. Observe whether the lord of the ascendant or ☽ be joined with the significator of the quesited's property, or be in good aspect with such significator. If this be so, and that significator be a fortune or very strong, he shall assuredly receive the money. If he be an infortune, and there be reception between him and the querent's significator, the querent will also receive his money, &c.; but if the quesited's significator be an evil planet, and there be no reception, he will hardly ever gain his desire, or with so much delay and difficulty, he would rather wish the thing undone.

In like manner if the lord of the 8th be in the 2d with reception, it is a sign he shall gain his money, &c. But if the lord of the 7th or 8th be in the 1st or 2d without reception with the querent's significators or lord of the 2d, he shall not have his desire, but may rather expect prejudice in the thing demanded.

If the lord of the 1st and ☽ be joined to a fortune that has dignity in the sign ascending or *intercepted* in the *ascendant*, the matter will be effected; or if joined to an infortune having such dignity, *with reception*, the business will be dispatched. Or, if the significators be joined to a fortune in the 10th or 11th, though without reception, the matter shall be perfected.

---

* When any planets are found in a house signifying anything, they may be taken as well as the lord of the house.

INTRODUCTION TO ASTROLOGY. 117

If one shall acquire Gain, or Profit, Salary, &c., from the Government, or any Nobleman, or Person of high Rank, &c.?

This question will serve for any other of the like nature, where the querent is much inferior in rank to the person he looks to for accomplishing his desires.

The ascendant, its lord and the ☽, represent the querent as usual, and the 10th and its lord the quesited. The 2d is the house of property for the querent, and the 11th for the person inquired about.

If you find the lord of the 1st or the ☽ joined to the lord of the 11th, or to any fortune in the 11th, not afflicted, you may affirm that the querent shall obtain his money, salary, or debt, &c. Or if it happen that the ☽ and lord of the ascendant be joined to an evil planet with reception, he may expect to succeed, but not without much solicitation, and many weary efforts. If there be any evil aspect between the significators, one being an infortune and without reception, the querent will never gain what he desires.

In this question be very careful to observe the planets' true essential dignities, and their mutual receptions, and by which of their mutual dignities they receive each other.*

Of the Time when the aforesaid Events treated of in this Chapter may happen.

Herein diligently note to what planet the lord of the ascendant or ☽ applies, by ☌ or aspect. Consider how many degrees are wanting of the perfect aspect or ☌, and say that it shall be as many days as there are degrees, if they be *both in cadent houses;* if both in *succeedent* houses, so many weeks; if both in *angles,* so many months. But if the matter cannot possibly be effected in days or weeks, but requires

* Reception by house is the most powerful; then exaltation, triplicity, term, and face: the latter is very weak.

much time, instead of months say years, and of weeks say months, and of days say weeks, &c. And if one planet be in an angle, and the other in a succeedent house, they shall signify months; one succeedent, and the other cadent, they denote weeks; and when one be angular and the other cadent, months.*

Some of the ancients have said, that if, at the time of a question, the planet which signifies the perfection of the thing demanded be in the same sign with the lord of the ascendant, the matter shall be brought to conclusion when they come to bodily conjunction; if the lord of the ascendant be the heavier planet, and whether there be reception or not. But if the lord of the ascendant be the lighter planet, not without reception, unless they be in an angle when the conjunction shall be effected, or that the other planet be in one of his own houses, especially that which is termed his joy.†

I have observed that reception by house, though the aspect were a ☐, or even ☍, brings things to perfection; but that other receptions avail not in this case.

As regards the time when; I find that if a fortune, or the ☽, or lord of the thing quesited, be in the ascendant, and have any essential dignities therein, the number of degrees between the planet and the cusp of the ascendant denote the time; days, if a moveable sign, and the business capable of being quickly perfected; months, or years, according to the sign and quality of the business.

---

* There appears a species of confusion in this arrangement, which is the reverse of the usual system, of allowing angles to produce events quicker than cadents. We should advise the student to be careful in his experiments before he adopt it.

† *Joys of the Planets:*

♏, ♄; ♐, ♃; ♏, ♂; ♎, ♀; ♍, ☿. These are not usually noticed by modern astrologers.

INTRODUCTION TO ASTROLOGY.

Fig. 6.

EXAMPLE.—A tradesman of *London*, in the year 1634, propounded the following queries. I have seen the experience of my judgment.

QUERIES.—1st. *If he should be Rich, or subsist himself without Marriage?*

2d. *By what Means he should attain Wealth?*

3d. *The Time when?*

4th. *If it would continue?*

1st QUERY.—*If the Querent should be Rich, or subsist himself without Marriage.*

I first considered the general disposition of the planets; and found the major number, especially the fortunes, swift and found the major number, especially the fortunes, swift in motion, well posited, and not afflicted. Also, that ♀, lady of the ascendant, was near *Cor Leonis*, a star of great virtue and influence; ☽ increasing in light, ♃ almost culminating. Hence I formed this general judgment, that he should live in good rank and quality among his neighbours, &c. (*quoad capax*) according to his calling. Secondly, whether he should be rich or not? I considered that the lord of the 2d is in the ascendant, and being also lord of ⊕, is near *Spica Virgina*, in 18° ♎.* Then ♃ (a general significator of wealth) was in his exaltation and angular, casting his □ to the cusp of the ascendant, which □ in signs of long ascension we usually repute a △.† Also, that ☽ separated from a ✶ of ♂, lord of the 2d, &c., significator of the thing demanded, and ☌ of ☿, and applied to ☌ ♀, the querent's significator; transferring the light and virtue of both ♂ and ☿, to the proper significator of the querent. The dispositor of ☽ is ☉, and he strong and powerful, the ⊕ in a fixed sign, and in the terms of ♂; from all which I judged that the querent would acquire an estate, and have a competent fortune; but as it is signified by an infortune, that he would attain it by labour and care. (*And so to this day he hath.*) And as ♂, lord of the 7th (the house of marriage), hath the most material signification of the thing demanded, viz. wealth, I advised him to marry, and said, that without marriage he should not so well subsist.

2d QUERY.—*By what Means he should attain Riches?*

In this scheme, ♂ being the planet signifying wealth, as lord of the ⊕ and the second house, and placed in the as-

* This star has now advanced to 22° ♎.

† Signs of long ascension, are ♋, ♌, ♍, ♎, ♏, ♐. Signs of short ascension, are ♑, ♒, ♓, ♈, ♉, ♊. In the former a ✶ is taken for a □, and a □ for a △; and in the latter, a □ is taken for a ✶, and a △ for a □. We advise the student to reject these distinctions, which only tend to create confusion.

cendant, signifies property got by the querent's own industry. And as ♂ is lord of the 7th, I said, he would marry a woman who would produce him a good fortune; and it more than he could well look for, and of a settled nature; which I judged by ♀, lady of his wife's house of property, being so well fortified. And as ☽ was lady of the 10th, (house of trade), and was transferring the light of ☿ and ♂ to ♀ his significator, I advised him to be diligent in his profession, and that he would thereby gain a good estate. (*He has since had a good fortune with his wife, money, and land, and been very successful in trade*). Jupiter, so strong in the 10th, was an infallible sign (according to natural causes) of plenty of trade, or a gainful profession.

3d QUERY.—*The Time when?*

All the significators oriental, and five planets swift in motion, promise property in a short time after the question; and ♂, the chief significator of the thing inquired after, being swift in motion, argues the same. The distance from the ascendant to ♂ being about two degrees, signified about two years, at which time he had a portion with his wife. The ☽ wanted 6° 27' of her ☌ with ♀: hence I concluded that about 1640 he should have very great trading, and live in excellent repute; and as ♀ is seated on the cusp of the 11th, (or house of friends), that he should have many good friends, &c., by whom he should increase his estate.

4th QUERY.—*If the Querent should continue rich?*

This I resolved by the cusp of the 2d, which being a fixed sign and ⊕ therein, and ♃ in his exaltation and angular, and ♀, the dispositor of ♂, being in ♌, a fixed sign, as also the ☽ in ♌, all implied that he should continue in a plentiful estate, and that the riches God should bless him with would be permanent, and that he should never be reduced to want or poverty.

There was only one thing arising out of the figure, of which I cautioned him. The ☉, lord of the 11th, beholds ⊕ by □, as also the cusp of the 2d; and as ☉ here signifies friends, I exhorted him to avoid confiding in solar men, though of much friendship with him. In all such cases describe the planet afflicting, and you give caution sufficient.*

CHAPTER XXVI.

OF THE THIRD HOUSE, VIZ. OF BRETHREN, SISTERS, KINDRED, NEWS, SHORT JOURNEYS, ETC.

THE chief, but not the only, questions regarding this house are those concerning brethren, cousins, or neighbours, and short journeys.

QUERY.—*Shall the Querent agree well with his Brother or Neighbour?*

The querent has the usual significators; the quesited is shewn by the lord of the 3d, the cusp of the 3d, and the planets therein. If the lord of the 3d be a benevolent planet, or be in the ascendant, or there be a fortune in the 3d, or the respective lords be in good aspect or mutual reception, or the lord of the ascendant throw a good aspect to the cusp of the 3d, no doubt unity will endure between the parties. If the evil planets, or ☋, be found in the 3d, unless very well dignified and aspected, it denotes discord, and the querent may expect little good from the quesited. If there be evil aspects between their significators, the same judgment holds; and if the significators are afflicted by being peregrine, retrograde, or combust, it shews hatred or untoward conduct.

---

* The description of ☉ in ♌, would herein answer the exact kind of persons who might injure the querent's property.

♄ or ☋ in the third, shews the neighbours are ill-mannered and the kindred selfish; if ♂ be there, the neighbours are dishonest, and the relations treacherous. If they be out of their dignities, these evils are increased; and if ill planets be in the ascendant, or ☋ be there, the querent is himself ill conducted.

Of an absent Brother?

The 1st, and its lord and ☽, are for the querent; the 3d for the quesited; and the 4th, his house of substance, &c.

Consider in what condition the lord of the 3d is, in what house, and how aspected. If he be in the 3d, free from evil aspects of the infortunes, you may judge that the absent brother is in health. If he be in his own house, but afflicted by the evil planets, without reception, judge that he is in health, but in great perplexity and sorrow; but if they so aspect him with reception, say, that he is in distress, but that he will shortly evade it, and rid himself of his troubles. If the fortunes aspect him by ✶ or △ without reception, or by □ or ☍ with reception, you may judge him to be in health, and well contented; and if they aspect him by ✶ or △, and there be reception, you may tell the querent that his brother is healthy and happy, and wants nothing in this world.

If the lord of the 3d be in the 4th, without aspects of the malefics, he is endeavouring to get property in the country where he then lives. If he be in the 5th, and joined by ☌, or good aspect to the lord of the 5th, if the latter be not much afflicted, he is healthy, jocund, and merry, and likes the society he is in. If it be a fortune, and there be a reception between the lords of the two houses, the 3d and 5th (his 3d), you are assured of his happy condition. Yet if it be a malefic, or he be in evil aspect with a malefic in the 5th, without reception, or if he be void of course while in the 5th, you may judge that he is restless, and discontented in his present abode. Generally, if he be afflicted in any but the 6th, 8th, or 12th houses, he is not very comfortable, yet not in ill health.

If he be in the 8th, and well aspected by a fortune, he is not in danger, yet he is indisposed. If he be joined to evil planets by bad aspects out of the 6th, he is in an infirm and dangerous state. The same, if the lord of his 6th be in the 3d, unless he have dignities therein. If, in this case, the lord of the 3d be ☌ with the lord of the 8th, or entering combustion at the same time, with other testimonies of his being ill, there is reason to fear that he will die.

If you find his significator in the 7th, he is still in the country he went to, and indifferently well.

If the lord of the 3d be in the 8th, he apprehends that he shall die; and there is great fear of his death if his significator be combust, in ☌ with the lord of the 8th, or afflicted by evil planets.

If his significator be in the 9th, he is gone to some country further off than when he first went, or is forming some clerical, legal, or scientific connexion, or is employed travelling.

If he be in the 10th, and well aspected by the fortunes, especially if with reception, he has got some good employment, or office, in the country to which he is gone. If combust and afflicted, there is fear that he is dead.

If he be in the eleventh, and joined to the lord of the 11th, it denotes he is well situated, with his friends, and happy; though if evil planets afflict him, he is not so well pleased with his present condition.

If he be in the 12th, and well aspected, he is engaged with horses or cattle, &c., keeping an inn, or is turned grazier, &c. If ill aspected in this or the 2d house, he is in trouble, and if in a fixed sign, probably in prison; yet, if his significator be retrograde, he will manage to escape. If in the ascendant, he is very pleasantly situated; and, unless ill aspected, he is much respected.

If any other person than a brother be inquired of, his condition may be known by applying the foregoing rules to that person's significator. As, for example, if the quesited be the querent's father, let the lord of the 5th (the 2d from the 4th) be considered for his substance. And if the quesited be a friend, let the 11th house represent him, and then the 12th will be his 2d, or house of property; the 8th will be his 10th, or house of honour, &c.; and so all round the 12 houses. But understand that, though every house has its 6th, 8th, and 12th, yet of every person inquired after, the 6th house of the figure shall signify his sickness, the 8th his death, the 12th his imprisonment.

Of Reports, News, Rumours, &c. whether true or false? and whether importing Good or Evil?

That which I found true by experience (in our late sad times of war) was this: if I found ☽ in the ascendant, 10th, 11th, or 3d house, separating by benevolent aspect from any planet, and then applying by good aspect to the lord of the 1st; I say, I found the report or rumour true, but always tending to the good of the parliament, let the report be good or ill. But if ☽ applied to the lord of the 7th by any good aspect, I was sure we had the worst, and our enemies the victory. If the ☽ was void of course, the news proved of no moment, usually vain and false, and soon contradicted. If the ☽ and ☿ were in □ or ☍, without reception, and neither casting a good aspect to the degree ascending, the news was *false*, and reported purposely to alarm us.

The time of erecting the figure was ever the hour when I

first heard the rumour; but, if another propounded it, then that very minute when it was first proposed.

If, on hearing of any matter, you desire to know whether it will be prejudicial to you or not, observe whether ♃ or ♀ be in the ascendant, or ☽ or ☿ in any of their essential dignities, in ⚹ or △ to the lord of the 11th; you may then judge that the party inquiring shall receive no damage thereby. But if the lord of the 6th, 8th, or 12th, be in the ascendant, or in evil aspect to the lord of the ascendant, or a malefic retrograde in the ascendant, or afflicting its lord, or the degree ascending, then the querent will be prejudiced by the matter. But if it concern the public, some damage has happened to their ministers or friends. In this case, if ♄ denote the evil, he shews plundering, loss of corn, or cattle, &c.; ♂ causes straggling parties to be cut off, and military violence, bloodshed, &c.; ☿ the miscarriage of letters, or evil to the literary community, messengers, &c.; ☉ causes distress to the king, or some chief or leader; ♀ causes ill to some gentlemen or their friends. The ☽ denotes violence by mobs, and if she be afflicted, injuries are done to the people.

If Rumours be true or false, according to the ANCIENTS.

If the lord of the ascendant, the moon, or her dispositor, be in an angle or a fixed sign, and in good aspect to the fortunes, or the ☉, you may judge the rumour is true. If they be in moveable signs, cadent, and ill aspected by the infortunes, judge the reverse; and consider the majority of the testimonies. When the angles of the figure, the ☽, and ☿, are in fixed signs, and these latter separate from infortunes and apply to fortunes, the rumour is true. Evil rumours hold true, or will be in some way verified, if the angles of the 4th and 10th are fixed, and the ☽ therein. If you have evil news, yet if either fortune be in the ascendant, or the ☽ fortunate, it is a strong argument that the rumours are false, and that they will turn rather to good than evil. Mercury, or the planet to whom he or ☽ applies, being retrograde or afflicted, or if either of these two be lord of the ascendant, it signifies that the rumour shall vanish to nothing, or shall be converted to good. If the lord of the ascendant be under the beams of ☉*, the matter is kept secret, and few shall ever know the truth.

Of Counsel or Advice given by a Neighbour, or Relation, Friend, &c.

Erect the figure when first the party begins to break their mind, and you shall know whether they really wish you well or not, and whether it be good to follow their advice.

If there be in the 10th house either ☉, ♃, ♀, or ☋, or if ☽ apply by good aspect to the lord of the ascendant, judge they come with an honest heart, and the advice is intended for your good. If ♅ ♄, ♂, or ☋ be there, or if ☽ apply by evil aspect, they intend deceitfully. *Haly* affirms, that if the sign ascending be moveable, and the ☽ and lord of the ascendant are both in moveable signs, the party comes to deceive.†

Of short Journeys, whether good to go or not?

By a short journey, I mean such distances as a person may go and come back in a day or two. Consider the lord of the ascendant, and whether he be swift in motion, and in the 3d,

---

* This signifies within a distance of 12 degrees of ☉. Modern authors say 17 degrees.

† If the advice be intended for your benefit, yet it may not be well to follow it. This may be seen by the lord of the 4th, and planets therein; for if malefics be there, or the lord of the 4th afflict the lord of the ascendant, it will end ill : if good planets be there, it ends well.—ZAD.

or in any of the dignities of the lord of that house; or in good aspect with its lord, or a planet therein; or if the ☽ apply to such aspect, or be in the 3d, or cast her ✶ or △ to the degree ascending, or be swift in motion; all these are arguments that the party shall go his short journey, and have success. The part of heaven in which the place lies to which he would go is known by the situation of ☽, the sign on the cusp of the 3d, or its lord, whichever may be strongest in essential dignities. If the chief significator be in a northern sign, he goes north, and so of the rest.

EXAMPLES.

In November 1645, a citizen of *London* having gone into the west of England, and no news being heard of him for many weeks, his brother, with great importunity, moved me to give my judgment concerning these particulars.

The figure, erected at the moment of the question, is on the following page; and the particulars of the judgment on each of three queries, which were put on the occasion, will be found to follow.

Fig 7.

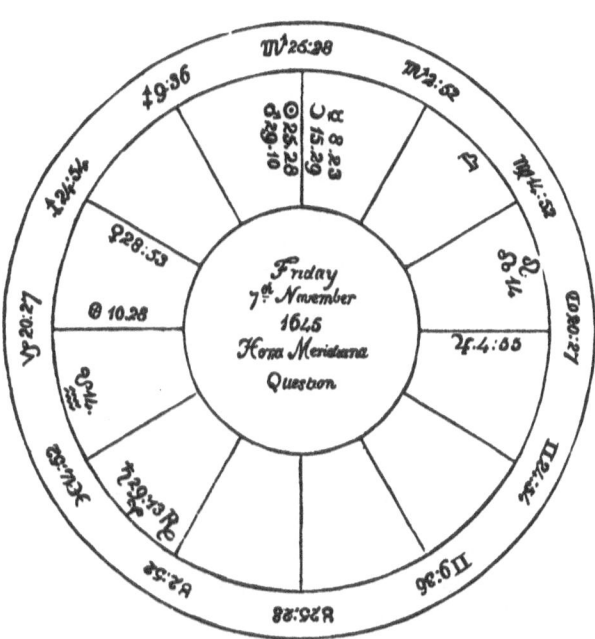

QUESTIONS REGARDING AN ABSENT BROTHER.

1st.—*If Living or Dead? if Dead, whether Killed by Soldiers? for at this time our miserable kingdom was full of soldiers.*

2d.—*If Living, when he should hear of him? and where he was?*

3d.—*When he should come Home?*

1st QUERY.—*If Living or Dead?*

The ascendant doth here represent the shape and form of

him who asked the question, with consideration had to ♄, lord of the sign. The querent was lean, spare of body, and a real *saturnine* man, &c.

♉ is the ascendant of the 3d house, and ♀ being lady thereof, represented the absent brother.

♀, the significator of the quesited, being noways afflicted, either by ☿, lord of the 8th in the figure, or ♂, lord of the quesited's 8th : and the separation of the ☽ being good, *viz.* a △ of ♃, and ☌ of ☿, who is in good aspect to ♃, and going to ☌ of ☉ on the cusp of the midheaven, I judged the absent brother was alive, and had had no manner of accident, but was in good health.

2d Query.—*When he should hear of him?*

♀ lady of the 3d applies to a friendly △ of ♄, lord of the ascendant, and ♄ being retrograde, applies also to the aspect of ♀ ; a very good argument that the querent should hear news of his brother very suddenly. And if you look into the *Ephemeris* for 7th November, 1645, you will find that, about four o'clock on that very day, the △ aspect between ♀ and ♄ was formed. I therefore advised the querent to go to the *carriers* of those countries where he knew his brother had been, and ask when they saw the quesited ; for I told him that it was probable that he should hear of him that very day. (*He has since confidently affirmed, that about the very moment of time, viz, about four, a carrier came casually where he was, and informed him that his brother was living, and in health.*)

Where he was?

His journey was into the *west*. At time of the question I find ♀, his significator, leaving ♐, a north-east sign, and entering ♑, a south sign ; whereon I judged he was in the south-east part of the county unto which he went. And as ♀ was not far out of the ascendant, and was in the oriental quarter of heaven, that he was not above one or two days' journey from London; and as ♀ was leaving ♐, and entering a sign in which she has dignities by *triplicity* and *term*, I judged the man was leaving the country where he had no possession or habitation, and was coming to his own house in London, where he had good property. As ♀ wanted one degree of getting out of the sign, I judged he would be at home in less than *one week;* for ♐ is a common sign, and one degree therein in this question might well denote one week. He came home on the following *Tuesday,* when ☽ came to ☌ ♀, she being then got into ♑, in her own *term* and *diurnal triplicity.* The two significators being in △, these two brothers always did, and do, live very amicably together.

Fig. 8.

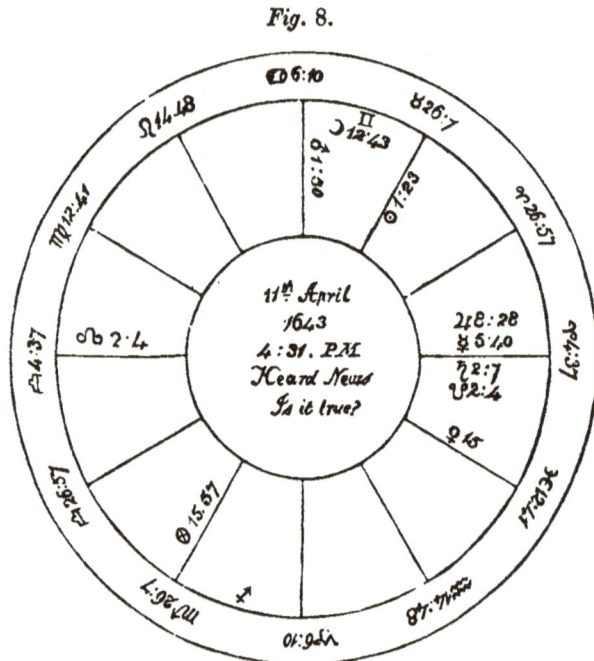

QUERY.—*If a Rumour or Report were true or not?*

In 1643, his Majesty's army being then *rampant*, several reports were given out that his Majesty had taken Cambridge, &c.: a well-affected person inquired of me if the news were true or false? whereupon I erected this figure, and gave judgment:—"*All that we heard was untruth, and that the town neither was or should be taken by him or his forces.*"

A Report that Cambridge was taken by the King's Forces; if true?

First, I considered that the angles were all moveable, and

that the evil ♂ vitiated the cusp of the 10th, and ♄ that of the 7th; one argument that the report was false.

Secondly, the ☽ was cadent, and in ♊, a sign wherein she is very weak: a second such argument.

Thirdly, the ☊ on the cusp of the ascendant was a sign of good to the Parliament, for the first house signified that honourable society. ♀, lady of the ascendant, was in her exaltation, but ♂, lord of the 7th, our enemies, in his fall, viz. ♋, and afflicted by □ of ♄. The ☽ separating from ♃ in the 7th, and transferring his light to ♀, gave reason to expect that there would come good to our side by this report or rumour, and no benefit to the enemy. The □ of ♄ and ♂ assured me that our enemies were so full of division and treason, and so thwarting one the other's designs, that no good should come unto them by this report. And so, in short, I judged that Cambridge was not taken, and that what we heard was false.*

Had this question been, *Whether the querent would have brethren or not?* then you should judge as follows:—

The sign on the 3rd ♏ is fruitful; ♋, the sign in which the lord of the 3d is found, is fruitful, and the ☽ applies to ♀; signs that the querent might expect both, but chiefly sisters, as the signs are mostly feminine.

---

* If the student erect a figure for 10h. 53m. A.M. Dec. 23d, 1834, he will find ♐ 15 on the 10th, and ☽ in ♎ 0:15 in the 7th, applying to □ of ☉, lord of the 7th. We erected this figure on hearing a rumour of several persons being cruelly slaughtered by soldiers at Rathcormac, in Ireland, for the purpose of collecting tithes. The ☽ being angular and afflicted, shewed that the *evil* report was true; and ♅ being exactly on the cusp of the ascendant, ♏ 23:30, was a similar testimony. ☋ was in ♐ 16:35 on the cusp of the 10th, shewing discredit to the government, arising out of the transaction. The coroner's jury found a verdict of *wilful murder.*

CHAPTER XXVII.

OF THE FOURTH HOUSE, AND JUDGMENTS DEPENDING THEREON.

This is the House of Parents, Lands, Tenements, Cities, Towns, Villages, Farms, Castles, Treasure found, &c., or of any Thing hidden in the ground; also of the Grave.

RULE.—*To Find a Thing hidden or mislaid.*

BE careful to consider to whom the thing hidden, &c. may belong: if the goods did belong to the querent, take the lord of the 2d; but if to his brother or sister, regard the lord of the 4th; if to his father, the lord of the 5th; if to his mother, the lord of the 11th, and so of other persons; if to a stranger to the querent, or one who is no relation, take the lord of the 8th. If you find the lord of the house of property is in any angle, judge the thing missing is within the house of him who is the owner. And if the lord of the property is in the ascendant, or disposed of by the lord of the ascendant, by house, or in the same sign with him, say it is in that part of the house wherein he most frequents, or lays up his goods, or such things as he most delights in. But if the lord of the quesited's property be in the 10th, it is then in his shop, if he keep one, or, if he be a gentleman, in his dining-room; if he be a farmer, it is in the common room of the residence, or first room after you enter the house. If the lord of the property be in the 7th, it is then in that part where the quesited's wife or his maid-servants have most to do. If in the 4th, it is where the most aged of the house lodges, or formerly did most frequent; or in the middle of the house, or in the most ancient part, or where his father or some elderly man lodged. The nature and quality of the place are known by the signs the significators are in; for if the sign of the second be *airy*, or the greater part of the significators, including the sign where ⊕ is, be the same, the thing is hid in the eaves, or the upper part of the room where it is, or on high from the ground; and if the thing be in an orchard or garden, it is higher than the ground, or upon some tree, line, &c., or is on the highest hill or part of the ground. If the said significators be strong, and in *watery* signs, it is in the dairy, or washhouse, brewhouse, or near water. If they be in *fiery* signs, it is near the chimney, or the walls of the house, or where iron is found. If in *earthy* signs, the thing is on the ground or earth, or near some pavement or floor; and if the thing lost be out of the house, it will be found near the bridge, stile, or gate, where people come into the grounds.

If the significator be going out of one sign into another, the thing is behind something, or fallen between two rooms, or near the threshold; and it is higher or lower, according to the sign being airy, &c.

If a thing be lost, and not stolen, consider the following points:—

1. The sign ascending, its nature, and the quarter of heaven it denotes.
2. The sign the lord of the ascendant is in.
3. The sign of the 4th house.
4. The sign the lord of the 4th is in.
5. The sign the ☽ is in.
6. The sign of the 2d house.
7. The sign the lord of the 2d is in.
8. The sign ⊕ is in.

Then examine the greater number of testimonies to discover what quarter of heaven the thing is in, as regards the parts of the house. Having found the bearing, or point of the compass, observe the nature of the sign, viz. *airy* signs, above ground; *fiery*, near a wall, or partition; *earthy*, on the floor; *watery*, near a moist place in the room, &c.

Bearing by Compass of the Signs.

♈ East	♌ E. by North	♐ E. by South
♎ West	♊ W. by South	♒ W. by North
♋ North	♏ N. by East	♓ N. by West
♑ South	♉ S. by East	♍ S. by West.

Of Buying and Selling Lands, Houses, Farms, &c.

The ascendant, its lord, and the ☾, are for the buyer, and the 7th, its lord, and planets therein, for the seller. The 4th, its lord, and planets therein, signify the land, or house, &c. And the 10th house, its lord, and planets therein, signify the price; that is, whether it will be sold cheap or dear.

If you find the lords of the 1st and 7th in good aspect, and the lord of the 7th apply by good aspect (or if by evil aspect with reception) to the lord of the ascendant, you may judge the seller has good will to the buyer; and if they are at all dignified, the purchase will be effected; but if the aspect be evil, there will be much bargaining and dispute before all be settled.

If the lord of the ascendant, or ☾, apply to the lord of the 4th, or this planet apply to them, or if they be in each other's places, viz. the lord of the 1st, or ☾, in the 4th, or the lord of the 4th in the ascendant, and there be any reception, the purchase will be effected.

But if there be no dwelling in houses as above, yet the ☾ transfer the light of the lord of the 4th to the lord of the ascendant, the bargain will be concluded, though by brokers or agents, rather than by the principals.

If none of the above rules hold, there will be no bargain made.

Of the Quality of the Land or Houses, &c.

If you find the infortunes in the 4th, especially if they be peregrine, or the lord of the 4th retrograde or afflicted, it will never continue long with the buyer's posterity, or benefit him.

But if ♃, ♀, or ☊, be in the 4th, or the lord of the 4th be strong and well aspected, the purchaser may expect good success with the property; and if a fixed sign be in the 4th, it will continue in the family of the purchaser.

If an infortune possess the ascendant, the tenants or occupiers are evil and deceitful, and will give trouble. If a fortune be there, or ☊, judge the reverse. In the former case, if the evil planet be retrograde, the tenants will decamp without paying their rent, or will throw up their leases.

If in the 10th house there be a fortune, and it direct, the timber will be profitable, or the house will let well. If it be retrograde, there are many trees, but they not profitable. If there be an infortune direct, there are few trees, or the house will not let well; and if he be retrograde, the timber will be stolen, or the rent will be either stolen after payment, or no payment be well and truly made. If there be no planet in the 10th, consider the lord of the house, and, as he may be strong or weak, judge the result of the profits, whether by timber, &c., or by letting the house, &c. But the angle of the 7th must be considered in like manner, to judge the quality of the grass, corn, or herbage, &c. As regards the description of the ground, look to the 4th house; and if you find a fiery sign on its cusp, the ground is in general hilly, dry, and hard; the more so, if the lord of the 4th be in a fiery sign, viz. ♈, ♌, ♐. If there be an earthy sign on the cusp, the ground is plain, level, and good pasture land, or for tillage. If there be an airy sign thereon, the ground is of a mixed nature, part hilly and part plain, partly good and partly bad. If the sign be watery, then there is plenty of water, a brook, or rivulet, &c., thereon. And if an infortune be in the 4th, and retrograde or peregrine, the land will partake greatly of the nature of that infortune; as if ♏ be the sign, and ♄ in it, the land is marshy or boggy, and full of rushes; if he be afflicted, so much worse is the land. And if the land lie near the sea, you may fear an overflow, or that the banks are damaged, &c. If ♄ be in the 4th in a fiery sign, the land is barren, and wants water; if he be afflicted, it is utterly stony and worthless. If ♄ be there in an airy sign, the land is defective; and if he be afflicted, especially in ♊, the management of it has been bad and unthrifty. If he be there in an earthy sign, the land is tolerably good, but heavy, clay land; and if he be afflicted, the farmers are dull, and too poor to manage it well.

In like way judge of the standing of a house or building: if it be a watery sign, there will be much damp; and if ♄ be there in ♏, it is overrun with rats.

Of the Cheapness or Dearness of the Land or Houses, &c.

This is known by the lord of the 10th; for if he be angular and strong, the price will be high, and the seller will stand upon his terms; but if he be weak, cadent, afflicted, &c., the price will not rise high.

If it be good for the Querent to take or lease the House, Farm, or Land, &c.

The 10th house, &c., will herein shew the profit or advantage to be made by the undertaking, having regard also to the usual significators of property, viz. the lord of the 2d, and ⊕, &c.

The 4th house will shew the end of the matter as regards the taking the property.

If there be a fortune ascending, or ⊕ be in the ascendant, or the lord of the ascendant be there, or be in ✶, or △ to the degree on the cusp and not afflicted, the querent will take the house or farm, &c., and find it a good bargain.

If an infortune ascend, the querent will not take the property; or if he have already taken it, he has no mind to it, and will quickly put it off to another party.

If you find the lord of the 7th in the 7th, or casting a good aspect to its cusp, or there be benefics therein, the man will keep his word in the bargain, but he will profit by it more than the querent.

If an infortune be in the 7th and not lord of the 7th, have great care of the covenants or agreements between you; for the landlord will be too hard for you, as he minds nothing but his own ends in the matter.

Consider the 10th house; and if a fortune be there or behold its cusp by good aspect, the parties, notwithstanding some rubs, will proceed in their bargain, and the land, &c. will be let to the querent.

If you find an infortune in or in evil aspect to the 10th, the bargain will be broken off. If it be land, they differ about the timber, &c., or upon the erecting of some new buildings; and if the thing be a house, &c., they differ about the repairs.

As to the end of the matter, see to the 4th house. If fortunes be there, or the lord of the 4th behold the cusp favourably, it will end well, and both parties will be pleased; but if an infortune be there, or the lord of the house aspect it by ☐ or ☍, the whole matter will end ill, and will please neither party.

QUERY.—*Shall the Querent enjoy the Estate of his Father?*

If in this question you find the lords of the 2d and 5th in reception and in each other's houses, there is no doubt that the querent shall have a competent fortune out of his father's estate. But if the lord of the father's property be retrograde or afflicted, then some part of the estate intended for the querent will be wasted or otherwise disposed of. If you would know why or how, see what planet impedites the lord of the 5th, and what house he is lord of. If it be the lord of the 6th, it may be one of the father's brothers, or sisters, or neighbours shall prevail on the father to alter his intentions towards the querent. If it be the lord of the 7th, it may be some female, or his wife, or some person with whom the querent has quarrelled, that will cause his father to alter his mind. If it be the lord of the 12th, it is some one of the mother's kindred, or it may be (especially if ♃), some minister or clergyman. Now, if, upon describing the party, the querent is well informed of who it is, and is desirous to gain the person's good will, and so to diminish their malice, let him do as follows: on the approach of any ✶, △, or ☌ between the planet signifying that party and the lord of the ascendant, let the day be observed in the Ephemeris when the ☽ separates from one and applies to the other, (by good aspect if possible), and on that day endeavour a reconcilement: and it is not to be doubted that he may obtain his desire, as I have found many times by good experience.*

If the lord of the 5th dispose of the ⊕, and be in the ascendant or 2d, the querent shall gain his desires. ♃ or

---

* This method of electing times for application to individuals for any favour, or to gain any point, may be safely practised after any other horary question, as well as this particular one.—ZAD.

♀ in the 5th, casting a ✶ or △ to any planet in the 2d, argues the same.

If ☽ separate from the lord of the 5th, and go immediately to ✶ or △ of the lord of the 2d or of the ascendant, it shews assured hopes of acquiring the property of the father.

If you find an infortune ill dignified in the 4th, the father has no inclination to part with his money; nor will it be well to move him much thereto, until that unfortunate planet be transited out of the sign. But if you cannot stay so long, observe when that planet is direct, swift in motion, oriental, in ✶ or △ with ♃ or ♀ or the lord of the ascendant, and then let the father be moved in the business. The observing those influences will not *compel* the father's mind, but will cause more benevolent intentions.

If the lords of the 2d and 5th apply to any good aspect by retrogradation, the querent will receive some property from his father suddenly, before he thinks of it. If there be any good aspect, reception, &c., between the lord of the 4th and any other planet, stronger than there is between the lord of the 4th and the lord of the ascendant, the father regards the party signified by that other planet better than the querent: if it be the lord of the 3d, or any planet in the 3d, then it is one of the querent's brothers, &c.

Of removing from one House or Place to another.

Observe the ascendant, the 4th and 7th houses, and their lords, planets therein, &c.

If the lord of the 4th be in the 7th, and he a good planet, and the lords of the 1st and 7th be good also and strong, it is then better to remain where you are. But if the lord of the 7th be with a good planet, and the lord of the 4th with an evil one, it is then not well to remain. If the ☽ or lord of the ascendant separate from ill aspects of the infortunes, and they lords of the 4th or 7th, or from the lords of the 6th, 8th, or 12th; or if an evil planet be in the ascendant or 4th; or if the lord of the 2d be weak, I advise the querent to remove. And if the lord of the 6th be in the ascendant, or afflict its lord or the ☽, I have found that the querent has ill health where he is, or is troubled by evil servants. If the lord of the 12th be the afflicting planet, he has backbiting, treacherous neighbours. And if the ⊕ was in the 6th, 8th, or 12th, or the lord of the 2d was in ill aspect to the lord of the ascendant, I have found that he went back in the world, &c. If the lord of the 10th afflict, I judged that he was unfortunate in trade, or had lost his credit. If the lord of the 4th afflict, he has been injured by repairing the house, &c. The lord of the 7th shews injury by an opposite neighbour, who undersells him, &c.

In giving advice which way to steer his course in hopes of better success, I observe what planet in the scheme is strongest, and has the best aspect to the lords of the ascendant or 2d; and according to the quarter of heaven the sign that planet is in signifies, I advise the querent to remove. I do not remember that any ever repented the following my advice, though many have afterwards returned me both thanks and rewards.*

If ☽ separate from a fortunate planet, stay; if she separate from an infortune, remove. An infortune in the ascendant, or a fortune in the 7th, remove; but a fortune in the ascendant, or infortune in the 7th, remain.

Of Treasure, Mines, &c. concealed in the Ground.

To discover mines or any other thing supposed to be concealed in any place, the querent must observe whether there

---

* Let the querent also attend to the places ruled by the sign in which the planet is; as London for ♊, Dublin for ♉, &c.

be any planet strongly dignified in the 4th house; and the nature of the treasure, mine, &c. may be judged of by that planet, if he have any affinity with the 7th house. The nature of the mine, &c. will depend on the nature of the planet. If ♄ be lord of the 7th and in the 4th dignified, he signifies good coal mines; or if the question were of stone, then there is a good quarry. And so judge of the others according to their nature and strength in essential dignities.

EXAMPLE.

If I should purchase the Houses of Master B.?

The inheritance of the house wherein at this present 1647 I live, and some others, being proffered me to buy in 1634, I had a desire to know if I should deal with the seller, and procure money in convenient time to pay for the purchase, my own money being in such hands that I could not call it in under six months' notice. Being desirous, I say, to purchase the said houses, and fully resolved upon it, I took my own question myself, at the time I found my mind most perplexed and solicitous about it. The time of the query to myself fell out according to the position of heaven following.

Fig. 9.

Resolution of the above Question.

The sign ascending is ♎, and the degree ascending the place of ♃ in my *radix:* I looked upon that as a good omen in the first place. ♀ is for myself, ☉ locally placed in the 7th is for the seller. ☉ receives ♀ in his exaltation; and as ♀ is near the cusp of the 7th, and no other planet there but the ☉, this signified that there was no other purchaser about it at present but myself. The ☉ so exalted and angular, denoted that the seller was high in his demands, (*and so he was,*) nor was he necessitated to part with it. Finding my significator received of ☉ and so near the cusp of the 7th, was an argument that I should proceed in the business, notwithstanding the many debilities of ♀. For as ☉ was lord of the 7th, so also was the lord of the 11th; signifying that my *hopes* should not be frustrated. And ♀ also was applying to △ of ♄, lord of the 4th, viz. the houses inquired after, and had no frustration, &c., before the perfect aspect; a strong argument that I should buy the houses. Both significators applied to the aspect, ♄ being retrograde, I also considered that ☉ was in △ to ♄, the ☉ being lord of my 11th and ♄ of the 4th; and as ♄ beholds the ascendant and has dignities therein, he, therefore, had signification of myself. Now, whether you consider him as having dignities in the ascendant or as lord of the 4th, the lord of the 11th and he applying by a △, argued assuredly that I should proceed and in the end conclude for the houses. The ☽ in the next place translating the influence of ♂, lord of the 7th, to ♄, having virtue in the ascendant, though by a □ out of signs of long ascension, did much facilitate the matter; but argued my contracting leisurely and slowly, because of the □ aspect. And as ☽ is afflicted and ♀ unfortunate, so I had much trouble and many meetings about it; the seller not abating one penny of £530, being the first money he demanded. As ☉ is near to a ⚹ of ♃, so did a *jovial* man endeavour to procure the purchase (after I began), but ♃ is cadent and in detriment, which shewed he should not prevail. ♀ angular and in aspect with ♄, and ☉ lord of the 11th (or 5th from the 7th), shewed that a daughter of the seller was my very good friend in this business, and suffered no interloper to intervene, though some offered fair to hinder me. As ♂, lord of my 2d, was retrograde, it denoted that I should get none of my own money to supply my occasions. ♃, lord of ⊕ in ⚹ to ☉, no ways impedited, but by being in detriment, in platic ⚹ with the lady of the ascendant, gave me such hopes,

L

that I doubted not of procuring money when he entered ♋, his exaltation, and ♂ became direct; which he did twelve days after, when a friend lent me £500.

The qualities of the houses are shown by ♑, the sign on the 4th, and by ♄, lord thereof, who having no material debilities (except being retrograde and cadent), and being also in △ to ☉, the houses were really old, but strong and able to stand many years. When ♀ and ☉ came to ☌ in ♉ (25th April), I bargained; and on the ☽ to ☌ ♀ (May 17th), I paid in £530, and my conveyance was sealed. As ♀ wanted 6 degrees of being ☌ with ☉, so was it six weeks and some days from the time of the question until I perfected what the figure promised.

As to the moles and scars on my body, it exactly agrees; for as ♀ is in ♈, which represents the face, so have I a mole on my cheek, about the middle of it; and as ♎ ascends, I have one on the reins of my back. The ☽ in ♍, afflicted by ♂, I have a red mole below the navel. ♃, lord of the 6th in ♊, a masculine sign, I have a mole near my right hand, visible on the outside; so have I one on the left foot, as ♓, the sign on the 6th signifies.

I had a hard bargain, as the figure every way considered manifests; and shall never live to see many of the leases yet in being expire. And as ♀ is in ♈, the sign opposite her own house, so did I do myself injury by the bargain; I mean in matter of money; but the love I bore to the house I now live in, wherein I lived happily with a good master full seven years, and therein obtained my first wife, and was bountifully blessed with the goods of this world, made me neglect a small hinderance; nor now, I thank God, do I repent it, finding God's blessing in a plentiful measure upon my labours.

CHAPTER XXVIII.

OF THE FIFTH HOUSE AND ITS QUESTIONS.

If one shall have Children, yea or nay?

HEREIN generally consider whether the signs ascending and on the 5th house be fruitful;* whether the lord of the ascendant, or the ☽ be in aspect with the lord of the 5th, and if so, whether the lord of the 5th be strong, and also the planet or planets in the 5th or in aspect with its lord. These are signs the querent shall have children before they die. Also if the lord of the 5th be in the ascendant, or the lord of the ascendant be in the 5th, it is a strong argument of children. If there be translation of light or collection between the significators, you may still judge that there will be children, but not so speedily as if it had been foreseen by the former manner of judgment.

If a Woman ask, whether she may have a Child?

If a married woman ask, consider whether the lord of the ascendant be in the 5th or 7th, or the lord of the 5th be in the ascendant or 7th, or lord of the 7th in the 5th, or the ☽ with him, or good planets in the ascendant, or with the lord of the 5th or in the angles; she may then conceive. But if none of these testimonies concur, and you find barren signs and planets in the aforesaid situations, (especially if infortunes be angular and fortunes cadent), she neither has conceived at present nor will hereafter. If good and evil planets be mixed, she may have children, but they will not live. If ♊, ♌, or ♍, be on the ascendant or 5th, and ♅, ♄, ♂, or ☉ in the 5th, it is a strong sign of barrenness. But ☉ rather causes the death of children than prevents their birth.

* Fruitful signs are the watery triplicity ♋, ♏, and ♓.

Whether a Man shall have Children by his Wife, or his intended Wife? Or, whether a Woman may by her Husband, &c.

Observe the ascendant, its lord, and the ☽; and if the lord of the ascendant or ☽ be joined to the lord of the 5th, they shall have issue by the party inquired of. If this be not, observe whether *translation* or *collection* of light occur between the significators, or whether ☽ or lord of the ascendant be in the 5th, or the lord of the 5th in the ascendant. These are all testimonies in the affirmative. If ♃ or ♀ be in the 5th no way afflicted, a child will be very speedily born; and if they, or either of them, be in the ascendant or 11th, there will be children, but not so speedily. But if the fortunes be afflicted while in those places, there is danger of the child being born dead, or dying shortly after birth. If there be signs of children, yet ♀ be afflicted by ♄ or ♂, there is danger of some accident, &c. to the mother before the birth.

If ♄, or ♂, or ☋, (and ♅, if afflicted), be in the 5th, or the two former cast their ☍ to its cusp, the woman is not with child, nor will be. The □ of the infortunes to the cusp of the 5th denotes no conception, unless they be strong and there be other good testimonies. The lord of the 5th, weak, &c., denotes a sickly child.

Whether a Woman be with Child or not? if she ask the Question.

She is so, if the lord of the ascendant, or ☽, behold the lord of the 5th by any aspect, or translation of light have passed between them. If the lord of the ascendant, or ☽ be in the 5th, free from affliction by the infortunes, or lords of the 6th, 8th, or 12th, or ☋. If ♃ be in the 1st, 5th, 7th or 11th, not in aspect to ♄, or ♂, and they slow in motion, or retrograde. If the lord of the ascendant, or 5th be in good aspect to a planet in an angle, with mutual reception. If the ☽ be in reception with any planet in an angle, and be essentially fortified. If the lord of the ascendant behold its cusp by good aspect, out of a good house; or if ☽ be in the 7th, and behold the lord of the 7th in the 11th; or if ☽ be in the 11th, and behold the lord of the 7th in the 7th. If the lord of the ascendant be in mutual reception by house, triplicity, exaltation, or term, with a planet who has the same reception exactly; that is, if each be in the other's house, &c. If the ☽ apply to the lord of the ascendant, or lord of the 5th, by good aspect from the 10th house, or by evil aspect if with mutual reception. If the sign ascending be fixed, and a fortune therein, or if the lord of the 5th be strong in the ascendant, or 10th, you may ever predict true conception.

She is not so, if you find none of the above testimonies, or barren signs on the 5th, or ascendant; or evil planets there, or afflicting their lords and the ☽.

If the Man ask the Question, unknown to the Woman.

She is with child, if the lord of the 5th behold a planet in an angle, with reception; or if the lords of the ascendant, or 5th, or 7th, or ♃, ♀, ☉, ☽, ☿, or ☋, be in the 5th, and be fortunate.—N.B. ☿ if in aspect to a malefic, and not in any aspect to a benefic, cannot be relied upon.

She is not with child, if ♃ or ♀ be afflicted. If ♀ be joined to ♄ or ♂, (or to ♅, if he be ill aspected), and they be combust, retrograde, or in ♌, ♍, or ♑. If ♄ or ♂ be in the 5th, in □, or ☍, to its lord, they denote no conception; but if other testimonies be more powerful, and denote conception, they shew danger of abortion.

The lord of the ascendant joined to a retrograde planet, or

to one in a cadent house, or received by a retrograde or combust planet, or if no aspect or translation of light be between the lords of the 1st and 5th, are all signs of no conception; but judge by the majority of testimonies.

Is the Child Male or Female?

The lords of the ascendant, the 5th, and the ☽, and the signs on the ascendant and 5th being masculine, denote a male; if they be, on the contrary, feminine, the child will be a female.—N.B. Unless this be a part of the question, do not attempt to give a judgment; nor then either, unless there be a great majority of testimonies on one or the other side. The sign the dispositor of the ☽ is in may also be considered.

Whether the Child shall live or die?

The lord of the 5th retrograde, combust, or cadent, or being in his fall or detriment, and afflicted by the lord of the 8th of the figure, or the 8th from the 5th, (which is the 12th), are signs of death. Or if the lord of the 5th, being weak, be afflicted by an evil planet in the 8th or 12th, unless some opposite testimonies occur, it may be expected the child will speedily die. If the lord of the ascendant be in the 5th, and be afflicted as above, or if ♅, ♄, ♂, or ☋, be in the 5th, especially if retrograde, they denote the same.

Whether there shall be twins?

If suspicion be of twins, and you find, upon that question, the ascending sign be double-bodied, and a fortune therein, or the same of the 5th house, and ☉ and ☽ be in double-bodied signs, and the lords of the ascendant and 5th be the same, you may judge twins. But unless all, or nearly all, these testimonies concur, it is not safe so to judge.—N.B. The dispositor of the ☽, that is the planet in whose house she is, may also be considered. Moreover, if the ☋ be with either ♃, ♀, or the ☽, or that all these be in either ♊, ♍, ♐, or ♓, it is a farther testimony of the woman bearing twins.

How long the Woman has been pregnant?

Observe the lord of the ascendant, the 5th, or the ☽; see which is nearest from any aspect which is past, and then judge according to the nature of the aspect. If the separation be from a △, say she is in the 5th month of her conception, or the 3d; if it be a ✶, she is in the 2d or 6th month; if a ☐, she is in the 4th month; an ☍, gives the 7th month; and if it be a ☌, then she has been pregnant only *one* month.

Of the Time when the Birth shall take place?

Observe when ♂ or ☉ are in ☌ with the lord of the 5th, or there be a ☌ of the lord of the 5th with the lord of the ascendant in the 5th house; about that time the birth may be expected. Observe, also, when the lord of the ascendant goes out of one sign into another; that is also a probable period for the birth. See, also, how far the lord of the 5th is from the cusp of the 5th, and give to every sign one month. Judge according to the majority of these testimonies.*

OF AMBASSADORS OR MESSENGERS.

The lord of the 5th and the ☽ may be considered to represent the ambassador or messenger. The planet to whom

---

* This is rather a difficult point to decide; and unless the querent have great anxiety on the subject, which in some cases may happen, we advise the student to avoid giving judgment, or at least till he has well satisfied himself, by experience, of the right method. We believe it will generally be found, that at the time of the birth the ☉ is passing some aspect of the cusp of the 5th, or its lord.

either of them apply shall shew the cause and nature of the message.

If you find the application be from a fortune by □, ☍, or ☌, and there be reception between them, or collection or translation, and that planet be in the 10th, or lord thereof, the embassy is on some high and important matter of a political nature. If the planet who is received, or translates, or collects, be lord of the 11th, he comes to renew leagues of friendship. If the lord of the 5th be afflicted or weak in the 7th, and the lord of the ascendant and he be in evil aspect, and ♂ aspect either of them evilly, there is no sign of any peace or permanent benefit arising from this embassy or message. According as the lord of the 5th and ☽ be well affected to the ascendant, its lord, and planets therein, you may predict advantage to the querent or his nation, according as it be respecting a public or private matter.

Of a Message sent for Money.

The message is shewn by the ☽, the messenger by the lord of the 5th: the other significators as usual.

If the lord of the 5th separate from the lord of the 7th, and apply to the lord of the ascendant, you may judge the messenger has effected the thing he went for, and is returning home. If the lord of the 5th separate from the lord of the 2d, he brings money. The answer the messenger brings is of the nature of that house from whose lord the lord of the 5th separates, and also of the nature of the planet himself. Therefore, if he separate from a good planet, it gives hopes of a good answer; the contrary, when he separates from evil planets. If the lord of the 5th apply by □, or ☍, to an infortune, before he is separated from the lord of the 7th, the messenger has had some impediment in effecting his business by the party to whom he was sent, and has also sustained some hinderance on his journey before he arrived at the place. But if this application to an infortune happen *after* the lord of the 5th was separated from the lord of the 7th, the messenger will have delays and misfortunes on his return. If you find an infortune (especially ♂) in the 9th, he will hardly travel safe for thieves; but if a fortune be there, his going and returning will be safe.

If there be reception, (though they apply by □ or ☍) between the lords of the 5th and 7th, the messenger will be well received; but the evil aspect shews some delay or excuse framed by the party to whom the messenger is sent.

As to the messenger's return; when the lord of the 5th comes to a ✶ or △ of the lord of the ascendant, that day, or near it, the messenger is heard of; or when ☽ separates from the lord of the 5th, and applies to the lord of the ascendant, the querent shall have intelligence of his messenger. The application of the *significator* to a ponderous planet shews more certainly the day. Use discretion in judging the nature of the journey, its length, &c. And, according to the nature of the signs and houses in which the applying planet may be found, expect the return to be in days, weeks, months, &c.

INTRODUCTION TO ASTROLOGY.

Fig. 10.

QUERY.—*If the Person asking the Question should ever have Children?*

Judgment upon the preceding Figure.

The ascendant is here ♍, a barren sign; the sign of the 5th is ♑, an indifferent sign in this question, but rather barren, as being the house of ♄. The lord of the 5th, ♄, is retrograde in ♐; and the lord of the ascendant, ☿, is in ♊, both signs more barren than fruitful. The ☽ is in the terms of ♂, and in □ to ♄, lord of the 5th. ☿, lord of the ascendant, is in the terms of ♄, and afflicted by ♂, and going to ☌ of ♄, who is lord of the 6th as well as 5th; ☋ also in the ascendant. All these are strong arguments of barrenness; and I therefore delivered the following judgment, viz., that the querent neither had been, nor ever would be, pregnant, being naturally barren; for finding the chief angles afflicted by malefics, it was certain that the evil which prevented her from conceiving had been long upon her, and would continue. I found no one promising testimony; so I declared, positively, that she never would have any children, according to the rules of the science.

The ☽ being in □ to ♄, and ☿, lord of the 1st, applying to his ☌, the querent was very sickly, afflicted with wind and cholic; ☋ in the ascendant, shewed great pain in the head; and ☿ in ♊, shewed the same.*

The querent's moles, &c. agreed exactly with the figure, viz. one mole close by the navel: one upon the right ancle; one towards the right knee, on the inner side of the thigh; one near the member shewn by the ☽ in ♍; and one on the outside of the right arm.

* See the Table of the Parts in Man's Body the planets rule in each sign.

Fig. 11.

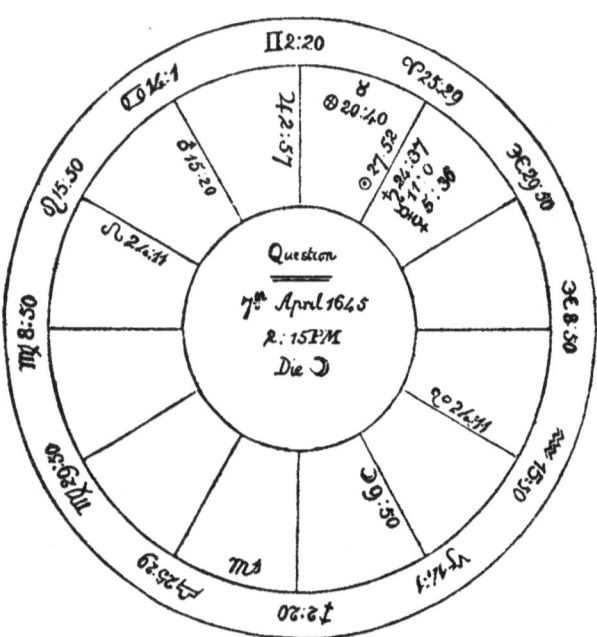

QUESTION.—*A Female being with Child, whether it were a Male or Female; and about what Time she should be delivered?*

1st QUERY.—*Is the Child a Male or Female?*

In this case I followed the method of taking only the plurality of testimonies of the proper *significators*, whether masculine or feminine, and so gave judgment.

Arguments of a Girl.

♍ the sign ascending .... *feminine.*
♑ the sign on the 5th house .... do.
☽ in a sign .... do.
☿ lord of the ascendant, with ♀ a planet .. do.

Arguments of a Boy.

☿ lord of the ascendant in a sign...... *masculine.*
♄ lord of the 5th, a planet .... do.
♄ lord of the 5th, in a sign .... do.
☽ in a house .... do.
♄ in a house .... do.
♃ a benefic in an angle, in a sign...... do.
☿ applying to aspect of ♂, a planet .. do.

Here are seven testimonies of a boy, and only four of a girl; I therefore affirmed that the lady carried a son; (*and so it proved*).

2d QUERY.—*How long ere she should be delivered?*

The sign of the 5th is moveable; so is ♈, wherein both the lords of the 1st and 5th are situated. These argued but a short time; but as ♄, lord of the 5th, is a ponderous planet, and was slow in motion, I considered him much in this query; and also ☽, because she was situated in the 5th. I took the distance between

$$\begin{array}{rr} ♄ \text{ in } ♈ \ldots\ldots\ldots\ldots & 24° \ 37' \\ ☽ \text{ in } ♑ \ldots\ldots\ldots\ldots & 9 \ \ 50 \\ \hline \text{Difference} & 14 \ \ 47 \end{array}$$

Also between ♄ and ☿:

$$\begin{array}{rr} ♄ \text{ in } ♈ \ldots\ldots\ldots\ldots & 24° \ 37' \\ ☿ \text{ in } ♈ \ldots\ldots\ldots\ldots & 11 \ \ 0 \\ \hline \text{Difference} & 13 \ \ 37 \end{array}$$

158   INTRODUCTION TO ASTROLOGY.

Finding only one degree and ten minutes between the aspect of the ☽ and ♄, and that of ☿ and ♄, I gave for every degree one week, and so judged that, about *fourteen weeks* from the time of the question, she should be delivered.

The birth took place on the 11th July following, when ♂ transited the degree ascending, and ☿ the ☍ of ☽, viz. ♋ 9°. The ☉ also was that day in ♋ 27° 48′, the perfect ☐ to his own place in the figure, and ☽ in ☌ with ☿ in ♋. The time was thirteen weeks and four days after the question.

CHAPTER XXIX.

OF THE SIXTH HOUSE.

Viz. Sickness, Servants, Small Cattle, &c.

In the first place, we ought to take the figure for the exact moment of the person falling sick, or rather of being obliged to take to his bed.*

Secondly, if that cannot be had, accept of that time when first any person spoke to a physician, &c. regarding the patient. And if it was with his consent, the ascendant will signify him; but if unknown to him, the ascendant will denote the querent; and the house describing his relation to the person speaking of the sickness will describe the patient. (This is, supposing the physician to be an astrologer, which they formerly were; but if the patient's friend speak to an astrologer, the same rule holds.)

Thirdly, or let the physician note the time of his own first

* If the illness be produced by an accident, then take the time at which it occurred.

speaking with the patient,* and let a figure be erected for that moment.

Then consider carefully, first, the ascendant and planets therein; secondly, the 6th house, and planets therein; thirdly, the sign and house wherein the Moon is; fourthly, how she is affected or afflicted, by what planet, in what house that planet is, and of what house he is lord.

What Part of the Body is afflicted?

If the ascendant be afflicted by an evil planet, and he retrograde, combust, peregrine, slow in motion, or in □ or ☍ to the lord of the 4th, 6th, 8th, or 12th, the disease is then *in the head*, or in that part or parts of the body which the planet or planets signify in the sign then ascending.

For example; if ♋ ascend, and ♄ therein, the sick party is afflicted in the head, because the ascendant signifies the head; and also has some disorder in the bowels, reins, or secrets, because ♄ in ♋ signifies those parts; or else with some rotten cough, as ♄ denotes coughs, and ♋ rules the breast. If the lord of the ascendant, ☾, or lord of the 6th, be in a sign signifying the same member or parts as ♄, or if the sign on the 6th represent the same, your judgment will be more certain; I may say, infallible.†

I also would observe, in like manner, the 6th house, its

* Our author adds, "or when first the *urine* was brought to him." This makes it evident that the water doctors, as they were termed, even until a very recent period, had recourse to astrology to ascertain the nature and result of their patients' diseases. We are quite sure, from long experience, that these may be accurately learned by the science; and we believe that many medical men call it to their aid even now. The day is coming when this will be generally the case.

† In all cases where the ☾ is afflicted by either ♄ or ♂, we should regard the rules for that situation as of the chief importance; we have never known them fail.

sign, lord, and planet in it. Also observe carefully the sign and house where ☽ is, her separation and application. And you may then venture safely to give judgment as to what part of the body of the sick person is grieved, and of the nature and quality of the sickness.

The Cause and Nature of the Sickness.

The significators in *fiery* signs, and *fiery* signs on the ascendant and 6th, shew feverish and hot complaints, hectic fevers, erysipelas, &c.

Earthy signs argue long and tedious diseases, agues, intermittent fevers, and such complaints as proceed from melancholy, consumption, &c.

Airy signs shew corrupt blood, gout, cutaneous diseases, scrofula, &c.

Watery signs shew diseases that proceed from cold and moisture, coughs and disordered stomach, &c.

Diseases signified by the Houses.

1st. All diseases in the head, eyes, face, ears, nose, mouth, foul breath, &c.
2d. The throat, scrofula, quinsey, glandular swellings in the neck, sore throat, &c.
3d. The shoulders, arms, and hands.
4th. The stomach, breast, and lungs.
5th. Back, hind parts of the shoulders, liver, heart, sides, and stomach.
6th. Lower part of the abdomen, the intestines, liver, and reins.
7th. The hams, the flank, the small intestines, bladder, matrix and members of generation.
8th. The spine, rectum, and groin.
9th. The hips and thighs.

INTRODUCTION TO ASTROLOGY. 161

10th. The knees and upper part of the leg behind the knees.

11th. The leg from the knee to the ancle, the shin-bone, shank, &c.

12th. The feet, ancles and toes, with all hurts or disease incident to them.*

Whether the Disease will be long or short.

Have regard to the time of year, and consider that diseases commencing in the winter are usually longer, and those in summer shorter.

Diseases which proceed from ♄ are more permanent, and are generally regulated much by the motion of the ☉. Those of a hot and dry nature, which are influenced by ♂ and ☉, are short, and regulated by the motion of ☽. ♄ causes long chronic complaints, falls, bruises, blows, &c.; ♃ and ☉ shorter; ♂ short, violent, and quick, such as cuts, bleedings, &c. ♀ a mean between both, and such as proceed from intemperance; ☿ various and changeable, such as fits, &c.; ☽ such as return at periods, as the falling sickness or epilepsy, giddiness, swimming in the head, gout, periodical illness in females, &c.†

Signs of a short Disease.

When the cusp of the 6th, the ☽, and the lords of the 1st and 6th, be in *moveable* signs, or the lord of the ascendant swift in motion, or going out of his own house into another, so that it be not the sign of the 6th or 12th, or if a fortune be in the 6th, you may judge that the disease will soon terminate.

---

* For the diseases signified by the *signs*, see CHAPTER XV; and for those of the *planets*, see the nature, &c. of each, at page 35.

† ♅ causes all uncommon and extraordinary complaints; or gives remarkable features to the sickness.

M

Signs of a long Disease.

The lord of the 6th evil or afflicted, and placed in the 6th, fixed signs on its cusp, or the significators, especially the ☽, in fixed signs, are testimonies of a long and durable disease: and if ♄ be lord of the 6th and in a fixed sign, or retrograde and slow in motion, he extremely prolongs the disease; but if he be in a moveable sign, or in any of his own terms, or be swift in motion, he is not then so unfortunate.

General Signs.

The disease continues but a short time if ♓ be on the cusp of the 6th. If the ☽ apply by ill aspect to the lord of the ascendant, the disease will increase. If ☽ be in the 6th in ill aspect to ♀, the disease is brought on by intemperance, either evil diet or surfeit; and if ♀ be in ♏, there is evidence of a scandalous disease. But if the patient be a female, it may be the whites or other diseases of the matrix.

The last degrees of any sign being on the cusp of the 6th, denotes that the disease is almost at an end. If the lord of the 6th apply by ill aspect to the lord of the ascendant, it is a token of the disease increasing; the same, if the lord of the 6th be in the 8th or 12th house. If the lord of the ascendant be in the 6th, and the lord of the 6th in the ascendant, the disease has been of long continuance, and will continue until one of the significators leaves the sign where he is. And if, at the time of transiting out of the sign, he meet the evil aspects of the infortunes or lords of the 4th or 8th, and they slow in motion, and it be from signs evilly aspecting one another, it is a strong sign that the sick person will then depart this life. The lord of the 6th afflicted by the □ or ☍ of the lord of the ascendant, the disease is grievous and hard to cure. If the lord of the 6th be in the ascendant, the disease will continue, but the pain at times is small. If he be in a cadent house, the disease is not important, nor will it endure. Good planets in the 6th promise a good end to the disease; evil, the contrary. The lord of the 6th, afflicted in the 6th, 8th, or 12th, or an infortune in the 6th, denotes a disease not easily curable. The lord of the ascendant and ☽ free from ill aspects, both being unafflicted and strong, and not in the 6th, 8th, or 12th, is a fair testimony of recovery and health. The lord of the 1st in the 4th or 8th, if not afflicted, denotes not death; but if unfortunate, it shews great difficulty ere the party be cured. If, however, he be unfortunate by retrogradation, being combust, &c., he may possibly be cured, but will afterwards relapse. If he be in evil aspect with ☽, there is danger; but, above all, if ♄ be lord of the ascendant, and be slow or retrograde, there is reason to fear a long and tedious sickness. If ♄ be strong and well qualified, the reverse.

When the lord of the ascendant is angular, strong, and unafflicted, the querent is in no danger. The ☽ slow in motion and in any aspect with him, it prolongs the infirmity, though there be at present hopes of a cure. If she be swift in motion when aspecting the lord of the ascendant, the cure will be effected in a little time. The ☽ decreasing in light, and coming to ☌, □, or ☍ of ♄, unless the disease be already leaving the patient, is very dangerous. The ☽ in ☌ with an oriental planet, who is swift in motion and direct, denotes a brief sickness; if joined to a retrograde and occidental planet, the contrary.

If ♏ ascend, the patient has been the cause of his own sickness by folly, anger, peevishness, or the like; especially if ♂ be therein. Both lights cadent and their dispositors unfortunate, the sickness will be severe; but if the fortunes assist, though the disease will be of long continuance, the party will recover beyond all expectation: the stronger the fortunes are, the more confident you may be in your judgment. If ♂ be lord of the ascendant and in the 6th, but in good aspect to ♀, there is no danger; if even in □ or ☍, not much.

The lord of the 6th combust, retrograde, in his fall or detriment, and in the 8th, in ☌, □, or ☍ of ♄ or ♂, you may fear that the disease will never leave the patient till death. If the ☽ also be applying to the same aspects of the lord of the 8th, your judgment will be certain. The ☽ or lord of the 1st, in ☌, □, or ☍ to a benevolent planet, but he retrograde, the patient will recover, but not speedily, for it denotes relapsing out of one disease into another. When ☽ leaves ☍ of ☉, and is swiftly applying to the □ or ☍ of ♂, it threatens a fatal end to the disease; but if she receive a ✶ or △ of ♃ or ♀, the sick shall recover. If the ☽ be in the ascendant, and in ☌, □, or ☍ to ♄ or ♂, or any other evil planet, it is a token of severe illness and danger, unless she be in mutual reception with the planet afflicting.

Testimonies of Recovery.

The ☽ applying to a fortune, powerful, denotes that the party will be restored to his former health. If reception be between the lords of the ascendant and 8th by house or triplicity, the fortunes assisting the degree ascending, or that on the 6th, or the ☽ by ☌, ✶, or △, the sick will perfectly recover. The lord of the ascendant, being a benefic planet, or any fortune in an angle and no ill aspects cast thereto, signifies health. A certain sign of recovery is, when ☉, ♃, ♀, or ☽ be in the ascendant, and no ways afflicted by the lord of the 6th or 8th house; the more so if in the houses of the lights or benefics. The ☽ in her own house, or the houses of ♃ or ♀, and in any aspect to those benefics, and no way afflicted by ♅, ♄, or ♂, denotes health and life. Whenever ☽ ☌ ♃ occurs, it denotes recovery, but if in ♑, less than in any other sign. If ☽ apply to the lord of the ascendant by good aspect, and be unafflicted (by the lord of the 8th or 6th especially), recovery is promised.

When, at the first falling sick of the party, ☽ is void of course, and at her next crisis meets a ⚹ or △ of ♃ or ♀ in the exact degree which forms the perfect critical aspect, the patient will undoubtedly recover, be he never so ill at time of asking the question. If at the commencement of a disease, ☉, ☽, and the lord of the ascendant, are free from ill aspects of the infortunes or lord of the 8th, there are assured hopes of life.

Arguments of Death.

The lord of the ascendant and ☽ in ☌ with the lord of the 8th, without interposing aspects of fortunes.

The lord of the ascendant cadent, and the lord of the 8th in an angle, especially if the latter be an infortune. The ☽ applying to a planet in the 8th, and afflicted; and the lord of the ascendant applying to the lord of the 8th or to evil planets therein, are very dangerous. The ☽ transferring the light of the lord of the 8th to the lord of the ascendant, usually denotes death. So when the lord of the 8th is in the ascendant, the lord of the ascendant and ☽ both being afflicted; or the lord of the ascendant being in the 8th and afflicted, and ☽ also weak and in no dignity. The lord of the ascendant under the Earth, and in ill aspect to the lord of the 8th in the 8th, or if the two lords be in ☌ in the 4th house. It is a very ill sign when the lord of the ascendant is in ☌ with the lords of the 4th, 6th, 8th, or 12th.

The lord of the ascendant combust in the ascendant, or the lord of the 8th in the 10th, and the lord of the ascendant in the 4th, 6th, or 12th, and afflicted by malefics, are very evil.

The lord of the 8th retrograde and conjoined with the ☽, or in ☐ or ☍ to her, shews death. The lord of the ascendant in ♌ or ♒, and evilly affected by the lords of the 6th or 12th, shews little hopes of recovery; and his being conjoined with *Aldebaran, Antares, Caput, Algol,* or other violent fixed stars, is also evil. And if both lights be afflicted by ♄ in an angle, it is testimony of a tedious, long illness.

The ☽ in the 4th with ♂, or the ☉ with ♄, are testimonies of death; also the ☽ near the cusp of the ascendant in ☐ of ♂ from the 4th. The ☽ combust in the 8th, or if lady of the 6th and combust in the ascendant or 4th, the same; and especially if the lord of the 8th be afflicted.

The ☌ of ☽ with ☉ is a very ill sign, especially when she has not yet passed ☉; however, when the ☌ is in ♈ or ♌, it is not quite so evil.*

In all cases the multiplicity of testimonies must be observed, the strength of the afflicting planets, and the absence of assistance to neutralize the evil influence, before you predict death.

To know whether the Querent be really ill or not.

If the ascendant be not afflicted, nor its lord out of all his essential dignities, nor afflicted by ♄, ♂, or the lord of the 6th, he is not. Or if no planet afflict the 6th house by its presence, or the ☽ be not afflicted in the 8th or 12th, or if you find ♃, or ♀, or ☊ in the ascendant, or ☉ in the 6th, or the ☽ and lord of the ascendant in good aspect, or ♃ or ♀ casting a ✶ or △ to the cusp of the ascendant or 6th, the party is not really sick, but at the utmost some slight indisposition has occurred, which will shortly be rectified.

Whether the Disease be in the Body or Mind, or both.

If the ascendant, ☉, and ☽ be all afflicted, the disease is

* We should say, if it be in ♋, where ☽ disposes of ☉, it is not so evil.

then through the whole body; but if the planets which dispose of ☉ and ☽, or if the lord of the ascendant, or two of them, be afflicted, the disease is more in the mind. If the ascendant, the ☽, and lord of the ☉ are all, or two of them, afflicted, and the lord of the ascendant and the dispositor of the ☽ free, the affection is in the mind and not in the body.

If ♄ afflict the ☽, he shews trouble in the mind, vexation and care; but if ♃ be in the planet afflicting the ☽, the contrary; for he never oppresses the mind, but always the body.

If the lord of the house in which ☽ is, and the lord of the ascendant are afflicted by ☉, or combust, or under the beams of ☉, the distemper is bodily. But if the ruler of ☽ and the ruler of the lord of the ascendant be *much* afflicted, the grief is more mental than bodily. Also if the degree ascending and that degree where ☽ is be more afflicted than the lords of those signs, the disease is more in the mind; but if the lords be more afflicted, the reverse.

When the dispositors of the lights are very much afflicted and very weak, and the degree ascending have a □ of ☽ but no ill aspect of ♄ or ♂, the person is much tormented in mind. In these cases ☉ causes the mind to be troubled by pride, self-conceit, haughtiness, &c. ♀ argues luxury, or a lasciviousness which disturbs both body and mind. ☿ shews foolish fancies and fearful imaginations.

Of the Crises, or of Critical Days.

If the disease be not chronic, you will find great alteration in the patient near those times when ☽ arrives at a distance from her first place, when the patient was taken ill, of 45, 90, or 135 degrees. To learn whether these *crises* will be good or evil, see how she is aspected at those times. If she be in good aspect with a benevolent planet, it promises ease and an improved condition; but if she there meet with evil aspects of malevolent planets or the lords of the 6th or 8th, he will be worse, and the medicines do little good. I have always observed that, when the ☽ came at the *crises* to ☌, □, or ☍ of that planet which did afflict the ascendant, ☽, or lord of the ascendant, or when she came to such aspect of the lord of the 6th or planets placed in the 6th, the patient suffered much, the disease ran high, and medicines given about that time worked little or no good. When she came, however, to ✶ or △ of the lords of the ascendant, 9th, 10th, or 11th houses, I observed some interval of ease or amendment. So when the lord of the ascendant came to any good aspect of the ☉ (if he had not power or dominion in the disease), I found the patient's *mind* much relieved.

How long it may be before Recovery.

When there is reason to believe that, by God's blessing, the sick person shall recover, and it be desired to know when, observe which planet is lord of the ascendant, and what benevolent planet he is in aspect with; then see what house they are in, (that is the one which *applies* to the other's aspect), whether angles, &c., and what signs they possess, whether moveable, &c. Then according to discretion and quality of the disease, so frame the measure of time. In general, I judge in so many days as the aspect wants degrees of being perfect, if the sign be moveable and the planet angular; but if swift in motion, I am the more certain that the patient will begin to amend in so many days. If the sign be common, in which the application is, I neither judge days, weeks, nor months, but use discretion, having first observed the nature of the disease.

The ancient rule was as follows:—

    Moveable signs shew .... *days.*
    Common ditto .... *weeks.*
    Fixed ditto................. *months.*
    Angles are equivalent to ...... *moveable signs.*
    Succeedent houses to.......... *common signs.*
    Cadent houses to .... *fixed signs.*

It is well to observe, also, the quick or slow motion of the ☽, the sign she is in, and her situation as to angles, &c. I often find that when the lord of the ascendant quits the sign he is in, and enters a sign in which he has dignities, the patient recovers at that time, or feels an alteration for the better. If a common sign be on the 6th, 28° or more, I say, that the disease will *vary* in two weeks.

JUDGMENT OF THE DISEASE FROM THE AFFLICTION OF THE MOON AT THE FIRST ILLNESS OF THE PATIENT, OR THE TIME OF ASKING THE QUESTION.*

Whoever shall be first taken ill, or compelled to take to his bed when the ☽ is afflicted by ♄, or by ☿, if he have the nature of ♄, will, in a great measure, suffer as here described.

The ☽ in ♈, in ☌, □, or ☍ of ♄.—Headache or heaviness in the head, much discharge at the nostrils, dulness, or weariness of the eyes, humours falling into the throat; weak pulse, and a heavy drowsiness of mind; loathing at the stomach, violent unseasonable perspiration, internal heats, and externally cold. The patient more afflicted at night than by day.

The ☽ in ♉, in ☌, &c. of ♄.—Fevers proceeding from obstructions near the heart, liver, and lungs, occasioned by sur-

---

* The student may rely that he will find these rules, when they apply, to be infallible.—ZADKIEL.

feits, high living, &c. The pulse high and immoderate, the body inflated, lungs oppressed, ulcerated, &c. If the ☽ be not supported by benefics, there is danger of death within 14 days.

The ☽ in ♊ in ☌ ♄ . &c.—The disease has its origin in the mind by too much care, or a multiplicity of business, or otherwise by fatigue in travelling or over-exercise. There is danger of a small fever; the pain is dispersed over all the body, but chiefly in the joints. The vitals are afflicted, the pulse rare, and weak; there are frequent perspirations, symptoms of spleen and consumption. If ♂ also afflict, without assistance, the patient will hardly live 10 days; but if ♃ or ♀ assist, the sick person may recover after a long period.

The ☽ in ♋ in ☌ of ♄, &c.—The breast is much afflicted with tough phlegm, or slimy matter; there is cough, and much salivary discharge. Hoarseness, catarrhs, &c., with humours falling into the breast; the windpipe obstructed; slight fevers, agues, &c. holding a long time; also pains in the bowels, infirmity in the reins or secrets. If ☽ be decreasing, and near the body of ♄, the disease will continue a long time.

The ☽ in ♌ in ☌, &c. of ♄ .—The sickness arises from bad blood, the patient suffers with heat in the breast, heartburn, violent fevers, troubled pulse, much external and internal heat, faintness at the heart, swoonings, the stone; and sometimes the black jaundice. If there be no good aspects to prevent it, they frequently die when ☽ comes to ☍ of ♄ .

The ☽ in ♍ in ☌, &c. ♄ .—The illness arises from indigestion, obstructions in the bowels, &c.; shooting pains are felt under the ribs, &c.; flatulency, gout, or aches in the thighs or feet, &c. The patient generally is sick a long time.

The ☽ in ♎ in ☌, &c. of ♄ .—The disease has its origin in some surfeit of wine or rich food, meat ill digested, &c., or from excess of venery; the breast is affected, also the head; there is no appetite, a loathing in the stomach, cough, hoarseness, &c., and often great pain in the joints, knees, and thighs, with an itching in those parts, and fear of sciatica.

The ☽ in ♏ in ☌, &c. of ♄.—Denotes a disease in the *rectum* or *sphincter muscle*, piles, hemorrhoids, or fistula. There is very likely a retention of urine, or the reverse; stone in the bladder, dropsical humour, &c. It may be that it is gonorrhea, &c., or the diseases of the matrix.*

The ☽ in ♐ in ☌, &c. of ♄.—The patient suffers by pains in the joints, &c., or fever, extremes of heat and cold. Illness often happens by too great exertion of body or mind, and cold taken afterwards; there is much melancholy also. And if it be an ☍ of ♄, there is generally a spice of gout, tumours or swellings in the hands, thighs, or feet, &c. If ♂ have any ill aspect to ☽, it proves a violent burning fever.

The ☽ in ♑ in ☌, &c. ♄.—The disease proceeds from cold or melancholy. It brings heaviness of the breast and stomach, difficulty of breathing, dry coughs, the lungs oppressed, and a fever is approaching. The pain is greater at night than in the day. The patient continually complains of headache, or pain in the left ear, or of a rumbling noise in his head.†

---

* These latter especially, if ♀ throw an ill aspect, or the lord of the 5th house.

† We can speak personally as to this effect. We were taken ill in the evening of the 1st March, 1829, when ☽ was in ♑, 19°, and ♄ in ♋ 28°, and we suffered extremely during the night, and had violent pains in the left side of the head, and sensations of noises, as of the working of the piston of a steam-engine. A fever ensued, which confined us to bed for three weeks, having caught cold after taking mercury. The direction in our nativity was M.C. ☌ ☉, who, being in ☌ with ♂ at birth, partook of his ill qualities, and afflicted the ascendant by his mundane square.

The ☽ in ♒ in ☌, &c. ♄.—The illness is occasioned by too much toil of mind or body, want of sleep, or due refreshment. The malady comes on unequally with remission or intension.* The patient suffers by noise in the head, by wind, or faintness at the heart, or a rising and danger of suffocation by hysterical fits, &c.; and by sore throat.

The ☽ in ♓ in ☌, &c. ♄.—The complaint arises from cold,† and the patient is afflicted with continual fever, frequently sighs, suffers pains under the nipples of the breast, and about the heart; the throat suffers from much phlegm, or there is water in the chest, rotten cough, &c.

Whoever is taken ill when ☽ is afflicted by ♂ or the ☉, suffers in the following manner:—

The ☽ in ♈ in ☌, &c. of ♂.—The disease is from some distemper of the membranes, &c. of the brain. There is continual fever and restlessness, extreme thirst, foul tongue, or inflammation of the liver, heat and pain in the breast, high pulse, and often delirium. The patient is generally almost mad with pain, either cholic or cholera pains, &c. in the bowels. If after the ☽ leave ♂ she go to ☌ or ☍ of ♄, there is small hope of life; and if she decrease in light, and be slow in motion, there is scarce any.

The ☽ in ♉ in ☌, &c. of ♂.—There is an abundance of blood, continual fever, the whole frame disordered; sore throat, with inflammation in the neck, or hind part thereof; pain in the bones, broken sleep, and a foolish longing after wine and cold water. There is often putrid sore throat and also hoarseness, and strangury, stone, or gravel, with pain in the reins or kidneys, or disease therein.

* This till ☽ is past ☍ of her own place, when, if there be good aspects, the sick is recoverable.
† Especially wet feet, damp linen, &c.

The ☽ *in* ♊ *in* ☌, &c. ♂.—A violent fever, high and inordinate pulse; there are obstructions and corrupt blood, pains all over the body, heat in the reins, and sometimes spitting of blood; also lameness or fractures in the arms, pains in the joints, &c.

The ☽ *in* ♋ *in* ☌, &c. ♂. This shews a disordered stomach by having taken too much to drink, &c., riot, and excess. It often turns to dysentery, cough, and spitting of blood.

The ☽ *in* ♌ *in* ☌, &c. ♂.—Too much blood abounds, weak pulse, a disturbed brain, raving, and strong fits; loss of or depraved appetite; distempers of the heart, heaviness all over the body, and drowsiness. There is danger of consumption. The blood is over-heated, the body dry and parched; there is probability of pleurisy, fainting, and swooning. I ever fear this ☌ or ☍ more than in any other sign.

The ☽ *in* ♍ *in* ☌, &c. ♂. Flux in the bowels, small fevers, a failing pulse, cholic, flatulence, weakness in the legs, or near the ancles. If ☽ be afflicted by ♂ in ♍, diseases are not easily removed.

The ☽ *in* ♎ *in* ☌, &c. ♂.—The patient is grieved with plentitude of blood, and, from that cause, has high pulse, no rest, is feverish, and an inflammation all over the body. The patient has taken some surfeit by excess or disorder in his diet, or the blood is over-heated; or there is stone or gravel in the kidneys. Violent burning fevers often follow.

The ☽ *in* ♏ *in* ☌, &c. ♂.—There is generally some ulcer, lues, gonorrhea, &c., or, if a child, measles; it may be piles, or hemorrhoids. There is frequently some stoppage in the head by grievous colds; and as the blood is corrupt, so we find blotches, breakings out, &c. If there be reason to believe it, some scandalous disease may be judged, especially if ♀ afflict ☽.

The ☽ *in* ♐ *in* ☌, &c. ♂.—The disease is in general violent, and caused by gluttony or repletion. There is fever frequently very high, or choleric passion; but the pulse is often faint, and beats slow and feeble. Inordinate exercise has frequently been the cause of the disease; and he suffers pestilent fever, &c. It shews hand and foot gout, breakings out, sore throat, &c., and, at times, sore and inflamed eyes. Also, hurts by horses.

The ☽ in ♑ in ♂, &c. ♂.—Nausea abounds, vomiting and flux. A puffing up of the sinews, (such as cholera cramps), inflammation of the breast, and humours in the hands or fingers. The face is yellow and sunken, the body extremely wasted, and the blood corrupt. The pulse remits, and is slow. The yellow jaundice happens under these aspects.

The ☽ in ♒ in ♂ &c. ♂.—If ☽ be slow in motion, and decreasing in light, the disease proceeds from sharp and violent affections, or vehement passions. There is pain at the heart, swooning fits, high pulse, great pain in the chest, and much difficulty in breathing.

The ☽ in ♓ in ♂, &c. ♂. The body is full of gross humours, the disease is from too much drinking and excess, and is most prevalent in the night time. The party is troubled with a kind of delirium, (frequently it shews that they are yet drunk), they have vehement thirst, sharp burning fevers, and are desirous of wine. They have generally a looseness and much pain in the bowels, or a violent cough and great expectoration, and are almost suffocated with phlegm; the body is swollen, and there is danger of dropsy.*

---

* Where various diseases are named, the student must look to other testimonies to ascertain the exact complaint.

Fig 12.

QUESTION.—*A sick Doctor; what is his Disease? Is it curable?*

To learn what part of the body is affected, observe that, as the ascendant is not afflicted, you must look to the 6th house, and see if it be so. Therein we find ♄ in his fall; and as he naturally signifies diseases by his presence, I concluded that, from thence and that house I must require the part aggrieved.

♈ represents the head.

♄ in ♈ shews the breast.*

♂, lord of the ascendant, in ♌, signifies the heart.* The lord of the ascendant has just separated from a □ of ♄, being at that time in ♋, which signifies and rules over the breast and stomach. From all these testimonies I concluded that the parts of the body grieved were the head, breast, heart, and stomach; and that there was lodged in the breast or stomach some obstruction, which caused all his disease and suffering.

From what Cause the Sickness was.

The principal significator being ♄, and he in his own terms, and ☽ disposed of by him and applying to him, shewed such diseases as he causes, and which might exist in the head and breast. ♂, lord of the ascendant, was also in the terms of ♄, and applied to □ of ☉, who was in the terms of ♂. So that dry, melancholy diseases were shewn by ♄, and heat or fever by ♂. And, indeed, when I came to speak to him, he was suffering great pain and rumbling in his head, was very silent, dull, and melancholy; he slept very little, had a very dry cough, and complained of great weakness and pain in his breast and at his heart. His complexion was between black and yellow, as if inclined to jaundice; and he had also a lingering consumption and great weariness all over him, with pains in his joints, shewn by ☽ in an airy sign. The ascendant is ♏, which signifies the secrets, stone in the bladder, &c.; so the ☽ in ♒ shews the secrets and diseases therein, &c. Hence he had great difficulty in making water, voided red gravel, and suffered great pain in those parts.

Whether the Disease would be curable or not?

The author of the disease being ♄, shewed it would be of

* This will be seen by the Table at the end of this chapter.

INTRODUCTION TO ASTROLOGY. 177

some continuance, for he is a slow ponderous planet; besides, the angles of the figure are all fixed, and the lord of the ascendant, ☉, and ☽, are all in fixed signs. The lights are in ☐ aspect to each other from angles, and both in the terms of an evil planet; and the lord of the 6th in a fixed sign: all these shewed a long disease. The ☽ being in the 4th in aspect to ♄ in the 6th, and applying to ☐ of ☉, who has dignities in the 6th, and the lord of the 4th in the 6th, and lord of the 8th in the 8th, the testimonies were strong for his death: *he died the 14th August following*.

Fig 13.

QUESTION.—*What is the Disease? and will the Patient live or die?*

The ascendant is ♍, and it is afflicted by the presence of ♂, who is partly lord of the 8th house, as great part of ♈ is already therein. Hence from the ascendant chiefly we must learn the cause and nature of the disease, and part afflicted. A fixed sign ♒ is on the 6th, afflicted by ♅, and ♄, lord of the 6th, is in ♉, an earthy sign, of the same nature as ♍, the ascendant. The ☽, a general significator in all diseases, is also in ♍ in ☌ with ♂. All these shewed the patient to be greatly afflicted with the spleen, cholic, and obstructions in his bowels, small fever, flatulence, and a failing weak pulse. And as the ☽ and ♂ are in the *ascendant*, the patient was perplexed with distempers in the head, slept unquietly, &c. (*All which was true.*)

Will the Patient live or die?

All the significators promised death.

1st. ☉, light of time, was in close □ to ♄, lord of the 6th in fixed signs.
2d. The ascendant was extremely afflicted by presence of ♂, he being lord of nearly all the 8th house.
3d. The ☽ was afflicted by ♂ in the house of life.
4th. The ☽ separated from the ✶ of ☿, lord of the ascendant, in signs of long ascension, and did transfer his light to ♃, lord of the 4th and 8th houses, denoting death and the grave.

N.B.—The patient died the 28th of the month, when ☿ came to the □ of ♄ and ☌ of ☉ in the figure. The ☽ came then to ☍ ☉, and had transited the cusp of the 6th house the day preceding, viz. ♒ 14°.

INTRODUCTION TO ASTROLOGY.

A TABLE

SHEWING WHAT PARTS OF MAN'S BODY EVERY PLANET SIGNIFIES IN THE TWELVE SIGNS.

SIGNS	♄	♃	♂	☉	♀	☿	☽
♈	Breast Arms	Neck Throat Heart Bowels	Head Bowels Eyes	Thighs	Reins Feet	Secrets Legs	Head Knees
♉	Heart Breast Bowels	Neck Shoulders Arms Bowels	Throat Reins	Knees	Secret-Members Head	Thighs Feet	Throat Legs
♊	Heart Bowels	Breast Reins Secrets	Breast Arms Secrets	Legs Ancles	Throat Thighs	Head Knees	Shoulders Arms Thighs Feet
♋	Bowels Reins Secrets	Heart Secrets Thighs	Breast Feet	Feet	Arms Shoulders Knees	Eyes Throat Legs Knees	Head Breast Stomach
♌	Reins Secrets	Bowels Thighs Knees	Heart Bowels Knees	Head	Heart Breast Legs	Throat Arms Shoulders Feet	Arms Shoulders Bowels
♍	Thighs Secrets Feet	Reins Knees	Bowels Legs	Throat Neck	Stomach Heart Bowels Feet	Head Breast Heart	Arms Shoulders Bowels
♎	Knees Thighs	Head Eyes Secrets Legs	Reins Secrets Feet	Arms Shoulders	Head Intestines	Throat Heart Stomach Bowels	Breast Heart Reins Bowels
♏	Knees Legs	Thighs Feet	Head Arms Secrets Thighs	Breast Heart	Throat Reins Secrets	Arms Shoulders Back Bowels	Stomach Heart Bowels Secrets
♐	Legs Feet	Head Thighs Knees	Throat Hands Thighs Feet	Heart Bowels	Arms Shoulders Secrets Thighs	Breast Heart Reins Secrets	Back Bowels Thighs
♑	Head Feet	Eyes Neck Knees Legs	Arms Shoulders Knees Legs	Back Bowels	Breast Heart Thighs	Stomach Heart Secrets	Reins Thighs Knees
♒	Neck Head	Arms Shoulders Breast Feet	Breast Heart Legs	Reins Secrets	Heart Knees	Heart Bowels Thighs	Secrets Legs Ancles
♓	Arms Shoulders Neck	Head Breast Heart	Heart Bowels Ancles Feet	Secrets Thighs	Neck Throat Bowels Legs	Reins Secrets Thighs Knees	Thighs Feet

The DISEASES *each* PLANET *naturally signifies when it becomes the afflictor, and is posited in any of the* TWELVE SIGNS.

DISEASES OF SATURN.

♄ in ♈ signifies rheum, melancholy, vapours, cold in the head, obstructions, stoppage in the stomach, pains in the teeth, deafness, &c.

♄ in ♉ signifies swelling in the neck and throat, king's evil, scurvy, hoarseness, melancholy, and chronic distempers about the neck and throat.

♄ in ♊ signifies infirmities incident to the arms and shoulders, consumption, black jaundice, and diseases proceeding from bad blood.

♄ in ♋ denotes phthisic, ulcerations in the lungs, obstructions and bruises in the breast, ague, scurvy, cancer, &c.

♄ in ♌ signifies the heart afflicted by grief or poison, consumption of the reins or inward parts, vapours, weakness, and pains in the back, &c.

♄ in ♍ shews the blood corrupted, obstructions in the bowels, costiveness, weakness in the thighs, melancholy, gripings, stone, &c.

♄ in ♎ shews the blood corrupted, back and kidneys distempered, strangury, consumptive pains in the knees and thighs, sciatica and gout.

♄ in ♏ denotes swellings or distempers of the secret parts, melancholy, piles, palsy, gout in the hands and feet.

♄ in ♐ signifies weakness in the hips and thighs, old aches and bruises in those parts, and sciatica or gout.

♄ in ♑ denotes the gout in the lower parts, pains and obstructions in the head, ague, &c.

♄ in ♒ signifies disorders in the head and teeth, defects in the ears, pains in the joints, bruises, swellings in the legs, and sometimes a sore throat.

♄ in ♓ gives defluxions of rheum, king's evil, consumption, all distempers of the feet and toes, such as the gout, and illness by colds.

DISEASES OF JUPITER.

♃ in ♈ produces distempers in the head, a quinsy or swelling in the throat, chiefly from ill blood in the veins of the head; and causes strange dreams and imaginations.

♃ in ♉ brings distempers in the throat, wind in the blood, gripings in the bowels, and goutish humours in the hands and arms.

♃ in ♊.—A pleurisy, or some disorder of the reins.

♃ in ♋ gives the dropsy, the stomach offended, bad appetite, corrupt blood, scurvy, surfeits, &c.

♃ in ♌ indicates a fever, pleurisy, the heart ill affected.

♃ in ♍ indicates a consumption, obstructions of the lungs, melancholy, cold and dry liver.

♃ in ♎ shews the patient hath too much blood, whence arise obstructions, corrupt blood, fever, piles, tumours, inflammations, &c.

♃ in ♏ signifies the strangury, piles, the blood discharged with watery humours, whence arise dropsy, &c.

♃ in ♐ denotes some choleric distemper, arising from putrefaction of the blood; a fever, pains and swellings about the knees, &c.

♃ in ♑.—The patient is afflicted with melancholy, obstructions in the throat, &c.

♃ in ♒.—The blood abounds too much, whence it is corrupted, and many diseases and flying pains afflict the body. It gives lumbago.

♃ in ♓.—The blood is too thin and waterish, which breeds dropsy.

DISEASES OF MARS.

♂ in ♈ signifies the patient is almost distracted with a violent pain in his head, rheum in the eyes, want of rest, &c.

♂ in ♉ denotes extreme pain in the throat and neck, king's evil, weakness in the loins, and the gravel or stone.

♂ in ♊ shews the blood is corrupted; itch, breakings out, surfeit, fever, pains in the arms and shoulders, disorders in the secret parts, strangury, &c.

♂ in ♋ indicates pains in the breast and stomach, a dry cough, or a tumour in the thighs: accidents to the feet.

♂ in ♌ denotes affliction at the heart, choleric humours, gravel in the kidnies, pain in the knees, &c.

♂ in ♍ signifies choleric humours, obstructions in the bowels, bloody flux, worms in children, humours in the legs.

♂ in ♎ produces diseases in the reins and kidnies, stone or gravel, urine hot, lues, &c., as may be suspected.

♂ in ♏ shews a suspicion of some venereal distemper, or ulcer in the secret parts, pains in the bladder, pains in the head, overflowing of courses, &c.

♂ in ♐ produces pain or ulcers in the hips and thighs by humours settled in those parts, and an extreme heat in the mouth and throat.

♂ in ♑ denotes lameness in the knees, hands, or arms, or a flying gout.

♂ in ♒ signifies blood over-heated, pains in the legs, surfeit, or fever.

♂ in ♓ gives lameness in the feet, by corrupt humours settled there; sometimes the heart is afflicted, &c.

DISEASES OF THE SUN.

☉ in ♈ produces sore eyes, megrims, head disturbed, fevers, &c.

☉ in ♉ denotes tumours in the knees, quinsy or sore throat, breakings out and swellings in those parts.

☉ in ♊.—Blood inflamed, pestilential fevers, breakings out in several parts of the body, scurvy, pains and weakness in the legs.

☉ in ♋ shews the measles or small pox, a disordered stomach, hoarseness, dropsy or swelling in the feet.

☉ in ♌ indicates violent pains in the head, madness, stone, pains in the back, plague, spotted fever.

☉ in ♍ produces humours in the bowels, obstructions in the stomach, bloody flux, sore throat, or swellings in the neck.

☉ in ♎.—Inflammation of the blood, pains in the arms and shoulders, stone and gravel, the venereal distemper, &c.

☉ in ♏ indicates distempers in the secret parts, sharpness of urine, obstructions in the stomach, and female courses; also *phlegmatiæ dolens*.

☉ in ♐.—The thighs are afflicted by hot humours; a fistula, fevers, swoonings, &c.

☉ in ♑ signifies lameness about the knees, bowels disordered, and a fever.

☉ in ♒.—The blood inflamed, breakings out, reins disordered, gravel, stone, strangury, &c.

☉ in ♓.—The secret parts afflicted, strangury, and violent pains in those parts.

DISEASES OF VENUS.

♀ in ♈ indicates the disease is in the head from abundance of moist humours, lethargy, reins afflicted, and head disordered by cold.

♀ in ♉ signifies pain in the head or secret parts, swellings in the neck from moist humours in the head.

♀ in ♊ denotes a corrupted blood, king's evil, dropsy, and a flux of rheum.

♀ in ♋ shews the stomach is much offended with cold, raw, undigested humours; many times with a surfeit, &c.

♀ in ♌.—Some ill affection of the heart, love passion, &c., pains in the legs, of bad consequence.

♀ in ♍ shews some distemper in the bowels, a flux, or the worms, mucus in the bowels.

♀ in ♎ denotes a gonorrhea or distemper in the reins, or surfeit by too plentiful eating or drinking, and windy disorders.

♀ in ♏ produces some venereal distemper, and pain in the private parts, &c.

♀ in ♐.—Hip gout, surfeits, cold and moist humours.

♀ in ♑ produces gout in the knees and thighs, and swellings in those parts.

♀ in ♒.—Pains and swellings in the legs or knees from a cold cause, and the heart afflicted.

♀ in ♓ indicates lameness in the feet, swellings in the legs, a flux, windy complaints, &c.

DISEASES OF MERCURY.

☿ in ♈ shews the disease lies in the head and brain, vertigo and spasms in the head, and sometimes disorders of the womb.

☿ in ♉ produces defects in the throat, swellings in the neck, hoarseness, and also pain in the feet.

☿ in ♊ signifies windiness in the blood, gouty pains in the head, arms, &c.

☿ in ♋ produces a cold stomach, gripings, windiness, distillation of rheum, lameness in the legs and *knees* from colds, &c.

☿ in ♌ indicates tremblings, melancholy, pains in the back, occasioned by colds caught in the feet.

☿ in ♍ imports much wind in the bowels, obstructions, pains in the head, short breath, and wind cholic.

☿ in ♎ shews stoppage of urine, obstructions, blood disordered; breast, lungs, and reins afflicted.

☿ in ♏ denotes distempers in the secret parts, afflictions of the bowels, running pains in the arms and shoulders.

☿ in ♐ shews distempers in the reins, weakness in the back, stoppage at the stomach, coughs, swellings in the hips and thighs.

☿ in ♑ denotes stoppage of urine, goutish humours above the knees, pains in the back, melancholy, &c.

☿ in ♒ imports wind in the blood, running pains in different parts of the body, fluxes and disorders in the bowels.

☿ in ♓ signifies pains in the head, weakness in the legs and feet, a gonorrhea, or a distemper in the reins, &c.

DISEASES OF THE MOON.

☽ in ♈ signifies convulsions, defluxions of rheum from the head, lethargy, weakness in the eyes, and pains in the knees.

☽ in ♉ produces pains in the legs and feet, swellings, stoppage in and sore throat, &c.

☽ in ♊ denotes a wandering gout in the legs, arms, hands, and feet, surfeits, and great obstructions.

☽ in ♋ shews the stomach much afflicted, a surfeit, small-pox, convulsions, falling sickness, tympany, or dropsy.

☽ in ♌.—The heart afflicted, sore throat, quinsy, king's evil, &c.

☽ in ♍ signifies great pain and disorders in the bowels, melancholy blood, obstructions, weakness in the arms and shoulders.

☽ in ♎ denotes the reins are distempered, obstructions in the stomach, weakness in the back, whites in women, surfeits, pleurisy, &c.

☽ in ♏ shews the distemper is in the secrets, small-pox, dropsy, poison, the heart afflicted, swoonings, &c.

☽ in ♐ imports lameness or weakness in the thighs, distempers in the bowels, &c.

☽ in ♑ signifies the stone, weak back, gout in the knees, whites in women, &c.

☽ in ♒ signifies hysterics, swellings, and pains in the legs and secret parts.

☽ in ♓ shews cold taken in the feet, and body disordered thereby; swellings in the legs, dropsies, and the body overcharged with moist humours.*

CHAPTER XXX.

THE SEVENTH HOUSE, AND ITS QUESTIONS.

This House signifies Marriage, Love Questions, Lawsuits and Controversies, Contracts, Wars, Duels, open Enemies, Bargains, Thefts, Fugitives, and all matters regarding Strangers.

THE questions to be judged by this house being more difficult than those of any other house, I have been more lengthy in delivering the opinions of the ancients as well as moderns thereon; and have written several aphorisms concerning its questions.

APHORISMS AND CONSIDERATIONS

FOR THE BETTER JUDGING ANY HORARY QUESTION, ESPECIALLY THOSE OF THE 7TH HOUSE.

1. See the question be radical and fit to be judged.
2. Be not confident of the judgment if either the first or

---

* This table is taken from the old Arab writers on astrology, who flourished many centuries back: they used many terms inconsistent with the modern nomenclature of diseases; but as the human frame is still the same, so are its diseases, though called by different names. Thus, *Mercury in Aquarius* is said to cause " wind in the blood," by which, we presume, was meant spasmodic action, arising from debility.

last degrees of a sign ascend. If few degrees ascend, the matter is not yet ripe for judgment: if the latter degrees, the matter of the question is elapsed, or the querent has been tampering with other artists, or despairs of success. Meddle not with it at that time.
3. If ♄, ♂, or ☊ be in the 10th house unfortunate, it will end in the discredit of the artist.
4. Judge not upon every trivial motion or light question, or when the querent has not wit to know what he would demand.
5. Observe well the strength and condition of ☽; for it is far better that the lord of the ascendant be unfortunate than the ☽.
6. The evil planets shew tardiness and difficulty in every question, unless ☽ and they receive each other in the signification.
7. The benefics, ♃ and ♀, never import evil but when ruling evil houses; and if they be significators without reception, even then they put forward the matter.
8. If ☽ be void of course, there is no great hope of the question, unless she be in ♋, ♉, ♐, or ♓.
9. Observe from what planet ☽ last separated; for it will shew what has already happened: if from a fortune, good; but from a malefic, evil; according to the nature of the house the planet rules and is in.
10. The application of ☽ shews the present condition of the matter, and what may be expected. If ☽ apply to a planet in his fall, it denotes trouble and delays.
11. If evil planets promise good, it will be imperfect or less than is expected, and come with much effort; and if they foreshew evil, it will be greater than may be feared.
12. If malefics threaten evil, observe whether ☉, ♃, or ♀

cast any good aspect to them, for then the evil will be mitigated.

3. If the fortunes promise good, but are weak, or behold not the ascendant, they perform but little without reception.

4. A planet peregrine, viz. having no essential dignities at all, is very malicious.

5. Confide not too much in a fortune, unless he be in his essential dignities.

6. In a figure where both fortunes and infortunes are equally weak and ill placed, venture not a judgment, but defer the party for another time.

7. In all questions where the significator of the thing is combust, or in ☍ to ☉, he can bring nothing to perfection.

8. If one infortune be joined to another, the good they promise will come to nothing; but the evil they threaten will be more violent.

9. The lord of the ascendant out of his dignities, cadent, &c., shews the querent out of all hopes in the business.

10. A planet under the beams of ☉, (viz. within 12 degrees), has no fortitude;* if within *sixteen minutes* of ☉, he is in cazimi or heart of ☉, and then he is very strong.

11. If the dispositor of the significator be *oriental*, and he either ♄, ♃, or ♂, the matter is sooner performed; but if ♀ or ☿, later: the reverse, if they be *occidental*.

12. If the significator of the thing desired be in a *fixed* sign, it denotes stability, and that the thing shall continue, whether it be begun or is to be begun; if he be in *common* signs, it shews the probability of the matter,

---

* We should judge that, if the planet dispose of ☉ by house, this rule does not hold. We have no faith in the doctrine of Cazimi.

but not its conclusion; and if in *moveable* signs, a sudden resolution or concluding the matter one way or other. Hence we begin the foundations of buildings when the significators are fixed; short journeys when moveable; but things wherein a mediocrity is desirable, when they are in moveable signs.

23. The ☽ or lord of the ascendant, with ☋, brings damage, according to the house they are in. The ☊ is in like manner beneficial.

24. If in any question you find ☽ afflicted, there is seldom any good comes of the matter.

25. If ☽ or lord of the ascendant be in their fall, the querent despairs of the matter, nor does he much care whether it be performed or not.

26. Consider diligently the planet afflicting the significator of the thing demanded, and what house he is lord of, and where placed; from the nature of those houses require the cause obstructing.

27. The most powerful affliction to the ☽ is when she is combust, and if she applies to ☉ it is the worst.

28. If an infortune aspect your significator, and they be both peregrine or retrograde, you may judge that the mischief threatened is almost inevitable.

29. Take especial notice whether any frustration or prohibition be before the perfect aspect of the significators; the planet which frustrates hinders the thing demanded.

30. In all questions of gain, look well to ⊕: the querent will get by persons or things connected with the house it is in; but if it be afflicted, he loses in the same way.

31. In questions of marriage, an evil planet in the 7th shews ill agreement in the married state.

32. If the lord of the 8th be unfortunate in the 8th, the querent will suffer by the death of some female; or, concerning debts due to him, by dead men.
33. In what house you find ♃ or ♀ well dignified, expect benefits by men or things signified by that house; as if in the 3d, by kindred; in the 4th, by your father or lands, &c.; in the 5th, by play, pleasure, &c.; and so of the others. And beware of slander or damage through that house where ☋ falls.

QUESTIONS CONCERNING MARRIAGE.

Whether a Man shall Marry?

If a man ask this question, let the lord of the ascendant, ☽, and ♀, also planets in the ascendant, be his significators. Then if ☽ aspect favourably ☉, ♀, or lord of the 7th, or the lord of the 1st aspect the lord of the 7th, or be in the 7th, or the lord of the 7th be in the ascendant, or if most of these significators be in fruitful signs, or disposed of by ♀, the man shall marry.

Whether a Woman shall Marry?

Follow the same rules as above, but, instead of ☽ and ♀, substitute ☉ and ♂. If ♂ have no aspect or familiarity with ☉, it is a strong testimony of the negative.

The Time of Marriage.

The degree of the application of ☽ to ☉ or ♀, or of ☉ to ♂, or the lords of the 1st and 7th to good aspect, or to □ or ☍, if with strong mutual reception, or of the lord of the ascendant to the cusp of the ascendant, or the lord of the 7th to the cusp of the ascendant, must be noticed. And if the significators be swift, and the testimonies of marriage strong and numerous, moveable signs give days, weeks, or months, as the applying planet be angular, succeedent, or cadent; and common signs, in like way, give weeks, months, or years; and fixed signs give, in like manner, months or years.

Of Marriage with any particular Person who may be desired.

If the lord of the ascendant or ☾ (or if the querent be a woman, the ☉) be joined to the lord of the 7th in any of his dignities in the ascendant, 10th, or 11th, the querent shall obtain the party desired.

If both significators behold each other by ✶ or △ out of the ascendant and 11th, or out of the 7th and 9th, or 7th and 5th, and no frustration or retrogradation of the chief significators happen before the good aspect be completed, the match will be perfected, if the *querent* please. For we always suppose a FREEDOM OF WILL to do or not to do. And if there be a ☐ or ☍ between the significators, without reception, the matter will come to nothing.

A ☐ aspect with reception will perfect the matter, but with some difficulty. If no reception be, there may be hopes, but no grounds to judge favourably.

When the lord of the ascendant is in the 7th, the querent loves best; and when the lord of the 7th is in the ascendant, the quesited loves best.

The match may be brought about, though there be no aspect between the significators, if there be any good translation of light; more especially if the planet who translates be a fortune, or be not retrograde, combust, or unfortunate, or afflicted by ♄ or ♂. The person signified may be known by the description of the planet, according to the sign he is in, and the way he is aspected; and the quality of the person, from the house he is lord of. A masculine diurnal planet shews a man, and a feminine nocturnal planet a female, or an effeminate man, and *vice versâ*.

Testimonies that the Marriage shall be hindered.

Observe the planet who receives the light of the significators. If he be a heavy planet, and have the □ or ☍ of a malefic, or be cadent, the intended match shall be broken off, though at present never so feasible.

Remark which party's significator is strongest; that party shall first marry after this dissolution.

If the significators apply by an evil aspect without reception, or if there be no good aspect between the luminaries, there will be no marriage; unless the lords of the ascendant and 7th be placed in each other's houses, and the other signs be very decided for the match.

If the evil ♄ be in the ascendant, he renders the querent cool, and but little inclined to marriage; unless he be very strong or well aspected. If he be in the 7th, he has the same effect on the quesited. He is generally an enemy to marriage, whereas ♀ assists marriage, and inclines the parties thereto.

What shall be the Cause of the Marriage being prevented?

Consider the evil planet who intercepts his rays between the significators, and hinders the marriage; and observe what house he is lord of, and where he is situated. If he be lord of the 2d, want of money will be objected to the querent, or he may fear to marry from lack of means.

The lord of the 3d denotes that it will be caused by the querent's kindred or neighbours, or by means of some short journey.

The lord of the 4th shews that his father will not agree,

or it may (especially if a feminine planet) be the mother of the quesited; or it may be for want of some settlement of houses or lands, &c.

The lord of the 5th causes obstacles by means of children, or by the querent having a character for loose living, &c.

The 6th denotes sickness in the querent, or opposition by some relation of his father, or by means of servants, or some private enemy of the quesited.

The lord of the 7th, or a planet therein, denotes a public enemy of the querent, or a lawsuit, or a rival.

The 8th denotes a lack of money on the part of the quesited; or, if other testimonies concur, it may be that the querent's death may intervene to prevent the match.

The 9th, in like manner, shews opposition by the relations of the quesited, or the interference of some lawyer or priest, or that the querent may go a long journey or voyage, and so the match be hindered.

The 10th and its lord shew the father of the quesited, or the mother of the querent, or some person having authority over the querent.

If it be the 11th house or its lord, then the friends of both parties dislike the match; or those who first introduced the parties, or endeavoured to bring it about, will now try to dissolve the connexion.

If it be by the lord of the 12th, or by a planet therein, there is some under-hand dealing or secret enmity to the querent. The affair shall be much retarded; but the querent shall never know by whom; or some private scandal will do much wrong, and quite break off the matter.

In the same manner that you may thus learn who will *oppose* the querent, you may ascertain who will *assist* him in his desires. And by varying the houses, you may know the persons who will aid or hinder the quesited.

To describe the Person and Qualities of the future Wife or Husband.

For the man, observe the planet the ☽ is nearest in aspect with and *applying*; as if with ♀, say she is fair, slender, and pleasant. And according as that planet is found in any of the twelve signs, describe her person; and as it is aspected and dignified, her qualities; observing also the sign on the 7th house. And if there be any planets in the 7th, take that planet nearest the cusp; unless ☽ aspect a planet there, then take that planet. For a woman, judge by the planet ☉ applies to, in like manner; as if ☉ be in ✶ or △ to ♄, he is grave and laborious; if ♃, honest; if ♂, violent; if ♀, fond of pleasure and agreeable; if ☿, active and industrious; and if ♅, strange and eccentric. If ☉ and ☽ are applying to ☐ or ☍, there will be contention and discord.

Whether the future Wife or Husband shall be rich or not?

Observe the lord of the 8th and planets therein. If ☽ apply by good aspect to the lord of the 8th, or good planets be there, or the lord of the 8th have a good aspect to the querent's ⊕, or other significators of property, the future wife or husband will be rich. If evil planets be in the 8th, or its lord afflict the ☽ or ⊕, the querent will gain little by marriage. And if ♄ and ♂ be both in the 8th, he gains nothing; and though the party may have property, the querent will be cheated of it, or lose it in some manner. The persons or means by which the property will be injured, may be discovered by observing what houses the afflicting planets are lords of for the persons, and what houses they are placed in for the means; as ☿, lord of the 8th, being in the 9th, and throwing a ☐ to ⊕, might denote a lawsuit respecting the future wife or husband's property.

Whether the Marriage be legitimate or not?

If the significators of either party be afflicted by ♄ or ♂, or joined to ☋, it denotes some dispute about the marriage; and if other testimonies agree, a lawsuit may be the consequence.

How the Parties shall agree after Marriage?

If the figure promise marriage, observe whether the lords of the ascendant and 7th are in good aspect; or if the ☽ behold with good aspect the planet disposing of her by house or exaltation, and the luminaries be in good aspect, they will agree.

If the lords of the ascendant and 7th be in □ or ☍, or the ☽ be afflicted, and behold the ascendant by ill aspect, or ♄, ♂, or ☋, be in the ascendant, or 7th, they will live unhappily. If the ill planets, or ☋, be in the 1st, the querent is to blame; and if it be ♂, is given to quarrel, or be loose in conduct, according to the sign; and if they be in the 7th, it is the quesited. And judge the same way according as the significator of the 1st or 7th be afflicted. The ☽ in her fall, or □ or ☍ of ♄ or ♂, or any retrograde planet, and at the same time throwing any aspect to the ascendant, it is the man who brings on disputes, &c. If the ☉ do the same, under the same circumstances, it is the woman.

The lord of the 7th angular, and the more weighty planet, the quesited will strive for mastery; and if neither the lord of the ascendant nor 7th be in angles, then note the weightier planet, for he points out the party who will rule.. If ♀ be afflicted, it is worse for the man; and if ☉, for the woman. The ☽ afflicted, is evil for both. The lights in evil aspect shew discord.

The Cause of Contention.

If the afflicting planet be lord of the 3d, and be in the 1st or 7th, he denotes quarrels, or injuries by neighbours or kindred. If it be an *infortune* who afflicts, and he be in the 10th, it shews continual brawls. If he be in the 4th, a divorce or willingness thereto; or some hindrance in the dowry or fortune of the female. Evil planets in the 10th or 4th lead also to contention by means of the parents of the parties. If ☽ behold the ascendant, and be unfortunate, it denotes brawling, separation, or dishonest living. And if there be no application between the planet the ☽ separates from and that one to which she applies, there will be continual contention. If ☽ aspect evilly, or be in ☌ with ♄ or ♂, one of them shall die shortly, or have some misfortune; if in the 8th or 12th, (and she void of course), they meet troubles, grief, and sickness; and if in angles, long disagreements; and probably separation, if in a fixed sign. If this be in the 10th, and a masculine sign, the man is the chief sufferer; if in the 4th, and a feminine sign, the woman.

The Cause of Happiness.

The ☽ in ✶ or △ of good planets, shews gifts or benefits by friends; if in □, by the dead. If ☽ be in ☌ with good planets, by their own conduct or industry.

Arabic Aphorisms not to be trusted to, unless the other Testimonies concur.

The woman who departs from or loses her husband when ☽ is in the last 13° of ♐, shall never return or marry.

The man who shall engage to marry when ☽ is in the first 12° of ♑, shall lose his betrothed before marriage, or die within six months, or live in discord with her.

From what Part a Person shall Marry?

If the lord of the 7th be in the 9th, the querent shall marry a stranger. If the lords of the 1st and 7th be in one quarter of heaven, or in one house or sign, the person will marry one near to their own residence. Consider the sign of the 7th, the sign and quarter of heaven the lord of the 7th is in; and judge by the majority of testimonies from what direction the querent shall marry; as if most of the testimonies be southern, the south, &c. Mix the sign and the quarter of heaven, preferring the former.

Which of the two shall be most honourable in Connexions, &c.

If the lord of the ascendant be angular, and the lord of the 7th succeedent, the querent is best connected, and *vice versâ*. In like manner you may judge of any two individuals. A more assured way is, by observing which of the two significators is the most powerful in dignities. You may combine the two systems.

Whether a Lady have a Lover besides the Querent?

If there be any planet in the 7th, (if it be not lord of the 7th), she has one of the description of that planet. The lord of the 7th, or ☉ joined to ♂, she has a lover with whom she is familiar; but, (unless other and very evil testimonies accord), not improperly. The lord of the 7th void of course, or with ☋, or if no planet be in the 7th, judge that she has none: and if the lord of the 7th aspect only the lord of the ascendant, judge the same.

If either the lord of the 7th, or the ☉ be joined to the lord of the triplicity then ascending, and ☉ separate from the lord of the ascendant, it seems that she has some friend that she loves besides the querent.

The lord of the 7th, or the ☉, or both, separating from any other planet but the lord of the ascendant, and he not separated above three degrees, the lady did love another, but she has now left him. If the lord of the 7th be with ☋, she is blameless; unless there be another planet in ☌ with them, and then she is not. And if it be ☍, she is faulty in her desires and affections; and if evil testimonies concur, such as aspects of ♂, or the ☌ be in ♏, it may be feared in acts also.

If the ☉, or lord of the 7th, be in ☌ with ♂, and ☋ be there, she loves a martial man, yet he cannot prevail on her entirely. If ☍ be there, she is sore pressed to comply. If they be near, or within very few degrees, the gentleman resides near her house; and if in the same degree, he is in the house, if it be a fixed sign; or frequently visits the house, if it be a moveable or common sign.

If ☉, or lord of the 7th, separate from ♂, she had formerly a lover, but now they have forsaken each other. If ☉ be lord of the 7th, and be in ☌ with ♂ or ♃ in any sign whatever, the lady has loved or does love a person described by ♂ or ♃ ; and he has rank as an officer, gentleman, or clergyman. And if there be mutual reception, they still love one another, and many acts of kindness pass between them.

If the ☉ or lord of the 7th be joined to ☿, the lover is a young clerk or merchant; lawyer or writer; a witty, nimble fellow. His age may be judged by the number of degrees ☿ is in the sign.

If the lord of the 7th be joined to ♀ with reception, (and it be a female who is inquired of,) then she cares little for the men; but is fond of female society, is rather free in her language, but not naturally vicious. If it be a male who is the quesited, he is found much in female company, and is partial to such an one as ♀ may describe, according to the sign she is in. If the aspect be ⚹ or △ and with mutual reception, the lady is partial to him; but if the ☽ or lord of the 7th dispose not of ♀, she cares not for him, unless the aspect be very close and in angles. And if the aspect be evil, there is no mutual regard, without there be very strong reception.

The lord of the 7th joined to ♄, she loves, (or did love if they separate), an elderly person, or farmer, &c.

The lord of the 7th joined to ☉, she loves some person of consequence, according to her rank in life; and if with mutual reception, he may do what he please with her. If they separate, or there be no reception, the feeling is passed away or was never mutual.

If other planets aspect ☉ and the lord of the 7th, especially ♄ or ☿, she has other admirers, &c.

If the lord of the 7th aspect ☽, or the ☽ be in the 7th, especially if they be then in aspect, or ♂ be in aspect with ☽, she is given to change and acts discreditably, yielding up her affections upon slight solicitation.

Generally, you may consider that if ♂ be in the 7th, unless he be in his own house, the lady has a lover. If ♄, she loves one, but there is no familiarity between them; if ♃ be there, she is honest; if ♀, she is giddy and merry, and is thought to be wanton, but is not; if ☿, she had a friend, but has not now; and if ☽, she has not yet, but will have more than one. If ☉ or ☊ be there, she is virtuous and honourable, and has no lover other than the querent. ☋ denotes discreditable desires at least.

Whether a Gentleman have a Lover besides the Querent?

You may judge this question exactly by the rules for judging of a lady, if you substitute the ☽ for the ☉ and ♀ for

♂. You may in like way judge of *friends* by taking the 11th for the 7th.

Whether a Damsel be virtuous or not?

Behold the lord of the 7th, the cusp of the 7th, and the ☉; and if they be in fixed signs and well aspected, you may judge that she is correct. If ♂ be in ♌ and ♏ descend, she is suspected, but yet is honest. If ♏ descend and ♂ therein, it is suspicious; and if there be a moveable sign on the 7th, or the ☉ and ♂ be in common or moveable signs, and be ill aspected; and if ♂ and ♀ be in ill aspect, or the ☉ or ☽ behold ♂, and the evil stars aspect them from fixed signs, there is great reason to doubt. Yet if there be *any good aspect* to either the 7th or its lord, ♂, or ☉, it is not safe to judge the lady to be unchaste, though she may have been much tempted. The student will do well to avoid a positive judgment *unfavourable* on this head, unless *all* the testimonies are decided.

If there be great reason to doubt, then observe whether ☽ be in the last face of ♊, or in a moveable sign, and in the 5th house, and the lord of the 5th in the ascendant or 7th, and in a moveable sign, and either of them in aspect to ♂; or the lords of the 5th and 7th in ☌ in one sign. If all these, or nearly all, concur, you may be more confident that the lady is faulty.

Whether the Child conceived is the Child of him who is the reputed Father?

Observe the lord of the ascendant, and the ☽, who signify the querent; then observe the sign of the 11th, and its lord, which signify the issue in conception. If these significators behold one another by ✶ or △, with reception or not, the conception is legitimate, viz., the child of its supposed father.

If they aspect each other by □ or ☍ with reception, and perfect aspect: or the lord of the ascendant or ☽ be in the 5th, or the lord of the 5th in the ascendant, without the evil aspect of the infortunes, or if one of the fortunes behold the cusp of the 5th or its lord, then also is the child begotten by its reputed father. But if none of these things be, and ♄, ♂, or ☿, behold the 5th or lord thereof, there may be just suspicion that the child is conceived in adultery, or is not the child of the querent.

Whether a Woman living from her Husband shall ever return to him, or be restored to Favour?

This question will equally resolve a doubt concerning a mistress or *person beloved.*

If the woman herself propose the question, consider the lord of the 7th, (for the 7th is ever given to the banished or expelled party;) and if the lord of the 7th behold the ascendant with a perfect aspect, and the lord of the ascendant behold the 7th, or its lord, without doubt she shall again come into favour. If the lord of the 7th do not behold the ascendant, but another planet, who is not afflicted, behold the ascendant, the woman shall be received again through some person who shall interpose his friendship with the husband or friend. If none of these things be, observe ☽ and ♂; and if ☽ be above the earth, and ♂ behold the ascendant with ✶ or △, she shall return quietly, and without much trouble.

If ☽ be under the earth and ♂ above, and behold the ascendant with ✶ or △, she shall return, but with trouble and delays, and with much publicity. If ☽ aspect the ascendant favourably, and be not afflicted, she shall return, but with solicitation. If ☽ decrease in light, but be not near the beams of ☉, and behold the ascendant, she will return easily and speedily.

If ♂ be retrograde, and hasten to aspect with ☾, she will of her own accord return; but if ♂ and ☾, or the lords of the 1st and 7th, separate from good aspect, they have no mutual desire to return, nor will the lady much respect the gentleman for the future.

OF RUNAWAY SERVANTS, CATTLE STRAYED, AND THINGS LOST.

The significator of the thing missing is the ☾; wherefore if you find ☾ applying to the lord of the ascendant, or to the lord of the 12th, (being herself in the ascendant,) or to the lord of the house of the ☾, the thing missing shall be found again. But if ☾ apply to none of these, nor be in the ascendant or 2d, the thing lost shall not be found.* If the lord of the house of ☾ be in the 3d, or in ✶ to the ascendant, there is some hope of finding the thing again during that aspect with the degree ascending. Also, if he separate from the lord of the 6th, 8th, or 12th, and apply by any aspect to the cusp of the 2d, or behold the ☾, you may hope to find it. But if there be contrary indications between these, judge the reverse.

If the ☾ be aspected well by both fortunes, the thing lost is in the hands of some trusty person; and if ☾ or one of the fortunes behold the ascendant, he will restore it to the owner.

The Place where the Thing lost is.

This is shewn by ☾, according to the sign she is in; for if the sign be eastern, it is east; and if west, it is western, &c. Observe also the place of ☾ in the figure; for if she be in the ascendant, it is east, &c., but prefer the sign. If the lord of the house of ☾ be in human signs, (♊, ♍, ♒, or the first

---

* This rule principally applies to cattle strayed.

half of ♐), it is in a place where men frequent. If in signs of small cattle, as ♈ or ♑, it is where they are found. If ☽ be in a fiery sign, it is where fire is; if in a watery sign, where water is, &c. If ☽ be in the same quarter as the lord of the ascendant, and there be not more than 30° between them, the thing lost is in the house of the owner, or about it; if they be above 30° and less than 70° apart, it is in the town where he resides; but if they be not in one quarter, it is far from the owner.

How the Thing was lost.

Observe from what planet the lord of the ascendant last separated. If from ♄, it was through forgetfulness of the owner; or through cold or illness which afflicted the loser, especially if ♄ be retrograde. If from ♃, it was through some abstinence, or ordering of laws, or by excess of care in managing affairs, or putting too much trust in the person by whom it was carried away or mislaid. If from ♂, or the lord of the ascendant be in the house of ♂, it was lost through fear or some sudden passion, provoking the loser to anger; or by fire, or by enmity, or upon some quarrel. If from ☉, by means of the king or some gentleman, or the master of the family, or by hunting or pastime. If from ♀, or in her house, by drinking, cards, &c., or making merry in a tavern, &c., or by singing or dallying with women. If from ☿, by writing, letters, messages, or going a message, &c. If from ☽, by too frequent use, or shewing the thing lost, or making it too common; or some messenger, widow, or servant lost the same.

If it be an Animal, and you would know whether it be stolen or not?

If you find the lord of the house of ☽ separating from any

planet, say that it went away of its own accord. If that lord be not separating, but another planet be separating from him, say that some person took it away. If the lord of the house of ☽ be in neither of these cases, look to the lord of the 2d house, and judge by him in the same way. And if you find no separation of either of these two lords, say that the animal is still in or near its place, and is not gone away.

Whether it be dead?

Observe the ☽; and if you find her in application to the lord of the 8th house from her, say it is dead. But if you find no such testimony, observe her dispositor; and if you find him applying to the lord of the 8th house from the Moon, say likewise that it is dead, or will shortly die; but if in neither of these you find application, take the lord of the 8th house of the figure in the same way; and if neither ☽ nor her dispositor apply to it, then the animal is not dead.

Whether the Thing missing be stolen?

If the significator of the thief, (usually the lord of the 7th, unless there be any peregrine planet in an angle), be found in the ascendant, or disposing of the ☽, or ☽ disposing of him, or the lord of the ascendant be disposed of by him or dispose of him, or unless he apply to the ☽ or lord of the 1st or 2d, or ⊕, or its lord by ☌, □, or ☍, or some planet be in the ascendant, and be in □ or ☍ to the significator of the thief, the thing is *not* stolen. Generally any ill aspect of any evil planet, or the lord of the 7th to the ascendant or 2d house or their lords, or ☽ or ⊕, or their lords, denote that the thing *is* stolen.

Whether a Thing lost shall be found?

If ☽ apply to the lords of the ascendant or 2d, or to her

dispositor, it shall be found. ☽ in the ascendant, or her dispositor in ✶ or △ thereto, give hopes; the dispositor of ☽ separating from the lord of the 6th, 8th, or 12th, and applying to the lord of the ascendant or cusp of the 2d, give hopes also; and if ☽ be in aspect to her dispositor, it is good. But ☽ afflicted by the lords of the 6th, 8th, or 12th, it is in the hands of an evil person, who will not part with it; especially if an *infortune* afflict the ascendant or its lord. ☽ in △ to the ascendant, its lord or ☉, or in the ascendant, or ☉ there, unless in ♎ or ♒, it shall be found.

The Kind of Place a Thing lost is in?

If ☽ be in a human sign,* it is in a place where men frequent; and if in a brutal sign (♈, ♉, ♌, ♑, and the last half of ♐), the thing is where animals frequent. If ☽ be in fiery signs, it is where fire is or has been, or near a fire, or on hills or high ground; if in watery signs, where water is or has been;† if in airy signs, where many windows are, or open places, garrets, &c.; if in earthy signs, in an earthy place, where houses are built of mud, clay, &c., and in brickfields. The ☽, or her dispositor, in a moveable sign, shews a place newly peopled, or a house newly built, or where there are hills and dales: if in a fixed sign, in a level plain country; if in a common sign, in a place of much water, according to the nature of the thing missing. Also ♊, ♍, ♐, ♓, shew, if it be not living things, within the house; but if cattle, &c., they shew ditches, pits, and among rushes, or in a market-

* The human signs are ♊, ♍, and ♒, also the first half of ♐. If the significator of any person or ☽ be in one of these signs, they are humane and civil in their manners.

† In this case ♋ generally denotes pure or running water; ♏ foul water, and filthy liquids, oils, dyes, &c.; and ♓ standing waters, spirituous liquors, wines, &c.

place. ♉, ♌, ♏, ♒, shew that the things are laid low or hid in the earth, or near walls, in hollow trees, &c. ♈, ♋, ♎, ♑, shew high places, roofs, ceiling, &c., but watery signs denote about the foundations of houses, or cellars, if water be there.

Of Animals missing.

If the lord of the 6th be in the 6th, they are small animals; if the lord of the 12th be in the 12th, they are large. If the lord of the 6th be in the 12th, they are in pound; and if in a fiery sign, locked up. If ☽ be in common signs, they are in rushy grounds; if in an angle, they are in enclosed ground; if in a succeedent, they are near enclosures; if in a cadent house, they are on commons. If in watery signs or ♒, near fish-ponds or other waters; and if in the last moiety of ♑, they are near ships, or on shipboard, or near some wood or timber-yard.

Whether it shall be restored?

The ☽ aspecting ♃ or ♀, it is in the hands of an honest man, who will restore it. If ♃ or ♀ have any aspect to the ascendant, or ☽ apply to the ascendant, it will be restored; and if ☽ be in the ascendant, it is restored without trouble or pain. The lord of the 7th, or 12th in the 12th house, the fugitive is imprisoned.

If the ☽ be within 30° of the lord of the 1st, the thing is with or near the loser; if ☽ be more than 30° off the lord of the 1st, it is far off.

If it be animals, and the lord of the 6th, (or if large cattle the 12th,) be fortunate by the good aspects of ♀ or ♃, or they be found in the 2d, 5th, or 11th, the animals will be had again. The same if the lord of the term in which ☽ is, or the lord of the cusp of the 4th be with the lord of the ascendant, or the lord of the 6th or 12th be in △ to ☉ out of angles.

Of a Fugitive, and whether he shall be found or return?

The lord of the 7th in the ascendant, he will return of his own accord.* If ☽ separate from the lord of the ascendant, and be joined immediately to the lord or cusp of the 7th, news will shortly be brought of him. The lord of the 7th combust, he shall be found against his will. The ☽ afflicted by ♅, ♄, ♂, or ☋, or a retrograde planet, he shall be found or return, after much suffering. ☽ separating from ♃ or ♀, he shall quickly come back; and if she aspect her own house by ✶ or △, he will return or shall be heard of within a very few days.

The lord of the 7th aspecting an infortune from the 7th, the querent will discover the quesited with some person, to whom he must give money before he can have him back. If the lord of the 7th be retrograde, it is a testimony of his return.

OF THEFTS.

The ascendant is for the querent, and its lord for him that has lost the goods; and it signifies the place from whence they were taken.

The 7th house and its lord, or the peregrine planet in an angle, signify the thief.

The 2d house, its lord, and the ☽, signify the things lost or stolen; and the 4th house, and its lord, shew the place where they are conveyed to, and then are.

The aspects of ☉ and ☽, the lords of the 1st and 2d, and

---

* If a servant, take the lord of the 6th in all these cases; and if the querent's child, the lord of the 5th, &c.

the dispositor of the ☽, by application to each other, shall shew whether they will be had again or not.

If the lord of the 2d and the ☽ be in the 7th, and the lord of the 7th behold them both by ⚹ or △ (though the aspect be several degrees distant), then are the goods taken away by some one, and not merely lost.

If ☽ be lady of the 2d, and going to ☌ of the lord of the 7th, then has the party mislain it; and the thing is neither lost nor stolen.

If ☽ be lady of the ascendant, and in the 4th, and the lord of the 2d be in the 7th or 8th in ⚹ or △ of ☽, the thing is not stolen, but taken away in jest.

If ☽ be lady of the ascendant, and be in it, and ☉ lord of the 2d in the 10th, with the lord of the 7th, and the lord of the 7th □ ☽, then are the goods stolen and taken away. If ☽ be in the 3d, and in □ to the lord of the 7th, and the lord of the 2d be in the 7th, it was first taken in jest, but is now stolen, and will be hard to recover, unless ☉ and ☽ aspect the ascendant.

If ☽ be lady of the 5th, and in ♑, and ♀ lady of the 2d in the 10th, and ☽ in ☍ to the lord of the 7th, then has the party lost the goods as he went by the way, or left them in some place. If ☽ be in ♋ in the 8th, and the lord of the 2d in the 5th, and neither of them behold the lord of the 7th, and he be in the 7th, the goods are taken away in jest by the master of the house, and he will deny it. If ☽ be in the 4th in ☍ to its lord, and the lord of the 2d in the 12th in ⚹ to the lord of the 7th, then has somebody taken away the things in jest. If ☽ be in the house of the lord of the 7th, and be in the 12th, not beholding the lord of the 7th, and the lord of the 2d be in the 6th, then are the goods removed in jest; and if, in this case, the lord of the 2d did last separate from the ruler of the ☽, they will scarcely be had again. If the ☽

separate from the lord of the 2d by □, they are taken away and stolen; and the same, if the ☽, being lady of the 2d, separate from the lord of the house wherein she is.

If the lord of the ascendant separate from ♃, (he not being lord of the 7th, or peregrine in an angle), or from the lord of the 2d, the querent has lain it down and forgotten it, and so it was lost; but, when both the lords of the 1st and 2d separate from ♃, this is surer. If (in such case) the lord of the 2d, or ♃, separate from the lord of the ascendant, then did the party lose the goods by the way as he went, or in some place where he was, or they fell out of his pocket accidentally, and they are neither found nor stolen. But if there be none of these separations, see if the peregrine planet, or lord of the 7th apply to ♃, or the lord of the 2d; then, if they do, the goods are absolutely stolen. If the lord of the 2d, or ♃, apply to the significator of the thief, he came easily by them, and did not come with intent to steal; but, seeing the thing unprotected, he was tempted to steal.

If the significator of the thief aspect the lord of the 1st or 2d, or the cusp of the 2d, or ⊕, or ☽, or their dispositor, or the planet in whose term ☽ is, or if he be in the ascendant, it is stolen; but, if there be no *evil* aspect to any of these, it is not stolen.

Of the Age of the Thief.

Guido Bonatus says, that if the thief's significator be ☿, he is very young; if ♀, rather older, but yet a young female; ♂ shews him of full age; ♃ of middle age, and ♄, elderly. If the ☉ be his significator, and be between the ascendant and 10th, he is young, and so increasing in age until he come to the angle of the earth. If the ☽ shew the thief, his age will correspond to her age; and in all cases judge *also* by the position the thief's significator has reached in the sign where he is found. If he be just entered the sign, quite young; if in the middle of the sign, of middle age; and if towards the end of the sign, elderly; and if ♄ aspect him any way, it adds to his age. Oriental planets denote also younger persons, and occidental planets elderly persons. You must consider all the testimonies before you judge the thief's age.

Whether the Thief be Male or Female?

The significator of the thief being masculine, and in a masculine sign, and the ☽ in a masculine sign, it is a male; *et e contrâ*. The angles of the figure masculine shew a man; and if feminine, a woman. If ♀ or the ☽ be the significator, or ☿, when aspecting them, it is a female; ♄, ♃, ♂, ☉, and ☿ aspecting them, a male.

Whether one Thief or more?

If the significator be in a fixed sign, it denotes one only; if he be in double-bodied signs, it denotes more than one, especially if there be more than one planet in the sign, and they peregrine. Also, when ☉ and ☽ are in angles, and in ☐ aspect, it shews more than one. If the significator be in ♋, ♏, or ♓, it is a testimony of there being more than one; the angles being moveable, the same. The ☽ in the ascendant, and in a double-bodied sign, shews more than one. And if the significator be in aspect with more than one planet, unless he be in a fixed sign, it shews plurality.

Of the Colour of the Thief's Clothes.

This must be judged in a general manner; and by the colours of the signs and houses of the significator, and the planets ruling them. Thus, ♄ is black; ♃ green, spotted, or ash; ♂ red; ☉ tawny, or saffron, or sandy; and if you mix the colours according to the signs and planets, &c., you will judge very nearly the general colour of the thief's clothes. Thus, ♄ and ♃, mixed, give dark green, or green spotted with black; ♄ and ♂, a dark reddish brown, or tawny; ♄ and ☉, a blackish orange, and shining; ♄ and ♀, a whitish grey; ♄ and ☿, a black blue; ♄ and ☽, a deep russet, or grey; ♃ and ♂, a tawny, light spotted; ♃ and ☉, a deep, shining red; ♃ and ♀, a greenish grey; ♃ and ☿, a spotted green; ♃ and ☽, a high-coloured green; ♂ and ☉, a deep red, or scarlet; ♂ and ♀, light red, or crimson; ♂ and ☿, a tawny red, or brick colour; ♂ and ☽, a light red, glistening.

You must observe, that if the significr be ♄, in his own house, ♑, and not in close aspect with any other planet, the thief will be dressed all in *black;* because both sign and planet rule that colour. But if he were in the 1st house, which rules *white*, he would have some *white* about his person. Also, if it were ♂, who rules *red*, and he were found in ♏, which rules *brown*, he would denote a rusty, dirty, reddish brown; but if he were in ♌, which rules *red and green*, and ♃ were in aspect, there would be much *green*, as well as *red*, about the dress; and so of the others.

The relation the Thief bears to the Owner.

The lord of the 7th, or significator of the thief, being in the ascendant, it is one well known to the querent, or one who frequents his house; and is in no way suspected.

If the significator of the thief be in the 2d, it is one of the household, or an acquaintance; but if in a feminine sign, it may be the querent's wife or maid-servant; and it is in the loser's power, and may be recovered by money.

If he be in the 3d, it is one of his near kindred or neighbours; or some messenger, or other person, often in his sight.

If in the 4th, it is his father, or some elderly person, or one who resides in the house, &c., of his father; or he is a labourer or farm-servant.

If in the fifth, it is his son or daughter, or one of the near relations of his brother or sister, or near neighbour; or one of the household of his father, or his kept mistress, or some one connected with taverns, theatres, &c.

If he be in the 6th, it is a servant, or the querent's father's relation; or it is some person in bad health.

If he be in the 7th, it may be his own wife or lover, or some female who has been suspected of having connexion with the querent: or it is some person with whom he deals publicly, or one who is his open enemy.

If in the 8th, it is a stranger; yet it is likely to be one who is, or has been, at times employed about the house, such as an occasional gardener, or charwoman, washerwoman, &c.

If in the 9th, it is some traveller or vagrant, or some person employed about churches, &c.; or a person in connexion with some jailor, or master of a workhouse, &c.

If in the 10th, it is a person of respectable circumstances, or some master tradesman, &c.; one not necessitated to turn thief; and, generally, a person who lodged in the house, or visited it frequently when the thing was taken.

If in the 11th, a friend, or one who is trusted, and has done the querent some service; or one connected with a neighbouring clergyman, or the household of the querent's mother.

If in the 12th house, it is a stranger, or some poor, common thief or beggar; a person in miserable circumstances, who partly lives by thieving or thief taking.

Other Particulars of the Thief.

If the thief's significator be in the end of a sign, or applying to a planet in the 3d or 9th, he is going off; and if it be a superior planet, and leaving a sign, he is undoubtedly leaving his house or lodgings, &c.

If his significator be in an angle, he is still in the town; if succeedent, he is not far off; but if cadent, he is far gone.

If it be in an angle, he is in a house; and if ☽ be in an angle, in his own house, &c.; if in a succeedent, in a field or enclosure; and if ☽ be succeedent, it is his own, or where he resides; and if in a cadent house, he is on a common or open place, and if ☽ be cadent, it belongs to the town, &c. where he lives.

If the lord of the ascendant and the significator of the thief be together, the thief is with the querent. And if the thief's significator be in the ascendant, the thief will be at the querent's house before the querent. But if the significator be in the 7th, he is hid at home, and dare not be seen. The direction in which the thief lives may be judged by the sign and quarter in which the significator is.

The ☽ denotes also the door of the thief's house. If she be in a fixed sign, the house has but one door; if in a moveable sign, the door is high above the earth, and it is probable that there is another smaller door. If ♄ aspect the sign of the ☽, the door has been broken, and often repaired, or is old or black. If ♂ aspect it, the gate or door has some mark of fire. If ♄ and ♂ both have a friendly aspect to the sign the ☽ is in, the door is iron, or is very strong. If ☽ be afflicted, it is broken or injured; and if ☽ be decreasing, and near ☉, the gate, &c. opens on the back premises, and there is no front door to the street; if she increase, and is near ☉, it is low down, and there is a step to descend in entering. But if ☽ be in a moveable sign, there are steps up to it.

Whether the Goods are in the Hands of the Thief?

If the thief's significator be in aspect to, and disposed of by another planet, they are not in his hands; otherwise they are.

The Place where the Goods are.

The nature of the place is judged by the lord of the 4th house. If he be in a moveable sign, it is in a place high above the ground; in a fixed sign, in the earth; and in a common sign, it is under the eaves of a house, &c.* And you must judge also by the quality of the sign; as ♈ shews a place where small cattle are, as sheep, hogs, &c. ♌ shews a place of animals that bite, as dogs, foxes, &c.; ♐ a place of animals that are ridden, as horses, mules, &c., and their stables. ♉, ♍, and ♑ shew a place of large cattle, as ♉ oxen, kine, &c.; ♍ and ♑ shew camels, mules, asses, &c.; ♍ also shews barns where corn is kept, and a place about the earth. ♑ denotes goats, hogs, &c.; ♊ shews a wall or partition in a house; ♎ a high part, or near a closet or little house; ♒ shews near a door, above another door or gate in a high part; ♏ shews a place of unclean water; ♓ a place always moist. But if the ☽ be in the same sign with the lord of the 4th, judge by her more than him.

In what Part of a House Things lost, stolen, or concealed may be.

If the thing lost be in the house, (whether stolen or not), behold the lord of the 4th, (or, if a planet be in the 4th, take him in preference.)

If it be ♄, it is in a dark or secret place; and if he be in

---

* We should pay more attention to the nature of the sign, as fiery, earthy, &c.; and judge as in the rules for things mislaid.

aspect with ♂, or in the house of ♂, it is in or about some dirty place, where people seldom go, a privy, &c.

If ♃, a place of wood, bushes, &c.

If ♂, a kitchen or place where fire is kept; if aspected by ☿, a shop.

If ☉, the hall, dining-room, or chief room where the master frequents.

If ♀, a bed, or among bed-clothes, or where females much frequent. In this case ♎ would shew the top of the bed.

If ☿, a place of books, pictures, carving, &c.; and if ♍, where corn is.

If ☽, it is in a pit, cistern, or washing place.

Description of the House or Place where the Things are that are lost, &c.

The ☉ describes the house, and also its front entrance. If he be in an airy sign, it is high, &c., and its colour may be known by the sign and house he is in. The ☽ describes the cellar, pump, or place holding the water; as, if she be in ♒, it is a cistern, high above the ground, &c.; if ♏, a low pit or pond; if ♍, a deep well. ♀ shews the place of mirth, female apartments, &c. ☊ denotes the stairs or ladder to climb by, &c. ☋ describes the place the wood is in, or the animals are kept. ☿ denotes the room, &c.; if in a common sign, it is a cupboard, or small room within another; if in a fixed sign, it shews a house having no cellar, or a single chamber. If ♃, ♀, or both, be in the 10th, the door has a fair appearance, and opening; if ♄ be in the 10th, the door is near some ditch, pit, or deep place; if ♂ be there, there is a fire-place near the door, or place for killing animals; if ☿ be there, near the door is a place where tools or instruments are kept; if ☉ be there, then there is some seat or porch near the door; and if ☽ be in the 10th, there is near the entrance a door to go under ground, a trap or cellar door, or some other convenience in very common use.*

The Nature of the Thing stolen.

This is judged by the lord of the 2d house. ♄ shews lead, iron, things of a black or dark blue colour, wool, black garments, heavy things, earthy materials, agricultural implements, carts, &c. ♃ oil, honey, silk, fruit, men's clothes, merchandize, horses, &c. ♂ arms, pepper, brass, red clothes, red wine, and red things; generally sharp-pointed, cutting, and hot things, horses for war, &c., and all warlike engines or instruments. ☉ gold, brass, yellow clothes, diamonds, and things of value. ♀ women's dresses, or ornaments, such as rings, ear-rings, &c., white cloth, and white wine. ☿ shews money, paper, books, pictures, and party-coloured dresses, &c., and scientific instruments, writing-desks, &c. The ☽ all common commodities, such as crockery, &c. cattle, poultry, and also silver.

Whether the Goods shall be recovered or not.

The ☽ in the 7th, aspecting the lord of the 7th with a △; a fortune strong in the ascendant; ♃ in the 2d direct; in ☽ the 10th in a △ to a planet in the 2d; ☽ in the 2d in △ to the lord of the 2d; ☉ and ☽ going to △, or ☉ and ☽ aspecting the cusp of the 2d with a △; or the lord of the 2d in the ascendant or 4th, well aspected by application; ☽ in the 2d, going to □ of ☉ in the 12th, in signs of short ascension: *all these are signs of its recovery*.

Also, if the lords of the term and house of the ☽ be both

---

* These minute particulars may be found useful in many other questions, such as where fugitives, &c. are; and they might be of use in discovering criminals.

increasing in light and motion,* and free from affliction, it shall be recovered, and be uninjured.

Generally, if there be a diminution of their light and motion, the thing is already partly destroyed. If there be good aspects to the lords or cusps of the ascendant, or 2d, or to ⊕ or its lord, by planets in angles, it will soon be recovered.

The lord of the 8th in the ascendant, or with its lord, shews recovery; the lord of the 7th in the 8th, denies it: ♄, ♂, or ☋ in the ascendant, or 2d, shew dividing and loss of the thing.

The lord of the 2d in the ascendant shews recovery; and the lord of the 1st in the 2d the same, after long search. If the 2d or its lord be afflicted, all the things lost shall not be recovered. If both luminaries be under the earth, it is a strong testimony against recovery.

If both ☉ and ☽ aspect the ascendant, the thing cannot be lost, but will shortly be discovered.

Of the Time of the Thing being recovered.

Observe the *application* of the planets that signify recovery, and determine the number of days, weeks, or months, as they may be in moveable, common, or fixed signs, in angles, succeedents, or cadents. And if the significators are swift in motion, it hastens the recovery; if slow, it retards.

Of the Thief's Person.

In addition to the planet's general description in the sign he is in, observe the aspects he has, and take all these into consideration. Moreover, if the significator be oriental, and in ♌, ♍, or ♐, the person is *large;* if occidental, and in ♋, ♏, or ♓, the body is *smaller.* If the planet have *south*

---

* This means, going faster than they were the previous day.

latitude, he is nimble; if in *north* latitude, slow in his motions. If going out of one sign into another, he is weak and feeble.*

* ♄ shews one of a pale, swarthy, dark complexion; hard, rough skin; hairy body; small, leering eyes; jaundiced look; lean, crooked, or ill made; beetle browed; thin beard; thick, negro lips; bow-legged, or one who knocks his knees or ancles one against the other, and shuffles in his gait. He has a down look, his eyes always on the earth; is seldom free from cough and bad breath. He is crafty, revengeful, and malicious; dirty, a great eater, covetous, and seldom rich.

♃ denotes a full face, white and red mixed; full eyes; good make, light beard, but this depends chiefly on the sign; thick hair, good teeth, but some defect in the two front teeth; moderately curling hair. If in a watery sign, fat and plump; in an earthy sign, large make: in an airy sign, strong—a person who bears a good moral character.

♂ denotes a full face, red or sunburnt; a sharp, fierce countenance; eyes fiery and ferocious, with rather a yellow tinge; hair and beard reddish; but this depends on the sign, unless he be with fixed stars of his own nature, such as *Aldebaran, the Lion's Heart, &c.* In earthy signs it is a sad brown; in watery, lighter or flaxen; in airy, curling or crisping; in fiery, strong and wiry. He is strong, broad shouldered, proud, scornful, drunken, and debauched; with a mark or scar, generally in the face.

☉ denotes a round full face; sanguine complexion; short chin; curling hair; fair, comely, sometimes swarthy or bronzed; bold, ambitious, vain, slow of speech; outwardly decent, but secretly vicious and lascivious.

♀ gives a fair, round face; full or large eyes; red, plump lips, the lower larger than the upper; black eyelids, smooth brown hair; person well-shaped and handsome; rather short than tall; face pleasing, with smiles and dimples.

☿ middling complexion; darkish hair, or a sad brown; long face; high forehead; black or grey eyes; thin beard and whiskers, often hardly any; slender, small legs; one quick in walking, and full of talk and business.

☽ a round face, more white than red; in watery signs, freckled; and if in ♋, and in no aspect to ♂ or ☉, very pale and white, or wan—a person generally short and full; and one who is dull and heavy, and also very vulgar and ill-mannered.

N.B. The above descriptions are partly taken from *Wilson's Astrological Dictionary;* a very useful work for the young student.

Signs of the Thief being taken.

If the lord of the 7th (or thief's significator) be in the 1st or 7th, in ☌ with the lord of the ascendant, or a retrograde planet. If the ☽ separate from the thief's significator, and apply to ☌ of the lord of the 1st; or go from ☌ of the lord of the 1st to him. Or if ☉ and ☽ be in ☌ with him; or if he be going to combustion, or be in ☌ with an infortune in the 7th. He is captured if ☽ be in the 7th, applying to ☐ of ♂, the ☉, or ☿; ☽ separating from ☐ of ♄ or ☿, and applying to ☐ of ☉, or separating from ☌ ♄, and going to ☐ ☿; or in the 8th, in ☍ ♂, or in the 7th, going to the lord of the 8th.

The Thief escapes.

If his significator be in aspect with a fortune; if he be in aspect to ♃ or ♀, they being in the 11th, he escapes by friends; if in the 3d, by strangers, or by law quibbles, &c.

OF BATTLE, WAR, DUELS, PRIZE FIGHTS, OR OTHER CONTENTIONS.

The lord of the ascendant, planets therein, and ☽, are for the querent or challenger, or him who attacks; the 7th house, its lord and planets therein, for the adversary. Behold whose significators are most angular, best dignified and aspected, and expect victory for that party. If evil planets be in the ascendant, and fortunes in the 7th, the adversary shall overcome, and *vice versâ*: also the lord of the 7th, in the ascendant, betokens victory to the querent, and *vice versâ*.

Whether any one shall return safe from War, or any dangerous Voyage, &c.

The lord of the ascendant, strong, well aspected, and his

dispositor a good planet; good planets in the ascendant, or aspecting its cusp, are all good testimonies; and the reverse are evil. If the lord of the 7th, and the 7th house, be fortunate, (though the first be not,) the party returns, though not without great crosses and hinderances; *et e contra.* Observe how ☽ is disposed; for her application to the good planets is fortunate; *and the contrary.* Evil planets in the 8th are signs of fear and death; ♄ shews bruises and hurts by falls, &c., and losses; ♂ denotes wounds by weapons; ☋, injuries and disgrace.

If an evil planet be with the lord of the ascendant, and a good one in the ascendant, he will suffer great loss or be sorely wounded, but not die.

♄ in the 1st, or with its lord, shews loss to the querent by one whom he will meet; ♄ in the 1st, and an evil planet with its lord, he shall be wounded by wood or stone; ♂ shews wounds by fire or iron, and if ☋ be in the ascendant, and ♄ afflict its lord, he shall receive a wound, and be nearly killed. It is evil if ☉ be with the lord of the 7th, or be in the 8th.

The lord of the ascendant in the 8th, or with its lord, or the lord of the 8th in the ascendant, denotes the querent's death. And the lord of the 7th in the second, or with its lord, shews the death of the adversary.

If the lord of the 7th be strong, and have good aspects from the 10th, or its lord, the querent will gain honour. And if the cusp of the 2d and its lord, and ⊕ or its lord, be fortunate, then he gains money by the war, &c.

In the same manner as the 8th house and its lord shew death, the 12th and its lord denote imprisonment.

And if the question concern the general result of a war or expedition, it must be judged on the same principles.

Of Partnership.

If good planets be in the 1st and 7th, the partnership shall be and do well. And if the lord of the 7th be strong, and in fixed signs, it shall endure. If the two lords agree in aspects, and by mutual reception, the partners will accord well together. But if they disagree, the fault will be with that party who has ♅, ♄, ♂, or ☋ in their house.

The significators of substance will shew the means of each party; and as they may be about to receive good or ill aspects, will they thrive or lose by the concern. The 8th, its lord, and planets there, are for the quesited's property.

If ☽ separate from one fortune, and apply to the other, they will neither of them gain much by the concern. If she leave a good planet and apply to an ill, they begin well but end ill: and if she separate from one evil planet, and apply to another, they begin with complaining, continue with jealousy, and end with lawsuits. An evil planet, or ☋ in the 2d, the querent gains but little, will be cheated, or get into debt: if they be in the 8th, judge this of the quesited. And if the lord of the 7th or 8th, □ or ☍ ⊕, the querent may hope but little gain from his partner, who will embezzle the common stock, &c.

Of removing from Place to Place.

The lord of the ascendant and planets therein stronger than the 7th, and planets there, it is better to remain. If there be a benefic in the 7th or ☊, and especially if ☽ separate from an infortune, remove; an evil planet there, or the lord of the 1st or ☽ leaving a benefic, remain.

The 8th house shews the property of the querent in the place he desires to remove to: if evil planets be there, it is better to remain. (*See also p.* 141)

Of Lawsuits, and their Success.

The lord of the ascendant or ☽ joined to the lord of the 7th, or in ✶ or △, with reception mutual, the parties will easily agree together, and make up the quarrel. But if one dispose of the other, and the reception be not mutual, they will agree without a lawsuit, but not without the interceding of friends. If they be in good aspect without, or in evil aspect with, reception, they will accord, after one effort at law. That party shall be most ready to agree whose significator is disposed of by the other. If they hasten to a mutual good aspect, and the lord of the 9th or 10th interpose an evil aspect, they will be led to dispute by a lawyer or by the judge. If there be any translation of light by the ☽, or other planet, between the two significators, it denotes that they will be reconciled by a third person, described by that planet.

Observe whether the lord of the ascendant or 7th be strongest or most powerful, and best aspected; for that one shall gain the day. If they compound, the first motion thereto comes from the lighter planet, who is disposed of by the other. If the lord of the ascendant be in the 7th, the adversary will overcome, and *vice versâ*. If either lord of the 1st or 7th be retrograde, he shews that the party does not believe that he has right on his side; nor will he stand to it very stoutly.

If the lord of the 10th, which denotes the *judge*, be direct, he will proceed fairly, and endeavour to settle the cause speedily. But if he be retrograde, the judge will not act fairly according to law, nor strive to terminate the cause. If the lord of the 10th throw an evil aspect to either significator, the judge will be against that party.

If ☉ or ☽ be in the ascendant, or aspect its lord, or be in either of his houses, it is a good testimony for the querent;

and if, on the contrary, the lord of the 7th be so situated, it is in favour of the quesited. If the lord of the 10th receive both significators, the judge will settle the matter before it comes to full trial.

If the lord of the 10th be in the 10th, in his own house, the judge will do justice, and decide the case with honour to himself, unless the lord of the 10th be ♄. If the lord of the 10th be only in his own term, or triplicity, the judge will determine the cause, but he is indifferent about it. If a planet having no dignities, or not in reception with the lord of the 10th, be in the 10th, the parties will not be satisfied with that judge or court. If ♄ be judge, he will not decide aright; and if ♃, ♀, ☉, ☿, or ☽ be in any aspect to him but ☍, there will be an ill report against him, of which he will clear himself; but if it be ☍, he will have a hard report against him, which will long continue. And if ♂ ☍ to ♄, the judge will be sorely defamed; and if also ☉ □ ♄, he may be disgraced.

In deciding as to the result, observe well the lord of the 4th, and how he aspects the significators, or the lords of their substance; also the *application* of the ☽. If both significators aspect one planet, some person will intercede between them. If the ascendant and 7th be in fixed signs, both parties are resolutely bent on the suit; if common signs, they will continue it long also, and remove the cause out of one court into another; and if moveable signs, they are not very determined, and will soon bring it to an end.

That party who is weakest, and most afflicted by the infortunes, shall receive most prejudice by the contention.

Of making Purchases or Sales.

If ☽ be joined with the lord of the 7th, the querent may make the purchase. The lighter planet of the two houses

(1st and 7th) will be the occasion of the sale. Judge the nature of the commodity by the house by which it is governed; as the 4th for a house, the 12th for large cattle, the 9th for books, &c., the 10th for merchandize.

If infortunes be in the 7th, be cautious of the seller; he will try to trick the purchaser. The fourth house will shew the final result: but if ☽ be void of course, there may be many meetings, &c., but scarcely any bargain concluded.

Whether a City, Town, Castle, &c. besieged, shall be taken or not.

The ascendant and its lord are for the querent and for the besiegers; the 4th signifies the place besieged or to be besieged, and the lord of the 4th the governor; the 5th and planets therein the ammunition, soldiers, &c. in the place.

If you find the lord of the first strong and fortunate, or joined to the lord of the 4th in the ascendant, or with the ☽ or lord of the 10th, or any where but in the 6th, 8th, or 12th, and the lord of the 1st dispose of the lord of the 4th; or if ☽ dispose him, and be not disposed of by him, it is an argument that the place shall be taken. Or if the lord of the 4th be in such houses as behold not the 4th, and be with infortunes, and weak, it will be taken, and the governor may be wounded. If infortunes be in the 4th, without some strong aspect of the fortunes, it will be taken. If ☋ be in the 4th, it will be taken, and some parties will try to betray it, or some principal work or fort therein: the sign will shew which part of the town, &c. In this case the governor does not expect to preserve it.

If the lord of the 4th be in the 4th, strong and not afflicted, neither retrograde nor combust, nor besieged of the infortunes, or if the lord of the 7th be there, *free from all impediments*, or if ♃, ♀, or ☋ be therein, and no reception between the lords of the 1st and 4th, then shall not the city, &c. be taken; and if there be both a fortune and infortune in the 4th, it shall not be taken, if the fortune be the nearest to the cusp, or first transit that degree; and this more certainly, if the lord of the ascendant be weak or unfortunate, especially if a light planet. But if the lord of the ascendant be strong, or fortune therein, and the ☽ behold the cusp of the 4th, it shall be surprised or surrendered. An infortune in the 2d, or its lord, &c. afflicted, the querent lacks means to pursue the siege with vigour.

Of Commanders in Armies: and whether they shall be victorious or not.

If there be an infortune in the ascendant, it shews that the querent has no great justice on his part, or cause of quarrel. And if an infortune □ the ascendant, the party shewn by it (viz. that for which the querent asks) will not manage their affairs well or discreetly. If a good planet be in the ascendant, or aspect it by ✶ or △, it shews a good cause, and that it will be well managed.

An evil star in the 2d, and having no dignities therein, or aspecting its cusp by □ aspect, denotes that either there will be no war, or that the querent will gain nothing by it; a benefic testifies the reverse. If ♃ (or ♂ well dignified) be in the 3d, the querent's party will have good warlike stores, &c., and will consist of good, brave soldiers; but if ♂ be there, ill dignified, they will be bad characters, and ill disciplined.

If an infortune be in the 4th, the campaign will be held in a difficult country. If the sign describe a hilly country, it will offer obstacles by woods and bad roads; and if it shew a moist country, it will be unfit for military occupations, by reason of rivers, marshes, &c.; and so the army can do no good service.

If ♂ be in the 5th, well dignified, or a fortune aspect it, the army on the querent's side will be good soldiers, and well behaved; but ♄ there, or ☋, denotes the contrary.

If a fortune or ☊ be in the 6th, the ammunition train, artillery, &c. will be good; if ♂ be there, the horses will be fierce, wild and unbroken. If ♄ be there (without dignities), they will be unserviceable, slow, and worn out.

A fortune in the 7th, the arms and instruments of war will be plentiful and serviceable. If an infortune be there, or afflicting it by evil aspect, they will be the reverse. In the former case, the enemy will be brave and no fool, and will fight fair; in the latter case, the enemy will fight rather by craft and treachery, than fair manhood.

A fortune in the 8th, shews that there will not be many men slain on the querent's side; nor any very important battle be fought. If ♄ be there, there will be much plundering and destruction, and many prisoners be taken; also much death by sickness and want, &c. If ♂ be there, then expect much bloodshed.

A fortune in or aspecting the 9th, the enemy is well situated, and will strive to gain by false reports, alarms, &c.; he is politic. If an infortune, he will wear himself out by marching, and will be often deceived by false intelligence; and if a fortune be in the 3d at the same time, the querent's side will gain by this conduct of the enemy.

A fortune in the 10th, or aspecting its cusp by ✶ or △, shews that the commanding officer is expert and capable. But if ♄, ☋, or ♂, (unfortunate), be there, or afflict the 10th house by ◻, the commander on the querent's side will be extremely incapable and unworthy, and meet only disgrace.

A fortune or ☊ in the 11th, shews the officers are clever, and understand their duty, and will well support the commander; but an infortune, or ☋, the reverse.

If a fortune (or ♂ well dignified) be in the 12th, it denotes that the enemy is well prepared, and will defend themselves well. An infortune there, shews that they are weak and will disagree among themselves, and fear their own forces. If ☋ be in the 12th, the querent may expect treachery; and if the lord of the 12th be there, and have any dignities in the ascendant, the querent's side will suffer by desertion.

Whether the two Armies will Fight or not.

Observe the ascendant and its lord, the ☽ and lord of the 7th, if they be ☌ in any angle they will fight. If the lords of the 1st and 7th be not in ☌, but are in ☐ or ☍ from angles, they will engage; or if there be any planet which transfers the light of one to the other by ☐ or ☍, there will be a fight, if there be no reception between them. But if there be none of these, and the heavier planet receive the lighter, there will be no serious engagement.

Whether the Querent have any Adversaries or open Enemies.

If the question regard not any relation, take the 7th house for any open enemy, if any person be specially considered; but if it be simply as to enemies in general, look to the 12th house. If it be as to some individual enemy, see whether the lord of the 7th, or planet therein, throw a ☐ or ☍ to the lord of the ascendant, or ☽; this denotes that the quesited is envious or inimical. If the aspect apply, the enmity will increase; and if the enemy's significator dispose of the querent's without reception mutual, the querent will suffer by him: the manner how may be learned by the house he is in. If the aspect be past, the injury is done, and the enmity is dying away, unless the querent's significator, or ☽, be about to receive another ill aspect.

If the quesited's significator be placed in the 12th, or in any good aspect with any planet which is in ☐ or ☍ to the ☽, or lord of the ascendant, without reception, there is enmity to the querent.

If the question be general, the lord of the 12th and planets therein must be taken; and they shew private enemies to the querent, unless a benefic planet be in the 12th, and throw a ✶, or △, to the querent's significators. If there be many planets in the 7th, it shews many open enemies; and if in the 12th, many secret foes. The ☐ shews envy and malice, which may be reconciled; the ☍, if without reception, denotes irreconcilable enemies. If an evil planet in the 12th throw a good aspect to the querent's significator, it shews that there is some person who under pretence of friendship wishes to injure the querent. The same if the lord of the 11th be in the 12th. The house the lord of the 12th is in, will describe what person will injure the querent.

Fig. 14.

JUDGMENT ON THE FIGURE ABOVE.

State of the Querent's case.—A gentleman had been a long time an earnest suitor unto her for marriage; but she had continually slighted, and at last had given him a positive denial; after which she sorely repented her conduct, and wished she had her former opportunity. She was in this state when she propounded her question to me.

The ascendant and ☉ are for the querent; ♄, lord of the 7th, and ☽, are for the gentleman. The querent was moderately tall, of round face, sanguine complexion, grey eyes, light brown hair, occasioned by ☉, lord of the ascendant, being in the terms of ♂, and she was of cheerful modest countenance, comely, and well spoken.

Finding ♄, in the south angle, in ☌ with ♂ in ♉, a fixed, earthy sign, I judged the quesited to be of middle stature, not tall, nor handsome; a long face, not well composed; a wan, pale complexion; hair dark, or of a sad chesnut colour, curling and crisp; his eyes fixed, always down-looking, musing, stooping forward with his head, some impediment in his walking, as treading awry, &c. (*All this was confessed.*)

Finding ♄ so elevated, and in ☌ ♂, I judged that he was gloomy and angry, discontented, scorning his former slights, (as all saturnine people do); and I judged him much incensed by a relation, a gentleman of respectability, shewn by ♂, lord of *his* 3d and 10th, and that this gentleman and he lived either in one house, or near each other; this being shewn by the significator's being in his 4th angle and fixed; (*and so it was.*)

I said the gentleman had no inclination for her, as the ☽ was void of course, and applied to ☍ of ☉, lord of the ascendant, which shewed that she herself was her own enemy. She then confessed the truth, and implored my advice how, consistent with honour, she might, if possible, bring it on again; and she appearing in great distress, I began to consider what hopes she had in the figure. I found ☉ applying to ⚹ of ♄; this argued her desire and affection towards the quesited: but as there was no reception it gave little hopes. Finding reception between ♃ and ☽, and ☉ and ☽, and also that ☽ disposed of ♄ in her exaltation, and ♃ in her house, and that ♃ was very near a ⚹ of ♄, *applying*, and not separating; and also that ♃ was in his exaltation, he being a fortune, and ever assisting nature and the afflicted, and that he was able to take off the malice of ♄; I was confident, from the exactness of the aspect, that the quesited was intimately acquainted with a person of rank and worth, (such as ♃ represented), whom I exactly described, and the lady very well knew. I directed her to apply to him, and acquaint him with the full extent of her folly, and I assured her that in him she would find all honour and secrecy; and I doubted not but, by God's blessing, he would again revive the business, and bring her to her heart's content. But finding that ☉ and ♄ came to ✶ aspect on the 27th of the month, I advised to hasten all before that aspect was over; and as on the 19th of June ♄ and ♃ came to a ✶, I told her that the gentleman should first move the quesited on that day near noon. My counsel was followed, and by that gentleman's means the match was brought on again, and completed within twenty days, to the content of the sorrowful (but to me unthankful) lady, &c.

I acquainted this lady, that shortly before her lover had been offered a match, and that the lady was well descended, of good fortune, and described by ♀; but that she need not fear his marrying her, as some officer or gentleman, who had been in the army, shewn by ♂, would prevent that. She well knew both the parties, and confessed that such a matter had been.

Had the query been, *who should live longest?* I should have judged the female, because ☉ is going to ☌ ♃, and ♂ afflicts ♄.

If, whether the quesited were rich? I should say he had a good estate, as ♃, lord of his 2d, was direct, swift, and in his exaltation, &c.

If, would they agree? I should say they would, as ☉ and ♄ are applying to ✶; yet ♄ with ♂ shews a man who looks

232   INTRODUCTION TO ASTROLOGY.

to have authority, one choleric as well as melancholy, jealous without a cause, &c.; yet the ✶ of ♃ mitigates his ill manners by means of education.

If, will the querent be honest? I answer, her significator ☉ is no way afflicted by ♂; her ascendant is *fixed*, and there is reception between ♃ and ☽, which are arguments of a virtuous woman.*

In this manner you may examine any figure for discovery of what is necessary, &c.

* We should rely much on her significator ☉ being in ♂ with ♃.

Fig. 15.

Judgment on the above Question.

The querent was of tall stature, ruddy complexion, sober, discreet, and well spoken, &c. The quesited was very tall, slender, lean, and of a long visage, with black hair. His tallness I attribute to ♃ being in the terms of ☿, and the cusp of the 7th being also in his terms. Indeed, a significator being in the terms of any planet, does vary the party from his natural constitution; so that he will retain a tincture from that planet, according as he is dignified.* The darkness of his hair I attribute to the aspect of ♄ to ♃, and ☽ being in the term of ♃.

☿ is here the querent's significator; and being retrograde, and under the beams of ☉, shewed that she was in distress and fear that the quesited would not have her. And she had some reason for it; for ♃ was in his exaltation, and near the ✶ of ♀, an argument that the man stood upon high terms, and had been tampering with another: yet, as both significators were in *semi-sextile* aspect, and in good houses, I gathered hope that there were some mutual sparks of love. And when I found ☽ separating from □ of ♃, and hastening to △ of ☿, thus conveying the light of the quesited's significator to the lord of the ascendant, which he received willingly by his retrograde movement, I was confident that the match would be suddenly brought about by a person described by ☽; who did, indeed, though with a little difficulty, produce the marriage to the content of both parties.

* We should rather consider that ☿ in ♊ aspecting the cusp of the 7th; and the ☽, the *man's* general significator, being in ♎ and aspecting ♃, shewed his tallness. ♊ and ♎ are tall signs.

Fig. 16.

JUDGMENT UPON THE ABOVE FIGURE.

The ascendant, ☿ in ♒, and ♂ in ♊, taken together, signified and described the querent, (the servant's master). He was short of stature, corpulent, of good complexion, and ruddy, fresh colour. His fatness I attribute to the north latitude of ☿, which was one degree; also the ascendant was in the terms of ♂, and face of ☉, who was in partile △ to ☽ in a moist sign, which shews a full body, and phlegmatic.

The servant was shewn by ♂ (lord of the 6th) and ♏.

He was a well-set short fellow, large joints, broad and full face, dark brown hair, his teeth irregular, complexion obscure and sunburnt, yet his skin clear; his age about nineteen.

I observed that he went away from his master the preceding Sunday, when ☾ was in ♊, a western sign, where ♂ now was; and that ☿, the common significator of servants, was in ♒, a western sign, but south quarter of heaven.

I judged, therefore, that he went westward at first, and that at the time of the question he was west from the querent's house; and this I judged, because ♂ was angular, otherwise I should have judged by ☾. As ♂ and ☿, lord of the ascendant, were hastening to a △ out of angles, I judged that in a day or two he should have his servant again.

Upon the Friday following he came home, and said he had been at Kingston upon Thames; which, if true, he was nearly west, but a little south; and near a great water, (viz. the Thames), as the ☾ in ♋ might signify.

Fig. 17.

JUDGMENT UPON THE ABOVE FIGURE.

The queries to me were, *What part of the city they should search?* and, *should he be found?*

The querent was described by the sign ascending, and *Cauda* (☋) therein; and, indeed, he was *saturnine*, and vitiated both in body and mind; that is, he was a little deformed in body, of small stature, and extremely covetous in disposition, &c. The sign of the 6th signifies a dog, as it would have done a sheep, hog, &c., or any small cattle.

The sign ♊ is west and by south, the quarter of heaven westerly; ☿, the dog's significator, is in ♎, a western sign, and is in a south-western quarter of heaven; the ☽ is in ♍, a south-west sign, verging to the west angle. The plurality of testimonies shewed that the dog ought to be *west* from where the owner lived, which was at Temple-bar; therefore I judged that the dog was about Long Acre, or upper part of Drury Lane. As ☿ was in a sign of the same triplicity with ♊, which signifies London, and applied to △ of the cusp of the 6th, I judged that the dog was not out of the lines of communication, but in the same quarter; of which I was more satisfied by the △ of ☉ to ♄. ☿ being in an airy sign, I said the dog was in some garret or upper room; and, as ☽ was under the beams of ☉, and ☿, ☽, and ☉ were in the 8th house, that he was kept privately, or in great secrecy. But as ☉, on the following Monday, formed a △ to ♄, lord of the ascendant, and ☽ formed a △ to ♂, who has dignities in the ascendant, I intimated that he should then have news of his dog; and this proved true; for a gentleman of the querent's acquaintance, coming accidentally to see a friend in Long Acre, found the dog chained up under a table, and knowing him to belong to the querent, sent him home about ten o'clock on the Monday morning, to my very great credit.

Usually I find that all fugitives go by the ☽; and as she varies her sign, they waver and shift their flight, declining more to east, west, north, or south. But you must judge by the significator or the ☽, according to which is strongest; or if both be equally strong, take that which best describes the fugitive, with regard also to that one which is nearest in aspect to the cusp of the house from whence signification is taken. That is, if the fugitive be a servant or small animal, the 6th; if a large animal, the 12th; if a son or daughter, the 5th; and if a wife, the 7th, &c.

INTRODUCTION TO ASTROLOGY.

Fig. 18.

JUDGMENT ON THE ABOVE FIGURE.

Here ♏ ascends, and partly describes the querent's person; ♂, his mind and disposition; ♂ in □ to ☿ and ♄, shewed him ill-conditioned, arrogant, proud, wasteful, &c. As ♂ is in 25° 2' of ♌, he has entered his own *terms*, and is in his own *face*, I therefore refused him for the thief's significator. In the next place, ♄, though in the west angle, (the house of theft), is in his own *term* and *face;* I also passed him by. But finding ☿ in an angle, having no essential dignity, and in partile ☌ of ♄, and □ of ♂, I took him to signify the thief. But whether he described a male or female was the question. The angles are part masculine, part feminine; no certain judgment could, therefore, be formed from thence. The ☽ was in a masculine sign, applying to a masculine planet, (♂), and ☿ was in ♂ with ♄, and □ to ♂, both masculine planets; I judged, therefore, that the sex was male.

As ☿ ever signifies youth, and as ☽ was so near the ☉, separating, I said he was a youth, of some 15 or 16. I described him of reasonable stature, thin visaged, hanging eyebrows, with some scar or blemish in his face, because ♂ casts his □ to ☿; bad eyesight, as ☿ is with evil fixed stars, *(the Pleiades,)* of the nature of ♂ and ☽; dark hair, because of his closeness to ♄; a scurvy countenance, and one formerly accused of theft and knavery.

The youth's significator being in ♂ with ♄, lord of the 3d and 4th houses, I judged him the child of some neighbour; and as ☽ is in ♊, and ☿ in ♉ in the 7th, I said he dwelt either opposite to the querent, or a little south-west. The ⊕ being in the ascendant, and disposed of by ♂, lord of the ascendant in the 10th, and as ☽ applied to his ✶, and was within about four degrees of the aspect, I judged he should not only hear of, but have his money again within four days. He believed not one word I said, but would need persuade me that a woman servant, shewn by ♂, was one thief, and ♄ another; but I stood firm to the art, and would not consent to this, as both ♄ and ♂ were essentially dignified. The event proved me right, both as to the person and the return of the money, which was within three days after.

Fig. 19.

EXPLANATION OF THE ABOVE FIGURE.

Living in the country in 1637, I had bought at London some fish for my provision in Lent; it came down by the barge to Walton. On Saturday, the 10th February, one of the watermen, instead of bringing my fish home, acquainted me that their warehouse was robbed last night, and my fish stolen. I took the exact time I first heard the report, and erected this figure accordingly; endeavouring to give myself satisfaction as to what became of my goods, and, if possible, to recover part or all of them.

Judgment.

I first observed that there was no peregrine planet in an angle but ♃, whom I found on the cusp of the 7th house. I considered the signification of ♃ in ♏ a moist sign, and the significator of my goods, ☿ in ♓, a moist sign; and that ⊕ was in ♋, a moist sign. Discretion, together with art, led me to think he who had my goods must be a person whose profession, or calling, was to live upon the water; and that they were in some low room, in a moist place, because ⊕ was in ♋, and ☽ was in ♉, an earthy sign, and under the earth.

I was confident I should hear of my goods again, as ☿, lord of the 2d, was applied to by ⚹ of ☽, who was lady of ⊕, and yet without hope of recovering them, as ☿ was in his fall, and detriment; but as he was in his own terms, and had a △ to ⊕, there were hopes of regaining some of my goods.

There being no waterman in Walton described by ♃ in ♏, I examined what fisherman there was of that complexion; and as ♂, lord of the 7th, was leaving ♏, his own sign, and entering another, I inquired if any fisherman of the nature of ♂ and ♃ had lately sold any land, or was leaving his own house and going to another; such a one I discovered, who lived near the Thames side, a mere fisherman, but a jovial fellow, though much suspected of thievery. He was of good stature, thick, and full-bodied, fair complexion, and red or yellowish hair.

I procured a warrant from a justice of peace, and reserved it privately until Sunday, the 18th of the month; and then, with a constable and the bargeman, I searched only that one house of the suspected fisherman. I found part of my fish in water, part eaten, part not consumed; all confessed. I asked the woman for seven *Portugal onions* which I had lost also; but she, not knowing what they were, had made pottage with them. I freely remitted the remainder of my fish, though the hireling priest of Walton affirmed that I had satisfaction for it. But he never hurt himself with a lie.

Thus you see, that the peregrine planet in an angle describes the thief; and that either ☉ or ☽ in the ascendant gives assured hopes of discovering who it was. The ☽ applying to the lord of the 2d, argues recovery; if they both be essentially dignified, *complete;* but if accidentally fortified, *partial.* If both be peregrine, and they apply, there will be a discovery, but no recovery.

Fig. 20.

A Figure erected to know whether Sir WILLIAM WALLER *or Sir* RALPH HOPTON *should overcome; they being supposed to be engaged near Alsford* ♀ *29th March*, 1644.

JUDGMENT ON THE ABOVE FIGURE.

The ascendant is for our army, the ☽, ♃, and ♀, for our generals, viz. Sir William Waller, and Major-General Browne, a valiant and prudent citizen of London, who may justly claim a large share of honour in that day's service. Sir Ralph Hopton is signified by ♄, lord of the 7th; his army by ♑ in the descending part of heaven which is usually given to the friends and assistants of the enemy. There are only ♂ and ☳ in the 9th; so it appears that Sir Ralph had no supplies ready to attend that day's success, &c. From the ☽, having principal signification of us and our army, being in her exaltation with ♃, I concluded all was and would be well on our side, and that the victory would be ours. From her separation from ♃, I said, I verily conceived that we had already taken some ammunition from them, or performed some service against them. This I was confirmed in by ☉, lord of our substance and assistants, being posited in the 10th house, in the very degree of his exaltation; (the 19th). And though I thought by the proximity of ♄ to ☉ we should not gain the whole, or have a perfect victory, without diminution of some part of it; yet I was confident we should obtain a considerable proportion of their ammunition, and have a victory, the only thing inquired after; for the ☽ applied to ♀, and then to a ✶ of ☿, he being angular. I told the *querent* that within eleven or twelve hours after the question we should have perfect news, and it satisfactory. For, considering that the fight was within fifty miles of London, I ordered my time with discretion, not allowing days for the time, but *hours;* and this because ☽ is distant from ♀ 11°, but is withal swift in motion, and increasing in light. These were also signs of our success, and the enemies' defeat. It appeared, by a letter from the army on that same Friday, that our generals took on the previous day 120 commanders and gentlemen, 560 common soldiers, and much ammunition. Thus the enemy was worsted, as appeared by ♄, (the Lord Hopton's significator), being *sub radiis*, in his fall in no aspect to any planet, wholly peregrine, and unfortunate, and aspecting the cusp of the 7th by □. All this argued that he would bring loss to his army, and dishonour to himself by the fight, &c.

INTRODUCTION TO ASTROLOGY. 245

Fig. 21.

QUESTION.—*Whether his Excellency* ROBERT *Earl of* ESSEX *should take* READING, *having then surrounded it with his Army ?*

JUDGMENT ON THE ABOVE FIGURE.

The General Essex is here shewn by ♂, lord of ♏, and his Majesty by ☉, lord of the 10th, the forces that were to relieve Reading by ♀ in ♓, and ☉ in ♉ ; also the town by ♒, the sign on the 4th ; the governor, Sir Arthur Acton, (reputed an able soldier), by the lord of the 4th, ♄ ; and their ammunition and provision by ♃, lord of the 5th, and by ♀ located therein.

The significator of his Excellency ♂ is well fortified, and afflicted in no way but by being in his fall. This figure manifests that it is of great importance in questions of warfare to have ♂ friendly to the querent. The ☽ separated from *nothing*, and was void of course; and, indeed, there was little hope of its being gained in the time it was. She applied to ✶ of ♂ from signs of long ascension, which was equivalent to a ☐; which argued that his Excellency would have much difficulty and some fighting ere he could get it. But as ♂ and ☽ were in reception, viz. ♂ in her house, and she in his terms and face, and near *Cor* ♌, and in the house of honour, I judged that his Excellency would obtain and take Reading, and gain honour thereby. Finding ☉, his Majesty's significator, in the 7th in a fixed sign, I said that he would send forces to relieve the town, and oppose all he could; but that he would not prevail, as ♂ was better fortified than ☉. The King did come in person, and was beaten back at Causham Bridge.

Finding that ♒ was not afflicted, I judged the town strong, and able to hold out; and ♀ being in the 5th, that they wanted not ammunition. Having well weighed all things, and that ♄, lord of the 4th, signifying the Governor, was in his fall with ♉, and that ☿ and ♃ were not far from ♉, I said, (and sent somebody word), that the most certain way, and which would assuredly occasion the surrender of the town, was to set division among the principal officers, and incense them against their chief officer, and that about eight days from the time of the question his Excellency would be master of the town; yet rather by composition than by blood. This because ☉ and ♂ were separated from their ✶ aspect, and ♂ was also separated from the ☐ of ♄; as also because the ☽ applied so directly to ✶ of the lord of the ascendant, without any frustration, &c.

INTRODUCTION TO ASTROLOGY. 247

The town was delivered for the Parliament's use on the 27th April, three days after the time I said; but it is observable that they began to treat on the very Monday before, just eight days after the figure was set.

The Governor was hurt in the head, as ♄ in ♈ with ☍ shews; nor did they want provisions, &c., as ♀ in the 5th signifies.*

Fig. 22.

* The well-known instance of a military siege, the capture of the Castle of Antwerp, being so applicable to this question, and the time of its commencement by the opening of the trenches being so well authenticated, we are induced to offer to the student's notice a figure we erected for that time.

JUDGMENT ON THE PRECEDING FIGURE.

This figure is erected for the latitude and longitude of Antwerp, and is an exact representation of the heavens at the time the French troops opened ground, (or began the siege), before the citadel of Antwerp. By it the student will perceive that the rules laid down by our author, being founded in truth and nature, are infallible; and that they hold equally true in the 19th as they did in the 17th century. They must eventually put the sceptic to silence, and convince the world of the truth of planetary influence.

The ascendant and its lady, the ☽, are for the besiegers, the 7th and its lord for the besieged, the 4th is for the town, and its lord for the governor. The 10th is the house of honour for the besiegers, and we find ♃ potent therein, denoting decidedly that they should gain honour by the siege. The ☊ in the ascendant shewed success to the French, and ☋ in the 7th the reverse to their enemies. The lord of the 4th, ☿, is in his detriment, cadent, and in exact □ to the evil ♄, denoting disgrace to the governor, who is thereby shewn to be extremely obstinate, as, indeed, he was. The malefic in the 4th denoted that the place should be taken, and, as ☽ was in close □ to ♂, it would be by much loss of men and bloodshed on the part of the besiegers. The ☽ is in the *terms* of ♂, and he in her *exaltation* and *triplicity*, which reception denotes courageous conduct on the part of the besiegers; and although the ☽ is in □ to ♂, yet, there being mutual reception, it shews success in a martial exploit; but with much difficulty, because of the □ aspect. The garrison were denoted by the 5th, and its ruler ♀; and as ♀ is in the 6th, (the 12th from the enemies' ascendant), it shewed that all the enemies' party would be made prisoners, which was the case.

The citadel capitulated when a breach had been effected; and they surrendered to the French on the 23d December following; when the ☽, the besiegers' significator, crossed the cusp of the 7th house; thus entering the 7th just as the besiegers entered the place itself. It deserves notice that on the day ☿ fell retrograde, and ☽ crossed the cusp of the 5th (Dec. 15th), the besiegers carried the horn work.

The student will observe, that the lord of the 7th was peregrine, having no essential dignity whatever; and that the ☽, besides her aspect and her mutual reception with ♂, the chief significator of warfare, is in her own face, and disposes of ♄ by triplicity. Hence the besiegers are decidedly the strongest party, and should, by the rules of the science, certainly prevail.

The student may rely that the figure of the heavens at the first moment of commencing any enterprise whatever, will infallibly point out, to those who really understand astrology, its final result.

CHAPTER XXXI.

OF THE EIGHTH HOUSE, AND ITS QUESTIONS:

THESE ARE DEATH, DOWRY, THE WIFE'S SUBSTANCE, &c.

QUERY.—*Whether an absent Person be dead or alive?*

Take care to learn whether the *quesited* be any relation to the *querent*: if so, look to the house signifying that relation; and if not, look to the 7th for the quesited's significator. If the lord of the quesited's ascendant be in the 4th or the 8th, either from his own house or in the figure, it is one argument that the party is dead. If, also, his significator be in the

12th, or his own 12th in □ or ☍ to a malefic, or if ☽ or ☉ be unfortunate in like way, you have strong testimony that he is deceased.

If the significator of the absent be strong, and in a good house, and separated from a fortune, he is not dead. If he be afflicted, and was lately in ☍ or □ of an evil planet, I judge that he has been in trouble or misfortune, according to the nature of the house from whence afflicted; but not dead, unless the lord of the 8th afflict him also, and the lights be afflicted.

Of the Death of the Querent?

If any one ask concerning the probable length of his life, or when he may probably die, observe the ascendant, its lord, and ☽; also, the lord of the 8th, an unfortunate planet in the 8th, and that planet to whom the lord of the 1st or ☽ be joined by ☌, □, or ☍; and you may determine the death of the querent, according to the number of degrees between the significator and the aspect of the afflicting planet. If the lord of the ascendant be in ☌ with the lord of the 8th in an angle, it notes so many years; for in this question angles do not accelerate death, but show that life and nature are strong. If in a succeedent house, months; though if the sign be *fixed*, it gives half years, half months. In a cadent house, weeks. But you must always consider whether the significators are extremely afflicted; if not, the querent may live longer, and only be *near* death at the time threatened. The lord of the ascendant is more to be considered in this case than the ☽; and, therefore, his ☌ with the lord of the 8th or ☉ is to be most feared.

Observe that the ☽ being strong even, yet if the lord of the ascendant be afflicted extremely, she does not denote health or life, but only success in his affairs, &c. Aspects by separation are not to be considered, but only those by application.*

What manner of Death the Querent shall die?

This judgment is chiefly shewn by the lord of the 8th, if in the 8th, or any planet therein or nearest to its cusp, and having dignities in the 8th house; or from the planet which afflicts the lord of the ascendant, and has dignities in the 8th. If it be either ♃ or ♀, or that they be in the 8th house, or aspect its cusp by ✶ or △, they shew a natural death by such diseases as they shew in the sign they are in, and the part of man's body it governs. If evil planets be there, they shew violent deaths, or fevers, and long and painful illnesses; and if the figure be violent, it may be by accidents, &c. The ☋ with the significator of death is very evil; and if it be ♄, (and ♀ assist by her □, &c.), it shews fear of poison. The lord of the 1st and 8th being the same planet, shews that the querent brings on his own death by imprudence, &c.

Whether the Wife's Fortune will be great, or easily obtained, or whether the Person inquired of be rich or not?

The cusp of the 8th, in terms of ♃ or ♀, gives good hopes of wealth, or if ♃ or ♀ be therein. If they be essentially strong, and free from combustion, &c., they denote much wealth; but though well dignified, if they be combust, slow, or retrograde, they shew trouble in procuring the fortune, &c. The lord of the 8th in the 8th, and strong, and no way afflicted, gives good hopes of some estate or legacy to fall to the quesited; this is more sure if either the lord of

---

* If the fatal ☌ or aspect fall in the term of ♃ or ♀, or exactly in their ✶ or △, there is much less fear of death.

the 4th or 10th be in good aspect with the lord of the 8th from angles. If ⊕ be in the 8th, and in ♌, or ♒, or any of the houses of ♃ or ♀, or they in good aspect to ⊕, the quesited's fortune is good. The dispositor of ⊕ in good aspect to it, or ♃ and ♀, shew the same thing. If all these happen, the quesited is very rich.

If ♄ or ♂ be in the 8th and peregrine, the party is poor, or there will be contention about the property. The lord of the 8th combust, shews slow performance, and little ability of what is promised; and if ☋ be in the 8th, and no planet there, fraud is intended, or more will be promised than can be performed.

The lord of the 8th in the 2d, or in ✶ or △ to its lord, the querent shall have what is promised; in ☐, with difficulty; in ☍, with much wrangling; if without reception, never. But weigh well what the particular figure promises besides these general rules.

Whether the Querent shall suffer by a particular Thing of which he is in fear?

If you find the ☽ afflicted, or the lord of the ascendant unfortunate and falling from an angle, or especially if he be in the 12th, and the ☽ with him, there is ground for his fear; and he may expect to be accused, &c. of much of which he is not guilty. If the lord of the 1st ascends into the 11th or 10th, or be joined to a fortune, he shall not be injured. If he apply to infortunes, the thing threatened is true; but if to a fortune, and not at the same time to an infortune, it is false or ungrounded. The ☽ in △ to ☉ discovers all suddenly. The ☽ cadent, and applying to a cadent planet, the supposed danger will be nothing, or come to nothing in the end.

Fig. 23.

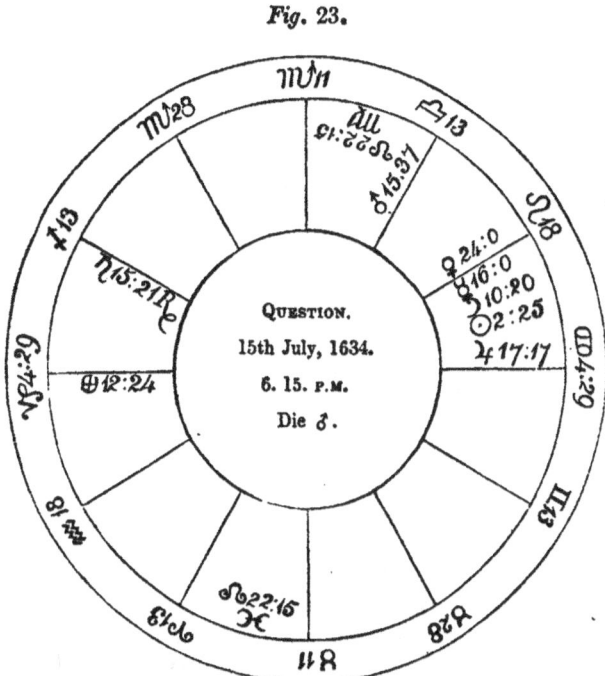

QUESTION.—SHALL THE QUERENT RECEIVE THE PORTION PROMISED?

Judgment.—The querent's significator retrograde in the 12th, shewed he had been in despair of it, which he confessed. The female is signified by ♃ and ☽; ♃ in his exaltation, and ☽ in ♌, a fixed sign, argue that she thinks well of herself, is confident, &c., yet modest and virtuous. The ☽ being near ☉, she had a scar near her right eye.

Finding ☉ lord of the quesited's 2d in his own house, and

♀ in her 2d, and also that ☽ separated from ☉, and transferring his light to ♄, lord of the ascendant and 2d and ⊕, I assured the querent that he had no cause to fear the non-payment of his wife's portion; that all promised would be paid; and that, to his farther comfort, she would prove a chaste and virtuous woman, but somewhat proud. I have since heard, from his own mouth, that this judgment proved exactly true.

CHAPTER XXXII.

OF THE NINTH HOUSE AND ITS QUESTIONS. LONG JOURNEYS, VOYAGES, ARTS, SCIENCE, CHURCH PREFERMENT, LAW, &c.

Of a Voyage, and its Issue.

If there be good planets in the 9th, or its cusp be well aspected, or the lord of the ascendant or 10th be there, and well affected, it is good. But if ♅, ♄, ♂, or ☋ be there, it is always evil. If the lord of the 9th be with an evil planet, he shall not speed well. ♄ shews losses and sickness; ♂ shews danger by thieves or pirates: and ☋ much the same as ♂, but more of cozening and cheating. The house of substance from the 9th is the 10th. Fortunes there shew wealth; infortunes loss. If benefics be in the 9th, a good voyage; if malefics, many hardships, &c.

What Wind and Weather the Querent will experience.

The lord of the ascendant with good planets, and they strong and in friendly aspect, and the lords of the 1st and 9th in △ out of ♊, ♎, or ♒, shew fair weather and favourable winds. The significators in ☍, out of fixed signs, shew detention by foul winds; and if near violent fixed stars, storms and contrary winds will drive him back.

Of a long Journey, and its Issue.

If a fortune be in the ascendant, say he will have good success before he sets out, or in the commencement of his journey; if it be in the 10th, then he will have success on the journey; if in the 7th, at the place to which he goes; and if in the 4th, it will be on his return, and when he is come home. In this case ♃ gives benefits by clerical persons, judges, magistrates, or gentlemen, according to the querent's situation in life and the house ♃ rules, and the nature of the ruler of ♃. As if it be ☉, by a king, or nobleman, or person in power; if ♄, it will be by old people, or ancient matters, or farmers, &c. Let him apply to such a person in his affairs as ♄ describes, according to the sign he is in and the aspects he receives. If it be ♀, it will be by women, pleasure, sport, &c.; or by dealing in linen, silks, jewels, spices, &c. If ☿, by writing or merchandize, letters of introduction, &c. If ☽, by some female, probably a widow, or by a sailor, or by carrying news, &c., or by play.

Of the Length of the Journey, &c.

The lord of the 9th, or planet therein, or ☽ in moveable signs, swift and oriental, shew a short time absent. If they be in fixed signs, slow and occidental, it shews a long and tedious journey and absence. If they be in common signs, they shew change of mind, and a varying of his journey, going to other places, &c. According as the ☽ is assisted or afflicted, judge results to happen. As, for example, if ☽ be in the 6th, or in ☍ to its lord, it shews sickness or impediments from servants. The lord of the 4th, and the 4th house, denote the final issue.

Of the Return, &c., of a Person who is gone a long Journey.

The lord of the ascendant in the ascendant or midheaven, or aspected by planets therein, shows that he is thinking of returning. But if he be in the 7th or 4th, his return is prolonged; and he is not thinking of leaving the place he went to. The lord of the ascendant in the 3d or 9th, applying to a planet in the ascendant, he is on his journey homeward. The same may be judged if he be in the 8th or 2d, and apply to a planet in the 10th; but in this case observe also the ☽, and whether she aspect the ascendant, or a planet therein. If the lord of the ascendant or ☽ apply to a retrograde planet, or the lord of the ascendant be himself a retrograde, and behold the ascendant, he is coming; but if his significator be afflicted, it shews some hinderance which makes him tarry. The dispositor of the ☽ afflicted, shews hinderance also.

If you find ☿ or the ☽ in the ascendant or midheaven, judge that letters or some news shall come shortly from the party; for ☿ is the significator of letters, and the ☽ of news. If they separate from a fortune, it denotes good news; and if from an infortune, the contrary.

The planet from whom the lord of the ascendant of the quesited is separated, is the significator of the state and condition in which he lately was; the planet to whom he applies, of the state in which he now is; and the planet to whom he afterwards applies is the significator of him to whom he intends to come.

If the quesited's significator be going out of one sign into another, judge that he went out of the place he was in, and entered another, or that he has undertaken another journey. Observe in which of those signs he was stronger, better aspected and received, &c.; and so judge of his corresponding condition.

Observe, that combustion in all questions of one absent,

shews some great evil; such as imprisonment, &c.; and if it be in the house of death, or ☉ be lord of the house of death, it generally denotes death.

Ever consider for whom the question is asked, and take his proper significator. The lord of the 7th for a husband (or for any one who is no relation), the lord of the 3d a brother, 5th a son, &c.; and note how the fortunes are placed; if strong in the figure, well aspecting the significator of the quesited, or in his house, judge health and prosperity; and the reverse by infortunes.

OF PROFIT BY, OR PROFICIENCY IN, ANY SCIENCE, &C.

The ascendant, its lord, and the ☽, are for the querent; and the 9th, its lord, or planet therein (if more than one, the nearest to the cusp), for the science.

See whether the lord of the 9th be fortunate or not, oriental, angular, &c.; and whether he behold the lord of the ascendant with ✶ or △. If he be a fortune, and aspect the lord of the ascendant, the man has scientific knowledge, and will gain thereby; the more so if there be reception. If the aspect be □ or ☍, the man has talent, but shall do no good by it. If an infortune aspect either the lord of the ascendant or 9th, the man has wearied himself, but to no purpose, for he will never attain the knowledge he desires. If infortunes be in the 9th, or its lord afflicted, the party has but little scientific knowledge.

The ☽ must also be observed with the lord of the 9th; for if they both apply to fortunes, the man is scientific; if to infortunes, the contrary.

If the question be put regarding another person, you must in this case give the ascendant for the quesited.*

* We do not agree with our author on this point; for unless the quesited has given his *consent* to the question, we think he should have the same significators as in any other question; the 7th, 5th, 3d, &c.

258 INTRODUCTION TO ASTROLOGY.

EXAMPLE.

The author having given no good example regarding this question, the reader is here presented with a figure, which will no doubt prove interesting.

The editor being in company with two other artists, a general desire was expressed to know the future destiny of astrology, and the following figure was erected.

Fig. 24.

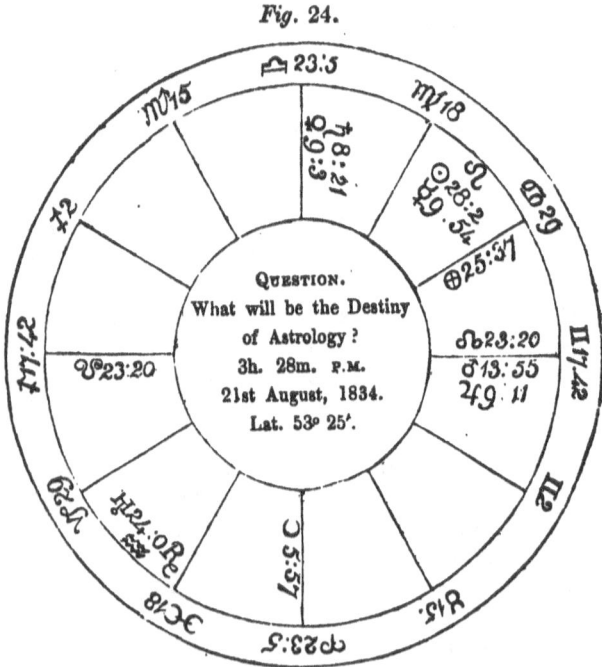

JUDGMENT ON THE ABOVE FIGURE.

The first thing to be observed in this figure is that ☿, the natural significator of science, is lord of the 9th, and is, therefore, the significator of the science of astrology. He is found cadent, and almost peregrine, having no essential dignity but his term, by which may be seen the present enfeebled state of the science; but as ☿ has passed through four degrees of his term in a *fixed* sign, this points out, that for four years it has been in some measure more in credit than previously. And this is the case, as it is about four years since the Editor's publications began to call attention to the science. And as ☿ has just passed a ✶ of ♃, who describes the person asking the question, it is shewn that the science has been much benefited by such a person, about nine months before, because ☿ is past the ✶ of ♃ by 43', which shews about nine months, taking a degree for a year. And the fact is, that the *Grammar of Astrology* was published about nine months before the time of the question.

The ☋ in the ascendant shews the difficulties the Editor has had to encounter, and the contumely he has had to meet in bringing the science forward again.

The presence of ♄ in the 9th, denotes the discredit in which the science is generally held; and being in ☌ with ♀, it shews that injury has been done to it by elderly females, who pretend to practise divining, &c., but who are held in great contempt by the public, as may be seen by the ☽ (the general significator of the public) being in ☍ to both ♀ and ♄, from the house of enemies to the science.

The next aspect formed by ☿, is the ✶ of ♂, who being lord of the 11th house of the figure, and placed on the cusp of the 11th from the ninth, denotes *friends*. This shews, that in about four years from the time of the question, the science will gain many friends among persons denoted by ♂ in ♊, such as writers of public spirit, booksellers, &c.; and there is no doubt that about that time it will suddenly and rapidly gain ground in public opinion. The next aspect formed by ☿, is the ☍ of ♅, from which he is distant 14°; this may shew that some *sudden* mischief may be done to the interests of the science by means of female agents, as ♀ is in exact sesquiquadrate aspect to ♅. But as ♅ is retrograde, and not angular, this will not be very important. The ☉ is in the 12th from the 9th, and denotes secret enmity to the science by men in power, the ☉ being in ♌; and as he disposes of ☿, it shews that the hand of power at present keeps it down. As ☿ is 18° from ☉, I judge that, about the year 1852, some important honour will be done to the science; probably by the present penal laws being repealed, which forbid the acceptance of any remuneration for practising it. As ☿ has 20° to pass before he reaches ♍, his own dignities, and as ♄ will then have entered ♊, and be disposed of by ☿, I judge that about 20 years hence the science will be publicly honoured; and as ☿ has afterwards 18° to pass in a common sign (signifying months), I conceive that about 18 months after that, when ☿ crosses the cusp of the 9th house in this figure (about the year 1856), the science will rapidly rise in public estimation, and be publicly studied in colleges, &c.

The ☉ enters ♍ after two years, as he is two degrees off, which will cause the ruling powers to relax something of their severity against the science; and as he then has 18°, (equal to 18 months, being in a common sign,) to go before he passes the cusp, there will be some person of rank who will assist the science at that time; viz. three years and a half from the time of the question, or the year 1838.

The ☽ must now be considered; she is hastening to ☍ of two planets in the 9th, which shews that there is yet much opposition to be expected to the science by the public, and especially by rash and violent people, which ☽ in the house of ♂ always denotes. But after the influence of the ☍ of ♄

and ♀ is passed away, the ☽ meets nothing but favourable aspects. It is very remarkable that the ☽ is aspected by every one of the planets before she passes through ♈. The first aspect she forms after ☍ of ♄ and ♀ is ⚹ of ♃, which denotes popularity for the works of the Editor, connected with the science. The next is △ of ☿, which shews an increase of students, and public discussion. The next is ⚹ of ♂, denoting increase of powerful friends, who will boldly advocate the cause of the science. The ⚹ of ♅ is of little import; but the △ of ☉ being the last aspect she forms before leaving the sign, decidedly shews that at last the science will receive the highest patronage, and be publicly honoured; and as ☉ is in ♌, a fixed sign, this will be permanent. Finally, the cusp of the 4th is in the term as well as house of ♂, and is ruled by ☉, by triplicity, and face; and ☉ casts a △ thereto; ♂, lord of the 4th, is in ☌ with ♃, in ⚹ to ☿ and ☽, and △ to ♄ and ♀; and he rules the ☽ by house and face, and the ☉ by face. All these are decided testimonies, that in the end the cause of truth shall triumph, and the reality and utility of the science be permanently established. ☿ in a fixed sign, and so powerfully aspected by ♄, ♃, ♂, (lord of the 4th, the house denoting the end of the matter) ♀ and ☽, is another strong evidence that AS-TROLOGY IS DESTINED TO FLOURISH WHILE THE WORLD ENDURES!

N.B. It is remarkable that ☿ had just passed the ⚹ of ♀, lady of the 2d (or house of property), from the 9th, and lady also of the 10th in the figure, and 9th (house of law) from the 9th. This shewed the benefit resulting to astrology, by the repeal of the law which taxed Almanacs, and which greatly injured the science. It is also remarkable, that ♃ was exactly passing over the 2d degree of ♊, the cusp of the 10th (house of honour) from the 9th, about the 7th

262   INTRODUCTION TO ASTROLOGY.

February, 1835, when the last sheet of the former edition of this work went through the press; and at the same time ♄ was in ♎ 23° 6′, having just quitted the 9th house, where he had injured the interests of the science.

Fig. 25.

A WOMAN ASKS OF HER HUSBAND, WHO IS AT SEA;
IF ALIVE? WHEN RETURN?

Judgment. — The lord of the ascendant, ☿, shews the querent. He being with ☽ and ♄ in ♈, which rules the face, she was extremely disfigured in the face by small pock, had weak eyes, &c., and was full of grief and sorrow for her husband, occasioned by ♄ afflicting ☿. She had also a lisp, and spoke ill; for ♄ in a bestial sign afflicting ☿, causes impediments in speech, especially if also ☽ be afflicted.

♃ signified the quesited, who being in the 10th, and lately separated from ⚹ of ♀, now in the 9th, and lady of the 3d, it shewed that he had been lately some voyage south-east. And as ♃ was no way afflicted and swift in motion, as well as angular, I judged the man was alive and in health. But as ☿ who disposes of ♃, is lord of his 8th (viz. the 2d house), and as ☽ is so exceedingly afflicted by ☿ and ♄, I said he had been in much danger and peril of his life by treachery and plots of his adversaries; for ☿ is lord of the 7th from his ascendant, and ♄ of his 12th.

Moreover, ♃ is accidentally but not essentially fortified, and is in his detriment, and near *Oculus* ♉, a violent fixed star; intimating that the man had endured many sudden and violent chances.

Finding ♃ more fortified than ☽, she almost entering ♉, a southern sign, and ♃ in ♊, a western sign, and south quarter, I judged that the quesited was in the south-west of England, in some harbour, as ♃ was angular.

When She should hear of Him, or see Him?

The ☽ separates from ♄, and applies to ☿, the querent's significator; shewing that after much expectation, &c., she should hear of him, and in about three days, as ☽ is so near ☿, and in a moveable sign, (*and so she did*). But as ☿ is in a moveable sign, and ☽ afflicted by him and ♄, the news she heard was false, for she heard that he was in town; but it was not so. Considering that ☿ and ♃ hastened to a ☌ in ♊, ☿ being therein very potent, and that this was about the 5th May following, I judged that she would about that time have certain news of her husband, if he did not then come home. The second week in May she did hear from him, but he did not come home till July. He had been several voyages in the west, was taken prisoner by the king's forces, and, at the time of the question, was in Barnstaple.

Fig. 26.

QUESTION.—WHETHER PRESBYTERY SHALL STAND?

Judgment.—The angles of the figure are not fixed, but the cusp of the 9th, from which this judgment is to be deduced, is ♉, a fixed and stable sign; and we must also judge from

♄ therein in the terms of ♃, who is the general significator of religious matters. ♃ is now stationary, and is leaving his exaltation, and is impeded by ♂; after leaving ♋, he enters the fixed sign ♌, and is in the terms of ♄. We find ♀, who rules the 9th, in her detriment, and in the 12th house from her own, the 9th. She has twenty-one degrees to pass through in the 8th house before she get into her own sign ♉, and where she would be fixed. But before she reaches ♉, she meets the □ of ♃, (shewing that the gentry of England will oppose it), and then of ♂, (lord of the ascendant of England, ♈), hence the whole commonalty of the kingdom will disapprove of it), and all three planets at the time of the aspect in the term of ♄.

There is not a single planet fixed, except ♄, nor essentially dignified, except ♃; the ☽ entering *via combusta*, ♂ and ☿ in their fall, ♀ in her detriment, and ♃ impeded by ♂. The ☽ separates from ♀ in the 8th, and then goes to □ of ♂ and ♃. From these configurations we shall form our judgment, THAT POSTERITY MAY SEE THAT THERE IS SOME VERITY IN ASTROLOGY.

The position of ♄ in the 9th, who is naturally of a severe, surly, rigid, and harsh temper, may argue that Presbytery will be too strict, sullen, and dogged for the English constitutions; little gentle or compliant with the nature of the community. And that there shall spring up among themselves many strange opinions and distractions even, concerning this very Presbytery; that they shall grow excessively covetous, contentious, and desirous of more than belongs to them; worldly, envious, and malicious one against the other; that among them some juniors, represented by ♀,* shall be light in

---

* The reason of this is, that ♀ in the house of ♂ shews persons given to pleasure.

judgment, wavering, and decline the strictness of their discipline; and that the elders, represented by ♄, shall not be respected on account of their excessive rigidness, nor shall their orthodox opinions be consented to.

Observe, that ♄ is peregrine, and supported by no favourable aspect of either fortune ; there is reception between ☽ and him, but no aspect: ☿, lord of the 10th, signifying authority, is fast separating from ♄, as if the gentry or supreme of the kingdom do already decline from the severity of the austere Presbyterian clergy, fearing thraldom rather than freedom to ensue from their power.

Three whole years from hence shall not pass, ere authority itself, or some Divine Providence, will inform our judgment with a way in discipline or government either nearer to the former purity of the primitive times, or better beloved of the whole kingdom of England; or authority shall in this space of time moderate many things now strongly desired. For some time we shall not discover what shall be established, but all shall be even as when there was no king in Israel ; a confusion among us shall yet awhile remain. The soldiery then, or some men of fiery spirits, will arise, and keep back their contribution from the clergy, and will deny obedience or submission to this thing called Presbytery. It will then come to be handled by the magistracy, and the grand authority of the kingdom. Also, by the plurality of the clergy, or men of sound judgment, it will be contradicted, disputed against, disapproved ; and these shall make it manifest that this very Presbytery, now maintained, is not the same that the commonwealth of England will entertain as a standing rule to live under.

From what I find by this figure, I conclude *that Presbytery shall not stand here in England.**

* We have given this judgment at great length, as its complete fulfil-

Fig. 27.

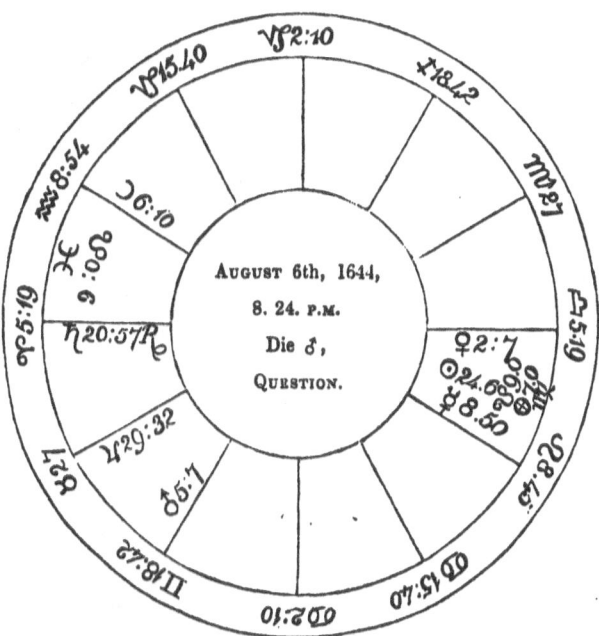

QUESTION.—WHETHER THE QUERENT SHOULD OBTAIN THE PARSONAGE DESIRED?

Judgment.—In the first place, I find ☌ between ♃, lord of the 9th, and ♂, lord of the ascendant, but separating.

ment, by the re-establishment of the Episcopal church, being a matter of history, is a decisive proof of the truth of the science, and of its ability to decide the most important questions both public and private. The student will readily perceive that the prediction of the downfall of the Presbyterian church, as far as regards England, is made according to the strictest rules of the doctrines laid down by our author.

2dly. Neither the ☽, nor lord of the ascendant, in the 9th. 3dly. There is no planet translating the light of ♃ to ♂. 4thly. There is no reception between ♃ and ♂. 5thly. ♄ is impedited in the ascendant, and by his presence afflicts the querent, and causes him to despair of success. 6thly, The ☽ separates from a △ of ♂, and applies to ☍ of ☿, lord of the 3d; which intimated that some neighbour of the querent, either with a letter, words, or cross information, would wholly destroy the querent's hopes; and that mercurial men, viz. scholars or divines, would be his enemies: and as I found ♀ in ♎, opposing the ascendant, I judged that some female would inform against him, or prejudice him in his suit.

From all this I persuaded him against proceeding any further in the matter; but the parson being covetous, would proceed, and did: and when he thought to have success, behold a scurvy letter, revealing some unpleasant truths concerning a female, dashed the good man's hopes, *et exit*.

The querent was ♄ and ♂ exactly, had wit and volubility of tongue; and as ☿ and ☽ were in ☍, he under the earth, she in the 12th, he could never discover which of his neighbours it was that thus injured him; nor would he ask me. If he had, it must have been ♄, lord of the 12th, viz. some farmer or dealer in cattle, a sickly, repining character, living north-east, about fifteen furlongs, from him.

CHAPTER XXXIII.

THE TENTH HOUSE AND ITS QUESTIONS.—VIZ. OFFICE, DIGNITY, PREFERMENT, GOVERNMENT, TRADE, OR PROFESSION, &c.

THE usual significators are for the querent; and the 10th house, its lord, and the ☉, for the place, preferment, &c., inquired after.

If the lord of the ascendant or ☽ be both joined by good aspect to the ☉, or by ☌ or good aspect to the lord of the 10th, and this planet behold the 10th, or be therein, the querent shall gain the thing sought for, if he use proper endeavours.

Or if none of the significators be joined to the lord of the 10th, yet if the lord of the ascendant or ☽ be in the 10th, unafflicted, he shall gain it; and also, if the lord of the 10th be in the ascendant; and very easily, if the two lords be going to a good aspect.

The lord of the 10th joined to ♃ or ♀, and in the ascendant, he gains the office, &c., easily; if joined to ♄ or ♂, and either of them in the ascendant, but well dignified, it will be gained, but with difficulty.

The lord of the 10th receiving ☽, or the lord of the 1st, denotes success. And if there be translation of light from the lord of the ascendant to the lord of the 10th, it denotes that it will be gained by means of such a person as the planet translating the light describes.

If the lord of the ascendant apply to ☌ of the lord of the 10th, and there happen no previous abscission by any other planet before the ☌ be complete, the querent will gain his desire, but he must labour hard for it.

If any planet be in ⚹ or △ to the lord of the 10th, or the

☉, let the querent make application to such persons as they describe; for they may greatly befriend the querent by means of their influence.

If the promising planet in any case be in an angle, the matter will be readily completed; if in a succedent, but slowly; and if in a cadent, the affair goes backward at times; but may, at last, be performed, if the planet be otherwise well dignified.

If an evil planet behold ☽ or the ascendant by □ or ☍, without reception mutual, he hinders the querent by means of that person who is to solicit the cause, &c. for him.

The best sign of all is, when the two lords be joined together, and the ☽ separate from the lord of the 10th, and apply to the lord of the ascendant; but it she apply to either, it is good.

If the lord of the ascendant apply to good aspect of the lord of the 4th, it denotes success; but if the lord of the 4th be joined also to the lord of the 10th, the matter shall be effected, but only after much delay and vexation.

Whether a Person shall remain in the Office he holds, or not?

Observe whether the lords of the 1st and 10th be in ☌, or any aspect; and note whether the more ponderous planet of the two be in any angle but the 4th; if so, he shall not be removed. But if the heavy planet be in the 4th, or approaching it from the 5th, he will leave his office. Yet, if there be reception between the two lords, he shall recover it again; and if the reception be mutual, he returns speedily, and with more honour than before.

You may judge the same if the lord of the ascendant be joined to a planet in the 3d or 9th, or to their lords, and after separation be joined to a planet in any angle, except the 4th.

But if the two lords (of the 1st and 10th) separate from each other, then he returns no more to his office, but loses it entirely.

If the lord of the ascendant, or 10th, or the ☾, are disposed of by any planet in an angle, (except the 4th), and that planet be slow in motion, he shall not be removed until that planet be combust or retrograde, or leave the sign he is in; but much about that time he will be removed, unless some powerful aspects intervene.

If the ☾ be joined to the lord of the 10th, and he in the 10th, the officer or governor, &c., shall not be removed.

If the lord of the ascendant, or ☾, be joined to the lord of the 10th, and he more weighty than either of them, and in the 10th, 11th, or 5th houses, free from impediment, though he behold not the 10th, the officer shall be transferred to some other place or office; but if he behold the 10th, he shall remain where he is.

If the ☾ be joined to any planet not in his essential dignities, though with reception, (unless it be ♃ or ♀ by ✶ or △), the querent shall leave his employment, office, &c. If either the lord of the 4th, or ☾, be in the 4th, and ♈, ♋, ♎, or ♑, be on its cusp, he will leave it; and this is more certain if ☾ be then joined to the lord of the 4th, and be peregrine. The same may be feared if ☾ be in ♑, and afflicted, or if she be void of course, and the lord of the ascendant be afflicted.

Whether a King expelled his Kingdom, or an Officer having lost his Place, shall be restored?

The ascendant and its lord are for the querent, be he king, duke, or gentleman, &c. Observe, that if the lord of the 1st be in ☌ with the lord of the 10th, and the more ponderous planet behold the 10th house, then the king or ruler, &c. shall be restored.

If the planet do not behold the 10th house, observe whether ☽ be joined to any planet in the ascendant, or 10th, which also will denote his restoration. If ☽ be in ♈, ♋, ♎, or ♑, he returns the sooner. If the lord of the 10th be joined to a planet in the 10th, or the ☉, (but not by ☌ to ☉), it denotes the same. The lord of the 10th a lighter planet than the lord of the 4th, and separated from him, argues the same.

If the lord of the 10th be lighter than the lord of the ascendant, and be joined to him, he shall return to his office, &c. So also, if ☽ be joined to the lord of the 10th, and behold the 10th house, unless disposed of by a peregrine planet under the earth.

The lord of the 1st aspected and received by a planet not afflicted, he returns; if not received, he will not.

The ☽ joined to a planet in the 9th, (it not being a fortune), shews that the king, &c. recedes from his kingdom, &c. If it be a fortune, and in ♈, ♉, ♋, ♌, ♎, ♑, ♒, he will return; and if it be in ♊, ♍, ♐, or ♓, he obtains office, power, &c. in another place.

The lord of the 10th, or ☽, being afflicted by ☌ of an infortune in any angle, the king, &c. shall never be restored.*

Of the Profession, Trade, or Employment of which any one is capable.

Consider the lords of the ascendant and 10th, and the

---

* This rule will answer the question of the re-election of any Member of Parliament for any place he has formerly represented; as well as the restoration of any minister, &c. to power, or the return of any individual to any office or employment.

INTRODUCTION TO ASTROLOGY. 273

cusps of those houses, the ☽, and also the places of ♂ and ♀; for these two planets are the significators of trade or employment. Observe which of the two (♂ or ♀) is the most powerful, and note the sign he may be in; also consider the four angles, and any planet in them. If they be in fiery signs, or the majority of them, (viz. ♂, ♀, the planet in an angle, and the cusps of angles, especially the 10th), and ♂ have any dignity in the place of the lord of the 10th, or the ☉, say the querent will make a good tradesman, &c. in any business where *fire* is used, or of its nature; and if the lord of the 10th be in his exaltation, he will do well in serving the king, or any high nobleman, &c.

If the significator of the employment, (usually the lord of the 10th, or a planet, especially ♂ or ♀, in the 10th, near the cusp), be in ♈, *weak*, he will make a good cattle-dealer, groom, farrier, grazier, &c.; if *strong*, a coachmaker, veterinary surgeon, &c., where he has to do with horses or great cattle, in a respectable way.

If the significator be in ♉, then husbandry will best suit him; or gardening, corn-dealing, grazing, &c.; or if ♀ be the significator, such things as appertain to women's affairs, a soap-boiler, fuller of cloth, scourer, &c.

If the significator be in ♊, he will make a writer, clerk, bailiff, &c., or a surveyor, painter, astronomer, astrologer, geometer, schoolmaster, &c.

If he be in ♋, he will be fitted for a variety of occupations; but he will be likely to go to sea, or to deal in liquids, such as wines, beer, &c.; and he will be fond of political distinction.

If he be in ♌, he will make a good horse-jockey or coachman; a smith, watchmaker, glassblower, huntsman, or cowdoctor; or to do with any trade which uses fire.

If in ♍, he will make a good secretary to a person in

T

power, a schoolmaster, accountant, stationer, printer; he will be an excellent politician, or be a good astrologer, &c.

If in ♎, he will be a good poet or orator; singer, or musician; silkman, or linendraper, &c.

If in ♏, he may prove a good surgeon, apothecary, or physician; or a brazier, founder, brewer, vintner, waterman, or malster.

If in ♐, he will do very well to make a clergyman, to study chemistry, to buy and sell cattle, or to be a cook or butcher.

If he be in ♑, he will prove a good chandler, victualler, farrier, farmer, dealer in wool, lead, or farming commodities.

If he be in ♒, he will make an excellent ship-carpenter; and if any planet aspect him out of a watery sign, he may prove a good sailor or ship-master, or a painter and ornamenter of ships, or a merchant.

If he be in ♓, he makes a good jester, singer, player, &c., or brewer, or fishmonger; but generally the genius is dull, and the party given to sottishness.

As fiery signs shew workers at the fire, whether goldsmiths, &c., or bakers, &c., so earthy signs shew occupations connected with the earth, as potters, ditchers, brickmakers, gardeners, &c.; airy signs import singers, gamekeepers, actors, &c.; and watery, sailors, fishermen, watermen, laundresses, waiters in taverns, &c.

INTRODUCTION TO ASTROLOGY.

Fig. 28.

JUDGMENT ON THE ABOVE FIGURE.

The ascendant and ♀ are for the querent, the 10th house for the office or preferment he expected.

Finding ☽ strong in the 10th, was one argument that he should succeed. In the next place ☽, applied to △ of ♄, who has exaltation in the ascendant, and who receives ♀ by house, and is received by her again by exaltation. The ☽ applying to △ of the lord of the 4th (♄), argued that in the *end* he should obtain the office; but as ☉ was in the 7th in ☌ to the ascendant, with ☋, and was lord of the 11th, I judged that he employed as a friend a *solar* man, who was false, and did rather envy than feel friendly to him. I concluded, that with some difficulty he would obtain the office, notwithstanding the opposition a pretended friend offered; and so it came to pass within three weeks, and he then discovered that his friend was false; who had a great scar in his face, his hair of a blackish colour, shewn by ☉ being so near ☋. The separation of ☽ from ☐ of ☿, argued that he had delivered many petitions about it, hitherto without any success.

CHAPTER XXXIV.

OF THE ELEVENTH HOUSE, AND ITS QUESTIONS, VIZ. OF FRIENDS, HOPES, PROPERTY OF THE KING, &c.

If the lord of this house be strong, fortunate, and well aspected, it foreshews the obtaining the thing hoped for; also the love and concord of friends, &c., if that be the question.

Whether any one shall have the Thing hoped for?

Observe whether there be any good aspect or reception between the lord of the ascendant and 11th, or translation of light, or that the lord of the ascendant be in the 11th, or the lord of the 11th in the ascendant. All or any of these give reason to expect it. But if there be none of these, note the ☽, and if she be not well qualified with the lord of the 11th, nor any benefic, or ☋ in the 11th, judge the contrary.

The lord of the 11th in an angle, received by the lord of the ascendant, you may judge in the affirmative.

If the receiver of the ☽ be in a common sign, judge that he shall have but part of the thing hoped for. If in a moveable sign, he shall have but a little, a mere sign of the thing; but if the receiver be in a fixed sign, he shall have the whole or complete thing. Yet, if the receiver of ☽ be unfortunate, the matter shall get some injury or hurt, &c. after he is in possession of it.

If there be mutual reception between the receiver of the ☽ and the ☽, he shall obtain the thing, and more than he looked for. And if the lord of the ascendant be also received, he shall obtain whatsoever he hoped for, that is feasible or possible.

If the querent's significator or ☽ apply to a fortune, not cadent, he may expect the thing desired.

N.B. if the querent *name* the thing hoped for, then judge of it by its own proper house, &c.; as, if it be money the 2d, if it be children the 5th, &c.

*Of the Sincerity of Friends.**

Good planets in the 11th, or ☋ there, or good aspects between the lords of the 11th and ascendant, denote the friends of the querent to be sincere; and if they throw good aspects to the cusp of the 2d house, its lord, or ⊕, it denotes gain thereby. Evil planets, and evil aspects in like manner, denote false friends and losses. The lord of the 12th in the 11th, denotes a secret enemy under the guise of friendship. ☿ in the 11th, shews wavering, unsteady friends, unless he be in a fixed sign.

* These rules are not found in our author.

CHAPTER XXXV.

OF THE TWELFTH HOUSE, AND ITS QUESTIONS, VIZ. OF IM-
PRISONMENT, GREAT CATTLE, PRIVATE ENEMIES, BANISHED
MEN, &c.

If a question be asked regarding secret enemies, who are not named, observe the lord of the 12th, and planets therein, how they aspect the lord of the ascendant, and from what houses, &c. If the lord of the 12th behold the lord of the ascendant from the 6th, 8th, or 12th, or from the 4th, 7th, or 10th, then there are some who privately wish ill to the querent.

To know who a private Enemy is.

Observe how the lord of the 12th is affected, and whether he be with good or evil planets, and how he behold the lord of the ascendant. If he be in the 6th, or joined to its lord, it shews the secret enemy is afflicted with some secret disease or malady; if the lord of the 6th be in the 12th, he is also sickly. If the lord of the 12th be in the 10th, or with its lord, he is in favour with the king or some person of rank; and if he be strong, it will not be well for the querent to meddle with him, especially if he aspect the lord of the ascendant or ☽ by □ or ☍. If the lord of the 12th be with the lord of the 4th or 8th, or in those houses, he is sickly or near dying, or is repining, and very miserable. Consider and judge farther, as in former cases directed.

Whether a Person committed to Prison shall be discharged?

First learn your ascendant exactly, by knowing what rela-
tion the quesited bears to the querent. If ☽ be swift in motion, it denotes a short stay in prison; if she aspect a

planet in the 3d or 9th by ✶ or △, or by □, if with reception), he shall soon leave the prison; the same, if she aspect the lord of the 3d or 9th, and be not in an angle. As you judge by ☽, judge also by the lord of the ascendant. But these aspects must be by application.

The lords of the angles being in angles, is an ill testimony; and so much the worse if the lord of the ascendant be in the 4th, or if either he or the lord of the 12th dispose of each other. It is still worse if the lord of the ascendant be disposed of by a planet in an angle, especially a malefic; and worst of all if that malefic be in the 4th; and if he be the lord of the 8th, he may expect to die in prison. The ☽ disposed of by the lord of the 12th, or any malefic, is a sign of a long stay; and it is still worse, if her dispositor be in an angle, and especially in the 4th. If, however, the disposing planet be in a moveable sign, or swift in motion, it shortens the time; but a retrograde planet shews a long detention. If the lord of the ascendant, or ☽, be combust, it shews a long imprisonment.

The ☽ and ☿ in moveable signs, when ☿ is lord of the ascendant, shews speedy enlargement, especially if they aspect a fortune. If ♃ ascend, or be in ☌ with ☽, or ♀ be in the ascendant in ☌ with ☽, or ☿ be in ☌ with ♃, and aspect the ☽, or ☽ apply to ♃ or ♀, he will be discharged. The dispositor of ☽ with a fortune denotes the same.

Whether a Prisoner of War shall escape or be exchanged, &c.

If the lord of the ascendant separate from the lord of the 4th, and apply to a fortune; or if the lord of the ascendant be cadent, or leaving an angle, he shall escape. Also if he separate from combustion, or ☽ get from under the beams of ☉.

If at the time of being taken, or of the question, a fixed

sign ascend, or the ☽, or lord of the ascendant, be in a fixed sign, or in ♓, it denotes long imprisonment. The same if a fixed sign be on the 12th, or its lord be angular, and in a fixed sign. The ☽, or lord of the 1st, in ♉ or ♌, and in ☍ to ♂, shews danger of being slain by the sword, or by quarrelling; if in ☍ to ♄, it shews irons or severe punishments. (If it be an ordinary prisoner, these may shew sickness, want, and ill treatment, or accident, &c.)

An infortune in ♒, shews a long imprisonment. If the lord of the ascendant be in his fall or detriment, and the ☽ in ♒, the same; also the ☽, or lord of the 1st, in the 8th or 12th. If ☽ apply to a fortune, and the lord of the ascendant and the cusp of the ascendant be fortunate, it denotes liberation.

Note.— ♀ is better than ♃ in this question, especially if in aspect to ☿ or ☽. If ☽ be with ♄, and ♃ behold them by □, and ♂ by △, it denotes that, after a long confinement and suffering, he shall break prison and escape.

If a felon, &c., be imprisoned when ☉ ascends or rules the ascendant, he shall escape (the ancients declare) within a month; if ♀, within 40 days; if ☿, he has long imprisonment; if ☽, his state will depend on and change according as she has applications with other planets; if ♄, he has long confinement; if ♃, short; and if ♂, he shall be ill-treated, beaten, put into irons, &c.

Fig. 29.

JUDGMENT ON THE ABOVE QUESTION.

The prisoner's person is described by ♐, the cusp of the 12th, and by ♃ in ♌. The way he went, and intended to go, is here shewn by the cusp of the 12th ♐, and by ♌, where ♃ is, and by the sign and quarter of heaven wherein we find ☽.

All of them considered, they signify, unanimously, that the prisoner would go eastward, or full east, (*and so he did*). The closeness of ☽ to the ascendant shewed that he was not yet out of town, or, at least, that he would not be far from town. And as ♃ was in the 8th, I judged that he lay obscure for awhile, viz. a night; but that then he would go away, (*which he did*).

I confidently affirmed, that he should be taken again by some man of authority; for ☽ separated from △ of ♃, his significator, and applied to ☍ of ☉, both in angles. It never fails, but that if the ☽, or the significator of a fugitive, be afflicted by an unfortunate planet in the 7th house, that fugitive, or prisoner, is again taken. In the next place, I found ♃ and ☿ in ⚹, ☿ in his own house, and applying to ♃; therefore I judged that the querent should have news of the prisoner by letter, or by some young man, within six or seven days, or when the significators came to ⚹ aspect; which was six days afterwards. The truth is, that on the next Friday he had a letter to tell where he was, and on the Sunday he apprehended him by authority.

Fig. 30.

QUESTION.—A LADY ASKS WHEN HER HUSBAND, WHO IS IMPRISONED, SHALL BE DELIVERED?

Judgment.—The lady's husband is signified by ♃ lord of the 7th; he is in ♋ retrograde, and had the day before been in △ to ☉. The ☽ applies to ✶ of ♄ retrograde, then to △ of ♃, with a most forcible reception. From hence I made not many words, but told the lady she need not trouble herself to make friends to apply to his majesty, for that I was

284 INTRODUCTION TO ASTROLOGY.

assured that either he was, or would be, within three days, discharged from his imprisonment by means of a *solar* man, a commander who would release him and furnish him with what was necessary for his convenience.

The truth is, he was released, and the garrison where he was prisoner taken the day before the question was asked, (when ☉ was in △ to his significator), by an honest parliamentary colonel, who plentifully relieved him with money, and all convenient necessaries. ♃ in his exaltation, retrograde, *in a moveable sign*, and in △ to ☉, shewed short imprisonment; the more so, as ☉ is lord of the 4th, and the △ so perfect.

Fig. 31.

May 13th, 1644,
12: 29 P.M.
Die ☽.
Time of setting off on a
Journey for WAR.

The Time of His Excellency ROBERT *Earl of* ESSEX *last setting forth into the West of England.*

Here ♒, the ascending sign, well represents his form of body, for it was comely, &c. ♄, ☿, and ♀, his mind, they having all dignities in the ascendant. ♃ has also much to do with his qualities, being lord of ♓, an intercepted sign in the ascendant.

I first considered that the ☽ separated from a △ of ♄, and applied to a □ of ♂, lord of his house of substance, assistants, &c., and also of the 9th, his house of journeys. This intimated he should have but slender success, and lose much by his present march. Finding ☋ in the ascendant, I judged that he would be betrayed in his councils; and seeing ♄, lord of his ascendant, peregrine, and in his fall in the 2d, the ☽ in her detriment, and ⊕ disposed of by ☿, lord of his 7th, signifying his enemies, and that ♃, the general significator of wealth, casts a □ to the ascending degree, I gave this judgment:—that his Excellency must expect no success from this employment; that he would have no honour by the journey; that he would be extremely crossed by men of great power here at London, who pretended great friendship to him; (♃, lord of the 10th and 11th, being in □ to his ascendant), that he would be betrayed wholly, and be in danger to lose all; that, in short, I was extremely sorry he had chosen so unlucky a time to set forth, &c. &c.

The issue was thus, (for I write to posterity): he prospered in the beginning, and daily men of good quality and authority jeered at me, and derided my prediction. I was quite content to be abused, provided that he might have had success. But observe, that on the 8th September following, came sad news, that on the 2d of September this worthy man had surrendered all his ammunition to his majesty, having only quarter for his soldiers; with some other articles, which were dishonourably performed, to the eternal shame of the royal party.

Fig. 32.

JUDGMENT ON THE ABOVE FIGURE.

The above remarkable era in the life of King Charles the First affords a striking illustration of the truth of the rules of the science as laid down by our author.

The King is here represented by the ascendant, the ☽, and the lord of the ascendant, because *he* began the WAR, as it were, by this act.*

* "The King had lain most part at York, or rambled into some other counties near adjacent, until August, and done little to any purpose.

Here we find ♄ peregrine, and retrograde in the ascendant, a decided testimony of ill success; the ☊ is also ascending, a sign of evil and treachery to the King. His second house is afflicted by ♂, who is in his detriment, and disposed of by ☿, the significator of his adversaries. The King's ⊕ is afflicted by ☌ of ♂, and by ☐ of ☿, having only the ✶ of ♃, who is retrograde, and in ☍ to ☉, the joint significator of his foes. Then we find the ascendant in ☍ to ☿, the significator of the enemy; and also the ☽ in ☐ to the ☉, cadent and peregrine. Each one of his significators is afflicted, and ♃, the lord of the 11th, his house of hopes, and of the 10th, the house of honour, and dispositor of ☽, is afflicted by the ☍ of ☉, by being retrograde, and by being within orbs of a ☌ of ♄, lord of the 12th, the house of disgrace and misfortune.

Now as regards the adversary, we find ☉ and ☿ both ruling the 7th, and placed therein in mutual reception, ☉ being in the house of ☿, and ☿ in the house of ☉. The ☊ is also in the 7th, and ♀ lady of their 2d, or house of substance and means, assistants, &c., is strong in her own house ♎, angular, and no way afflicted.

The general significator of *war*, ♂, is in his detriment, and is disposed of by ♀, a benefic in the 7th. The lord of the adversaries 10th, or house of honour, is ☿, and he is in reception mutual with the ☉, angular, and no way impeded,

For the several counties were generally nothing inclinable to his purpose; in most whereof, and in every county he came in, he rather received petty affronts than support. Yet at last he came to Nottingham, and there set up his STANDARD, (with a full resolution for war), the 22d August, 1642, under this constellation; having some few horse with him, but in great expectation of more aid from the Welsh, &c., whom he thought most doted on monarchy."—*Monarchy or no Monarchy*, p. 112.

except being retrograde; and he is in the term of ♂, and ♂ is in his term; another mutual reception.

All these things were decided testimonies that his Majesty should fail in all his endeavours, and eventually be ruined. The lord of the 12th being also lord of the ascendant, shewed that he had been himself his greatest enemy, and the cause of his misfortunes. The lord of the 12th, (house of imprisonment) being in the ascendant, shewed that he should be imprisoned; the more so from his being in ♓. And history tells us how truly the "signs of heaven" spoke on this occasion; for "all the remainder of his life, after this August 22d, 1642, was a mere labyrinth of sorrow; a continued and daily misfortune."

The student will perceive that his death was plainly foreshewn by the ☽ applying to ⚹ of ♀, lady of the 8th, or house of death, from signs of long ascension; in which a ⚹, it is said, has the same effect as a □ in other signs. The ☽ moreover is with *Antares*, a violent fixed star, (now in about 7° 30′ ♐) which is said to denote a *violent death*; which is farther shewn by the □ of ☽ to ☉, the latter being in an angle. The lord of the 4th being in ☍ to the ascendant, was also a token of his death; and perhaps ♏ being in the 8th, and ♂, its ruler, approaching *Caput Algol*, which is said to denote *beheading*, might intimate that; but all such minute points must be left to posterity to decide, when the science will be better understood.

The hour of the King's death was 4h. 4m. P.M., 30th January, 1648-9, when the heavens were as represented in the following figure. The student will see that ♄, lord of the ascendant in this figure, had exactly gained the □ aspect of the ☉ at that time, being in ♊ 9° 25′; and that ☉ was just transiting the ascendant of this figure; and that the cusp of the 10th (which denoted the King) is there the place of ♄

in this figure. The ☽ is in the 29th degree of ♑, a ☐ aspect to the cusp of the 8th, in this also; and ♃, part lord of the ascendant here, is in ☌ with the place of ♀, lady of the 8th. All these coincidences must be considered by the genuine searcher after truth as strong evidences of the truth of planetary influence, as evinced in *horary astrology*. The consequences and final result of the mad attempt of this unhappy King to make war upon the nation were here plainly depicted; and it is for the opponents of astrology to shew, that these things are merely accidental coincidence, or the fruit of *chance*, the deity they so fondly worship.

Fig. 33.

Exact Time of the Death of KING CHARLES I., 4 : 4. P.M. 30th Jan. 1648-9.

OBSERVATIONS ON THE ABOVE FIGURE.

King Charles I. was born at *Dumfernline*, in Scotland, about fifteen miles from Edinburgh, on the 19th November, 1600; at which time ☉ was in 9° of ♐. Hence, at the period of his death, ♄ was exactly in ☍ to the place of ☉ at his birth, and ♂ nearly in □ to that place.

The ☍ of ♄ to ☉ will ever be found to bring trouble, sorrow, disgrace, and often death, to the native. It will be seen that at the time of the King's setting up his standard at Nottingham, the ☉ was exactly transiting the □ of his own place at birth ; a decided cause of failure, discredit, &c. But although we mention these circumstances, we would remind the student that such transits can have but little effect unless evil directions be operating at the time; which, there can be no doubt, was the case in the nativity of the unfortunate and ill-advised King Charles the First.

If we regard this figure as that of the exact commencement of the COMMONWEALTH, we shall find that it will point out the result of that change in the government, as it would of any other thing which might then have commenced.

The ☽ is lady of the ascendant, and she is in her detriment and peregrine; hence the commonwealth was not *successful;* her being in a moveable sign, and moveable signs on the ascendant and 7th, and such signs intercepted in the other two angles, shewed that it would not be *permanent*. The lord of the 4th being also lord of the 12th, shewed that it would come to an end by means of the exertions of its *secret* enemies ; and as ♄ is also lord of the 7th, and rules the ☽, it shewed that its *enemies* would overthrow it at length. The end of it was clearly pointed out to be when ☽ came to ☌ of the lord of the 4th, ☿, and to the △ in signs of short ascension of the lord of the 8th, ♄, who is very powerful, as being in reception with ☿, and △ with ♃, and ruling both ☉ and ☽, and being also with ☋. If we calculate from the place of the ☽ to the △ of ♄, we shall find eleven degrees and a quarter, which would be equivalent to *eleven years and a quarter;* which, it is well known, was THE EXACT DURATION OF THE COMMONWEALEH.

APHORISMS, BY ZADKIEL.

1st. In all cases of hearing rumours or reports, receiving letters or messages, &c., if you erect a figure for the exact minute of hearing or reading the news, &c., the lord of the 3d in good aspect with the cusp of the 7th, or a planet in the 7th, shews that the news is *true*, and that you are not deceived; if he be in evil aspect, either semi-square, □, sesquiquadrate, or ☍, the news is *false*.

2d. Whenever any person applies to another on any business whatever, either by letter, message, or personally, the 1st house represents him who is the first mover in the matter, who either goes or sends to the other, and the 7th represents the person applied to. Therefore, when a person reads a report in a newspaper, or elsewhere, the 7th shews that person, because the report, &c. comes, as it were, to him.

3d. If you apply to a person for goods of any kind, and they are promised, the application of the lord of the 2d to the lord of the 8th, or a planet therein, shews the time when they will be received.

4th. If you receive a bill of exchange, the figure for that time will shew whether it will be paid. If ⊕ receive a good aspect of the lord of the 1st, it will be paid; but if ⊕ receive any evil aspect of the lord of the 1st, it will not be paid. *Probatum est.*

5th. The ⊕ always denotes *money*, whether in cash or bills; but *property*, whether in goods or lands, houses, &c., is always shewn by the lord of the 2d, or a planet therein.

FAC-SIMILE *of the* HIEROGLYPHIC *of the* GREAT PLAGUE *in* 1665, *published by* W. LILLY, *in the* YEAR 1651.

Fac-Simile of the ASTROLOGICAL HIEROGLYPHIC of the GREAT FIRE in LONDON, September 2d, 1666, published by W. LILLY, in the Year 1651.

APPENDIX.

EXPLANATION OF THE HIEROGLYPHICS.

THE first of these curious cuts, which have been exactly copied from our author's tract, entitled "*Monarchy or no Monarchy in England,*" is intended to represent a great mortality, in which the vast number of deaths should so far exceed the supply of coffins, that the dead must needs be buried in their shrouds, or merely stitched up in sheets, &c., as therein rudely represented.—The second cut is an *Astrological* Hieroglyphic, as may be understood by the horoscope being introduced therein; and the two children or twins are intended to represent the sign *Gemini*, which, in astrology, is known to rule London; and the twins are, therefore, intended to denote that city. Their falling headlong into the fire, describes the extensive injury to be done to London by that element fifteen years afterwards. The manner in which this was foreseen by the author has been explained in our remarks on his life.

These two Hieroglyphics, even if there had been only these, whereas there were several others equally pointing out future events, published with them, would ever remain undeniable monuments of our author's skill, and of the substantial truth of the science of astrology.

DESCRIPTION OF PERSONS ACCORDING AS THE SIGNIFICATOR MAY BE FOUND IN EACH OF THE TWELVE SIGNS.

Saturn *in the Twelve Signs.*

♄ *in* ♈

Gives a ruddy complexion, a spare, rawboned person, full-faced, dark hair, not much beard, addicted to boasting, resolute, quarrelsome, and very ill-natured.

♄ *in* ♉

Gives a person in no wise comely, but a heavy, lumpish, awkward appearance, dark hair, middle stature, not well made, rough in carriage, sordid, vicious, &c.

♄ *in* ♊

Represents a person of rather tall stature, dark, sanguine complexion, oval visage, dark brown or black hair, ingenious but unpolished, perverse, and generally unfortunate in most of his undertakings.

♄ *in* ♋

Denotes a person of middle stature, rather short than tall, sickly and feeble, meagre face, dark hair, languid eyes; the body sometimes crooked; jealous, malicious, and deceitful in his dealings.

♄ *in* ♌

Gives a person of moderate large stature, broad, round shoulders, wide chest, lightish hair, large boned, surly aspect, eyes sunk, apt to stoop. Qualities tolerably good, generous but passionate; not over valiant or courageous when put to the test.

♄ in ♍

Represents a person of a tall, spare body, swarthy, dark or black hair, and it plentiful; a long head, solid countenance; generally unfortunate; inclined to melancholy, retaining anger; a projector of many curious matters to little purpose; studious, subtle, reserved; inclined to pilfering and indirect dealings.

♄ in ♎

Describes a person above the middle stature, comely brown hair, oval face, large nose and forehead, clear complexion; one opinionated of himself, prodigal of expense. They are given to debate and controversy, and seldom leave any wealth at their death.

♄ in ♏

Represents a person of a mean stature, squat, thick, trussed body, broad shoulders, black or dark hair, which is usually short and thick; quarrelsome, mischievous; one who will undertake violent and dangerous actions, though to his own detriment.

♄ in ♐

Gives a large body, brown hair, good make, tolerable complexion; obliging disposition, not covetous, moderately frugal, rarely profuse, but somewhat choleric. One who will not bear an affront, yet willing to do good to all; a lover of his friend, and merciful to an enemy.

♄ in ♑

Personates a lean, raw-boned body, dark or black hair, middle stature, dark complexion, small leering eyes, long visage, and a stooping awkward posture in walking. One who is peevish, discontented, melancholy, covetous, of few words, fearful, retains anger, and is of great gravity.

♄ in ♒

Gives a reasonable full-bodied person, a large head and face, rather inclined to corpulency, middle stature, sad brown hair, a clear complexion, a sober, graceful deportment. Affable, courteous disposition; of an excellent, searching fancy, and generally very proficient in what they undertake in arts or sciences; a person of a pregnant genius, yet subject to be conceited.

♄ in ♓

Describes a middle-statured person, pale complexion, sad or dark black hair, a large head and full eye; sometimes the teeth are distorted. A person not very comely. Active to do mischief, malicious and given to contention and dissimulation. An uncertain, fickle person in everything; though often presenting a good outside, yet fraudulent and deceitful in the end. They are not loquacious, but deliberative, and do evil with malice aforethought. They are said to improve as they grow aged.

N.B. ♄ always gives bad teeth; and in this sign they are generally discoloured and rotten.

JUPITER *in the Twelve Signs.*

♃ in ♈

Describes a middle stature, but not stout, rather lean than corpulent, a quick and penetrating eye, a high nose, oval visage, with generally pimples or a peculiar redness in the face. They are of a free, noble, and generous disposition; very obliging, polite, and complaisant, especially to their friends.

♃ in ♉

Gives a middle stature, stout, well-set body, but, though

compact, not handsome; hair brown, rough, and curling. Complexion swarthy; and frequently the skin looks shining or oily. The disposition reasonably good, judgment sound, deportment good, behaviour free and charitable; fond of the female sex, and very humane and compassionate to the distressed.

♃ in ♊

Represents a well-made, compact body, plump, yet above the middle stature; sanguine complexion, though rather dusky; brown hair, and full, expressive eyes. The deportment graceful, affable, courteous, gentle, mild, obliging, and good-natured. An admirer of the female sex, and a lover of learning. But if ♃ be near *Occulus Taurus*, (in ♊ 6° 15', with 2° 36' south lat.) he will be addicted to women. And if near *Aldebaran*, (in ♊ 7° 30', with 5° 29' south lat.) he will be rash and unstable, inimical to himself, and disagreeable to others. If with the *Bull's North Horn*, in ♊ 20° 20', with 5° 22' north lat., he will be rash and violent.

♃ in ♋

Gives a person of middle stature, a pale, sickly, and unwholesome complexion; oval face; hair, dark brown; body, rather plump, but disproportioned. A busy, loquacious character, very conceited, and apt to intermeddle with other people's concerns. A lover of women, and fond of the water, whereon he is usually fortunate. Unless ♂ throw a good aspect to ♃, he is not courageous.

♃ in ♌

Represents a strong, and well-proportioned, tall body; the hair is a light or yellowish brown, and curling; complexion, ruddy; eye, full and fiery; person, rather handsome. The disposition is noble-minded, courageous, and magnanimous, but lofty, and proud, and ambitious; one who delights in warlike actions, is a terror to his enemies, and who scorns to bend to them; fond of contending for honours, &c., and full of daring and enterprise.

♃ in ♍

Gives a person of a reasonably full stature, well built, and what may be termed handsome; sad brown or black hair, ruddy complexion, but not clear or fair. One who is choleric, and given to boasting; studious, yet covetous, and by his rashness often meeting serious losses; he is not easily imposed or wrought upon by any person.

♃ in ♎

Renders the body complete and elegant, a handsome form, and inviting face; upright, tall stature, rather slender; clear complexion, a full eye, oval face, light brown hair, subject to have pimples or a rash in the face. Disposition and temper, mild; behaviour, winning, and obliging to all; partial to exercise and recreation; much esteemed, and honoured.

♃ in ♏

Gives a middle stature, stout, compact body; dark, coarse hair, fleshy and full face; muddy, dull complexion. Manners, proud and lofty; one who is ambitious, and desires to bear rule over his equals, resolute, covetous, ill-natured, and selfish; very subtle and crafty, therefore to be very warily dealt with.

♃ in ♐

Gives a fine, tall, upright body, good form and make, oval face, ruddy complexion, brown chestnut-coloured hair, full beard and whiskers; but the hair falls off early in life, especially about the temples; a good eye, and much expression in the face. The mind is just and noble; disposition courteous, humane, affable, and agreeable; manners, polite and accomplished. One fond of horses and hunting.

♃ in ♑

Describes a small stature, pale complexion, thin face, little head, not much beard, weakly person, dark brown hair, said to be darker than the beard. The mind is ingenious, but peevish, inactive, helpless, indolent.

♃ in ♒

Personates a middle stature, well set, brown hair, clear complexion, rather corpulent, compact make; and one of a cheerful, obliging disposition, hurtful to none; well conducted, and moderate in recreations; just and merciful, good-humoured, industrious, communicative, inclined to be scientific, and but little given to extravagance.

♃ in ♓

Describes a person of middle stature, obscure complexion, plump, fleshy body, lightish-brown hair. Disposition harmless, studious, and possessed of excellent talents and good acquirements; friendly, kind, and inoffensive. They delight in good company, and to be upon the water, where if ☽ throw not an evil aspect to ♃, they are found to be fortunate.

N.B. ♃ usually gives good teeth, and frequently an apparent mark in the fore-teeth. In an airy sign, he gives broad fore-teeth; in a fiery sign, crooked; in earthy they are discoloured; and in a watery sign, the teeth decay suddenly, and grow black and rotten, especially if he be in ☌ with ☋, or in any evil aspect of ♄ or ♂. If he be in a watery sign, in □, or ☍, ☿, the party has some defect in his delivery or speech. ♃ in an airy sign, the body is more strong and corpulent; in a fiery sign more square made, and strong; in an earthy, a well-composed body, and in a watery, more fat and comely.

Mars *in the Twelve Signs.*

♂ *in* ♈

Represents a middle-statured person, well-set, large boned; swarthy complexion, light hair, and curling, frequently red; austere countenance, and, if ♂ be oriental, ruddy, and smooth; bold and undaunted, confident, choleric, and proud; fond of war and dispute; one who often gains by those means.

♂ *in* ♉

Gives a middle stature, well set, rather short; dusky complexion, dark or black hair, which is rough and coarse; broad face, wide mouth; he will generally have some scar or other mark in the face, which is often ruddy, but never fair. He is gluttonous, debauched, given to drinking and wenching; also a gambler, and very quarrelsome, treacherous, and ill-natured. He is generally unfortunate, but, if ♂ be near the Pleiades, remarkably so.

♂ *in* ♊

Gives a tall person, with black or dark brown hair, (though if ♂ be in the first seven degrees of ♊, the terms of ☿, it will be light), sanguine complexion, and well proportioned body. He is restless and unsettled, but ingenious; unfortunate in most things, living in a mean way, generally shifting here and there, leaving his debts unpaid, and exercising his wits for a livelihood; in short, a *chevalier d'industrie*, or mere swindler. But good aspects of ☉, ♃, or ♀, will mitigate this evil judgment.

♂ in ♋

Describes a short figure, and a bad complexion, without much hair, and it brown; the body is generally ill made, and crooked. The temper is sour and bad; one who is given to sottishness; a mean, servile, unfortunate creature; usually he is employed in some low business, being incapable of better.

♂ in ♌

Shews a well-proportioned body, rather tall; light brown hair, oval face, sanguine or sunburnt complexion, large eyes, stout limbs, and a brisk, cheerful aspect. A lover of women, given to boasting; fond of robust sports, as hunting, riding, shooting, &c., and ready for warlike occupation at any time. He dresses well, and is a favourite with the ladies, but it is generally to his prejudice.

♂ in ♍

Produces a middle-sized body, and well made and proportioned; black hair or very dark brown; the first seven degrees give lighter hair than the rest of the sign, being the terms of ☿; the complexion is swarthy or darkish, and generally some scar, marks, or blemish in the face. A hasty, proud, revengeful, and spiteful mind; one who retains an injury, is hard to please, conceited, and generally very unfortunate in all he undertakes.

♂ in ♎

Gives a neat made, rather tall person; his face oval; complexion sanguine, and hair light brown, and soft, but, if in the last six degrees, his own term, it is more wiry and reddish. The disposition is brisk and cheerful, but fond of boasting, and very conceited; one who is fond of dress, effeminate in appearance, much attached to women, by whom he is also much beloved, and frequently ruined.

♂ in ♏

Produces a well-set form of middle stature, rather corpulent; swarthy complexion, black curling hair, broad and plain face. The temper is very unsociable, and rash; they are generally revengeful, ungrateful, quarrelsome, and wicked; yet of good genius and ready apprehension, excelling in mystery, &c.

♂ in ♐

Denotes a tall person, with a well-proportioned body, compact and well-made, sanguine complexion, oval visage; a quick, penetrating eye; the mind is cheerful, merry, and jovial; but disposition hasty and passionate, high-minded, and lofty, courageous, loquacious, and fond of applause; on the whole, a good character.

♂ in ♑

Represents a mean or small stature, thin, lean body, little head, thin face, bad complexion, being sallow and obscure; black, lank hair. An ingenious mind, witty, shrewd, and penetrating; generally fortunate, and succesful in his undertakings.

♂ in ♒

Gives a well-composed body, rather corpulent, and inclined to be tall (though frequently not above the middle size), fair or clear complexion; sandy hair; a turbulent disposition, and addicted to controversy, &c.; not very fortunate in general.

♂ in ♓

Represents a mean stature, rather short and fleshy; a bad complexion, far from handsome; a debauched look; light brown hair; sottish and stupid; a great lover of women (if in his own terms or those of ☿, sly and artful), deceitful, idle, and worthless; not friendly to any one.

N.B. If ♂ be in ☌, □, or ☍ of ♄, or with ☋, the disposition is very evil, especially if they be in angles; when the person he describes is very fierce and violent. He is the giver of courage and resolution, which, if he be weak and afflicted, are very deficient. If ♂ be in fiery signs, he is hasty and choleric; and there is generally observed to be a falling in of the cheeks, and a lightness of feature, with an angry look; in earthy signs, a sullen, dogged temper; in airy signs, more free and obliging; in watery, sottish, dull, and stupid, unless he be well aspected by ♃, ☉, or ☽.

The SUN *in the Twelve Signs.*

☉ *in* ♈

Describes a good stature, strong and well-made; a good complexion, though not very clear; light hair, flaxen or yellowish, and large eyes. The man is noble, valiant, and courageous; delighting in warlike actions and enterprise; he gains victory, is famous, and a terror to his enemies, &c.

☉ *in* ♉

Gives a short, well set, rather ugly person; dusky complexion, brown hair, large broad face, wide mouth, and great nose. A confident, proud, and bold man, fond of opposition, proud of his physical strength, and one who generally is victorious.

☉ *in* ♊

Represents a well-proportioned body, above the middle stature, sanguine complexion, brown hair. He is affable, courteous, and kind; not very fortunate, as he is so meek and mild-tempered, that he is controlled and imposed on by others.

☉ in ♋

Gives a mean, ill-formed body, deformed in the face, with a very unhealthy aspect; the hair brown. A harmless, cheerful person, but indolent, and not fond of employment; one who spends his time in sports and pastimes, dancing, &c., and is greatly addicted to women.

☉ in ♌

Gives a strong, well-proportioned body, and a very portly person; sanguine complexion, light brown or yellowish hair, a full face, and large staring eyes, very prominent; there is generally a mark or scar on the face. A very just, upright, and honourable man, who scorns to do any meanness; punctual, faithful to his friends, and magnanimous even to his enemies; in short, a right royal disposition; a very ambitious man withal, fond of rule and authority, and given to war and dominion, conquest, &c.

☉ in ♍

Makes a person something tall of stature, and slender, but very well proportioned, good complexion, dark hair, and much of it, but not black; the mind ingenious, cheerful, and fond of honest recreations, especially agreeable, convivial parties, &c.

☉ in ♎

Produces an upright, tall, and slender body, full eyes, oval face, ruddy complexion, light hair, and frequently a rash or pimples in the face. The mind is honourable, and disposition good; but the party is always unfortunate, especially in all matters of war or ambition.

☉ in ♏

Gives a remarkably square-built, full, fleshy person, broad face, cloudy complexion, dun or sunburnt; brown hair. The mind ingenious, but the temper rugged and overbearing; manners disagreeable, disposition ambitious; one who will not admit of an equal; they are fortunate upon the seas, or as surgeons, physicians, &c.

☉ in ♐

Makes a tall, handsome, well-proportioned body, oval face, sanguine complexion, or rather olive-brown or sun-burnt; light brown hair, but in the first eight degrees of the sign it is darker; one who is very lofty and proud-spirited, aiming at great things, austere and severe, and one who performs some honourable exploits, and often becomes ennobled, or receives titles, honorary distinctions, &c.

☉ *in* ♑

Represents a mean stature, ill-made, spare, thin body, oval face, sickly complexion; brown, soft hair, not curling, and if in the first six degrees of the sign, it is light brown; the party is just and honourable in his principles, a tolerably fair temper, and gains love and friendship by his agreeable conversation; one who is very hasty at times, and much given to women.

☉ *in* ♒

Describes a person of middle stature, well-made, corpulent body, round full face, clear complexion, and light brown hair (in the term of ♄ it is dark brown). The disposition tolerably good, free from malice or deceit, but yet vain, proud, desirous of bearing rule, and ostentatious.

☉ *in* ♓

Gives a stature rather short, body plump and fleshy, a round full face, and indifferent complexion; light brown hair; in the first eight degrees of the sign it is flaxen, and

x

very soft: the party is extremely partial to female society, very effeminate, fond of pleasures, &c., and though harmless to others, ruins himself by extravagance, debauchery, gaming, intemperance, feasting, &c.

VENUS *in the Twelve Signs.*

♀ *in* ♈

Describes a middle stature, rather tall and slender, light hair, (if in the term of ♃, dark), good complexion, a pensive aspect, and usually a mark or scar in the face, (often marked more or less with small-pox, according as ♀ may be afflicted or not). They are generally unfortunate both to themselves and others, unless ♀ have a ✶ or △ of ♃.

♀ in ♉

Gives a handsome person, though the stature is not great; the body is extremely well made, plump, but not gross; and if ♀ be well aspected, they are very handsome; the complexion is ruddy, but not fair; generally females are handsome brunettes, and have much the form and figure of the *Venus de Medicis*. The hair is generally brown, and, if ♀ be in her own term, it is very soft and luxuriant; if in the term of ♃, it is a shining black. The eyes are generally black, and very expressive. The temper is mild and winning, the disposition kind, humane, obliging, &c. They generally gain much respect from those with whom they converse, and are fortunate.

♀ *in* ♊

Gives one above the middle height, slender, upright, and well-made body. The complexion clear and fair, with soft brown hair; frequently brown or hazel eyes. They are good-humoured, loving, liberal, just and charitable; and rarely guilty of any thing dishonourable.

♀ in ♋

Represents a short person, a fleshy body, round, pale, and sickly face, with light hair; and if the ☽ be with ♀, and they in the ascendant, the face will be quite white and wan, and the hair very light coloured; but if ♀ be in the term of ♂, the hair may be reddish, and a tinge of colour appear in the cheeks. They have generally small grey or greenish eyes. The disposition is idle and dull; they are fond of low company and vicious pleasures and pursuits; if it be a female of the poorer classes, she is a frequenter of spirit shops, &c. They are very fickle and timid, put the best side outwards, and seem to be in earnest when they are not; ever mutable and inconstant.

♀ in ♌

Gives a person reasonably tall of stature, well-composed body, clear complexion, round face, full eye, freckled and fair skin, hair reddish, or if in the term of ♀, it may be flaxen. They are petulant and passionate, soon angry, and soon pleased again; free, generous, sociable, and good-humoured, but rather proud, and frequently indisposed, though not seriously.

♀ in ♍

Shews a tall, well-proportioned figure, oval face, dark hair, or, if in her own term, sad brown, and a dusky complexion. They are ingenious, eloquent, active, and clever, of an aspiring turn, but rarely successful in their pursuits; generally unfortunate.

♀ in ♎

Describes an upright, tall, elegant person, extremely well made, with a genteel carriage. The face is oval, and rather beautiful, having pleasing smiles and beautiful dimples; but they are frequently freckled; the hair is brown and soft, but rather grows long than plentiful. They are kind, affectionate, and very obliging; and generally well-beloved by all with whom they have any dealings. If ♀ be in the ascendant, and there be no afflicting aspects, but ♃ cast a △ from ♒, the party, if a female, will be a perfect beauty.

♀ in ♏

Denotes a short, stout, well-set, corpulent body, broad face and dusky complexion, and dark or black hair, (unless ♀ be in the terms of ♂ or ♀); one who has nothing very pleasant in the countenance. They are envious, debauched, and vicious; given to contention; and if ♀ be afflicted by ♄ or ♂, to very disgraceful actions; and if both ♄ and ♂ afflict, and there be no assistance by ☉ or ♃, they are possessed of very evil propensities.

♀ in ♐

Represents a person rather tall than otherwise, well made, clear or sanguine complexion, fair, oval face, and brown hair. They are generous, spirited, aiming at no mean things, rather proud, passionate, yet, in general, good-tempered, kind, and inoffensive. They delight in innocent recreations, and are, in short, very obliging fortunate persons.

♀ in ♑

Describes a small-sized person, short stature, a pale face, thin and sickly; dark hair, (but if ♀ be in her own term, a sad-brown). They are generally persons who love their belly, fond of enjoyment, not fortunate, subject to sudden changes in life and strange catastrophes.

♀ in ♒

Gives a handsome, well-formed person, clear complexion, rather corpulent or large body, brown hair, if she be in her own term, flaxen. A good disposition, quiet, affable, courteous, not at all inclined to vicious actions, peaceable, obliging to all, fortunate in his affairs, and respected by his friends and acquaintance in general.

♀ in ♓

Personates a middle stature, a fleshy plump body, a round full face, with a dimple in the chin, good complexion, between pale and ruddy. Good-humoured, just, kind, mild and peaceable, ingenious, but somewhat unstable, yet moderately fortunate in the world.

MERCURY *in the Twelve Signs.*

☿ in ♈

Gives a mean stature, spare and thin body, oval face, light brown and curling hair, dull complexion. A mind rather ill-disposed, addicted to dispute, to lie, steal, and many tricks and unworthy actions; in short, a mere knave.

☿ in ♉

Gives a middle-sized, corpulent, thick person, strong and well set, swarthy sun-burnt complexion, dark short and thick hair. He is idle, slothful, one who loves ease and gluttony, and who ruins himself among the female sex.

☿ in ♊

Shews a tall, upright, straight body, well formed, brown hair, good complexion, and a very intelligent look. An ingenious pregnant fancy, a good orator, a cunning lawyer, or clever bookseller; one who perfectly understands his own interests, and (if ☿ be not afflicted) one who is a subtle politician, not easily deluded by the most cunning knave he may encounter.

☿ in ♋

Personates a low, short stature, or squab figure, an ill complexion, a thin sharp face, small eyes, sharp nose, dark hair; one who is given to drink, light-fingered, ill-natured, dishonest, and very deceitful and changeable; a very mean little wretch, if ☿ be afflicted.

☿ in ♌

Gives a full large body, and good stature, dull, swarthy, sunburnt complexion, light brown hair, round face, full eyes, a broad or high nose. A hasty, proud, conceited, ambitious, boasting, and contentious troublesome character.

☿ in ♍

Denotes a tall, slender, well-proportioned person, dark brown hair, (or if ☿ be in the terms of ♃ or ♄, black hair), not a clear complexion, a long visage, and austere countenance. A very witty, ingenious, talented mind; and if ☿ be free from affliction, a profound scholar or linguist, and capable of any undertaking which requires great ability.

☿ in ♎

Personates a tall body, well made, but not thin; light brown, smooth hair, a ruddy or sanguine complexion. A just, virtuous, prudent man, a lover and promoter of learning, and having great natural abilities, and many acquired accomplishments.

☿ in ♏

Gives a short, mean, stature, full and well-set but ill-made body, broad shoulders, swarthy, dark complexion, brown curling hair. Not any way elegant or pleasing, yet ingenious and studious; very careful of his own interests, fond of the female sex, and partial to company and merry making.

☿ in ♐

Denotes a person of tall stature, well formed, not corpulent, but rather large boned and spare; an oval face, a large nose. and ruddy complexion. A man who is hasty but soon reconciled, rash in many things to his own injury, yet well disposed, striving after honourable things, but seldom attaining them; not very fortunate.

☿ in ♑

Gives a mean, small stature, often crooked make and bow-legged, a thin face and figure, dusky complexion, and brown hair. A very peevish, discontented, dejected, sickly, feeble person, yet active; one who is unfortunate to himself and disagreeable to others, owing to his suspicious nature and ill temper.

☿ in ♒

Shews a person of middle height, rather fleshy and corpulent, a good complexion and clear skin, with brown hair and full face. An ingenious, obliging character, inclined to study, fond of arts and sciences, very inventive, and remarkable for his talent, as well as being a humane, kind, charitable person.

☿ in ♓

Gives a short, squab, dumpy figure, though if in his own term or that of ♄, rather thin, pale face, brown hair, sickly look, and very hairy body. A very peevish, repining, foppish person, addicted to wine and women; very effeminate and contemptible.

The Moon *in the Twelve Signs.*

☽ in ♈

Describes a person of indifferent stature, rather fleshy or plump, round face, tolerably good complexion, light brown or flaxen hair. The mind is rash, angry, ambitious, and aspiring, often changing; and he undergoes various mutations in life; not often fortunate.

☽ in ♉

Gives a strong, corpulent, well-set body, rather short, pretty good complexion, dark brown or black hair. A gentle, obliging, kind, sober, just, and honest man; one who gains esteem, is much respected, and attains preferment according to his situation in life.

☽ in ♊

Describes a tall, well-formed, upright, comely person, brown hair, good complexion, between pale and sanguine. The mind is ingenious, yet crafty and subtle to excess; not of the best disposition, nor very fortunate, unless other good testimonies by aspects of ♃, ☉, or ♀ concur.

☽ in ♋

Represents a middle stature, well proportioned, and fleshy person, a round, full face, pale, dusky complexion, sad-brown hair. The mind is flexible, given to change; a merry, easy, pleasant, disposition, very harmless and peaceable, fond of good company; one who is generally well-beloved, and fortunate in most affairs; unsteady, but free from passion or rash actions.

☽ in ♌

Denotes a person above the middle size, well proportioned, strong, and large boned, sanguine complexion, light brown hair, large and prominent eyes, and full face. A lofty, proud, aspiring person, very ambitious, and desirous to bear rule; one who abhors servitude or dependence, and is generally an unfortunate person.

☽ in ♍

Describes a rather tall person, dark brown or black hair, oval face, rather ruddy, but tolerably clear complexion. An ingenious, reserved, covetous, melancholy, unfortunate person; not in general very well disposed, and one who seldom performs any very commendable actions.

☽ in ♎

Gives a tall, well-composed body, with smooth, light brown hair, handsome and pleasant cheerful countenance, fine red and white complexion. They are merry, jocund, and pleasant, and much admired by the female sex; very fond of amusement; and, if a female, she is courted by numbers, but yet unfortunate, unless ♀, the dispositor, be very strong and well aspected, &c.

☽ in ♏

Denotes a thick, short, and ill-shaped person, a fleshy obscure complexion, dark hair, often black, (especially if ☽ be in the term of ♃ or ♄). They are sottish and vulgar, malicious, brutish, and treacherous; and if it be a female, she is generally infamous in her desires, and if ☽ be afflicted by the □ or ☍ of ♄ or ♂, she is openly scandalous.

☽ in ♐

Represents a handsome and well-proportioned rather tall person; oval face, sanguine complexion, rather bronzed, and bright brown or shining chestnut hair. The disposition is good, open and generous, but hasty and passionate, yet forgiving; one who aims at great things, is fortunate, and much respected by those with whom he associates.

☽ in ♑

Gives a person of low stature, a thin, small, weak body, bad health, and feeble, especially about the knees; the complexion bad, black hair, and small features; one who is inactive, dull, not ingenious, generally very debauched in his conduct, and held in low esteem by his companions, &c.

☽ in ♒

Represents a middle-sized person, well made, and rather corpulent, brown hair, clear skin, and sanguine complexion. They are ingenious, affable, courteous, and inoffensive; a lover of curious and scientific studies, having much invention, and a person rarely guilty of unworthy actions.

☽ in ♓

Describes a person of a mean or low stature, but plump or fat, pale and bloated face, light brown hair, and sleepy eyes; one not inclined to action, unless of the worst kind; unfortunate both to himself and others; given to drink.

N.B. If ☽ be well aspected, and in a good house, the disposition is much improved.

EFFECTS OF THE ASPECTS BETWEEN THE SIGNIFICATORS.

♄ ☌ ♃.

If ♄ be significator, he gives the querent inheritance of estates, and profit by means of agriculture; his disposition is extremely moral and grave; he may gain a fortune by merchandize, or, probably, by preaching.

If ♃ be significator, the disposition is not so good; the querent seldom meets with much success in the world; he is very niggardly, and generally acquires property by some selfish and unusual means; though he seldom enjoys it like other persons. He generally lives hated by every one for his mean and deceitful ways, and dies in obscurity.

If ♂ be in □ to the significator, and in aspect with ☿, the querent is generally duped of his property, and dies a miserable death.

♄ ☌ ♂.

If ♄ be significator, the querent is of a rash, turbulent disposition, and generally very unfortunate; very often engaged in some public calling of the lowest order, and frequently ends his days in prison.

If ♂ be significator, the disposition is equally bad, but not quite so rash, being more sly and cowardly. Sometimes he gains favour from elderly persons, who assist him with their property, which he generally loses in the end, and becomes very unfortunate; especially if the significators be under the earth.

♄ ☌ ☉

Signifies losses to the querent by fire, (especially if they be in a fiery sign), or by men in power, who persecute him, and confine him within the walls of a prison for some contempt of the law; and he is seldom healthy or of long life.

If ☉ be significator, the querent is generally very disagreeable, deceitful, mistrustful, and unfortunate; always losing his property by some speculation, which in the end often brings him to ruin; particularly if the querent have anything to do with the government, or persons connected with the state.

♄ ☌ ♀

Shews gain to the querent by means of ladies, to a considerable extent; he is much attached to them, greatly addicted to pleasure, and very fortunate where females are concerned. If he be a man of property, he often wastes most of it by gaming or pleasure.

If ♀ be significator, the querent is very artful, sly, unfortunate, destitute of friends, often disappointed by death; and he loses considerably by persons older than himself, especially if he be in trade.

♄ ☌ ☿.

If ♄ be significator, the querent is subtle and crafty, fond of researches into antiquity; one of much gravity and considerable learning; though not always of the most agreeable manners.

If ☿ be significator, he is dull, suspicious, mean, cowardly, calculating, and covetous. Should he turn his attention to literature, he may gain some knowledge, although with great labour; and should he become an author, his writings may bring him into some disgrace.

♄ ☌ ☽.

If ♄ be significator, the person is restless and unsettled in his purposes, and often changes his residence. He is not very fortunate, though he may sometimes benefit by the populace, and by the lower order of females.

If ☽ be significator, he is poor, miserable, and dejected; of unpleasant manners, and sullen disposition; extremely unfortunate, and uncommonly covetous, though possessing scarcely any property. With much suspicious caution, he frequently commits the most unaccountable errors in affairs of the greatest consequence; as, through excess of prudence, he is very likely to doubt and deliberate in the moment of action.

♃ ☌ ♂.

If ♃ be significator, the querent is bold, proud, and ambitious; fond of martial exploits and enterprises; a good soldier or surgeon; though he may lose much by strife and contention, and sometimes receive wounds in quarrels.

If ♂ be significator, he is good, pious, and just; he is eminently successful in the law or the church; and often makes a fortune by those means.

♃ ☌ ☉.

If ♃ be significator, the querent is weak, servile, and credulous; he incurs the displeasure of men in power, by whom he is much oppressed, and often ruined; he has bad health; and is generally a vain, loquacious character, indulging in fanciful speculations about religion, and other matters, for which he is totally unqualified.

If ☉ be significator, the power of ♃ is so much destroyed by the power of ☉, that he has but very little effect; though the party will, in general, be very much given to religion, which, if ♃ be well dignified in other respects, and not ill-aspected, will be sincere, otherwise it is fanatical or hypocritical.

♃ ☌ ♀.

If ♃ be significator, it promises the greatest happiness; the querent is highly favoured by the female sex, by whose means he gains great advancement; he is rich, prosperous, and fortunate; very healthy, and greatly admired and respected. It shews great personal beauty.

If ♀ be significator, it denotes great beauty of person, (unless ♀ be in ♏ or ♑), riches, honours, ecclesiastical preferment; the person so represented is truly virtuous, pious, kind and beneficent to all, with the greatest goodness of heart, and a disposition that will command universal love and esteem.

♃ ☌ ☿.

If ♃ be significator, it denotes a person of great learning, a good lawyer or divine, of excellent abilities and much information.

If ☿ be significator, he is mild, humane, religious, fond of literature; possessing an elegant mind, and a gentle, engaging disposition; he is raised to eminence, and protected by powerful patrons; he accumulates great riches, and is, in general, extremely fortunate.

♃ ☌ ☽.

If ♃ be significator, the person so represented is restless and changeable, and seldom sufficiently settled to procure much wealth; he is, on the whole, very fortunate, often gains considerably by marriage, and is a general favourite with the fair sex; he is a great traveller, and is eminently successful in maritime affairs and among seamen, shipping, &c.

If ☽ be significator, he is fortunate in ecclesiastical affairs; or among mercantile men, magistrates, &c. He obtains great wealth, though he is liable to losses frequently by canting, hypocritical persons, who impose upon his natural kindness and generosity of disposition. He has, however, too much good fortune to be injured by those persons to any serious extent.

♂ ☌ ☉.

If ♂ be significator, the querent is in danger by fire, lightning, or infectious fevers; it has been said in this case, with great truth, "he has the favour of kings and princes," and it may be their frowns too, to his utter undoing; he may rise hastily, but, perhaps, to a precipice.

If ☉ be significator, the querent is brave, but headstrong and violent; he will probably attain some considerable rank in the army or navy; but he will be frequently wounded, and most probably die in battle, or be killed by some accident, or fall a victim to some contagious fever.

♂ ☌ ♀.

If ♂ be significator, the querent is kind and gentle upon the whole, though at times rather hasty; he is moderately fortunate, extremely fond of women, and not always very particular as to their respectability.

If ♀ be significator, he is wicked and debauched, a companion of prostitutes, from whom he generally receives great injury; a drunkard, frequently brawling in taverns or low public-houses; though he may sometimes meet with good fortune, he will quickly dissipate whatever property he may possess in the company of the most worthless of mankind.

♂ ☌ ☿.

If ♂ be significator, it represents the querent as possessed of considerable ability, a skilful mechanic, or a good mathematician; one of an acute sarcastic wit; if he be in the army or navy, for which he is well qualified, he obtains great reputation for his bravery, and is distinguished still more for the policy of his measures. He is never very scrupulous as to the means he employs; and will pay but little respect to the persons or possessions of others, when he can gain any advantage by sacrificing them to his own interest.

If ☿ be significator, he makes a cheat or swindler, a thief, robber, or treacherous miscreant; a frequenter of gaming-houses, rash, furious, and blood-thirsty.

N.B.—Any evil aspect of ♄ increases these evils, and a good aspect of ☉, ♃, or ♀, will much diminish them.

♂ ☌ ☽.

If ♂ be significator, it shews one of an unsettled life and temper, and a favourite of females; he is frequently a wandering adventurer, more remarkable for the variety of his fortune than his success or abilities. He is likely to die in a strange country.

If ☽ be significator, he is a bold, enterprising character; frequently in great danger of a violent death, quarrelsome, and given to duelling, &c. He may be a good surgeon or soldier; and is seldom noted for much humanity. If a female, she is extremely likely to be seduced.

☉ ☌ ♀.

If ☉ be significator, it denotes one of soft and effeminate manners, a pleasing address, a great admirer of the ladies. He is too much given to extravagance and dissipation.

If ♀ be significator, he is of short life, unfortunate, and oppressed; too sickly to make much exertion; very proud and extravagant.

☉ ☌ ☿.

If ☉ be significator, it gives some ingenuity, but not much sound judgment.

If ☿ be significator, he represents a person of mean and shallow abilities; one addicted to fraud and deception; incapable of learning anything which requires memory or judgment, and extremely superstitious. He may succeed well in trade or business, but for study he is wholly unqualified.

☉ ☌ ☽.

If ☉ be significator, it represents a restless and changeable person, who aims at great things, but seldom accomplishes them.

If ☽ be significator, the querent is extremely unfortunate, and generally sickly and unhappy, dejected, and oppressed by men in power. He is rash and violent, subject to burns and scalds, and has frequently some defect in the eyes; and if the ☌ happen near the *Hyades*, *Pleiades*, or *Præspe*, he is likely to be nearly blind. If the ☽ be applying, he is in danger of death, especially if it happen in the 8th house, or ☉ be lord of the 8th; but if ☽ be separating, the danger is not so great.

♀ ☌ ☿

If ♀ be significator, it represents one who is polite, mild, and courteous, fond of the elegant branches of literature; a pleasant companion, a favourite of females; and one of an excellent disposition.

If ☿ be significator, he excels in any pursuit that requires taste; a good painter, an excellent poet or musician, of a very humane disposition, and of the most prepossessing appearance.

N.B. It must be most carefully observed, whether these planets have any other familiarity at the same time; for should ♅, ♄, or ♂ be in □, it will make a most remarkable difference. Indeed, this must be scrupulously attended to in all cases, but especially, where ♀, ☿, or ☽ may be significator.

♀ ☌ ☽.

If ♀ be significator, it renders a man very mutable and uncertain; often promising, through goodness of disposition, much more than he is capable of performing.

If ☽ be significator, he is of an easy, happy, disposition, with little care beyond the enjoyment of the present moment; a great proficient in all elegant amusements, and of an easy and genteel address.

☿ ☌ ☽.

If ☿ be significator, the native is possessed of great abilities, though generally very unsteady in his pursuits. He frequently travels in some literary capacity.

If ☽ be significator, the effects are not very different; his intellectual powers are of the first order; he is much attached to learning, and gains great reputation by his abilities.

OF THE ✶ AND △ ASPECTS BETWEEN THE SIGNIFICATORS.

♄ ✶ or △ ♃.

If ♄ be significator, it gives riches by means of agriculture; and he is of a sedate and religious disposition.

If ♃ be significator, he is extremely grave, and frequently gains riches by legacies or mining concerns.

$$♄ \;\ast\; or \;\triangle\; ♂.$$

If ♄ be significator, it increases the courage of the person so signified, and renders him more open in his resentment.

If ♂ be significator, he is prudent and cautious, bigotted in religion, and, should other aspects befriend ♂, he may gain an estate.

$$♄ \;\ast\; or \;\triangle\; ☉.$$

If ♄ be significator, he is generous and noble, though somewhat austere in his behaviour.

If ☉ be significator, he is ostentatious, boastful, and conceited; he may be expected to gain by legacies, or to be successful as a farmer.

$$♄ \;\ast\; or \;\triangle\; ♀.$$

If ♄ be significator, he is prodigal and extravagant, wasting his money among females.

If ♀ be significator, he is modest, shy, and retired in his manners; he gains the favour of elderly people, and sometimes inherits their property.

$$♄ \;\ast\; or \;\triangle\; ☿.$$

If ♄ be significator, it gives ingenuity and subtilty, though his talents are mostly employed to little purpose.

If ☿ be significator, he is very cautious and prudent, and is addicted to the study of arts and sciences.

$$♄ \;\ast\; or \;\triangle\; ☽.$$

If ♄ be significator, the querent is changeable, jealous, and mistrustful.

If ☽ be significator, he is vain and conceited, mean in his actions, though without the excuse of rashness, as he does nothing without much deliberation.

♃ ✶ or △ ♂.

If ♃ be significator, it gives bravery, and the spirit of military adventure; he is a good soldier, surgeon, or chemist

If ♂ be significator, he is noble, generous, and ambitious and will rise rapidly in the army.

♃ ✶ or △ ☉.

If ♃ be significator, it makes one extremely fortunate, and very noble and courageous in his disposition.

If ☉ be significator, he gains money rapidly, is always respected, and possesses a most excellent disposition.

♃ ✶ or △ ♀.

If ♃ be significator, it causes beauty, love, riches, and real goodness of heart: this is the most fortunate aspect that can be formed.

If ♀ be significator, the person is virtuous, amiable, of a noble disposition, incapable of fraud or malice.

♃ ✶ or △ ☿.

If ♃ be significator, it gives great learning, sound judgment, and excellent abilities.

If ☿ be significator, he possesses solid sense, an open generous disposition, and real good fortune.

♃ ✶ or △ ☽.

If ♃ be significator, it makes a man very fortunate, beloved by females, and much respected by the poorer classes of society.

If ☽ be significator, he is just and charitable, sincere in his friendships, and generous to the full extent of his means

♂ ✶ or △ ☉.

If ♂ be significator, it gives a very noble disposition, and great mind; it causes one to rise rapidly in the army; he is uncommonly successful in war, and will gain much by the patronage of men in power.

If ☉ be significator, it confers great bravery, and a high spirit; he rises to grandeur by means of his courage and invincible military talents.

♂ ⚹ or △ ♀.

If ♂ be significator, it causes lewdness and dissipation; his disposition is not radically bad, but he is extremely thoughtless and improvident; he may gain by females, for he seems to possess a fascinating influence, which he never fails to exert to the utmost with the female sex.

If ♀ be significator, he is handsome, but proud, rash, and inconsiderate; and neither remarkable for prudence nor principle.

♂ ⚹ or △ ☿.

If ♂ be significator, this aspect gives great acuteness, penetration, and learning; the querent, however, is crafty, rather hasty, and extremely confident.

If ☿ be significator, he possesses great courage, is very ingenious in any mechanical trade, a good engraver or mathematician, and will succeed in any thing that requires presence of mind, acuteness, and ready wit.

If ☿ receive any aspect of ♅, he is extremely fitted to become a good astrologer, especially if ☽ assist ☿.

♂ ⚹ or △ ☽.

If ♂ be significator, it makes one restless and changeable, servile and talkative; he travels much, and receives much assistance from females.

If ☽ be significator, he is very passionate and changeable, with a high spirit and good abilities.

☉ ✶ or △ ☽.

If ☉ be significator, it confers riches and honour; the querent is fortunate with women, and is much respected by the multitude.

If ☽ be significator, he is proud and aspiring; he is generally successful, but his fortune is not permanent, unless both ☉ and ☽ be in fixed signs.

♀ ✶ or △ ☿.

If ♀ be significator, this aspect gives ingenuity, subtlety, and good nature.

If ☿ be significator, the querent possesses a refined and accomplished mind; he is neat in his person, and elegant in his manners; a lover of music and the fine arts in general.

♀ ✶ or △ ☽.

If ♀ be significator, it is a very fortunate aspect; it shews a person who is much assisted by female friends; and one who, though unstable, often obtains considerable property.

If ☽ be significator, the querent is gentle, obliging, amiable, and genteel in his manners, and is much admired by females; whose condition in life depends on the strength or debility of ♀.

☿ ✶ or △ ☽.

If ☿ be significator, the person signified is witty, ingenious, subtle, easily learning any thing to which he applies, and frequently acquiring many sciences without any assistance. He is somewhat reserved, and a little melancholy, but, from his extensive knowledge, he is always a useful and sometimes a pleasant companion.

If ☽ be significator, this is the most favourable aspect for learning or scientific speculation.

THE EFFECTS OF THE □ OR ☍ ASPECTS BETWEEN THE SIGNIFICATORS.

♄ □ or ☍ ♃.

If ♄ be significator, it shews much trouble by lawyers or [th]e clergy.

If ♃ be significator, he is always wretched and miserable, [vi]le, unfortunate, and beggarly.

♄ □ or ☍ ♂.

If ♄ be significator, it is the aspect of cruelty and murder, [an]d the person so signified is extremely unfortunate; he ge[ne]rally lives a most dejected life, and dies a violent death.

If ♂ be significator, the person shewn by him is very mali[ci]ous, treacherous, and blood-thirsty; one delighting in the [m]ost evil deeds, yet very cowardly, sly, and much addicted to [su]icide and secret revenge; of a cruel complexion: in short, [su]ch a character as Don Miguel of Portugal.

♄ □ or ☍ ☉.

If ♄ be significator, it is the aspect of infamy and con[te]mpt; the person is prodigal, ambitious, overbearing, hating [co]ntrol, very disagreeable in his manners, extremely unfortu[na]te, subject to the frowns of persons in power, and often [m]eets a violent death.

If ☉ be significator, the person is cowardly, spiteful, [tr]eacherous, malicious, unfeeling, covetous, repining, always [de]spising any thing of kindness and humanity; one who [ge]nerally leads a life of wretchedness, and frequently meets [wi]th a bad end, and sometimes dies in prison.

♄ □ or ☍ ♀.

If ♄ be significator, it shews dissipation, and the person [lea]ds a most detestable life, connected with the lowest order of prostitutes, by whom he is eventually brought to ruin and disgrace.

If ♀ be significator, the person is generally of an evil complexion, and not very handsome; very sly, artful, full of mischief, and much addicted to dissipation, though not suspected; mostly unfortunate.

♄ ☐ or ☍ ☿.

If ♄ be significator, it indicates a thief, cheat, or swindler; a low, cunning fellow, sly, envious, treacherous, and malicious, one who is always planning some scheme to deceive his most intimate friends; generally forming a bad opinion of every one, and not at all particular as to speaking the truth.

If ☿ be significator, the person is very artful, always involved in strife and contention, and much given to vilify the character of others, by whom he is tormented with lawsuits; it also indicates pettifogging attornies, who very seldom act honestly towards their clients.

♄ ☐ or ☍ ☽.

If ♄ be significator, it shews a wandering, unsettled and changeable person, not of a genteel form, but one who is down-looking, and inclined to stoop forward; always very fretful, and appearing full of trouble; not a good disposition, nor to be depended on. He seldom attains any high situation, but, if he does, he soon falls into disgrace again.

If ☽ be significator, (*which in some measure she always is of the* QUERENT), the person is extremely unfortunate, always in trouble with the lower order of mankind, from whom he receives many injuries; he is mean, cowardly, and very dejected; is rather unhealthy, seldom living a long life, and generally dying a miserable death.

♃ □ or ☍ ♂.

If ♃ be significator, it denotes violence, ingratitude, a furious temper, and danger of death by malignant fevers.

If ♂ be significator, it shews pride, ingratitude, insolence, and the hatred of the clergy on account of theological opinions.

♃ □ or ☍ ☉.

If ♃ be significator, it gives arrogance, prodigality, and much vanity, with a great desire to be distinguished, which is but very rarely gratified.

If ☉ be significator, the person represented wastes his property by riotous living and all kinds of extravagance.

♃ □ or ☍ ♀.

If ♃ be significator, it shews extravagance, dissipation, and all kinds of debauchery and intemperance.

If ♀ be significator, the person has many enemies among the clergy, and the legal profession, magistrates, &c., and he is equally void of virtue and prudence.

♃ □ or ☍ ☿.

If ♃ be significator, it gives trouble, contention, perplexities, lawsuits, and, in consequence, indigence.

If ☿ be significator, the person is frequently persecuted for his singular religious opinions; his understanding is weak, and he is often involved in strife and contention.

♃ □ or ☍ ☽.

If ♃ be significator, it shews one of many words, though of poor abilities; he is weak and foolish, and, if in a public capacity, is execrated by the multitude.

If the ☽ be significator, he is injured by faithless friends and deceitful relatives; and his property is impoverished by hypocritical fanatics.

♂ □ or ☍ ☉.

If ♂ be significator, it denotes a man of great ambition and violence; but his fortune is too evil to allow him to succeed.

If the ☉ be significator, he is restrained by no principle of honour or gratitude; his affairs are always deranged, and he makes use of the most violent means to retrieve them. Such a one frequently becomes a footpad, murderer, or housebreaker, and is either killed in some contest, or falls a victim to the laws of his country.

♂ □ or ☍ ♀.

If ♂ be significator, these aspects cause lust, excess, prodigality, disease, and injury by loose women, and complete waste of fortune.

If ♀ be significator, he is very treacherous, mischievous, base, and inconstant; or if it be a female, she is a prostitute, or very shameless.

♂ □ or ☍ ☿.

If ♂ be significator, it shews one of some ability, but his talents are applied to the most dishonourable purposes.

If ☿ be significator, it denotes a thief or assassin; one whose most solemn protestations are not to be believed; who will desert his benefactors at their utmost need: he is violent, furious, contentious, and despised by every one for his infamous life.

♂ □ or ☍ ☽.

If ♂ be significator, the querent described by him is a fit companion for the lowest and most unprincipled of mankind; he is very unfortunate, and is probably a wandering vagabond, who travels over the earth without a friend or a home.

If ☽ be significator, he is excessively abusive, malicious, and treacherous. He may travel into foreign countries as a sailor or soldier, amidst innumerable dangers and hardships, and die by pestilence, dysentery, or the sword.

☉ □ or ☍ ☽.

If the ☉ be significator, the person suffers losses, trouble, and much anxiety.

If ☽ be significator, he is obstinate and quarrelsome; he is exceedingly ambitious and prodigal; and is sometimes marked in the face, or his eyes are affected: the latter is especially the case if ☉ be afflicted by ♂, or either ☉ or ☽ are with the *nebulous* stars.

♀ □ or ☍ ☽.

If ♀ be significator, it shews a changeable, unsettled life, great troubles in marriage, and much ill-fortune.

If the ☽ be significator, it shews a dissolute, extravagant life, attended with indigence and poverty, and much trouble from females.

☿ □ or ☍ ☽.

If ☿ be significator, it no doubt gives some abilities, but such persons are too unsettled to apply very closely to any subject; they are continually shifting their situations, (especially if ☿ be in a moveable sign), nor are they very sincere in their professions of friendship, nor very scrupulous in the method by which they may attain their ends.

If ☽ be significator, they have a defect in their utterance, have but little ability, except a kind of low cunning, which they apply to dishonest purposes. But as ☿ is acted on by every planet having an aspect to him, it will be necessary to observe each aspect, and allow for its influence; for if ☿ have a △ of ♃, the □ of ☿ to ☽ will not be near so evil, though the person will be far from sensible, notwithstanding that they are tolerably honest and well-meaning.

OBSERVATION.—The student must always remember, that the true character and condition of the person signified can only be correctly learned by noticing all the aspects the significator may receive, as well as observing the nature of the sign and house it is in, and the degree of strength or weakness it possesses, as well as those planets which aspect it. Thus, if the significator be ♂, and he receive the ☍ of ☉, yet if ☉ be weak, and ♂ have also a △ of ♃, this benefic planet being strong, he may judge that the querent will suffer by the evil influence of ☉, by receiving a severe wound in a duel, or in honourable warfare; whereas if, instead of the △ of ♃, the □ of ☿ occurred, there would be little doubt that he would be killed by police officers, or die by the hand of the public executioner; the latter especially, if ☉ was in the 10th house.

A List of Fixed Stars which may be considered in Horary Questions; with their approximate Longitude, Jan. 1, 1835.*

NAMES.	LONGITUDE.			LATITUDE.			NATURE.		MAGNITUDE.
Ram's following Horn	♉	5	21	9	57	N.	♄	♂	SECOND.
The Pleiades	♉	26	55	4	31	N.	♂	☽	FIFTH.
The Brightest of the Seven Stars	♉	27	50	4	2	N.	♂	☽	THIRD.
Occulus Taurus, or the Bull's North Eye	♊	6	11	2	36	S.	♀		THIRD.
Aldebaran, or the Bull's South Eye	♊	7	31	5	29	S.	♂		FIRST.
The Bull's North Horn	♊	20	17	5	22	N.	♂		SECOND.
Bright Foot of Gemini	♋	6	46	6	48	S.	☿	♀	SECOND.
Castor	♋	17	48	10	4	N.	♂ ♀	♄	FIRST.
Pollux	♋	20	59	6	40	N.	♂		SECOND.
North Asellus	♌	4	45	3	10	N.	♂	☉	FOURTH.
Præspe, or the Claw of the Crab	♌	5	0	1	14	N.	♂	☽	NEBULOUS
South Asellus	♌	6	26	0	4	N.	♂	☉	FOURTH.
Hydra's Heart	♌	19	43	7	32	S.	♄	♀	SECOND.
Cor ♌, the Lion's Heart	♌	27	33	0	27	N.	♂		FIRST.
Vindemiatrix	♍	7	38	10	15	S.	♄ ♀	☿	THIRD.
Arista, the Virgin's Spike	♎	21	33	2	2	S.	♀	♂	FIRST.
South Scale	♏	12	48	0	22	N.	♄	♂	SECOND.
North Scale	♏	17	0	8	46	N.	♃	♂	SECOND.
Frons Scorpio	♐	0	54	1	2	N.	♄	♀	SECOND.
Antares, or the Scorpion's Heart	♐	7	29	4	32	S.	☿	♂	FIRST.
Right Knee of *Ophiucus*	♐	15	41	7	18	N.	♄	♀	THIRD.
Capricorn's Tail	♒	21	15	2	33	S	♄		THIRD.
Scheat Pegasi	♓	26	29	1	7	N.	♄		SECOND.

* These are the principal fixed stars, near the ecliptic, to which only the planets can approach. If the student require the places of the stars for the purpose of bringing them to the midheaven or ascendant in a nativity, he may learn their right ascension and declination in the Nautical Almanac for each year, and he may readily calculate their longitudes and latitudes therefrom by the rules we have given.

N.B. The longitudes increase about 50" ⅓ each year; the latitudes do not vary.

APPENDIX. 335

Rules to find the Zodiacal Latitude and Longitude of a Fixed Star, Comet, Planet, or the ⊕, &c. from the Right Ascension and Declination.

1st. If the right ascension be less than 180°, it is *north;* and if it be more than 180°, it is *south.*

2d. To the logarithm *co-tangent* of the declination add the logarithm *sine* of the right ascension, measured from ♈ or ♎; but if measured from ♋ or ♑, the logarithm *co-sine:* the sum (minus 10 in the Index), will be the *log. tangent* of the angle A.

3d. If the right ascension and declination be both *north*, or both *south*, add 23° 28′ to angle A, and it will give angle B.

4th. If the right ascension and declination be one *north* and the other *south*, the difference between 23° 28′ and angle A will give angle B.

Note.—If angle B exceed 90°, the latitude will be of the contrary name to the declination; but if angle B be less than 90°, the latitude will be of the same name as the declination.

To find the Longitude.

To the arithmetical comp. of the log. *sine* of angle A, and the log. *sine* of angle B, add the log. *tang.* of R.A. from ♈ or ♎, (or the log. *co-tang* of R.A. from ♋ or ♑). The sum will be the log. *tang.* of the longitude from ♈ or ♎, or the log. *co-tang.* of the longitude from ♋ or ♑.

To find the Latitude.

To the arithmetical comp. of the log. *co-sine* of angle A, and the log. *co-sine* of angle B, add the log. *sine* of the declination. The sum will be the log. *sine* of the latitude.

N.B. The arithmetical complement of a logarithm is found by subtracting it from . . . 10.00000
Example. The log. sine of 13° 10′ is . 9.35752
―――――――
0.64248

or it may be found with equal ease, by taking each figure (beginning at the *left* hand or index), from 9, except the last or right-hand figure, which must be taken from 10.

Thus: if from	.	.	.	.	9.99990
we take	.	.	.	.	9.35752
It gives	.	.	.	.	0.64248

the object of this being to perform each problem by addition, in lieu of the lengthy process otherwise required.

EXAMPLE.—Required the zodiacal longitude and latitude of Halley's comet, at noon, on the 18th October, 1835, Greenwich mean time?

Comet's right ascension, 16^h 25.31 equal in degrees to 246° 19', which, being more than 180°, is *south*. The declination is 0° 35' *north*.

Co-tangent dec.	.	0° 35'	$=$	11.99219
Sine R.A. from ♎	.	66 19	$=$	9.96179
Tang. angle A	$=$	89 22	—	11.95398
From angle A take	.	23 28		
It gives angle B	.	65 54		

Then for the Longitude.

To the *sine* angle A (arith. comp.)	.	.	0.00003
Add the *sine* angle B	.	.	9.96039
And Tang. R. A. from ♎	66° 19'	$=$	10.35791
Tang. longitude from ♎	64 20	$=$	10.31833
Take the long. of ♎ and ♏ from this	60 0		
It leaves . . . ♐ 4 20, the longitude.			

Then for the Latitude.

To the log. co-sine angle A (arith. comp.) .	1.95650
Add the log. co-sine angle B . . .	9.61101
And log. sine of the dec.	8.00779
It gives the log. sine of the latitude 22° 6′ =	9.57530

As angle B is less than 90°, the latitude is of the same name as the declination; which being north, the latitude is north also.

Hence the comet will be, at mean noon, Greenwich time, on the 18th of October, 1835, in ♐ 4° 20′, with 22° 6′ north latitude.

EXPLANATION OF TERMS USED IN THIS WORK.

Abscission.—See "Frustration."

Affliction.—A planet, or the cusp of a house, being in evil aspect to any planet, or ☌ to a malefic.

Angles.—The four houses which commence at the points where the ☉ rises, culminates, sets, and arrives at midnight; viz. the east, south, west, and north.

Application.—The approaching of one planet to another, or to the cusp of any house, either by ☌ or any aspect.

Ascendant.—The eastern horizon, or the cusp of that house which represents the party; as the cusp of the 5th is the ascendant for a child of the querent.

Aspect.—The being placed at certain distances from a planet, or the cusp of a house: as, if ♃ be 60 degrees from ☽, then they are both said to be in *sextile* aspect to each other. They are found to agree exactly with *the angles of regular polygons which may be inscribed in a circle.* An elucidation of this property of all astrological aspects may be seen in the "*Grammar of Astrology.*"

Barren Signs.—♊, ♌, and ♍.

Benefics.—The two planets ♃ and ♀.

Bestial Signs.—♈, ♉, ♌, ♐ (the first half excepted), and ♑.

Besieged.—A planet being enclosed between two others.

Bicorporeal.—See "Double Bodied."

Cadent.—Falling from an angle: these are the 3d, 6th, 9th, and 12th houses.

Cazimi.—The heart of ☉, or being within 17 minutes of the

exact longitude of ☉; which is considered a strong position, but, we think, erroneously.

Collection of Light.—When a planet receives the aspects of any two others which are not themselves in aspect. It denotes that the affair will be forwarded by a third person, described by that planet; but not unless they both receive him in some of their dignities.

Combustion.—The being within 8° 30′ of the ☉, which is said to burn up those planets near him, so that they lose their power. It is always an evil testimony.

Common Signs.—♊, ♍, ♐, and ♓.

Conjunction.—Two planets being in the same longitude. If they be exactly in the same degree and minute, it is a partile conjunction, and very powerful; if within the half of the sum of their two orbs, it is a platic conjunction, and less powerful.

Culminate.—To arrive at the midheaven.

Cusp.—The beginning of any house.

Day House.—That house ruled by any planet by day; as ♒ is the day-house of ♄; ♐ of ♃, &c. If the question be asked by day, or while ☉ is above the horizon, and it be required to know what house ♄ rules, look for ♒; and wherever it may be found, that is the house of ♄.

Debilities.—See "Dignities."

Declination.—The distance any heavenly body is from the equator.

Decreasing in Light.—When any planet is past the ☌ of ☉, it decreases in light; it is a testimony of weakness.

Decumbiture.—A lying down; the figure erected for the time of any person being first taken ill, and taking to their bed.

Degree.—The 30th part of a sign in the zodiac; or the 360th part of any circle.

Descendant. — The western horizon; or cusp of the 7th house.

Detriment. — The sign opposite the house of any planet; as ♂ in ♎ is in his detriment. It is a sign of weakness, distress, &c.

Dignities. — These are either essential or accidental. The former are when any planet is in its own house, exaltation, triplicity, term or face; the latter are, when any planet is in an angle, and well aspected, not afflicted, swift in motion, increasing in light, &c. The reverse of dignities are debilities.

Direct. — When any planet moves on in the regular order of the signs, from ♈ towards ♉, &c.

Direction. — The calculating the arc between two heavenly bodies, &c. It is a term chiefly used in nativities.

Dispose, Dispositor. — A planet disposes of any other which may be found in its essential dignities. Thus, if ☉ be in ♈, the house of ♂, then ♂ disposes of ☉, and is said to rule, receive, or govern him. When the dispositor of the planet signifying the thing asked after is himself disposed by the lord of the ascendant, it is a good sign. To dispose by house is the most powerful testimony; then by exaltation, then triplicity, then term, and lastly, face, which is a very weak reception.

Double-bodied Signs. — ♊, ♐, ♓.

Dragon's Head. — It is thus marked, ☊, and is the north node of ☽, or where she crosses the ecliptic into north latitude. It is always a good symbol, denoting success, a good disposition, &c.

Dragon's Tail. — It is thus marked, ☋, and is where the ☽ crosses the ecliptic into south latitude, or her south node. It is very evil, and in all things the reverse of ☊; it diminishes the power of good, and increases that of evil planets.

Earthy Signs.—♉, ♍, and ♑, which form the earthy triplicity.

Ephemeris.—An almanack of the planets' places. The best is White's, until the year 1834, when it ceased to give the longitudes for each day. For horary questions, the best now published is Partridge's Almanack.

Exaltation.—An essential dignity, next in power to that of house.

Face.—The weakest of all the essential dignities.

Fall.—A planet is in its fall when in the sign opposite to its exaltation. It shews a person in a weak and hopeless state, unless the planet be well aspected.

Familiarity.—Any kind of aspect or reception.

Feminine Signs.—These are all the even signs, reckoning from Aries; as the 2d, 4th, 6th, 8th, &c.

Fiery Signs, or *Fiery Triplicity.*—♈, ♌, ♐.

Figure.—The diagram which represents the heavens at any time: it is also called a scheme or horoscope.

Fortunes.—♃ and ♀; and the ☉, ☽, and ☿, if aspecting them, and not afflicted, are considered fortunate planets.

Fruitful Signs.—♋, ♏, and ♓.

Frustration.—The cutting off or preventing any thing shewn by one aspect by means of another. Thus, if ♀, lady of the ascendant, were hastening to the △ of ♂, lord of the 7th, in a question of marriage, it might denote that the match would take place; but if ☿ were to form an ☍ of ♂ before ♀ reached her △ of that planet, it would be a frustration; and would shew that the hopes of the querent would be cut off; and if ☿ were lord of the 12th, it might denote that it would be done by a private enemy.

Horary Questions.—So named from the Latin word *hora*, an

hour, because the time of their being asked is noted, and the figure of the heavens for that time is taken to judge the result. The word *hora* appears to be derived from the Egyptian name for the Sun, which Herodotus informs us was *Horus* or *Orus;* the Hebrew *or*, lux, light, or day, and *oriens*, eastern, all appear to have had the same origin. The Budhists call the Sun *Hiru*, which, with its Braminical name also, appears equally to have been derived from Egypt, the first cradle of astrology.

Horoscope.—The ascendant is sometimes so called ; but it is more generally a term for the figure of the heavens used by astrologers for predicting by nativities, mundane astrology, and horary questions.

Houses.—The Twelve divisions or compartments into which the circle of the heavens is divided ; also the signs in which any planet is said to have most influence.

Human Signs.—♊, ♍, ♒, and the first half of ♐. Any person's significator therein, shews them to be of a humane disposition.

Impedited.—This signifies being afflicted by evil stars. The ☽ is impedited in the highest degree when in ☌ with ☉.

Joined to.—Being in any aspect.

Increasing in Light.—When any planet is leaving ☉, and is not yet arrived at the ☍; after which it decreases in light. The former is a good, the latter an evil testimony, especially as regards the ☽.

Increasing in Motion.—When any planet moves faster than it did on the preceding day.

Inferior Planets.—♀, ☿, and ☽; so called because their orbit is inferior to that of the earth.

Infortunes.—♅, ♄, and ♂ ; also ☿ when he is much afflicted.

Intercepted.—A sign which is found between the cusps of two houses, and not on either of them.

Latitude.—The distance any star, &c., is north or south of the ecliptic. The ☉ never has any latitude. Latitude on the earth is the distance any place is north or south of the equator.

Lights.—The ☉ and ☽.

Light of Time.—The ☉ by day and the ☽ by night.

Longitude.—The distance any star, &c., is from the first point of ♈, or beginning of the zodiac.

Lord.—That planet whose house is occupied by any other, is said to be the lord or ruler of that other; and if his sign be on the cusp of any house, he is called the lord of that house. Thus, if ♈ ascend in any figure, ♂, who rules that sign, is the lord of the ascendant.

Masculine Signs.—They are the odd signs, viz. the 1st, 3d, 5th, &c.

Medium Cœli.—The midheaven.

Meridian.—The midheaven, or place where ☉ is at noon. The opposite point, or where ☉ is at midnight, the cusp of the 4th house, is the meridian under the earth.

Moveable Signs.—♈, ♋, ♎, and ♑.

Night Houses.—Those signs in which the planets are stronger by night than by day. See "Day Houses."

Nodes.—The points where any planet crosses the ecliptic in its path of latitude.

Occidental.—See "Oriental."

Order of the Houses.—They rank in power as follows:—1st, 10th, 7th, 4th, 11th, 5th, 9th, 3d, 2d, 8th, 6th, 12th.

Orb.—That distance round a planet to which its influence more particularly extends. The orb of the cusp of any house, a fixed star, or ⊕, is five degrees.

Oriental.—Planets found between the fourth house and the midheaven, rising, are in the eastern half of the figure, and said to be oriental. When they have passed the midheaven, and until they reach the 4th again, they are occidental. In nativities, the ☉ and ☽ are oriental from the 1st to the 10th, and from the 7th to the 4th, and occidental in the opposite quarters.

Peregrine.—Having no essential dignity whatever. A planet is not reckoned peregrine that is in mutual reception with any other.

Platic.—Any aspect which is not partile or exact, but only within orbs, or rather within the moiety of the two planets' orbs. As if ♄ be in ♈ 10°, and ☽ in ♎ 20°, the ☽ is still in ☍ to ♄; because the half of their joint orbs being 10° 30', she still wants 30' of being clear of his ☍.

Querent.—The person who queries or inquires.

Quesited.—The person or thing inquired about.

Radical.—That which belongs to the radix, or root; fit to be judged.

Reception.—The being received by any planet is being in that planet's essential dignities; it is a good testimony when mutual. See "Dispose."

Refranation.—When two planets are coming to any aspect, and one falls retrograde before the aspect is complete, it denotes that the matter will wholly fail.

Retrograde.—When any planet is decreasing in longitude. It is a very great debility.

Separation.—When any aspect is past, but is yet within orbs, the planets are said to separate from each other. It denotes that the influence is passing away.

Significator.—The planet which is lord of the house which rules the matter inquired after, is the significator of the quesited; the lord of the ascendant is the general significator of the querent. The ☽ is in general his consignificator.

Signs of Long Ascension,—♋, ♌, ♍, ♎, ♏, ♐. A ✶ in them is said to have the effect of a ☐, and a ☐ that of a △.

Signs of Short Ascension.—♑, ♒, ♓, ♈, ♉, ♊. A △ is said to have the effect of a ☐, and a ☐ that of a ✶.

Swift in Motion.—When a planet moves faster than its mean motion.

Table of Houses.—These are necessary to erect a figure of the heavens.*

Term.—An essential dignity. (See page 72.)

Testimony.—Having any aspect or dignity, &c., or being in any way in operation in the figure as regards the question asked.

Translation of Light.—The conveying the influence of one planet to another, by separating from the aspect of one and going to the aspect of the other. It is a very powerful testimony.

Triplicity.—An essential dignity. The zodiac is divided into four trigons, or triplicities; the fiery, ♈, ♌, ♐; the earthy, ♉, ♍, ♑; the airy, ♊, ♎, ♒; and the watery, ♋, ♏, and ♓; agreeing with the four elements into which the ancients divided the whole of the natural world.

Void of Course.—Forming no aspect in the sign it is in. When ☽ is so, it denotes in general no success in the question.

Watery Signs.—♋, ♏, and ♓.

---

* A complete set for London and Liverpool, answering for all the kingdom, follows the *Grammar of Astrology*.

Watery Triplicity.— ♋, ♏, and ♓.

Zodiac.—A belt which surrounds the earth, about eighteen degrees broad, in which the Sun and Planets continually move.

THE END OF INTRODUCTION TO ASTROLOGY.

THE

GRAMMAR OF ASTROLOGY,

CONTAINING

ALL THINGS NECESSARY FOR

CALCULATING A NATIVITY.

BY ZADKIEL.

DEDICATED TO THE UNIVERSITY OF CAMBRIDGE.

NEW EDITION.

CONTENTS.

BOOK THE FIRST.

Chap.	Page
I.—The alphabet	357
II.—The signs of the zodiac	358
III.—The natures of the planets	362
IV.—Of the aspects	368
V.—The qualities of the aspects	370
VI.—Of the figure of the heavens	372
VII.—Of the twelve houses of heaven	373
VIII.—To erect a figure of the heavens at birth	375
IX.—To find the planets' latitudes, declinations, &c.	382
X.—To judge the future fate by the figure of the heavens at the moment of birth	388
XI.—To judge of the effects of directions	404
XII.—Of mundane aspects and directions	407
XIII.—Of the mundane parallels	410
XIV.—Of the part of fortune	411
XV.—Of the hyleg and the hylegiacal places	413

BOOK THE SECOND.

I.—Zodiacal directions	415
II.—To direct ☉ to any aspect in the zodiac, except a parallel	418
III.—To direct ☉ to a parallel in the zodiac	421
IV.—To direct the moon in the zodiac to any aspect except a parallel	422
V.—To direct the moon to parallels of declination	424
VI.—To direct the ascendant to aspects in the zodiac	425
VII.—To direct the mid-heaven to aspects in the zodiac	426

CONTENTS.

Chap.	Page
VIII.—Of mundane directions to the angles; that is, to the ascendant or M. C.	426
IX.—To direct the sun or moon to any aspect in the world (except parallels) by converse motion	430
X.—To direct the sun or moon to any aspect in mundo (except the parallels) by direct motion	432
XI.—To direct the sun or moon to mundane parallels converse	433
XII.—To direct the sun or moon to mundane parallels by direct direction	434
XIII.—To direct the sun or moon to rapt parallels	ib.
XIV.—Of directions to the part of fortune in mundo	437
XV.—On turning the arc of direction into time, to learn at what age its effects will be felt	438
XVI.—Of secondary directions	439
XVII.—Of revolutions, lunations, transits, &c.	441
XVIII.—To rectify the estimated time of birth to find the true time	445
XIX.—A judgment for marriage in the nativity of Lord Byron's daughter	449
A glossary of astrological terms	455
Appendix	471

ABBREVIATIONS.

A. R. signifies Right Ascension.
Asc. the Ascendant.
M. C. the Medium Cœli, or Midheaven.
Mer. Dist. the Meridian Distance.
S □, the Semi-square Aspect, 45°.
SS □, the Sesqui-square Aspect, 135°.

DEDICATION.

To the UNIVERSITY OF CAMBRIDGE, the seat of Mathematical and Philosophical Learning, where truth has never been veiled by prejudice or disfigured by ignorance, this little effort at opening a road for the mathematical investigation of the elementary Philosophy of Plato and Aristotle, as taught by the "divine" Claudius Ptolemy, is most respectfully dedicated, (in grateful acknowledgment of the compliment paid him by the examination of that science by several members of their learned body since the first edition was printed) by their

Most respectful Servant,
ZADKIEL.

PREFACE TO THE SECOND EDITION.

THE various demands on my time, together with peculiar circumstances, have hitherto prevented me preparing a new edition of this work, which has been for some time past eagerly demanded by the public. The sale of a large edition, unaided by any attempts to build up its reputation by means of pretended Reviews (which are often merely disguised ad-

PREFACE TO THE SECOND EDITION.

vertisements) has clearly shewn that public approbation is now fixed upon the subject it contains, and that extensive research is in progress into those doctrines for the support of which it was intended. And I feel assured that, as the former edition has been the means of producing many hundred practical astrologers, both in this country and in America, some of whom are to be found in the Universities of both Countries, so I may safely rely upon the cause of Truth being farther advanced by means of the present work.

I have, in this edition, abbreviated some things of less importance, and added much matter interesting to the lovers of truth, who may desire to study the science of Astrology, as relates to the doctrine of Nativities.

As to the enemies of investigation, I shall not waste a word upon them; for happily its spirit is aroused, and will not be readily put to rest. They may rail, if they please; but they will never be able to "rail the seal from off the bond;" the laws of nature can never be destroyed; and while the student can go forth with this little book in his hand, and by it alone prove to demonstration the *facts* of the actual agreement of those laws with the principles of Astral Influence, he may smile at the impotent efforts of Bigotry and Ignorance.

That it may add to the store of true science, and thereby lead to the honour of God and the benefit of mankind, is the fervent desire of

THE AUTHOR.

INTRODUCTION.

It is not intended here to enter upon any laboured argument to prove the antiquity of the science of the Stars: it is enough for my present purpose (which is to teach the mere outline of the art, which may be filled up as the student has inclination) if I state that Astrology existed for many centuries prior to the Christian era, about which time it appears to have been taught chiefly by tradition, being handed down from father to son by word of mouth, as the art of palmistry now is among the gipsies. There is no good evidence of any perfect system of Astrology having been reduced to written rules, depending on mathematical principles, before the first century; though Sir Isaac Newton admits, in his Chronology, that it was in existence nearly 900 years before that period. Somewhere about the year 133, that celebrated astronomer, geographer, and astrologer, *Claudius* Ptolemy, compiled his notable work entitled " The TETRABIBLOS, or Quadripartite, being Four Books of the Influence of the Stars."* In this work he seems to have collected all that appeared of importance to him which was then known of the science; but as Ptolemy did not devote the whole of his time to this study, which, however, would require the entire application of any man's time to make himself thoroughly and entirely master

* Translated by J. M. ASHMAND.

of it, we may fairly suppose that some of the less important rules had not been tested by him personally, but were merely adopted as the current opinions of the day. This accounts for a few of his doctrines being in some degree erroneous; although the great majority of them are true to nature, and, if rightly understood, never did or can fail, while the system of the universe remains *unchanged*.

The principles of Ptolemy's doctrine do not appear to have been very clearly understood, or acted upon free from the superstitious trash of the Arab writers, before the years 1647 and 1657, when *Placidus de Titus*, a Spanish monk, first published the true system of astrology, founded on Ptolemy's mathematical calculations. His principal work was printed in Latin, and called the *Primum Mobile*, or First Mover.* It is remarkable that the only subsequent works of any value on that part of astrology which is of most importance, nativities, were written by an Englishman, Mr. Partridge, whose Almanac is still in existence. His works, the *Opus Reformatum* and the *Defectio Geniturarum*, are evidently made up from Placidus; but they are full of the soundest doctrines, and contain numerous examples.

No good translation of Placidus appeared in English until that made by Mr. JOHN COOPER in 1816; nor did any correct copy of Ptolemy's book, from which all we know of Astrology is originally derived, until 1822, when Mr. ASHMAND's excellent work appeared. The old translations of Ptolemy and Placidus, especially those by Dr. Sibly, are detestable, and have made numerous erring astrologers, and done the science infinite injury. All the host of English astrologers, such as Lilly, Colley, Sibly, Gadbury, White, &c.,† were immersed in error when they treated on *nativities:* they embraced the follies of the Arabian astrologers,

---

* Translated by J. COOPER. † PARTRIDGE excepted.

which consisted in mixing up the system of divination, called horary questions, with the genethliacal art, or the science of nativities; and those who open any of their works only lose their time.

In short, there exists no brief, cheap, elementary work on the science, except the *Grammar of Astrology*. It contains nothing that is not founded on actual experience.

The science of Astrology consists of four branches, or distinct parts, which are essentially different from each other: they are—1, *Nativities*, or the art of foreseeing, from the figure of the heavens at the moment of birth, the future fate and character of individuals; 2, *Mundane Astrology*, or the art of foreseeing, by the positions of the heavenly bodies at certain periods, the circumstances of nations, such as wars, pestilences, inundations, earthquakes, &c. &c.; 3, *Atmospherical Astrology*, or the art of foreseeing, by the positions of the planets at the periods of the Sun and Moon being in mutual aspect, and some other circumstances, the quality of the weather at any required time or place; 4, *Horary Astrology*, or the art of foreseeing, by the positions of the heavens, at any period when an individual may be anxious about the matter, the *result* of any business or circumstance whatever.

The GRAMMAR OF ASTROLOGY is intended to teach the principles of the science of nativities; and to render them so plain, by divesting them of the trash which designing or ignorant men have introduced, that persons of an ordinary capacity and a common share of industry may examine and decide for themselves whether there be any truth in astrology or not. To those who consider it sufficient to decide without examination, merely because others have decided before them, this work has no recommendation, inasmuch as the gauntlet of argument is not thrown down. But to those who think experience a safer guide than reason in natural philosophy, it will be peculiarly acceptable; as herein they will find the briefest possible rules and the best decided principles for judging which have yet appeared before the world, as far as the author is capable of forming an opinion from many years' experience and the examination of many hundred nativities.

If the cause of truth should thereby be assisted, either through public demonstration by the test of experiment of the utter fallacy of the doctrines of Astrology, or, on the other hand, by the conviction of the honest portion of mankind that the Almighty does, indeed, choose the heavenly bodies as the instruments of his *will* in bringing about the ends of Providence, this little work will very well bear the lash of critics, whose pride will not believe that "There are more things in Heaven and Earth than are dreamed of in their philosophy."

In perfect but humble confidence in the purity of his intentions in endeavouring to gain a hearing for Astrology, the Author can contemplate with perfect calm the bitterness of abuse of some men who call themselves, *par excellence*, philosophers; since he finds, by the steady sale of the first edition of this book, and the numerous other similar publications he has brought before the public, that there are many who will soar above prejudice, and resolve on seeing with their own eyes.

N.B.—To those who wish to pursue the science farther, I recommend the *Tetrabiblos of Ptolemy* and the *Primum Mobile of Placidus*, but let them avoid the translations by Whalley and Sibly. The best editions are those translated by ASHMAND and COOPER.

GRAMMAR OF ASTROLOGY.

FIRST BOOK.

CHAPTER I.

THE ALPHABET.

THIS consists of twelve characters, which represent the twel[ve] *Signs of the Zodiac*: they are these—

NORTHERN.		SOUTHERN.	
♈ Aries.	♋ Cancer.	♎ Libra.	♑ Capricorn.
♉ Taurus.	♌ Leo.	♏ Scorpio.	♒ Aquarius.
♊ Gemini.	♍ Virgo.	♐ Sagittary.	♓ Pisces.

Also of eight others, which represent the *Planets*, as fo[l]low:—

♅ Herschel.   ☉ Sol, the Sun.
♄ Saturn.   ♀ Venus.
♃ Jupiter.   ☿ Mercury.
♂ Mars.   ☽ Luna, the Moon.

And five others, which represent the *Aspects*, or position[s] which these planets bear to each other, as follow:—

☌ *Conjunction*, or when two planets are in the same place[.]
✶ *Sextile*, or when they are 60 degrees or two signs apart.
□ *Square*, or when they are 90 degrees or three signs apart.
△ *Trine*, or when they are 120 degrees or four signs apart.
☍ *Opposition*, or when they are 180 degrees or six signs asunder.

N.B.—There are also some called the *new aspects*; the[y] were discovered by the great Kepler, one of the ablest astro[-] logers of modern date, and are as follow :—The *Semi-Sextile*, or 30 degrees ; the *Semi-Square*, or 45 degrees ; *Sesquiquadrate*, or 135 degrees ; and the *Quintile*, or 72 degrees ; and *Biquintile*, or 144 degrees. The power of these is not so great as that of the old aspects. The Moon's nodes are thus marked,— ☊ north, ☋ south. Lastly, there is another character, which is called the *Part of Fortune*, ⊕.

The learner should practise writing the characters, and become well acquainted with the signs which are opposite to each other.

CHAPTER II.

THE SIGNS OF THE ZODIAC.

THESE may be divided into *north* and *south*. The first six, from *Aries* to *Virgo*, are *northern ;* the latter six, from *Libra* to *Pisces*, are *southern:* this is because the Sun and planets, when in the first six, are north of the equator, and when in the last six they are south of that line. When the Sun is in northern signs he is longer *above* the Earth than below, and the days are longer than the nights ; when he is in the southern signs, he remains longer *below* the horizon than above, and the nights are longer than the days.

Of course, when any planet is in a *north* sign it remains longer above the Earth than below; and, *vice versâ*, when it is in a *south* sign its stay is longer below the Earth.

Each point of the zodiac rises and sets once every twenty-four hours, occasioned by the earth turning round on its axis once every day ; therefore, when any given point be *rising*, the opposite point must be *setting*.

As the zodiac consists of 360 degrees from the *first* point of Aries until you come to that point again, and as these are

GRAMMAR OF ASTROLOGY.   359

divided into twelve portions or signs, they must consist of thirty degrees each. It is found that each of these signs, when it rises at the birth of an individual, possesses a *certain influence* to produce a particular form of body, and some peculiar mental inclinations. There is no reason to suppose, however, that the influence of Aries, or any other sign, proceeds merely from that sign alone; but it is more probable that when that sign is rising, *the whole face of the heavens* is such as to produce a *certain effect*. This may be caused as much by the distant stars in the *milky way* (that large shining band seen in the heavens on a fine night, which consists of innumerable millions of stars, and of which our Sun is supposed to be one) as by any others. In fact, Ptolemy speaks of these effects being produced by the "ambient," which means the entire of the heavens, and not the ascending sign alone.

GENERAL RULE FOR JUDGING THE EFFECT OF EACH SIGN.*

Aries.—This sign produces a dry, lean body, middle stature, strong limbs, large bones, long and meagre face, sharp sight, neck rather long and scraggy, dark eyebrows, swarthy complexion, hair reddish and wiry, thick shoulders; disposition angry and violent as the *Ram*.

Taurus.—A short, full, well-set person; full face and eyes, thick neck and lips, wide nose and mouth, swarthy shining face; a short, thick, broad hand; large shoulders; dark, harsh, and generally curling hair. Given to eating, unfeeling, melancholy, and slow to anger, but when enraged, furious as the *Bull*.

Gemini.—A tall, upright, well-made body, with good carriage, long arms, but hands and feet generally short and fleshy; hair blackish, eyes hazel, and having a sharp, quick, pene-

* These must not be confounded with the constellations of the same names.

trating wanton look : if a female, she has very fine eyes; body strong and active; step smart and quick; understanding good; imagination powerful; said to beget or bear *Twins*.*

Cancer.—A short, small person, with pale, sickly complexion, round full face, and generally small features; sad brown hair, small grey eyes; the upper part of the body larger than the lower; constitution weakly: if a female, prolific. Dull and timid as the *Crab*.

Leo.—A large noble person; full, tall stature, well proportioned; shoulders broad and well set; hair often yellowish and bushy, or curling; eyes large and staring, yet quick-sighted, if no evil planets ascend; countenance fierce; head round, complexion ruddy; step firm and majestic; if ☉ be rising, a haughty air; disposition free and courteous; heart bold and courageous as the *Lion*.

Virgo.—Middle stature, inclined to be tall; slender figure, neat and well formed; dark brown hair; dark complexion, well favoured, but not handsome; face more round than oval; voice weak and unmusical; mind ingenious; pleasant in conversation; given to study; fond of learning; but fickle, and bashful as a *Virgin*.

Libra.— Tall and elegantly formed, rather slender; hair smooth, and a light auburn or flaxen; face round and lovely, having great beauty; fine, clear red and white complexion, which in old age becomes pimpled or ruddy; eyes generally blue and beautiful; mind well principled; temper even as the *Balance*.

Scorpio.—Thick, well-set, middle-sized person; strong and robust; face somewhat broad and square; complexion dusky; hair dark brown, curling, bushy, and plentiful; thick neck; coarse hairy legs, often bow-legged, or club-

* If ♄ or ♃ be setting, the shoulders will be large and uncomely.

footed, or ill-made feet; mind thoughtful, reserved; active and deceitful as the *Scorpion*.

Sagittarius.—Well-formed person, rather tall; strong active body; rather long face and handsome, with generally a straight Grecian nose; fine clear eyes, and good ruddy complexion; chestnut-coloured hair, growing off the temples; inclined to baldness; daring and intrepid, fond of horses and *hunting*.

Capricorn.—Short, slender, ill-formed person; long thin face; generally ugly; chin long and pointed, protruding like that of the goat; thin beard; neck long and small; hair black and lanky; narrow breast; weak in the knees, with crooked ill-formed legs; the native has a skippish manner, jumping forward when addressing any one, and they nod on one side like a goat when it butts; mind subtle and witty, but *capricious* as *Capra* the *Goat*.

Aquarius.—Person stout, well-set, and comely, rather tall, not very, but never short; robust, strong, healthy appearance; a long and rather fleshy face; distorted teeth if ♄ be ascending; complexion clear and delicate, somewhat sanguine; hazel eyes; sandy or darkish flaxen hair. This sign gives more beauty than any other, except Libra; disposition gentle and benevolent; said to take delight on the *Water*.

Pisces.—Person short; large pale and fleshy face; the face is always full, but sometimes sanguine in complexion; if ☉ be rising, a good colour; a stooping, heavy gait, holding down the head when walking. If a female, the face is generally plump, and the skin clear and lucid, but very white; hair dark; and round shouldered, unless ☉ be rising; eyes sleepy; shoulders round; arms and legs short and fin-like; ill-made feet; disposition indolent, and too often given to drink, like the *Fishes*.

CAUTION.—These descriptions are rarely to be met with exactly. Every planet which throws an aspect to the ascendant has an influence both on mind and body; and if any planet be rising, it impresses its own character most powerfully on both. If the latter part of a sign be on the cusp of the ascendant, a portion of the next sign must be in the ascendant; and the native will partake of both influences. A person, for instance, having the latter part of Sagittary rising, and the whole of Capricorn in the ascendant, may have a fine head of hair and handsome forehead, but the rest of the face and person extremely ugly. The disposition also depends *chiefly* on the Moon and Mercury.

CHAPTER III.

THE NATURES OF THE PLANETS.

Herschel.—This is the most distant planet from the Sun; he takes 84 years to go through the 12 signs. He is frequently retrograde, appearing to go backward in the heavens. His diameter is to that of our Earth as 4.332 to 1.

The nature of Herschel is extremely evil. If ascending at the time of birth, he causes the native to be of very eccentric disposition, pursuing extraordinary and uncommon objects; one who despises the track of custom, and is very abrupt in his manners. Whatever good he may produce, when well aspected or situated, will be of a sudden description, and quite out of the common course of things. Persons whose minds are influenced by this planet are unsettled in life, partial to travelling, witnessing many strange scenes, very romantic and extraordinary in their ideas, and given to the study of antiquity; yet likely to strike out many novelties.

Saturn.—This planet is next to Herschel. He is at a great distance from the Sun, and exceeds this Earth in bulk nearly 1000 times. He goes through the zodiac in 29 years and a half; his diameter is to that of the Earth as 9.987 to 1.

The nature of Saturn is far more evil than that of Herschel: he is called the Greater Infortune, and he is undoubtedly the cause (subservient to the will of Providence) of the greater portion of human suffering. When he is rising or setting at birth, the person born will suffer much lingering sickness, and be very subject to blows, bruises, and falls. If he be on the meridian, or coming to the meridian, he causes perpetual trouble and disgrace: all the native's affairs go wrong, and, unless there be some very strong aspects of other planets to counteract this evil position, the native is the complete child of misfortune. If he be in the opposite situation, that is, near the north meridian, or cusp of the fourth house, his effects are nearly as evil. Persons born under his influence are nervous, fearful, bashful, cowardly, melancholy, and given to shed tears. They suffer from chronic diseases, and are liable to mental infirmities. Their dispositions are thoughtful, malicious, and reserved; they are firm and obstinate in their opinions, but adhere strongly to their attachments.

Jupiter or *Jove* is next to Saturn in the solar system. He is the largest of all, in bulk exceeding that of the Earth nearly 1300 times. He is very nearly twelve years in going round the zodiac: his diameter is to that of the Earth as 10.86 to 1.

His nature is eminently benefic, and he is called the Greater Fortune. When rising at birth, he confers much strength of constitution, enabling the native to overcome very evil directions, which would otherwise prove fatal.

The persons under his influence are healthy, cheerful, and *jovial* in disposition, and are open, sincere, generous, and quite free from fraud or meanness of any kind. They are generally much esteemed, from pursuing always very honourable, magnanimous conduct; and they are the favourites of fortune. If Jupiter be approaching the meridian at birth, the native will (unless very evil aspects occur to counteract his influence) become extremely wealthy, and arrive at distinction. This is verified in the nativities of Queen Victoria and the Duke of Wellington.

Mars.—This planet is between the Earth and Jupiter; he is rather less in size than our globe, and goes round the Sun in about six weeks less than two years. His red fiery appearance renders him very conspicuous in the heavens: his diameter is to that of the Earth as 0.517 to 1.

Mars is a very evil planet, but his nature is quite different from Saturn. He causes all hot and violent diseases, and persons under his influence are subject to cuts, burns, and other violent accidents. They are rash, angry, and always ready to rush into quarrels and bloodshed. They feel no pity. If Mars be in the ascendant of any person's nativity, they become liable to receive cuts or have marks in the face; they are fond of war and danger; if in the 10th house, or on the meridian, they are generally observed as warlike characters, and may gain honours as such. In George the Third's nativity he was so situated, and during his reign England was perpetually at war.

Venus.—This beautiful planet is situated nearer the Sun than is the Earth. She goes round the Sun in 32 weeks, and is very nearly the same size as our globe: her diameter is to the Earth as 0.975 to 1.

Her nature is decidedly benefic, but her power nothing equal to that of Jupiter. She assists to strengthen the constitution if ascending at birth, but she gives such a strong inclination for pleasure, that the native often injures his health in its pursuit. She was ascending when George the Fourth was born, and gave him that remarkably refined *taste* which he possessed, and also a fondness for dissipation. Persons born under her influence are generally of a mild, quiet disposition. If on the meridian, she renders the native respectable in life, unless in ill aspect to Saturn, when he will generally be very mean in his conduct. She partakes very much of the nature of those planets to which she is in aspect, and no judgment can be formed of her effects without taking this into *full consideration*. If well aspected, the native will gain chiefly through the means of females; if ill aspected by ♂, the native is not chaste.

Mercury.—This planet is the nearest to the Sun of any yet discovered. He is very small, being only 3200 miles in diameter, and travels very swiftly, going round the Sun in 12 weeks and 4 days: his diameter is to the Earth's as 0.398 to 1.

His influence, when in no aspect with any other planet, and if in the ascendant, causes great restlessness and desire of change; fondness for travelling, and a busy turn of mind, addicted to literature: but as this planet is the chief ruler of the *mental* faculties, great care must be taken to note what aspect he forms with other planets, for on that will *chiefly* depend the mental disposition of the native. If close to the Sun, the native never has any great abilities for science; his mind is rather contracted and superficial, though he may be well adapted for any kind of plodding business. If at the same time he be afflicted by the evil aspects of the malefics, and the Moon also be weak and afflicted, the native will be of very weak mind; and if the ascendant also be afflicted by the presence or ill aspect of evil planets, and there be no good aspect between the Moon and Mercury, or between them and the ascendant, the native will be an idiot or become insane. This may be the case even where Mercury is distant from the Sun, as occurred in the nativity of George the Third, where Mercury was 12 degrees and a half from the Sun. In that king's nativity, Mercury had the sextile aspect of Jupiter, which preserved his mental faculties for several years; but being in conjunction with Saturn, and in semi-square with Mars, and the Moon being also in square to Mars, and in no aspect to Mercury, and neither of them in aspect to the ascendant, the royal native, under ill directions, lost his reason.

The Sun.—The glorious body which gives us light and heat is less noticed than the Moon in the judgment of a nativity; though, if astrology were all fancy, his appearance would have been likely to say much in his favour. The Earth is distant about 95 millions of miles from the Sun, which in bulk exceeds that of the Earth in the proportion of 1,384,472 to 1 : its diameter is to that of the Earth as 111.454 to 1. The human mind strives in vain to comprehend its immense bulk. Just as difficult is it to comprehend how he keeps all the planetary bodies in perpetual play around his centre; for although the terms *attraction* and *gravitation* have been long in use, they are still as full of mystery as is that of *planetary influence.* The specific influence of the Sun is small; but it seems to be similar to that of Mars. If in the ascendant, or in aspect to it, he causes a degree of pride; when in good aspect to the Moon, he causes success in life; but if in evil aspect, he gives rashness, and injures the native's fortune. If in conjunction with any planet, he destroys the power of that planet in a great measure, and assumes the nature of the planet himself, to a certain extent. It is highly important that the Sun should be free from the ill aspects of the malefic planets, to produce success in life; and it is better that he have no aspect whatever to them, unless it be to Mars, when the Sun is near the meridian, as this may cause military preferment.

The Moon.—This beautiful globe *apparently* goes round the Earth in 27 days, 7 hours, and 43 minutes.* Her distance is 237,000 miles from us; and she is nearly 50 times her own size smaller than this Earth: her diameter is 2160 miles, that of the Earth at the Equator 7925.648 miles.

She has *most powerful influence* on every person, according to her situation at birth, or what is termed her MUNDANE POSITION; that is, her rising, setting, &c.; and also, as regards her aspect with other planets. If she be nearly in conjunction with the Sun, the native will be of weak constitution, and, if not very well aspected, and the Hyleg not strong, of very short life. Persons born during an eclipse of the Sun, when the Moon is nearly in a direct line with the Sun, are invariably very weakly, and are said never to live many years. The Moon has certainly, at all times, much to do with the stamina of the native's constitution; and, if she be much afflicted, his health will rarely be good, and his fortune will be as poor. The animal propensities depend almost wholly on the Moon; and if she be afflicted, the native will be idle and given to drinking, gluttony, and debauchery. The good aspects of Mercury and the Moon to each other are important, to give wit and ingenuity. If the Moon ascend at birth, the native will be very fond of novelty and roaming about; and if she be weak, will lead a very dissolute life. If the Moon be on

* I have said "apparently," because I have shewn that the Moon does not in reality go *round* the Earth, but moves in a curve which, though *sui generis*, is similar to that of the Earth.

the meridian, or approaching it, and at the same time in good aspect to Mercury, the native will be clever, and fortunate through his own talents; if in good aspect to Jupiter, he will gain wealth ; to the Sun, he will meet preferment ; to Venus, he will have many female friends, and be very agreeable in his manners; to Saturn, if Saturn himself be strong, he may gain by elderly persons, legacies, buildings, or agricultural pursuits ; to Mars, he may succeed in warfare, or as a surgeon, cutler, &c. But in all these cases, if there be any evil aspects to the Moon, or to the meridian itself, the good will be materially diminished.

When evil aspects are found between the Moon, Mars, and Mercury, the native is inclined to dishonesty. The Moon in good aspect to Mars gives courage ; and if Mars be evilly affected by other planets, boldness and impudence.*

CHAPTER IV.

OF THE ASPECTS.

THE aspects in the zodiac consist of certain distances, at which, when two bodies are found, they produce a peculiar effect. Many objections have been made to this part of the science ; the adversaries asserting that these aspects are merely arbitrary measures, and that they have no foundation in nature, there being no difference whatever in mathematics between the distance of 120 degrees and the distance of 122 degrees which can be the foundation of that peculiar effect which astrologers declare that the aspect called a *Trine* does produce.

* *Vide* the Nativity of Richard Carlisle, 8 A.M. 3rd December, 1790, at Ashburton, Devon.

GRAMMAR OF ASTROLOGY. 369

The objection is not of any great consequence; for if it can be proved (which it certainly can), that when the Moon, for example, arrives at a *trine* aspect of Jupiter, or 120 degrees from that planet in any nativity, certain remarkable effects appear which do not appear when she arrives at the distance of 122 or 123, or any other number of degrees: this *fact* demonstrates that there is something peculiar in the angle formed by 120 degrees, which constitute a *trine* aspect.

Having closely investigated this subject, I have discovered a very remarkable peculiarity in the angles which form both the *old* and *new* aspects. The fact is, that EVERY ASTROLOGICAL ASPECT FORMS THE EXACT ANGLE, OR SUPPLEMENTAL ANGLE, OF A REGULAR POLYGON, WHICH MAY BE INSCRIBED IN A CIRCLE.*

A TABLE OF THE ASPECTS AND THE POLYGONS WHOSE ANGLES THEY MEASURE.

30 deg. A *semi-sextile*, the supplemental angle of a regular *duodecagon*, or figure of 12 sides.

45 deg. A *semi-square*, the supplemental angle of a regular *octagon*, or figure of 8 sides.

60 deg. A *sextile*, the angle of a regular *triangle*, or figure of 3 sides.

72 deg. A *quintile*, the supplemental angle of a regular *pentagon*, or figure of 5 sides.

90 deg. A *square*, the angle of a regular *quadrangle*, or figure of 4 sides.

120 deg. A *trine*, the angle of a regular *hexagon*, or figure of 6 sides.

135 deg. A *sesquiquadrate*, the angle of a regular *octagon*, or figure of 8 sides.

144 deg. A *biquintile*, the angle of a regular *decagon*, or figure of 10 sides.

Note.—180 deg. the *opposition*, the amount of 2 right angles, which is the sum of the 3 angles of every triangle.

There is one polygon, a figure of 9 sides, that forms an angle of 40 degrees, which have not yet been found to constitute an astrological aspect.

* These angles of the *regular* forms of geometry are those under which the superior metals crystallize. Water crystallizes at an angle of 60°, that of the *Trine*.

This is a very curious and remarkable agreement between the aspects and the angles of regular polygons; and those who understand geometry, and who reflect on the properties of the triangle and other polygons, and on the nature of the circle itself, will find in it room for admiration of the works of the Almighty Creator, "whose ways are past finding out."

The student will perceive that these facts are merely offered as proof that the aspects are not *arbitrary*, but are, indeed, intimately connected with the great principles of geometry, upon which the architecture of the universe itself is founded.

CHAPTER V.

THE QUALITIES OF THE ASPECTS.

THE BENEFIC ASPECTS are the *semi-sextile*, the *sextile*, the *quintile*, the *trine*, and the *biquintile*. When planets are found situated at these distances from each other, they operate beneficially for the native; and if the aspect be not yet complete at birth, but may be wanting a few degrees, then the effect is less powerful; but it will be found to take effect at that period of life when it becomes complete, which will be explained under the head "Directions." If the aspect be past, the planet which, by its more speedy motion, is *separating* from the other, will still retain the effect of the aspect until it has separated several degrees.

THE MALEFIC ASPECTS are the *semi-quartile* or *semi-square*, the *square*, the *sesquiquadrate*, and the *opposition*. When planets are found at the distances which constitute these aspects, they act evilly for the native. The same observations hold good with regard to the *approaching* and *separating* as are made in the last paragraph.

Observe.—The more perfect or exact is the aspect, the more powerful will be the effect, whether good or evil.

The Conjunction.—This is when two planets are in the same degree and minute of any sign. If either of the lights (the Sun and Moon) be in conjunction with an evil planet, it injures the native's constitution; and if an evil planet be conjoined with the *Hyleg*, the native will be very liable to illness all through life.

If the Hyleg be conjoined with Jupiter or Venus, the constitution is strengthened thereby; but, if it be the Sun which is Hyleg, his conjunction with the benefic destroys its power to do good in a great measure, and its favourable aspects to the Moon, mid-heaven, ascendant, or part of Fortune, are of less avail.

The Semi-sextile.—This aspect is the weakest of all; it is of no importance in directions; but if, at birth, the Hyleg have an exact semi-sextile to a benefic, the health will be benefitted.

The Semi-quartile.—This, whether found at birth or formed by directional motion, is evil; but if the aspect be between the Hyleg and Jupiter, it rather strengthens the constitution.

The Sextile.—This is a powerful and benefic aspect.

The Quintile.—This is benefic, but if to the evil planets is of no avail, as it is much less powerful than the sextile.

The Square or Quartile.—This is a very powerful and evil aspect; and if the planet casting it be Saturn, and he in the 10th house, and the planet receiving it be the Hyleg, the native will always be ailing, unless very powerful aspects counteract; and even then the native will suffer greatly from ill health, especially if Saturn's nature be rendered more evil by ill aspects to Herschel or Mars.

The Trine.—This is the most powerful of the good aspects.

The Sesquiquadrate.—This is just like the semi-quartile.

The Biquintile.—Consider this just like the quintile.

The Opposition.—This is the most powerfully evil aspect. If the Hyleg be in opposition to Saturn or Mars, the native will be of very weak constitution.

The Zodiacal Parallel.—The old writers did not properly calculate these parallels, as they omitted the planet's latitude: this caused continual error, as they never could be correct, except on those rare occasions when two planets were exactly on the ecliptic. The zodiacal parallel signifies a parallel distance from the equator, or being in the same degree of declination; and whether of the same name, north or south, is of no consequence. The student should pay very particular attention to the declinations of the planets, as the ZODIACAL PARALLEL *is of more importance than any other aspect*. The effect of this position is exactly the same as that of a close conjunction, but *more powerful*.

CHAPTER VI.

OF THE FIGURE OF THE HEAVENS.

THIS is nothing more or less than a map or plan, in which is depicted an accurate representation of the heavens at any required time; as, for example, at the moment a child is born. It shews what stars are rising, setting, or coming to the meridian; and, also, what positions are held by the Sun, Moon, and planets, and also by any comet which may happen to be visible at the time.

It has two *grand divisions*, which are the *diurnal* and *nocturnal* hemispheres. The former is all that space contained between the eastern and western horizons *above the Earth;* the latter is all the remainder of the heavens which are, of course, *below the Earth*. It has two other *great divisions* caused by the meridian; they are the *south* and the *north* points. The former is that at which the Sun arrives every day at noon, being then in an exact *south* direction from the spectator on this side the equator; and the other is that point which is directly opposite to the south meridian, where the Sun is at midnight, called the *north* meridian, or *lower* heaven.

These *four* divisions, the *east, south, west,* and *north*, are evidently formed by nature. The *east* is that point where the Sun rises or ascends, and becomes visible; the *south* is that where he ceases to ascend, and, after appearing for a moment to be stationary, begins to descend; the *west* is that where he sets and disappears; lastly, the *north* is that where he ceases to descend, and begins again to ascend, and approach the eastern horizon.

Astrologers divide the heavens into *twelve* compartments, which they term HOUSES: these *four* points are the most important of those twelve houses, and are called the ANGLES. Planets, when found in the *angles* at birth, are far more powerful to good or evil, according to their natures, than in any other part of the figure. The most powerful angle is the *south*, or when a star is on the meridian above the earth; the next is the *east*, or when a star is ascending; the next is the *west*, or when a star is setting; the least powerful is the *north*, or the meridian under the Earth.

CHAPTER VII.

OF THE TWELVE HOUSES OF HEAVEN.

HAVING divided the Heavens into *four* quarters, which we have shewn to be formed *by nature*, we shall now shew how these are again subdivided into *three* each, comprising in all *twelve* divisions, called the TWELVE HOUSES.

If the first degree of *Aries*, the beginning of the zodiac, be rising in the east, the opposite point of the zodiac (the first degree of *Libra*) must be setting at the same moment. If, then, we examine the heavens, we shall find that on the meridian (north) will be found the first degree of *Cancer*, and on the opposite meridian (south) will be found the beginning of *Capricorn*. Each of the meridians, therefore, are 90 degrees distant from the east point, or ascendant; but, for the sake of clearness, we will consider only the south meridian. If the Sun be in the first degree of Aries when rising, and the Moon be in the first degree of Capricorn at the same time, she must be on the south meridian, and be also at 90 degrees distance from the Sun, which is a *square* aspect to that body. If the Sun rise in the first degree of Aries, the day and night are then equal, each being 12 hours long. The Sun rises, in this case, at six o'clock, comes to the south meridian at twelve, and sets at six in the evening; and if we suppose the Moon to remain *fixed* on the meridian, the Sun will, two hours after rising, be within sixty degrees of her, having passed *one-third* of the distance from the ascendant to the meridian or midheaven:[*] this is a *sextile* aspect. It appears, therefore, that *one-third* of the half of the arc formed by the Sun in his daily course being completed, he is found at a *sextile* aspect to the meridian. Of course, he must then be 30 degrees (a *semi-sextile*) from the horizon, or ascendant. Now this, being *one-third* of ONE QUARTER of the heavens, is *one-twelfth part* of THE WHOLE; and thus constitutes ONE HOUSE. In two hours more the Sun proceeds upwards another 30 degrees,

[*] This distance will always be the same by *oblique ascension*, there being always 90° of oblique ascension between the horizon and meridian.

and arrives at the distance of 60 degrees from the ascendant, and 30 degrees to the mid-heaven. This forms another *third* of the quarter contained between the east and the meridian, and becomes another *house*. When he arrives at the mid-heaven, at noon, he has passed a third *house;* whence it appears that there are *three houses* between the horizon and meridian, and the *beginning* of each is in aspect to *both* of those points. It is *this* circumstance of their being *in aspect*, and being found to operate *certain effects* which they do not when otherwise situated, that, no doubt, first gave rise to the divisions of the heavens into *twelve houses*. It is plain that, in passing from the mid-heaven to the western horizon, similar positions are formed; as also in passing from the western horizon to the north meridian, and again from the north meridian to the place of sun-rise, in the east. Each quadrant of the heavens produces *three* houses—each hemisphere contains *six;* there are, of course, TWELVE HOUSES.

Notice.—It matters not whether the Sun or any star be on the equator, and so divide the heavens into *equal* portions to constitute the houses, or be distant from the equator, and so divide the heavens into *unequal* portions; since *one house* in the course of any heavenly body will always measure exactly *one-third part* of the arc that body forms between the horizon and the meridian.*

CHAPTER VIII.

TO ERECT A FIGURE OF THE HEAVENS AT BIRTH.

THIS is merely to draw a map of the heavens as they may appear at the moment a child was born; and according to

* See note, page 374.

the situation of the signs of the zodiac, the Sun, Moon, and other heavenly bodies, will be the destiny of the native or child then born, unless by care and prudence any portion of that destiny, being foreseen, may be avoided.

Draw a circle to represent the heavens; within which draw a second and smaller circle, to represent the Earth. Then draw a straight line through the outer circle (as in *fig. 1*) to represent the horizon; E being the east, where the Sun rises, and W the west, where the Sun sets. Then draw another line at right angles from the first, to represent the meridian; S being the south, where the Sun is at noon, and N the north, where the Sun is at midnight. These four points are the angles, or cusps, or beginnings of the 1st, 4th, 7th, and 10th houses; which are of most consequence in every figure of birth or nativity. Proceed to divide each of the four quadrants of the figure into three parts, by drawing four other lines, which are represented by the *dotted* lines in the plate. You will then have the twelve houses ready for representing the planets and signs as they may happen to be situated.

TO INSERT THE SIGNS OF THE ZODIAC.

1st. Look in my Almanac (or, if previous to 1839, in *White's* Ephemeris) for the degree and minute of longitude the Sun was in at the noon *preceding* the time of birth; and then find, in the table of A. R., what degree and minute that answers to; note this down. Then take the mean or clock time of the birth after the last noon, and turn it into degrees and minutes by multiplying it by 15; add these sums together, and add to them the correction for the difference between mean and sidereal time (this for 1 hour is 9.86 sec., and for a minute is 0.16 sec.), and the amount will be the degree of *right ascension* on the meridian at the moment of birth.

Correct the time also for the "equation of time," if the Ephemeris be not calculated to *mean* time.

Remark.—The true moment of birth is that when the child first draws breath, which is generally known by its crying; and this may happen before the lower extremities of the child are born.

2d. Having found the *right ascension* of the meridian, or mid-heaven, at birth, look in the table of houses* what degree of longitude it answers to, and write that down on the cusp of the 10th house or mid-heaven, and the same degree of the opposite sign on the opposite (the 4th) house.

3d. In the next column in the table of houses you will find the degree on the 11th house, and at the head of the column, or in some part of the column, above the line of figures you are using, the sign which is on that house, which write down accordingly, and the same degree of the opposite sign on the opposite (the 5th) house.

4th. In the 4th column you will find the degree of longitude to be placed on the 12th house; place the same degree of the opposite sign on the 6th house.

5th. In the 5th column you will find the degree and minute of longitude on the ascendant, or which is actually rising at the moment of birth, and its opposite is, of course, on the 7th house, or descendant.

6th. Take the degree in the 6th column for the longitude of the 2d house, and its opposite for that on the cusp of the 8th.

7th. Take the degree in the 7th column for the longitude of the 3d house, and its opposite for the 9th house, and you will then have completed the cusps of the *twelve houses.*— (*See fig.* 2.)

Example.—In "Moore's Life of Byron" will be found a letter, written by Lord Byron, dated *Pisa*, 10*th December*,

* In my "Tables for calculating Nativities."

1821, which contains these words—"This day and this hour (one on the clock) my daughter is six years old." We will, therefore, take this as a well authenticated nativity, and erect a figure of the heavens for 1 hour, P.M., 10th December, 1815, at London.

1st. Referring to White's Ephemeris for the noon *preceding* the time of birth, which was the noon of the 10th Dec. 1815, we find the Sun's longitude was 17 deg. 37 min. of Sagittarius. The right ascension of 17 deg. of that sign is found to be 255° 52′, that of 18 deg. of the same sign is 256° 57′; then, by the rule of three, say, If one degree or 60 minutes give the difference between these numbers, 65 minutes, what will 37 minutes give? Ans. 40 minutes, which, added to the first number 255° 52′, make 256° 32′ for the Sun's right ascension at noon.

The correction for "equation of time" is thus made: The clock, at the time the Sun was on the meridian on the 10th December, 1815, was 7 min. 9 sec. slow, or after the Sun. Therefore when the clock denoted "noon," the Sun had passed the meridian 7 min. 9 sec., which in degrees amounts to 1° 47′ 15″, because 7 min. 9 sec. × 15 = 6435 seconds.

Therefore, if to the

	°	′
Sun's right ascension at noon	256	32
We add the correction above	1	47
We get the right ascension of the meridian at *mean* noon	258	19
To this add the mean time of birth 1 hour =	15	0
Add also the correction for the difference of mean and sidereal time 1 hour*	0	3
R.A. of M.C. at birth	273	22

* This difference is found by multiplying the hourly difference of *mean*

2d. This right ascension is found to answer to 3 deg. 5¼' of the sign Capricorn: we, therefore, enter ♑ 3° on the cusp of the 10th house or mid-heaven, and the same degree of the opposite sign ♋ on the 4th.

3d. In the next (3d) column will be found 22°; which shews that on the 11th house must be placed ♑ 22, and the like number of the opposite sign ♋ on the 5th house.

4th. In the 4th column will be found 17 deg. of Aquarius, as that sign is given at the head of the column; place this on the 12th house, and 17 of Leo on the 6th or opposite house.

5th. In the 5th column you find 7° 55', which denotes that 7 deg. 55 min. of Aries were ascending in the east: but this was when 3° *exactly* of ♑ were culminating; and as 1° of longitude on the meridian is seen to give 2° 34' on the ascendant, 5¼' will give 14', therefore say 7° 55' + 14' = 8° 9' of Aries rising; and after placing ♈ 8° 9' on the 1st, place ♎ 8° 9' on the opposite or 7th house.

6th. On the 2d house place what you find in the 6th column, viz. 22° Taurus; thus ♉ 22°, and on its opposite place ♏ 22°.

7th. On the 3d house place what you see in the 7th column, ♊ 15°, and on its opposite ♐ 15°. The figure will then display the signs of the zodiac as they were in the heavens at 1 P.M. 10 Dec. 1815, at *London*. (*See fig.* 2.)

TO PLACE THE PLANETS IN THE FIGURE.

Preliminary Observation.—The Ephemeris being calculated for the meridian of Greenwich, if the birth take place as

and *sidereal* time, 9".86, into the amount of mean time elapsed since noon. Thus 1 hour ✶ 9".86=9".86; and to turn this into degrees or "arc," say 9".86 × 15 = 148", which I call 3', as I lost 15" in the "equation of time."

380   GRAMMAR OF ASTROLOGY.

much as 15 miles to the eastward or westward of Greenwich, the time of birth must be corrected for the longitude of the place, to ascertain the time it was at Greenwich, before we find the planets' places.

Rule.—If the longitude be *east* of Greenwich, subtract 1 minute from the time given for every 15 miles of longitude; but if it be to the *west* of Greenwich, add 1 minute for every 15 miles of longitude.

Example.—If the birth be at Liverpool, the longitude of which is 3 degrees west, or 180 miles, add 12 minutes to the time given (since 180 divided by 15 gives 12), and you will have the time it was at Greenwich, for which the planets' places must be found.

TO FIND THE PLANETS' PLACES AT BIRTH.

Rule.—Find the amount of longitude in the zodiac traversed by each planet between the noon preceding and that which follows the time of birth. Then say, If 24 hours give that amount, what will the time of birth from the preceding noon give? and add the result to the planets' longitude at the preceding noon.

Example.—In the nativity of Lord Byron's daughter, ☉'s longitude at noon on the 10th December was ♐ 17° 37' (the seconds when less than 30 may be omitted; if above 30 call them one minute, and add it to the minutes;) on the 11th it was ♐ 18° 38', the difference is 61 minutes; then, If 24 hours give 61 minutes, what will 1 hour 7 minutes give?* Answer, 2 minutes 50 seconds, which, added to the ☉'s place at the preceding noon, gives ☉'s place in the zodiac at birth.

* Here the "equation of time" is allowed for, because the planets' places in *White's* Ephemeris *were* given for *true* or apparent noon, when the ☉ was on the meridian.

Thus ☉ at noon preceding ♐   17° 37′ 21
Longitude gained since noon   2 50

☉'s longitude at birth........ 17° 40′ 11″

ANOTHER BRIEF METHOD USED BY THE AUTHOR.

Divide the amount of longitude made in 24 hours, and also the time since noon, by 12; then multiply the quotients together, and the result is the answer in minutes of a degree, the last figure being a decimal.

Example.—Longitude made in 24 hours 61 minutes, divided by 12, gives 5; time since noon, 67 minutes, divided by 12, gives 5½; then 5½ multiplied by 5 gives 27½: the last figure being a decimal, the answer is 2.7½, or 2 minutes and 7½ tenths of a minute, which may be called 3 minutes.

In like manner find the ☽'s longitude at birth. Thus ☽ longitude on the 10th is ♈ 5° 5′, ditto on the 11th, ♈ 17° 20′, difference in 24 hours 12° 15′; this divided by 12 gives 1° 1¼′, which, reduced to minutes, is 61¼, and multiplied by 5½ produces 33.6¾, or 33 minutes 6¾ tenths, equal to 34 minutes: this, added to ☽ longitude on the 10th at noon, ♈ 5° 5′, gives her longitude at birth ♈ 5° 39′.

Having found the other planets' places, proceed to place them in the figure as follows:

1st. ☉. On the cusp of the 9th is ♐ 15°; but as ☉ *is farther on* in ♐, place him inside the house: if he had been in less than 15° of ♐, he would have gone by the cusp of the 9th, and should have been placed just outside.

2nd. ☽. On the ascendant is ♈ 8° 9′; and as ☽ is not so far on in the sign, she *appears* to have passed the cusp, and must be placed just above the 1st house.

3rd. ♅ is not so far on as the cusp of the 9th, and must be placed just outside the same.

4th. ♄ is in ♒ 8° 36', and falls just outside the cusp of the 12th house, which is in ♒ 17°; he is, therefore, in the 11th.

5th. ♃ in ♏ 2° 15', and ♀ in ♏ 1° 32', both fall in the 7th, because ♏ 22° are on the cusp of the 8th.

6th. ♂ being farther on in ♈ than the cusp of the 1st, is in the ascendant, in ♈ 20° 26'.

7th. ☿ being in ♐ 0° 32', falls farther outside the 9th than does ♅, and is near the middle of the 8th house.

☊. The ☽'s north node is in ♐ 24° 57', and falls in the 9th house, farther on than ☉; the ☋, the south node, is always opposite to it, and is of course in ♊ 24° 57' in the 3d house. The figure is now complete, except as to the ⊕, for which see Chap. XIV.

CHAPTER IX.

TO FIND THE PLANETS' LATITUDES, DECLINATIONS, &C.

1st. *The Latitude.*—THIS is given in the Ephemeris for every day at noon for the Moon; and the proportional part may be found by either of the rules given for finding the longitude.

The Sun never has any latitude. The other planets' latitude is given for every 6th day; and the proportional part may be found by the golden rule with great ease.

Example.—The latitude of Mercury on the 7th of December, 1815, was 1° 33' north, and on the 13th it was 0° 49' north, difference 44 minutes; then if 6 days give 44 minutes, what will 3 days and 1 hour (the time between the 7th day at noon and the time of birth) give? Answer, 22 minutes, which, taken from the latitude of Mercury at noon on the 7th, as he is decreasing in latitude, leaves his latitude at birth 1° 11' north.

Observe.—If the planet pass from north to south, or from south to north latitude, *add* the amount of each to find the *difference*.

2d. *The Declination.*—On this depend most of the other data for ascertaining the arcs of direction, by which the period of the various events in life is known. It should be accurately calculated. In my Tables it is given for every even degree of longitude and latitude in which the planets can be found; but as they are seldom in an even degree, it is necessary to take the proportional part both for the longitude and latitude.

Example 1.—The Sun is in ♐ 17° 40', the declination of ♐ 17° is 22° 50', that of ♐ 18° is 22° 56', difference 6 minutes; then say, As 60 minutes are to 40 minutes, so are 6 minutes to 4 minutes, which add to the declination of ♐ 17°, as the Sun is *increasing* in declination, and the Sun's declination will be 22° 54', and as he is in a southern sign, it is *south*.

Example 2.—To find the Moon's declination in the nativity of the Countess of Lovelace, look for the Moon's longitude ♈ 5° 39' in the Table (the ☽ having 5° 11' south latitude). Opposite the longitude of 5 degrees of ♈, under the column of 5 degrees south latitude (nearly the latitude of the Moon), are found 2° 36'; and in the same column opposite 6 degrees of ♈ are found 2° 12', the difference is 24 min.; then say, 60 : 24 :: 39 : 15.36, 15 min. 36 seconds *minus*.

Next look for the difference between 5 degrees of latitude and 6 deg. opposite the 5th degree of longitude: this will be found to be 55; then say,

$$0 : 55 :: 11 : 10.5, \text{ or } 10.5 \; plus.$$

Then, as the difference for the minutes of longitude is *minus*, and the difference of the minutes of latitude is *plus*, subtract one from the other.

```
15' 36" minus
10  5  plus
```

And you will have, difference 5 31 *minus*, to be taken from the first number 2° 36', which is opposite 5 deg. longitude, and in the column of 5 deg. latitude. As the seconds are over 30, call this correction 6 min., which, taken from 2° 36, leaves the Moon's true declination 2° 30', which is *south*, since the Moon, though in a northern sign by longitude, is still south of the equator by reason of her great south latitude.

Observe.—If both corrections be *plus*, or both *minus*, add them together to find the true correction, which if *plus* add to, and if *minus* take from the number opposite to the *even degrees* of longitude and latitude which the planet has just passed.

3d. *The Right Ascension.*—This is found in my Tables by the same process as the declination : if less than 180 degrees it is north, and if it exceed 180 degrees it is south. It is counted from the beginning of ♈, and is the measure of a right sphere or circle, which passes over the meridian once in 24 hours ; and as it amounts to 360 degrees, and as 1-24th of 360 = 15, there pass that number of degrees over the meridian every hour; and *one degree*, being the equivalent to 1-15th part of an hour, is equal to 4 min. in time. Hence it follows, that an error of 4 min. only in the supposed time of a birth will cause an error of *one entire degree* in the right ascension of the meridian. And as all the aspects of the planets to the meridian or to the ascendant are measured by right ascension, the error of only *one minute* in noting the time of a birth will cause an error of 15 minutes of a *degree*, or one quarter of a degree in the arc of direction ; and as the time of events is ascertained by the right ascension of the Sun, which increases about *one degree* in *one day*, and as one day after birth answers to one year of life, the result is, that an error of *one* minute in the time of a birth will cause an error of a quarter of a year in the expected time of an event. This causes predictions to be incorrect as to time, unless the estimated time of birth be scrupulously exact, or the true time be found by comparing the arcs of direction with some events which have occurred to the native.

4th. *The Meridian Distance.*—This is found by taking the difference between the A.R. of the midheaven and the planet, if it be above the horizon; and the difference between the A.R. of the cusp of the 4th house or north meridian, if the planet be below the horizon. The A.R. of the fourth house is found by adding 180 degrees to A.R. of the midheaven or 10th house, and if it exceed 360 degrees, take that number from it.

Example.—To find the meridian distance of Saturn in the nativity of Lord Byron's daughter:—

A.R. Saturn	311°	17'
A.R. of the Meridian	273	22
Saturn's Meridian distance	37	55

6th. *The Semi-Arc.*—This is the half of the planet's duration above or below the horizon, and may be measured in hours or minutes, or in degrees and minutes of a degree.

Rule 1.—Seek in the Table of Ascensional Difference for the elevation of the pole (which means the latitude of the country) where the native was born, and opposite to the declination of the planet will be found the ascensional difference,* after making proportion where required.

---

* Or, by logarithms, the *sine* of the asc. diff. = tang. pole + tang. dec.

Rule 2.—If the planet have no declination, it is on the equator, and must be just 12 hours (or 180 degrees) above the Earth, and the same time below. But if it have declination, it must have ascensional difference, which is the extent of time it will be above six hours in passing from the horizon to the meridian, or less than six hours in so doing. If taken in degrees, it is the extent above or beneath 90 degrees, which it describes in passing from the horizon to the meridian.

Rule 3.—If the planet be *above* the Earth, and in *north* declination, add the ascensional difference to 90 deg. to find its semi-arc; and if it be in *south* declination, subtract the ascensional difference from 90 degrees for its semi-arc.

Rule 4.—If the planet be *below* the Earth in *north* declination, subtract; but if it be in *south* declination, add the ascensional difference to 90 deg. to find its semi-arc.

Note.—Having found its semi-arc, either above or below the Earth, you may find its other semi-arc by subtracting the one you have from 180 degrees.

Example 1.—What is the semi-arc of Saturn in the nativity of the Countess Lovelace?—Saturn is *above* the Earth, and in *south* declination; he is a shorter time above the Earth than below; therefore his asc. diff., which is found under the pole or latitude of London 51° 32', and opposite Saturn's declination 18° 57' to be 25° 36', is to be taken from 90°, which leaves 64° 24' for his semi-arc *diurnal*.

By logarithms thus:—

$$\begin{aligned} \text{Tang. } 51° 32' &\ldots\ldots 10.09991 \\ \text{Tang. } 18\ \ 57 &\ldots\ldots\ \ 9.53574 \\ \hline \text{Sine } 25\ \ 36 &\ldots\ldots\ \ 9.63565 \end{aligned}$$

The Tables give one minute less.

Example 2.—The Sun's asc. diff. under the same latitude and 22° 54' declination is 32° 7', which, taken from 90°, gives 57° 53' for the Sun's semi-arc; this doubled is 115° 46′, and turned into time is 7 hours 43 min. 4 seconds, the time of the Sun's stay above the Earth.

These are the only data required to proceed to calculate the arcs of direction, by which not only the nature of the events which shall befall the native may be foreseen, but also the period when they shall occur (to within a few days) may be undoubtedly ascertained.

For the purpose of reference, we will here give them all in

A SPECULUM (OR TABLE OF DATA) IN THE NATIVITY OF LORD BYRON'S DAUGHTER.

Planets.	Latitude.	Declin.	Right Ascension.	Meridian Distance.	Semi-arc.	Remarks.
♅	0.4 N	21.35 S	246.3	27.19	60.8 D	The Moon, though above the Earth, apparently by her longitude, is in reality under the horizon, owing to her great latitude: she is, in fact, farther from the horizon than Mars, as will be found by taking her meridian dist. 86° 7′ from her semi-arc 93° 9′; the diff., which is always the planet's dist. from the horizon, being 7° 2′, while the diff. of Mar's merid. dist. and semi-arc is only 4o 39′.
♄	0.51 S	18.57 S	311. 7	87.55	64.24 D	
♃	1.8 N	11.12 S	210.27	62.55	75.34 D	
♂	0.25 N	8.23 N	18.42	74.40	79.19 N	
☉	* *	22.54 S	256.35	16.47	57.53 D	
♀	2.35 N	9.36 S	210.17	63.5	77.43 D	
☿	1.11 N	19.7 S	238.24	34.58	64.8 D	
☽	5.11 S	2.30 S	7.15	86.7	93.9 N	
⊕	—	2.30 S	81.55	11.27	93.9 N	

CHAPTER X.

TO JUDGE THE FUTURE FATE BY THE FIGURE OF THE HEAVENS AT THE MOMENT OF BIRTH.

Remark.—The word fate does not here imply *inevitable* fate; for though the planets produce a certain *influence* on the native's affairs, yet that influence is capable of being *opposed* by the human *will*, and may by that means be either overcome entirely or greatly mitigated. If, however, it be *not attended to*, but allowed its full scope, it will then certainly produce its full effect; and the reader must remember *that astrologers, in predicting events, always pre-suppose that this last circumstance will be the case.*

RULE TO JUDGE OF THE PERSON.

Consider the planets in the ascendant, if there be any, and the sign ascending, and also those planets which throw an aspect to the cusp of the ascendant; and make a judicious mixture of these.

Example.—In the nativity of Lord Byron's Ada, we find the Moon and Mars ascending and placed in ♈. The native will be of moderate stature, rather lean neck, &c., and her eyes quick and darting, with a resolute glance. She will have some colour, occasioned by Mars; but yet the Moon tends to give paleness; and I have no doubt that she has some cut or mark in the face.* Her hair will be rather strong, and of a reddish tint, though the Moon again tends to correct this, which is produced by Mars. The Sun is on the cusp of the 9th house, throwing a trine aspect to the ascendant, and Saturn, being in the 9th degree of ♒, throws a sextile aspect to the ascendant. The Sun causes a bright golden-tinted

---

* I have, since this was first published, learned that it is a large mole.

hair, and Saturn causes dark hair: the result is, that I judge that her hair is what is called a bright auburn colour, inclining to redness in a very small degree. The words of Ptolemy are, "Mars, ascending, gives a fair ruddiness to the person, with large size; blue or grey eyes, a sturdy figure, and a moderate growth of hair." He says, "the Moon generally contributes better proportion and greater delicacy of figure." Hence, I conclude that this native is a well-made elegant person, of extremely good carriage. There is a conjunction of Venus and Jupiter in the figure; and I have observed this produces fine blue eyes. She has then, in addition, beautiful eyes, and is a fine specimen of the beauty of English females. Her head is formed exactly as the *generality* of *English* heads,— large at the top, and coming to a point at the chin, extremely similar in contour to the face of the ram, being born with the sign of the ram ascending.

RULE TO JUDGE OF THE MIND.

Consider the sign ascending and the planets in the ascendant (if there be any), and those which aspect the ascendant; but consider *chiefly* the Moon and Mercury, how they are situated, and how they are *aspected;* and remember, before judging of the effect of any planet upon the ascendant, the Moon or Mercury, to observe how that planet is itself affected by aspects of other planets; because the rules in Chap. III. are to be understood of the planets when pure from the admixture of others. Every planet *acts* upon every other it aspects, except the Moon and Mercury, which are purely passive.— N. B. ☿ governs the intellect, and the ☽ the sensual faculties.

Example.—In Ada's nativity we find Mars in the ascendant in trine aspect to the Sun: this, in the words of Ptolemy, renders her "noble, imperious, irascible, warlike, versatile, and powerful in intellect." The Sun in trine to Mars "co-operates to increase probity, industry, honour, and all laudable qualities." The Sun being in good aspect to the ascendant, causes a degree of pride or feeling of dignity. Mars has the zodiacal parallel of Venus, which Ptolemy says "renders the mind cheerful, docile, friendly, complacent, joyous, playful, frank, delighting in songs and dancing, amorous, fond of the arts and of dramatic personation, * * * brave * * * sensible, cautious, and discreet; * * * *quick in anger*, extravagant in expense, and jealous." The Moon having the conjunction of Mars, will render the native bold and enterprising, and the more so as it falls in the ascendant. To this the good aspect of the Sun contributes to add an indomitable spirit, which, if occasion should offer, will display the native to the world a perfect heroine. The Moon and ascendant being in a moveable sign will, however, add to the versatile character of the native, "who will be," says Ptolemy, "susceptible of change." The most remarkable feature in this nativity, as regards the situation of Mercury, is his trine aspect to the Moon; as good aspects between the Moon and Mercury are the best evidence of intellectual ability. The native has undoubtedly great talent. A farther proof of this is, Mercury being several degrees from the Sun, as this planet, when within a few degrees (6 or 7) of the Sun, is much weakened. Mercury in conjunction with Herschel, and the Moon in trine to Herschel, renders the native eccentric and fond of curious studies. The close zodiacal parallel of Mercury with Saturn will tend to add seriousness to the native's character, and, says Ptolemy, she will be "inquisitive, loquacious, studious * * mystical * * improvident, cunning, familiar with business, quick in perception, *petulant*, accurate (in judgment), meditative, fond of employment."

In short, this is no common-place nativity; this scion of

the great Byron will inherit much of his wonderful mind, and be a shining star among the fair nobility of England.

THE DURATION OF LIFE.

This point should be decided, if it be the nativity of a child we are about to judge, before any other matter; as, if the heavens deny life, other matters are of no consequence. The hyleg being supported by benevolent planets in conjunction, parallel, or good aspect, and being at the same time angular and free from *affliction*, that is, the evil aspects of evil planets, is the *chief* sign of life continuing; and in proportion as the luminaries and ascendant are well aspected by the benefics and among each other, and free from evil aspects of malefics, the benefics being in angles, will the constitution be strong. If the hyleg, the lights, and the ascendant, be all afflicted, the evil planets being angular, their ill aspects close, and there be no assistance to the hyleg by the good planets, the child will die in infancy: if there be some assistance, but yet the evil exceed the good, the constitution will be weak, and the first train of evil directions will destroy. The *last aspect* formed by the ☉ and ☽ is of great importance, and must be well considered.

N.B. Weigh well all the testimonies before you decide.

Example.—In Ada's figure of birth, the ☉ being in the 9th house, is the hyleg. He has the mundane sextile of Jupiter and Venus nearly, being within 9° 21' of the ✶ of ♃, and 11° 14' of that of ♀. He has also the semi-quartile of the benefics in the zodiac, which assist to strengthen the constitution, for any aspect of the benefics has this effect, but the good aspects most. The benefics being in an angle, and in conjunction with each other, are powerful, but their power is something diminished by being in ☐ aspect to Saturn. The Sun has also the *trine* of the Moon in the world, the

Moon being 7° 2′ inside the ascendant, and the Sun 2° 31′ inside the 9th, which houses are four houses apart, a trine aspect. There is nothing more to strengthen the Sun, and as he has nearly a □ aspect of ♄, being only 7° 2′ off, and is within 9° 7′ of a parallel to Saturn from the meridian by rapt motion, and is in semi-quartile to Saturn in the zodiac, and in zod. parallel to Herschel, who is evil, though not so much so as Saturn, the hyleg is certainly not very strong in this nativity. The evil of Saturn is somewhat abated by his having a mundane △ to the two benefics. As to the Moon and ascendant, they are so near that they may be judged of together. The presence of the Sun in △ to them both certainly strengthens those points; but Mars being in the ascendant and close to the Moon, and Saturn within 5° 46′ of a semi-quartile, and Mercury and Herschel near the middle of the 8th in sesquiquadrate to the ascendant, weakens both of them extremely. The evil clearly preponderates, and (as may be seen in the Table of Directions) there being many ill directions in infancy to the hyleg (the Sun) and to the Moon and ascendant, I am certain that this lady had *much ill health in infancy,** and that she has *by no means a strong constitution;* consequently she cannot be expected to be free from many serious attacks of illness, and it may be judged that she will not live to a great age.

HURTS, INJURIES, AND DISEASES.

The ascendant and its opposite, and the planets afflicting the hyleg, must be considered; and judgment must be inferred from their general character. If the Moon be afflicted by the Sun, the native is liable to injuries in the eyes, especially if at the same time she be afflicted by malefics and near nebulous stars, such as the Pleiades. And if the ☉, being

* Since this was printed I have heard that this was the case.

hyleg, be afflicted by Saturn, that evil planet being angular, the native is liable to die of consumption.* If the ☉ be setting at birth, and in the sign Leo (particularly when in close ☌ with the *Asselli* in 6° of Leo), and be afflicted by evil planets, the native is liable to injury by *fire;* and if the Moon at the same time be much afflicted by Mars, and Mars be descending, the native is extremely likely to be burned to death. Observe, that if both ☉ and ☽ be afflicted in or near the ascendant, the native is liable to violent *injuries* or *hurts;* and that if the lights or afflicting planets are in or near the 7th, especially near the cusp, then considerable *diseases* ensue.†

Example.—In the nativity we have been considering, the Moon being in the ascendant, in close conjunction with Mars (only 1° 34′ distant), I judge that the native will be liable to suffer some injury or accident by a blow or cut in the face, and may even have to undergo a surgical operation. The period when this is most likely to occur depends on the directions. This position renders her also liable to brain fever, &c. and flow of blood to the head.‡

DISEASES OF THE MIND.

Observe the positions of Mercury, the Moon, and ascendant. If these be unconnected with each other, and be afflicted by Mars and Saturn, these evil stars being in angles, and no assistance given by the benefics, the persons born will be subject to epilepsy or falling fits, and to insanity. If " Saturn

* As was the case with young Napoleon.

† As this work is merely to teach the elements of the science, the student is referred to Ptolemy (Book iii. chap. 17), for further information on this head.

‡ This latter complaint I have, since the first edition of this work came out, learned that she suffered when a girl.

be so posited by day and Mars by night," the former diseases will occur; but "when Saturn may have dominion by night or Mars by day (especially if in Cancer, Virgo, or Pisces), the persons born will become insane." (See Ptolemy, Book iii. chap. 19.)

Example.—George the Third was born at 7h. 46m. A.M. June 4th, 1738. Mars was on the cusp of the meridian, squaring the ascendant, and in zodiacal square to the Moon. Mercury was conjoined with Saturn, and neither the Moon nor Mercury in any aspect to the ascendant, or to each other. Under ill directions the royal native became *insane*, according to Ptolemy's rule; and but for ☿ having a ✶ of ♃, he would have been so much earlier in life. The conjunction of Venus with Mercury assisted also; but being with Saturn and applying to zod. ☐ of ♂, she could not prevent the disease entirely.

THE FORTUNE OF WEALTH.

The position of the part of Fortune, the Sun, and more especially the Moon, and the aspects to these, must be referred to for this matter. If they be in good position, that is, angular, and well aspected of the benefics and among themselves, the native will enjoy *much wealth*. If they have a cadent situation, be under the earth, and afflicted by ill aspects of the malefics without any assistance from the benefics, the native will always be poor. If there be a mixture of these circumstances, the native will have a middling portion of riches.

Jupiter has most power to give wealth. If he be with the ⊕, and in parallel with or good aspect to the Moon, and angular, then wealth will flow in upon the native amain. If in ill aspect to the ☽, he causes poverty, through extravagance.

Saturn, when strong, will, if throwing good aspects (not being in conjunction or parallel), give the native wealth by agriculture, buildings, &c., and, if ♃ assist, by inheritance.

Mars in the same way gives wealth by military means. "Venus by means of friends, especially females, and by the dowry of wives. Mercury by the sciences and by trade." But ☿ being afflicted by ♅ causes losses by public bodies, and by writings, and sudden accidents. The ☽ with ♃ in an angle brings riches; if with ♄, poverty.

THE FORTUNE OF RANK.

"The disposition of the luminaries, and the respective familiarities, exercised by the stars attending them, are to be considered as indicative of the degree of rank or dignity." (Ptolemy, Book iv. chap. 3.) In addition to this rule, I consider the mid-heaven. If the luminaries be well placed and aspected, and there be good stars on the mid-heaven or approaching thereto, or in good aspect to that point, and the luminaries be *in good aspect to each other*, the native will rank high in the world. If the lights be cadent, and in no good aspect to the benefics or each other, and the meridian have no good aspects of the lights or benefics, the native never gains any fame; and if ♄ afflicts the meridian, he meets disgrace. If Mars be strong, and in good aspect to the meridian and the lights, he may gain martial fame. ♃ in the mid-heaven, and the Sun and Moon in ⚹ to each other, the Moon having the △ of ♃, is one of the best positions for rising in the world. This was the case with Arthur Duke of Wellington, who rose by the power of his stars to the highest rank. I have never seen this in any other nativity. ♃ in the 10th house, if not much afflicted, will alone cause the native to do extremely well in the world. His being there in ⚹ to ☽ and ⊕, raised Queen Victoria to the throne. ♄ in that house, if not extremely well aspected, will bring him to shame and beggary.

THE QUALITY OF EMPLOYMENT.

The planet nearest the Sun and that which is in the mid-heaven, (or aspecting), especially if in familiarity with the Moon, has most influence in this question. If Mercury alone rule, he makes writers and travellers, merchants, &c.; connected with Saturn, he causes them to "become managers of the affairs of others." If Jupiter aspect him, they will be pleaders, painters, &c., or hold office about eminent personages. Venus ruling makes wine merchants, dealers in colours, dyes, perfumes, drugs, &c., and dealers in garments or apparel, &c.; if connected with Saturn, she makes persons have to do with amusement, players, jugglers, &c.: if with Jupiter, persons attending exhibitions, &c., and I believe priests, who have much personal decoration, as Catholic priests, bishops, &c., and they will gain by females. Mars ruling alone makes martial men, and, if in Cancer or Pisces, naval men. The Sun joined with him, being near the mid-heaven, or in aspect, makes persons dealing with fire or metals, the latter especially, if in Taurus or Leo. "If Mars be separated from the Sun, he makes shipwrights, smiths, agriculturists, stonemasons, carpenters, and subordinate labourers," &c. "If Saturn bear testimony, in addition to Mars, persons become mariners, workers in wells, vaults, &c. under ground, painters, keepers of cattle, cooks, butchers," &c. If Jupiter join with Mars, they will be soldiers, innkeepers, tax-gatherers, mechanics, &c. If Mercury and Venus become joint arbiters of employment, they produce musicians, dancers, poets, weavers, and painters, &c., and sculptors, if ♂ aspect ☿. Jupiter in connection with them makes magistrates and senators, as also teachers of youth.* Mercury joined with Mars makes surgeons, statuaries, boxers, &c. N.B. If Mercury be most powerful, they will be scientific; and if Mars be strongest, they will be more violent or wickedly inclined, and cruel in their practices. If Saturn join these two, they will be thieves (especially if the Moon be in ill aspect to Mercury) and swindlers: if ☽ be in ill aspect to ♂, they will be robbers or assassins. If Jupiter join ☿ and ♂, they engage in honourable warfare, and are industrious. If Venus and Mars rule together, persons will be dyers, workers in tin, lead, gold, silver, medical drugs, and also physicians. Saturn with them makes undertakers, grave-diggers, mutes, &c. Jupiter will bring them support, by being placed to govern over women, &c., and as holders of sacred offices.

If the ☽ be near the mid-heaven, she causes many *changes* of employment; and in Virgo or Scorpio, says Ptolemy (to which may be added Gemini and Pisces), and in connexion with ☿ (and especially if ♀ be on the mid-heaven), she makes astrologers.† This is the more likely, if Herschel be strong and aspected by ☿ or even the ☽.

♄ has *especial* influence over architectural, agricultural, and laborious employments.

♃ over honourable and lucrative offices, and the church.

♂ over military and naval matters, and occupations where fire and iron are much used.

♀ has influence over ornamental matters, decoration, and amusement.

* Especially when ♎ is on the mid-heaven, and ☿ rise nearest before the Sun.

† It is remarkable that ♀ was in the mid-heaven at the birth of the late author of the Prophetic Messenger, and the author of the True Prophetic Messenger, and also of the Author; the Moon in each case having much connexion with ♀ and ♅, and also some other similar affections.

☿ rules literary and scientific occupations, and travelling.

☽ causes *changes*, and some connexion with matters influenced by the sign she occupies.

☉ produces public employments.

♅ causes employment out of the common course of life.

Observe.—These are merely the general elements of the science on this head; and if the learner would ascertain further particulars, he should study Ptolemy (Book iv. chap. 4). And here let me advise him to make due allowance for the different state of society under which Ptolemy wrote, and not trust to modern strictures on that great philosopher.

MARRIAGE.

As regards men, observe the Moon and Venus. If the ☽ be found between the eastern horizon and meridian, or in the opposite quadrant, she causes them to marry early in life, or after they have passed their prime, to women younger than themselves. If she be in the other quarters of the figure, they will marry late in life, or to women older than themselves. If she be configurated with Saturn, it delays marriage; and if within a few degrees of the Sun, or in evil aspect to the Sun, the same: if both these testimonies concur, the ☽ being at the same time occidental, they never marry. If the ☽ be oriental, and especially if angular, and in aspect to many planets, they being strong, and she be situated in ♊, ♐, or ♓, they may marry more than once. If the ☽ *apply* to ♄ by aspect, the wife will be morose and grave; if to ♃, well conducted and economical; if to ♂, bold and refractory; if to ♀, cheerful and handsome; and if to ☿, a clever sensible woman. If ♀ be connected with ♃, ♄, or ☿, the wives will be provident and attached to their families. If she be connected with ♂, they will be violent and ill-conducted, especially if it be by evil aspect. If the ☽ be in good aspect to the ☉, and the ☉ be not afflicted, or if ♀ be strong, the native marries a person of respectable connexions. If good planets be found in the 7th house, the individual (whether male or female) is happy in marriage; and if evil planets be there, the reverse. Herschel in the 7th is evil; and if he afflict the Moon in a man's nativity, or the Sun in a woman's, he destroys domestic happiness. The description of the wife will be much like that of the planet to which the ☽ forms the nearest aspect, considered with the sign he is in, as given in my edition of Lilly's Introduction to Astrology. But the sign on the 7th house may also be regarded. No one, it is said, marries a person born under the same sign as himself.

For the marriage of women regard the Sun, Venus, and Mars. If the ☉ be oriental, they marry early, or to men younger than themselves, as did Queen Victoria; if the ☉ be occidental, they marry late, or to elderly men. If the Sun be angular, and in aspect to many planets, especially from ♊, ♐, or ♓, they marry more than once. Saturn configurated to the ☉ (if the ☉ *applies* to him) gives steady husbands, but morose; Jupiter gives honourable, noble characters; Mars violent, rash, unfeeling men; Venus amiable, handsome husbands; and Mercury clever, intelligent, and provident characters. If ♀ be with ♄, or in aspect to him, the husband will be dull and laborious; if with ♃, just and honest; if with ♂, rash men and adulterous; if with ☿, clever, but fond of change. If the ☉ or ☽ apply to ♅, the wife or husband will be eccentric. If the ☉ have no aspect with Mars, and Mars be weak in the figure, the female native does not do well in marriage; and if the ☉ be in ill aspect to ♄ at the same time, she will be likely to live single. The 7th house shews in part the description of husband. In Queen Victoria's figure we find ♐ there; and Prince Albert is a fair ♐ man in some measure, though ♂ in ♈ aspecting the ☉, renders him somewhat like ♈.

Example.—In the figure of the heavens at Ada's birth we find the ☉ in △ aspect to ♂, this planet being angular and strong; and this is a proof that the native, if she live, will marry. As the ☉ is occidental and cadent, I judge that she will not marry very early in life, or, if she do, that it will be to a man some years her senior.* The ☉ has no other application than the △ of ♂, and therefore, though he be in ♐, I judge that she will never marry more than once. The planet the ☉ applies to being ♂, does not promise a very good husband; but yet, as there is a benevolent conjunction of ♃ and ♀ in the 7th house, I believe that the evil effect of Mars will be corrected; and besides, as ♂ has the parallel declination of ♀, who is very powerful, being angular and joined with ♃, the native's husband will be a good man, fond of his wife, and well conducted; but he may be what is called hasty, and at times a little irregular. ♂ in ♈ shews a man who is very respectable, and probably one who holds some high military rank.† He will be a tall, fine-looking man, with bushy, curling hair, reddish; one who is noble and courageous.

CHILDREN.

The 10th and 11th houses, and their opposites, must be considered. If no planets be in the 10th or 11th, consider whether there be any in aspect to them, or placed in or aspecting the 4th or 5th houses. The ☽ (especially if in ♊ or ♐, and angular), ♃, and ♀, give offspring; and the ☉,

---

* She has, since this was published, married a man eleven years her senior.

† She married Lord King, who has since been created Earl of Lovelace. I am informed that the above description is quite correct.

♂, and ♄, deny children, or allot but few. ☿ acts according as he may partake of the nature of the three former or three latter: and if oriental he gives children, if occidental he does not. If children are promised by other planets, yet ♂ or ♄ be found in the 5th house, especially in ♌ or ♍, the native will lose many children, and have much trouble by them. If the benefics only be in the 5th, the native has much happiness by his children.

Example.—In the nativity of Lord Byron's daughter, we find ♄ in the 11th house, and ♂ in □ aspect to the cusp of the 5th: these are testimonies of no children; but as ♃ and ♀ throw a ✶ to the 10th, she may have some children born; but I judge that she may hardly expect to have above *one* who will live to adult age.*

TRAVELLING.

The Sun, Moon, Mars, and Part of Fortune, are to be considered. If they, or the most of them, be cadent, the native will travel. If the ⊕ alone be cadent, it will cause many journies; but the Moon is the chief significator of journeying and voyages.†

Examples.—In the nativity of the Countess of Lovelace, we find the Sun cadent in the 9th, and ⊕ cadent in the 3d; hence I conclude that she will take several journies in the course of her life, and be rather given to travel. In the nativity of this young lady's celebrated father, the Moon and Mars were both cadent in the 9th, and the Sun in the 3d, while the ⊕ was just falling from the 7th angle; and he, it is well known, spent most of his days in travelling.

---

* She has since had a son born, when the ☽ par. ♀ D.D. came up.

† ☽ being in ♊ or ♐, causes many changes and journies, especially if rising, or close to the M.C.

THE KIND OF DEATH.

If the ascendant and the hyleg be well aspected, and if ♃, ♀, ☽, or ☿, well aspected, be placed in the 8th house, the native dies a natural death. A violent or remarkable death happens when both the malefics attack both ☉ and ☽, or even only one, and at the same time the ascendant be afflicted. If an evil planet be placed in the 8th house, it is an additional testimony of a violent death; but if it be there when the other testimonies do not occur, then it merely shews a painful death. ♄ causes slow lingering deaths, and ♂ causes them to be more sudden.

Rule.—The nature of the death is to be judged of chiefly by the directions in operation at the time :—

Saturn causes all cold diseases, coughs, agues, rheumatism, consumption, dropsy, &c.; and if violent symptoms are perceived, he brings death by blows, falls, suffocation, &c., the latter especially in ♏.

Jupiter brings death by quinsey, impure state of the blood, liver complaints, diseases of the lungs, &c. If violence attend the death, it may be by sentence of a judge.

Mars causes death by fever, wounds, spitting of blood, erysipelas, childbirth, &c. If by violence, he kills by gun shot or swords, suicide or *fire*.

Venus produces death by cancer, scurvy, dysentery, diabetes or wasting away, fistula, and putrid diseases. If violence attend, she causes poison

Mercury kills by fury, madness, melancholy, epilepsy, coughs, and obstructions. If violence concur, he brings death by accident in sport or by robbers.

The Moon.—When the ascendant or ☉ be hyleg, the Moon will assist in causing death by cold phlegmatic diseases, and if she be placed in ♋, ♏, or ♓, by drowning.

The Sun will assist to cause death by his ill aspects to the ascendant or ☽ if they be hyleg, and then he acts like Mars, and if in *Leo*, will produce death by FIRE, if other testimonies accord.

Observe.—The benefics cannot cause death of themselves; and their □ or ☍ aspect will frequently save life when they fall amidst a train of evil directions. But if the influence is too powerful for them to save, or they be themselves vitiated or too weak to save, then they assist to cause death in the manner described. Herschel cannot kill by himself, but his ill aspects assist to destroy life; and where they concur, will produce something sudden, singular, or extraordinary in the nature of the death.

Rule.—DEATH IS ALWAYS CREATED BY A TRAIN OF EVIL DIRECTIONS TO THE HYLEG AND OTHER VITAL POINTS. And remember that if the *hyleg* be not afflicted, the *life* will not be destroyed, however evil the directions, and however much they may injure the health.

Example.—In the nativity of Ada, we find the Moon in conjunction of Mars in the ascending angle; and the Sun (hyleg) applying to a parallel of Saturn; thus we may conclude that the native will die, eventually, of some *feverish* complaint; and though it may carry her off rather suddenly (♅ being in the 8th), yet I judge that it will proceed from natural causes. It is not unlikely that the position of Mercury in the 8th house (he having the declination of Saturn, and therefore partaking of his evil nature) may bring on the disease through a severe cold or cough, and that considerable delirium may attend. N.B. This judgment is necessarily only of a *general* nature; as, according to the rule, we must look chiefly to the directions in operation at the fatal period.

CHAPTER XI.

TO JUDGE OF THE EFFECTS OF DIRECTIONS.

Rule.—CONSIDER well the general nature of the planet casting the aspect, and also the manner in which he is situated as regards other planets at birth; and observe, also, what other directions are near at the time; and then, according to the native's situation in life, judge of the effect.

1st. *Saturn* to an ill aspect of the ascendant brings cold diseases and lingering complaints; in a watery sign, danger of drowning, dropsy, &c.; in a fiery or airy sign, danger of falls, blows, &c.; in an earthy sign, accidents by being crushed or bruised, or buried alive. His ill aspects to the M. C. cause injury to the native's affairs by death of relations, being wronged by elderly persons, and a general tendency to disgrace, trouble, and misfortune. His ill aspects to the Sun produce similar effects, with much evil to the native's *father*, quarrels with persons in power or with his relations, especially his father. To the Moon, much mischief to the native's health, and many troubles; his affairs go wrong, and he is generally unfortunate, and very unpopular. To the ⊕, loss of property by various means, often imperceptibly. The △ or ✶ of Saturn to the ascendant or the ☽, renders the native grave and steady, and these aspects to either of the five moderators (viz. ☉, ☽, ⊕, ascendant, and M. C.) will produce benefits by old persons, legacies, &c. also by dealing in land or houses, or with saturnine people or things.

2nd. *Jupiter.*—The good aspects to either of the moderators produce prosperity, increase of wealth, new friends, honourable employment, the birth of children or their settlement in life, and an improved state of health* and much happiness. This planet never causes *marriage*. The *semiquartile*, □, ☍, or S S □, will cause quarrels with clergy-

* The ⊕ does not affect *health*.

men, magistrates, landlords, &c., losses in trade or by travelling, &c.; but unless ♃ be extremely ill aspected at birth, his ill aspects by direction will not cause any permanent evil.

3rd. *Mars.*—His evil aspects produce accidents by fire, fire-arms, cuts, blows, injuries by animals, &c.; also violent diseases, especially if thrown to the hyleg, death of relations, &c. In airy signs he causes falls; in fiery, fevers, hurts by fire; in earthy, pestilential complaints; in watery, scalds, fluxes, peril by water, and inflammations. He causes losses by robbers, fraud, &c.; and by means of military men, or persons in power, he brings various injuries. But although his *conjunction* with ☉ is reckoned an *evil* aspect, it will (if he be well aspected at birth) sometimes cause military honours, or success in the native's trade or profession, when it is to the *mid-heaven*. His ⚹ or △ causes military employment, or advancement, the birth of children (generally males), journies and success in trade or employment, especially if a surgeon, chymist, or dealer in metals. His good aspects frequently cause marriage in a female nativity, except those to ⊕, which give increase of wealth only.

4th. *The Sun.*—The Sun acts in a medium manner between the nature of Jupiter and Mars. If he come to ☌ of the ascendant, being at birth well aspected, he may give fame and reputation, and the native is successful in all matters connected with people in power. If he be ill aspected, he is likely to give disease in the head; and if in a fiery sign, or if the Sun be afflicted by Mars, it causes fevers. The ☌ with the M. C. will cause honours, if well aspected at birth; but if in conjunction with Mars at birth, he may very likely cause evil. The ☉ coming to ☌ with ☽ will cause journeys; and if ☽ be well situated, it gives some preferment; if otherwise, it brings sickness, especially humours in the head, diseases in the eyes, &c. It frequently happens that the native marries under this direction, especially if others tending to produce marriage accompany it; but as it generally makes him fickle and extravagant, such marriages are not fortunate, unless ☽ be very well situated at birth. The good aspects of the Sun to the ascendant, M. C., ☽, or ⊕, also his arrival by direction to his own ⚹, produce benefits, preferment, increase of wealth, *marriage*,* children, &c. If he be well placed and aspected at birth, his return to his own declination will also cause benefits, good success, &c. His evil aspects cause disease, disgrace, loss of friends, death of relations, and many evils. His arrival at his own semi-quartile is evil; his own square extremely so.

5th. *Venus*.—Her good aspects produce health, and give an inclination to enjoy pleasure and amusement. She causes benefits by females, marriage, the birth of children, their settlement in life, &c. Her evil aspects cause trouble by females and by free living, producing disease and discredit, disappointment in marriage, slander, and many vexations. If the train of directions which causes death have amongst it a □ or ☍ of Venus, and she be evil at birth, it may cause the native to be poisoned. The M. C. to the ☍ of ♀ will sometimes cause marriage, but then it is rash and attended with trouble.

6th. *Mercury*.—The good aspects cause journeys, removals, much activity in business, and successful law-suits. Also satisfaction by means of children or young persons, literary characters, booksellers, &c., and literary fame or success. His evil aspects cause trouble by similar means, and also frauds by young persons, servants, &c. The situation of ☿ at birth must be particularly noted, especially those planets he is in zodiacal parallel with, as he partakes strongly of the nature of those planets he is connected with by aspect or declination, and will act accordingly. If he be evil at birth, and should

---

* Fortune produces wealth only.

come to ☌ or ill aspect of the ☽ or the hyleg, he frequently causes mental diseases, epilepsy, &c.

7th. *The Moon.*—Her good aspects to the ascendant or M. C. generally cause changes in life for the better, long journeys, voyages, removals, &c.; to the Sun, they give honours and emoluments, profitable employment, popular favours, &c. and marriage; to the ⊕, the same, or benefit by females, going to sea, &c.; to her own ✶ or parallel, either in the world or the zodiac, the same; but these latter will depend on her condition. Her ill aspects cause the reverse, and if to the hyleg, will give cold or dropsical diseases; if in a watery sign, danger by water. Her ☌ with the ☉ will cause fevers if the Sun be evil at birth, and the moon be hyleg. It causes an unsettled state of affairs, losses, many changes, journeys, and much vexation, if the Sun be evil; also diseases in the eyes, if it fall near the Pleiades, Hyades, or other nebulous fixed stars. If the Sun be fortunate at birth, it may give marriage or preferment, and profitable journeys.

8th. *Herschel.*—This planet is not yet thoroughly understood. His conjunction, parallels, or ill aspects produce evil, generally of an unexpected, sudden, or uncommon nature, but in a far less degree than either Saturn or Mars. His good aspects produce benefits in the same way. He causes benefits or troubles by means of public bodies and public writers.

CHAPTER XII.

OF MUNDANE ASPECTS AND DIRECTIONS.

THERE are some modern astrologers who question the reality of mundane aspects. But this can only arise from lack of sufficient experience, combined with the difficulties which arise from imperfectly rectified nativities. I would refer such doubters to the nativity of ELIZABETH OF CLARENCE, born

5^h 5^m P.M. 10th Dec. 1820, as an instance of the effect of *mundane* aspects. She died at the age of four months, on the 4th of March, 1821. The public papers gave the time of birth; and it will be seen that there is no zodiacal aspect to account for death, the hyleg having only the semi-square of ♄. But there are the *mundane* squares of ♅, ♂, and ☉, the latter within three degrees, and being extremely evil from being near ☌ with ♂, and in *mundane* SS □ with ♄. The ☽ has also the *mundane* S □ with Saturn.

The positions of the planets as regards their relative distances from each other in the twelve houses produce this kind of aspects, which are extremely powerful in their operation. If they occur at birth, they act upon the native all through life; if they are found afterwards, they influence him for some weeks (sometimes months) at that period of life to which their arc extends.

A mundane ✶ is when two planets are two houses apart. Thus ☉ on the meridian at noon and ♃ on the cusp of the 8th house are in mundane ✶. If ☉ be half through the 9th, and ♃ half through the 7th, they are still two houses apart, and in mundane ✶. If ☉ be on the cusp of the 9th and ♃ be in the 7th, he will, when he arrives at the cusp of the 7th, be arrived by direction at the ☉'s ✶: and if ♃ at birth be just below the 7th and the ☉ in the 9th, he will when he arrives at the same distance below or past the 9th (in proportion to his semi-arc as compared with ♃'s semi-arc), be also arrived at ♃'s ✶.

A mundane □ is the distance of three houses apart. Thus, if ☽ be rising at noon or midnight, when ☉ is on the meridian, they are in mundane □, being three houses apart; the same if ☽ be setting at those times.—*Example:* In Ada's nativity we find ♅ a short distance outside the cusp of the 9th, and ♄ a short distance outside the 12th house; they are, therefore, nearly in mundane □ ; and as it is an evil aspect, they mutually increase each other's evil.

A mundane △ is four houses apart. Thus in Ada's figure of birth the ☉ being near upon the cusp of the 9th and ☽ near the 1st house (which are four houses apart) we say that the luminaries are in mundane △. The effect is fortunate, and upholds the native's honour and character.

A mundane ☍ is six houses apart. Thus, a star rising and another setting are in mundane opposition.

A mundane semi-quartile is one house and a half apart.

A mundane sesquiquadrate is four houses and a half apart.

A mundane quintile is one-fifth of two-thirds of the semi-arc of the planet you direct *more* than the ✶.

A mundane biquintile is one-tenth of the planet's semi-arc *more* than the sesquiquadrate.

Remark.—These mundane aspects are all measured by the semi-arcs of the planets; therefore

A semi-quartile is one-half of a planet's semi-arc.

A ✶ is two-thirds of ditto.

A □ is an entire semi-arc.

A △ is equal to a semi-arc and one-third more.

A sesquiquadrate is equal to a semi-arc and a half.

And observe, that whenever an aspect is measured between two planets, any other aspect may be ascertained, if it also fall in the same hemisphere, by merely taking the relative proportion of the semi-arc of the planet to be directed. Thus, if we know the distance between two planets, that is the arc of direction to the *conjunction;* then one-half of the semi-arc of the planet which is directed, added to that, will give the arc of direction to the *semi-quartile;* by adding *one-sixth* part of the semi-arc to this, we have the arc of direction to the ✶; *one-third* more of the semi-arc will give the □, and another *third* the △ : to which add *one-sixth* for the *sesquiquadrate.*

N.B. If the planet directed should pass the horizon in forming either of these aspects, that is, if the arc of direction should be longer than the planet's distance from the horizon, then its other semi-arc must be used for those aspects which fall beyond the horizon. Great care is to be taken to avoid errors by taking the wrong semi-arc: this may be done by observing, that if the aspect fall above the earth, the semi-diurnal arc is to be taken; and if below the earth, the semi-nocturnal arc *of that planet which is directed* is to be taken.

CHAPTER XIII.

OF THE MUNDANE PARALLELS.

These are as important as any mundane aspect in their effects, both at birth and when found by direction. They consist of equal proportional distances from the meridian; thus, if two stars, having the same semi-arcs, are at an equal distance from the meridian on opposite sides, they are in mundane parallel.

Example.—If ☉'s semi-arc be 60°, and he be 20° distant from the meridian, while ☽, having also the semi-arc of 60°, be 20° distant from the meridian, they are in mundane parallel. If, however, the ☉ be so situated while the ☽ has the semi-arc of 120°, or double that of ☉, she will require to be 40° distant from the meridian, or double the ☉'s distance, to be in mundane parallel with him.

Example.—In the nativity of Ada, ♄ is placed in the 11th, at the distance of 37° 55' from the meridian, his semi-arc being 64° 24'. The Sun is in the 9th, approaching to a parallel distance from the meridian with Saturn; the ☉ has the semi-arc of 57° 53', which is less than that of ♄; therefore, when the Sun is at a distance of 34° 5' from the meridian, he will be in mundane parallel with ♄, because the ☉'s semi-arc bears *the same proportion* to 34° 5' as ♄'s semi-arc bears to his distance from the meridian, which is 37° 55'.

CHAPTER XIV.

OF THE PART OF FORTUNE.

WHATEVER distance the Sun is from the Moon (measured by oblique ascension), so far is the Part of Fortune from the Ascendant: hence, if the ☉ be exactly ascending at birth, the place of ⊕ will be exactly that in which the Moon is at that time; therefore, to find the right ascension of ⊕, observe the following:—

Rule.—Add 90° to the A.R. of the M.C., and it will give the oblique ascension of the Ascendant. From the oblique ascension of the Ascendant subtract the oblique ascension of the Sun (having first added 360° to the former, if it be less than the latter); to the remainder add the A.R. of ☽: the sum will be the A.R. of ⊕.

Example.—In Ada's nativity, the A.R. of the M.C. is	273°	22'
To which add	90	0
Oblique Ascension of Ascendant	363	22
Subtract ☉'s oblique ascension	288	42
Remainder	74	40
To which add ☽'s A.R.	7	15
It gives the A.R. of ⊕	81	55

TO FIND THE SITUATION OF THE PART OF FORTUNE IN THE FIGURE AT BIRTH.

Rule.—Find its distance from the nearest meridian; bearing in mind that the ⊕ is always under the horizon before the full Moon, at which time it is on the cusp of the 7th house,* and that after full Moon it is always above the horizon.

Example.—In Ada's nativity the ⊕ is under the horizon, because the ☽ had not reached the full. The A.R. of the meridian under the earth is 93° 22′, from which, if we take the A.R. of ⊕ 81° 55′, the remainder is 11° 27′, the distance of ⊕ from the meridian, which, as it does not amount to *one-third* of the semi-arc of ⊕ (93° 9′), shews that ⊕ is in the 3d house.

N.B. The semi-arc of ⊕ is always that of the ☽, if they are both above or under the horizon; but if one be above, and the other under the horizon, the ⊕ will have the opposite semi-arc to ☽, which may be found by taking the semi-arc of ☽ from 180 degrees.

Observation.—Mr. Wilson, in his "Dictionary of Astrology," p. 306, says that the Part of Fortune "is really nothing but a phantom hatched in the figurative brain of Ptolemy, which has no influence whatever." I certainly must demur to this *dictum*, as I have found by experience that, if calculated in the manner I have here explained, and the directions to it be correctly calculated also, and no *false* directions made (such as aspects in the zodiac, which do not apply to ⊕), there will be found very considerable effects. I respect Mr. Wilson as a friend of truth; but I think that in treating of Astrology he has, in some few instances, thought too much of reason and too little of experience. It is true, that we cannot *explain* the *influence* of ⊕, nor can we explain *that* of any planet; but we must remember, that "two bodies, at a distance, will put one another into motion by the force of attraction; which is unexplicable

* If ☽ have no latitude.

by us, though made evident to us by experience, and so to be taken as a principle in natural philosophy."⁀ These are the words of the great Locke; and they justify our faith in the influence of ⊕ if made evident "*by experience,*" though it be, indeed, "unexplicable" by reason, in our present state of knowledge.

CHAPTER XV.

OF THE HYLEG AND THE HYLEGIACAL PLACES.

THE *hyleg*, or giver of life, is first the ☉, if found in a hylegiacal place; 2d, the ☽, if she be so found, when ☉ is not; lastly, the luminaries being neither of them in hylegiacal places, the degree ascending becomes hyleg. The *hylegiacal places* are from 5 degrees above the ascending horizon to 25 degrees below it, measured by oblique ascension; also from half way between the ascendant and mid-heaven unto 5 degrees beyond the cusp of the 9th house; lastly, from 5 degrees below the 8th house to 5 degrees below the 7th or descendant.

N.B. The ascendant or ☽ receiving evil aspects by direction will at all times be likely to affect the health, whether hyleg or not. And if the Moon be beyond the exact 5 degrees of any hylegiacal house, yet if within a short distance, she will cause a great deal of danger; and if the hyleg be at the same time afflicted, though only slightly, the native will very probably die. It has been said that if ⊕ be in a hylegiacal place when neither luminary is so situated, it becomes hyleg. This doctrine has never yet been confirmed by my own experience; nor should I direct to it as hyleg, because I have hitherto found that its chief effects were upon the native's pecuniary circumstances. Lilly, speaking of the directions to ⊕, says, "thereby to be certified of the state of riches and goods moveable, the times of increase or decrease, &c." And I believe the effects of ⊕ are confined to these subjects chiefly, though it may affect his family affairs.

N.B. The planet in ☌ with ⊕ will greatly influence the *nature* of the native's property, which will be according to the character of that planet.

SECOND BOOK.

CHAPTER I.

ZODIACAL DIRECTIONS.

The ☉, ☽, ascendant, and mid-heaven, only can be directed in the zodiac.* The principle on which these directions are to be made is the subtraction of the oblique ascension of either of the first three, taken under its own pole, from the oblique ascension of the place of the aspect taken under the same pole.

The pole of the ☉ or ☽ is a certain elevation they have from the meridian towards the horizon: hence, if they be exactly on the meridian they have no pole, and the arc of direction must be found by right ascension: hence also the mid-heaven itself, having no pole, must be directed by right ascension only. If the ☉ or ☽ be exactly on the horizon, they will have the polar elevation of the horizon itself; which is always *the latitude of the country*. The ascendant, when it is directed in the zodiac, must always be directed under the pole or latitude of the place of birth.

There being some difference of opinion as to the proper mode of calculating poles, it may be proper to explain the nature of the pole of a star, or house.

If we examine the horizon of any place on the equator, we shall find the poles of the heavens therein, and in a line with the poles of the Earth. Now, if we quit the equator and proceed towards either pole of the Earth, we necessarily raise

---

* Some modern artists, as well as *Placidus*, dispute the power of the *angles* thus directed. I have had innumerable proofs of its existence.

that pole of the heavens by an arc exactly equal to the extent of the latitude we arrive at from the equator. If, therefore, we were to reach London, in latitude 51° 32′ N., we should find that the north pole of the heavens had become *elevated* above the horizon by an arc exactly equal to that latitude. Wherefore we say, that *the elevation of the pole of the horizon, or 1st house, is the latitude of the country*. If we reached 90° of latitude, or the pole of the Earth, we should elevate the pole of the heavens to our zenith.

The circles of latitude are *small circles of the sphere* having their planes parallel with the plane of the *equator*. And the CIRCLES OF POSITION of all bodies between the meridian and horizon are analogous to these circles of latitude, being *small circles of the sphere*, having their planes parallel with the plane of the *meridian*. The *circle of position* of a planet, &c. has a certain point where it and the pole of the planet intersect the equator. It may be found by the following analogy:—

> As the semi-arc of the planet
> Is to 90° of the equator,
> So is the meridian distance of the planet
> To the distance in Right Ascension of its *circle of position* from the meridian.

Having found the *circle of position's* distance from the meridian, we have only to find the difference between it and the distance of the planet itself, and we obtain the *ascensional difference* of the planet *under its own pole*. Then to discover the POLAR ELEVATION of the planet, &c., say,

> As Rad. Sine 90°
> Is to the Co. Tang. of Declin.
> So is Sine of Ascensional Diff.
> To Tang. of pole.

Observe here that the *ascensional difference* of any place in a given latitude (or polar elevation) is exactly that which any *body* has as determined by its distance from the meridian; *ascensional* difference being in both cases the difference between *right* and *oblique* ascension. Therefore the proportion of the stars' ascensional difference, as connected with its semi-arc, may be taken to find its polar elevation.

To learn the ascensional difference (as, for example, that of the Sun with 23° 28′ declination in the latitude of London) say,

As Rad. Sine 90° 10.00000
To Tang. 23° 28′ 9.63761
So Tang. Lat. 51° 32′ 10.09991

To Sine Asc. Diff. 33° 7′ 9.73752

Suppose, then, that the Sun is one-third of his distance from the meridian to the horizon below the meridian, and we would know his *polar elevation*, say,

As Rad. Sine 90° 10.00000
To Co. Tang. 23° 28′ 10.36239
So Sine of ⅓ of 33° 7′=11° 2′ 26″ 9.28211

To Tang. of the Sun's pole 23° 48′........ = 9.64450

This is the pole of the 11th and 9th houses in the latitude of London, each being one-third of the distance from the meridian to the horizon. To prove it correct, we have only to seek for the ascensional difference in the latitude of 23° 48′; thus,

As Rad. Sine 90° 10.00000
To Tang. Dec. 23° 28′ 9.63761
So Tang. Pole 23° 48′ 9.64450

To Sine Asc. Diff. 11° 2′ 20″ .... = 9.28211

By these formulæ have the poles of the houses (as divided by the immortal PTOLEMY, and demonstrated by *Placidus*) been calculated. They have ever been found to agree with events in nature, as they do with the true principles of geometry.

Observe.—The place of the aspect or promittor must be taken *without latitude* in all directions in the zodiac, except those of the ☽ ; for when ☽ is directed to any point, the latitude she will have when she arrives at that point must first be ascertained.* If the ☽ be directed to the conjunction of any planet, and when she arrives at the longitude of that point she should have great latitude of an opposite nature to the planet, so that there shall be 6 or more degrees difference of latitude between them, the direction will have little or no effect. If, for example, ♀ have 5 degrees *north* latitude, and ☽, when she comes to ☌ of ♀, have 5 degrees of *south* latitude, then the ☌ will have no power. If it should be to an ☍, however, then the exact *opposite* place of ♀ would have 5 degrees of *contrary* latitude, and the aspect (if ☽ had 5° south and ♀ 5° north latitude) would be perfect. Therefore we must observe, that if, on coming to an ☍, the ☽ have extensive latitude of the *same* name as the planet, the direction is weak.

CHAPTER II.

TO DIRECT ☉ TO ANY ASPECT IN THE ZODIAC, EXCEPT A PARALLEL.

FIRST. Find the ☉'s polar elevation from the meridian, by the analogy in the previous chapter.

* Partridge directed ☽ also *sine latitudine ;* but I doubt the power of such directions.

GRAMMAR OF ASTROLOGY.   419

Example.—In Ada's nativity, (from which we will take all our examples), the ☉'s semi-arc is 57° 53′, and ☉'s meridian distance is 16° 47′.

1st. Add the arithmetical complement of the proportional logarithm of ☉'s semi-arc	9.5073
To the proportional logarithm of 90°	3010
And the proportional logarithm of ☉ meridian distance ..	1.0304
	.8387
The sum is the proportional logarithm of the difference of its circle and that of the meridian	26° 2′
2d. Subtract the ☉'s meridian distance	16 47
The difference is ☉'s ascensional difference *in his pole*	9 15
3d. Rad. s. 90°	10.00000
To logarithm sine of ascensional difference, 9° 15′........	9.20613
So logarithm co-tangent of ☉'s declination 22° 54′ = ...	10.37426
To logarithm tangent of the POLE of ☉ = 20° 50′	9.58039

SECOND. Ascertain the oblique *ascension* of ☉ under his own pole, if he be ascending, or his oblique *descension*, if he be descending.—N.B. ☉ is ascending from midnight till noon, and descending from noon till midnight.

Rule 1.—Add the ascensional difference to the A. R. if the declination be *south*, but subtract it from the A. R. if the declination be *north*: the result is the oblique *ascension*.

Rule 2.—For the oblique *descension* do the reverse: add the ascensional difference if the declination be *north*, subtract it if the declination be *south*.

Example.—The ☉'s A. R. is	256° 35′
The declination is *south*, therefore subtract the ascensional difference	9 15
It gives ☉'s oblique descension under his pole..........	247 20

E E

THIRD. Find the declination of the place of the aspect, and look in the tables* for the logarithm of its *tangent;* to which add the log. tangent of ☉'s pole. The sum will be the log. *sine* of the *aspect's* ascensional difference under that pole. With this *ascensional difference* find its oblique ascension or descension, as you did that of ☉ †.

LASTLY. Subtract that of ☉ from that of the aspect, and the remainder will be the ARC OF DIRECTION.

Example.—Direct the ☉ to □ of ☽ in the zodiac. The ☽ is in ♈ 5° 39′: when ☉ comes to ♑ 5° 39′, he will form a □ aspect to the place of ☽ at birth.

The declination of the aspect ♑ 5° 39′ is 23°21′ its log. tangent	9.63519
The logarithm *tangent* of the ☉'s pole 20° 50′ is	9.58039
Their sum is the log. *sine* of the ascensional difference of the *aspect* under ☉'s pole 9° 27′	9.21558

Then from the A. R. of ♑ 5° 39′ which is..............	276	9
Subtract the ascensional difference, as its declination is south	9	27
It leaves the oblique descension of the aspect under ☉'s pole	266	42
From which subtract the oblique descension of ☉ under ☉'s pole	247	20
And this will be the ARC OF DIRECTION of ☉ □ ☽ in zodiac...	19	22

To those who think the above a tedious operation, we observe, that if the ☉'s pole, &c. be once found, in all other of the directions you have only to go through the last two heads of the rule. And, moreover, the whole of these as-

---

* The best extant are "*Logarithmi* VI *Decimalium, auctore G. F. Ursino;*" but a less expensive and very convenient set have been published by Taylor and Walton.

† By adding it to or subtracting it from A. R. of the aspect.

pects *in zodiaco* may be worked by means of the *semi-arcs*, without reference to poles or the use of logarithms. The invariable rule is this:—

As the semi-arc of the significator (⊙, ☽, or asc.) is to its distance from the meridian, so is the semi-arc of the place of the aspect to its 2nd distance. The sum or difference of aspect's PRIMARY AND SECONDARY *distance from the meridian is the* ARC OF DIRECTION.

Example.—As semi-arc ⊙ is to ⊙'s meridian distance, so is the semi-arc of ♑ 5° 39' to its second distance, which add to its primary meridian distance.

CHAPTER III.

TO DIRECT ⊙ TO A PARALLEL IN THE ZODIAC.

Rule 1.—LOOK in the table of declination for the declination to which you desire to direct the ⊙, which you will find in the column marked 0 at the top; then note what longitude it answers to in the first column, and find the A. R. answering to this longitude.

Rule 2.—The log. tang. of the dec. + log. tang. of the pole of ⊙ = the log. sine of the ascensional difference of the aspect under that pole.

Rule 3.—Find the oblique ascension or descension of the aspect, according as the ⊙ is ascending or descending; and from it take the oblique ascension or descension of the ⊙: the remainder is the ARC OF DIRECTION.

Example.—Required to direct the Sun to the parallel declination of Herschel, in Ada's nativity.

The declination of ♅ is 21° 35' south, which is the declination ⊙ will have when he reaches ♑ 22° 30', the A. R. of which is 294° 19'.

To the log. *tangent* of 21° 35'........................	9.59725
Add the log. *tangent* of the pole of ☉, 20° 50'	9.58039
The sum is the logarithm *sine* of the ascensional difference of the aspect under the pole of ☉, 8° 39'	9.17764
Then from the A. R. of the aspect	294° 19
Take the ascen. difference as before	8.39
It gives the oblique descension of the aspect under the pole of ☉.....................................	285 40
From this subtract the oblique descension of ☉ under his pole	247 20
And there remains the *arc of direction* of ☉ to a zodiacal parallel of ♅........................	38 29

CHAPTER IV.

TO DIRECT THE MOON IN THE ZODIAC TO ANY ASPECT EXCEPT A PARALLEL.

FIRST. As in case of ☉, find the ☽'s pole and her oblique ascension or descension under her pole.

1st. To find the pole of ☽, add the proportional log. of ☽'s semi-arc (taking its arithmetical comp.) to the proportional logarithm of 90°, and the proportional log. of ☽'s meridian distance; the sum is the proportional log. of the difference of the circles of position.

2nd. The difference between the meridian distance of ☽ and the difference of the circles of position = the ascensional difference of ☽ under her pole.

3rd. The log. *sine* of the ascensional difference + the logarithm *co-tangent* of the ☽'s declination = the log. *tangent* of ☽'s pole.

Example.—Find ☽'s pole in Ada's nativity.

Proportional log. of ☽'s semi-arc 93° 9' (its arith. comp.)	9.7139
Ditto log. of 90 degrees	3010
Ditto log. of ☽'s merid. dist. 86° 7'	3202
Ditto log. of the difference in circle of position 83 12	3351
☽'s asc. diff. in her pole .... 2 55 log. sine of this	8.70658
Add log. co-tangent ☽ dec. 2° 30'	11.35991
Sum is log. tangent of ☽'s pole 49° 22'	10.06649

SECOND. 1. To find the oblique ASCENSION of ☽ in her pole, *add* the ascensional difference if the declination be *south*; *subtract* the ascensional difference, if the declination be *north*, to or from the A. R.

2. To find the oblique DESCENSION, do the reverse.

Example.—A. R. of ☽ 7° 15' + ascens. diff. 2° 55' = oblique ascens. of ☽ in her pole 10° 10'.

THIRD. Find the oblique ascension or descension of the aspect under the pole of ☽, and subtract the ☽'s oblique ascension or descension from it: the remainder is the ARC OF DIRECTION.

N.B. The latitude of the ☽ in the aspect must be first noted to find her true A. R. and declination therein.

Example.—Direct ☽ to ☌ of ♂ in Ada's nativity.

Mars is in 20° 26' of ♈, at which, when the ☽ arrives, she will have 4° 45' south latitude, and 3° 34' north declination; then the log. tangent of this declination 8.79470 + the log. tangent of the pole of ☽ 10.06649 = the log. sine of the ascensional difference of the aspect in ☽'s pole 4° 10'=8.86119.

The A. R. of 20° 26' ♈ with 4° 45' south latitude is 20° 40' — the ascens. difference, the declination being *north*, 4° 10' = the oblique ascension of the aspect in pole of ☽, 16° 31'.

LASTLY.—*The aspect's* oblique ascension in the pole of ☽ 16° 30'— the oblique ascension of ☽ in her pole 10° 10' = the *arc of direction* of ☽ ☌ ♂ zodiac, 60° 20'.

N.B. To work this by semi-arcs, say, semi-arc ☽ : meridian distance ☽ :: semi-arc of ♈ 20° 26′ with 4° 45′ south latitude: second distance of ditto. Then difference of meridian distance and second distance = arc of direction.

CHAPTER V.

TO DIRECT THE MOON TO PARALLELS OF DECLINATION.

Rule 1.—Look in the Ephemeris for the days succeeding the birth, and see at what time the ☽ falls on the declination you require; then calculate by proportion the latitude and longitude she will have at that time.

Rule 2.—Find the A. R. for that latitude and longitude, and take from or add to it the ascensional difference given by the required declination under the ☽'s pole: the result will be the oblique ascension or oblique descension of the *aspect;* the ☽'s oblique ascension or descension taken from which will leave the ARC OF DIRECTION.

N.B. Find ☽'s pole as taught in Chap. IV.

Example.—I desire to bring ☽ to a parallel of ♂'s declination in Ada's nativity.

I find that the ☽'s declination on the 12th December is 7° 22′, and on the 13th it is 12° 16′; then, if the difference 4° 54′ is equal to 24 hours, what will the difference between the declination at noon on the 12th, 7° 22′, and the declination of ♂ 8° 23′, which is 1° 1′, amount to? Answer, 4 hours 59 minutes; at which time, on the 12th, I find the ☽ is in longitude 2° 30′ ♉, with 4° 10′ south latitude.

The A.R. answering to this latitude and longitude is 31° 58′. Then the logarithm *tangent* of the declination ♂ 8° 23′, 9.16841 + log. *tangent* of the ☽'s pole 49° 22′, 10.06649 = log. *sine* of the aspect's ascensional difference 9° 55′ = 9.23590.

Now, from the A.R. of the aspect 31 58
Take the ascens. difference under the ☽'s pole 9 55

It leaves the oblique ascension under the ☽'s pole 22 3
From which subtract the ☽'s oblique ascension in her pole.. 10 10

The remainder is the ARC OF DIRECTION of the ☽ to the
zodiacal parallel of ♂ 11 53

N.B. There are no directions more powerful than the parallels in the zodiac; they merit the greatest attention. It is observed that their effects are felt a few weeks before the arc of direction is complete.

CHAPTER VI.

TO DIRECT THE ASCENDANT TO ASPECTS IN THE ZODIAC.

Rule 1.—ADD 90° to the A.R. of the mid-heaven at birth, and it gives the oblique ascension of the ascendant under the pole (or latitude) of birth.

Rule 2.—Look in the Table of Declinations for the declination of the aspect, which is found in the column marked 0 at the top, opposite its longitude.

Rule 3.—Find the A.R. of that longitude without latitude.

Rule 4.—To the log. *tangent* of the pole of the ascendant add the log. *tangent* of the declination of the aspect: the sum will be the log. *sine* of its ascensional difference.

Rule 5.—Take this ascensional difference from the A.R. if the declination be *north*, or add it thereto if the declination be *south:* the result is the oblique ascension of the aspect under the pole of the country.

Lastly.—The oblique ascension of the aspect — the oblique ascension of the ascendant = the ARC OF DIRECTION.

Example.—Direct the ascendant to □ ♄ in the zodiac.

1. The A.R. of the mid-heaven is 273° 22', to which add 90°, and we have 363° 22'; as it is beyond 360°, deduct the circle from it, and we have 3° 22' for the oblique ascension of the ascendant under its pole.

2. The □ of ♄ falls in 8° 36' of ♉, the declination of which is 14° 23'.

3. The A.R. of 8° 36' of ♉ is 36° 12'.

4. Log. *tangent* of the pole of the 1st house, 51° 32',   10.09991
+ log. *tangent* of the declination of 8° 36' ♉ 14° 23,   9.40900

= log. *sine* of its ascensional difference 18° 50'   19.50891.

5. The A.R. of the aspect 36° 12'—the ascens. difference 18° 50' = oblique ascension of the aspect 17° 22'.

Lastly.—From this take the oblique ascension of the ascendant 3° 22', the remainder is the arc of the ascendant □ ♄ zodiac 14° 0'.

CHAPTER VII.

TO DIRECT THE MID-HEAVEN TO ASPECTS IN THE ZODIAC.

Rule.—THE A.R. of the aspect—A.R. of M.C. = the ARC OF DIRECTION.

Example.—Find the arc of the M.C. □ of ♂ in the zodiac.

A. R. of the □ of ♂ in (♑ 20° 26') 292° 7' — A. R. of M. C. 273° 22' =: the ARC OF DIRECTION 18° 45'.

CHAPTER VIII.

OF MUNDANE DIRECTIONS TO THE ANGLES; THAT IS, TO THE ASCENDANT OR M. C.

THESE are merely the divisions of the semi-arcs of the planets; thus, ½ is a semi-quartile; ⅔ a ✶; the whole of the semi-arc a □; one semi-arc and ⅓ of another a △; one semi-arc and a half, a sesquiquadrate, &c. A semi-arc always bearing the same proportion to the 12 houses as 90 degrees do to the circle or 12 signs of the zodiac, it follows that ⅔ of it form a ✶ aspect, as ⅔ of 90° are 60°, a ✶ in the zodiac, &c. &c.

To find the Arc of Direction to a Semi-quartile of the M.C.

Rule.—The difference between half the semi-arc and the meridian distance of the planet is the ARC OF DIRECTION; because, when the planet is exactly half its semi-arc off the M.C., it is in semi-quartile aspect to that angle.

Example.— ♄ semi-arc is 64° 24′; half is 32° 12′, which taken from ♄'s meridian distance 37° 55′, gives the arc of M. C. to the semi-quartile of ♄ 5° 43′.

To find the Arc of Direction to a ⚹ of M.C

Rule.—The difference between the planet's meridian distance and ⅔ of its semi-arc is the arc of direction.

Example.—2-3 of ☉'s semi-arc 38° 35′—☉'s meridian distance 16° 47′ = 21° 48′, the arc of direction of M. C. ⚹ ☉.

To find the Arc of Direction to a □ of M.C.

Rule.—The planet's semi-arc — meridian distance = arc of direction.

Example.—The semi-arc of ♃ 75° 34′—meridian distance of ♃ 62° 55′ = arc of M. C. □ ♃ 12° 39′.*

To find the Arc of Direction to a △ of M.C.

Rule.—If the planet be above the Earth, add one-third of its semi-arc (nocturnal) to the arc for its □ of M.C. If under the Earth, the difference between its meridian distance and ⅔ of its semi-arc is the *arc of direction.*

Example.—♃ being above the Earth, the arc of M. C. □ ♃ 12° 39′ + 1-3 of the semi-arc of ♃ (nocturnal) 34° 49′ = arc of M. C. △ ♃ 47° 28′.

INFERIOR ASPECTS.

To find the Arc of the Quintile to the M.C.

Rule.—If the quintile be in the 7th house, take ⅕ of the

* This is when ♃ sets or comes to the 7th house, which is asc. ☍ ♃.

semi-arc from the arc for the □. If it be in the 12th house, subtract from ⅕ of the semi-arc the distance the planet is from the ascendant.

Example 1.—The ☉'s semi-arc 57° 53' — ☉ meridian distance 16° 47' = M. C. ⊓ ☉ 41° 16' — 1·5 of ☉ semi-arc 11° 35' = M. C. quintile ☉ 29° 31'.

	°	'
Example 2.—Semi-arc of the ☽ (diurnal) is 86° 51', of which 1·5 is	17	22
Then 17° 22' is the distance the ☽ must be from the ascendant to form the quintile with the M. C.; and as ☽ is not yet risen, her distance from the ascendant 7° 2' must be added to it.............................	7	2
Arc of M. C. quintile of the ☽	24	24

To find the Arc of the Sesquiquadrate to the M.C.

Rule.—If in the 2d, subtract ⅛ of the semi-arc from the arc for the △; if in the 5th, add ⅛ of the semi-arc to the arc for the △.

Another Rule.—Take half the planet's semi-arc, and find the difference between it and the planet's meridian distance, which will be the arc to the semiquartile of the 4th house, or sesquiquadrate of the M.C.

Example.—1·6 of the semi-nocturnal arc of ♃ 17° 24' + arc for his △ to M. C. 47° 28' = 64° 52', the M. C. to the sesquiquadrate of ♃.*

To find the Arc of the Biquintile to the M. C.

Rule.—To the arc for the sesquiquadrate *add* ¹⁄₁₀ of the semi-arc if the aspect fall in the 5th house, and *subtract* ¹⁄₁₀ of the semi-arc if it fall in the 2d house.

N.B. This direction is of no consequence with the evil planets; it is but weak with the benefics.

---

* This is also asc. S. S. ⊓ ♃.

To find the Arc to the ☌ or ☍ of M. C.

Rule.—If the planet be *ascending*, its meridian distance is the arc to the ☌ M. C.; and if it be *descending*, its meridian distance is its arc to the ☍ of M. C. This needs no example.

TO DIRECT THE ASCENDANT IN MUNDO.

To find the ☌ or the ☍ of any Star with the Ascendant.

Rule.—If the planet be between the 4th house and the ascendant, its semi-arc — its meridian distance = the arc to the ☌. If it be between the 10th house and 7th house, its semi-arc — its meridian distance = the arc to the ☍.

Example.—Mars is between the 4th and ascendant; its semi-arc 79° 19′ — meridian distance of ♂ 74° 40′ = arc of direction of the ascendant ☌ ♂ 40° 39′.

To find the ✶ or △ of any Planet to the Ascendant.

Rule.—If above the Earth, its meridian distance — 1-3d of its semi-arc = the ✶; if below the Earth, and *east* of the 4th, 1-3d its semi-arc — its meridian distance; but if *west* of the 4th, + its meridian distance = *the* ✶.

If above the Earth, and *east* of the 10th, its meridian distance + 1-3d of its semi-arc; but if *west* of the 10th, its meridian distance — 1-3rd of its semi-arc = *the* △. If under the Earth, the meridian distance — 1-3d of its semi-arc = *the* △.

The *quintile* to the ascendant is 1-5th of the planet's semi-arc from the meridian, either above or below the Earth.

The *sesquiquadrate* is the semi-quartile from the M. C. if it fall in the 8th house; if it fall in the 5th, it is the sesquiquadrate from the M. C., or semi-quartile from the 4th house.

The *semi-quartile* is in the semi-quartile from the M. C. if it fall in the 11th; if it fall in the 2d, it is the sesquiquadrate from the M. C.

The *biquintile* is 1-10th of the planet's semi-arc *beyond* the middle of the 8th, or semi-quartile from the M. C. If it fall in the 5th, it is 1-10th of the planet's semi-arc to be taken from the arc to the sesquiquadrate of the M. C.

N.B. The shortest way is to find one direction to the ascendant or M. C., and then add or subtract the portion of the planet's semi-arc to find the others.

Example.—☉'s arc to △ of ascendant is 2° 30′ 40″; add 1-3d of the semi-arc of ☉ 19° 17′ 40″, and it gives 21° 48′, for M. C. ✶ ☉, which is ☉'s distance from the 8th; add 1-3rd again, and it gives 41° 6′, the arc for M. C. □ ☉ or ascendant ☍ ☉. Take from 41° 6′ the 1-5th of ☉'s semi-arc, it gives 29° 31′ for M. C. quintile ☉. Take half ☉'s semi-arc from 41° 6′, and it gives 12° 10′, the M. C. semi-quartile ☉, which is also ascendant sesquiquadrate ☉.

CHAPTER IX.

TO DIRECT ☉ OR ☽ TO ANY ASPECT IN THE WORLD (EXCEPT PARALLELS) BY CONVERSE MOTION.

WHEN ☉ or ☽, *above the Earth*, are moved onwards to form the aspect, from the east towards the west, or *below the Earth* from the west towards the east, it is termed a CONVERSE DIRECTION.

Rule 1.—As the semi-arc of the planet to whose aspect ☉ or ☽ is directed is to that planet's distance within or without a certain house, so is the semi-arc of ☉ or ☽ to the *second* distance of ☉ or ☽ from the house which forms the required aspect with that from which the planet's distance is taken.

Rule 2.—Find the apparent or primary distance from the said house, and take the sum or difference of the two distances according as the ☉ or ☽ falls short of or passes the cusp of the house, for the ARC OF DIRECTION. If the aspect is formed before the ☉ or ☽ passes the house, the *difference*, but, if they pass the house to form the aspect, the *sum* must be taken.

Example 1.—Required the arc of ☉ □ ♄ converse?

Semi-arc of ♄ 64° 24′: ♄'s distance from the 12th (outside) 4° 55′ :: semi-arc of ☉ 57° 53′: ☉'s second distance from the 9th outside, 4° 25′.

As the ☉ has to pass the 9th to form the □, add the distance of the ☉ from the 9th, which is the arc of ascendant △ ☉ 2° 32′, the *sum* is 6° 57′, ☉ □ ♄ converse.

Example 2.—Required the arc of direction of the ☽ to the □ of ☉ by converse motion?

Semi-arc of ☉ 57° 53′: ☉'s distance *inside* the 9th, 2° 32′ :: semi arc of the ☽ (diurnal) 86° 51′: second distance of ☽ *inside* the 12th 3° 48′.

To find the ☽'s primary or *actual distance* from the 12th, add 1-3rd her semi-arc *diurnal* to her distance from the 1st house 7° 2′: 86° 51′, of which 1-3rd = 28° 57′ + 7° 2′ = the ☽'s primary distance from the 12th 35° 59′ — her *second* distance to the 12th 3° 48′ = 32° 11′, arc of ☽ □ ☉ converse.

N.B. That semi-arc, whether diurnal or nocturnal must be taken where the planet is when the aspect is *completed*. The Moon at Ada's birth was under the Earth, but when she formed the □ with the place of the ☉ at birth, she was near the 12th house; of course, her *diurnal* semi-arc must be taken.

To work with proportional logarithms, the rule is to add the logarithms of the 2nd and 3rd numbers together, and take from their sum the logarithm of the 1st number, which will leave the logarithm of the 4th number. But a shorter method is to take the *arithmetical complement* of the logarithm of the 1st number, instead of the logarithm itself; and then add all three logarithms together, and the result will be the same. The arithmetical complement of a logarithm is what it wants of 10.0000. The common way to find it is to take each figure from 9, beginning at the left hand, except the right hand figure, which must be taken from 10.

Example.—What is the arithmetical complement of the proportional logarithm of ♄'s semi-arc 64° 24'.

Its proportional logarithm is 4464. As there is no index, the arithmetical complement will have 9 in the index; then 4 from 9 are 5; and 4 from 9 are 5; and 6 from 9 are 3; and 4 from 10 are 6; which will stand thus, 9.5536. If the index amount to 10 or more, reject 10 in the index; for instance, in the second example of ☽ ☐ ☉ converse, the logarithm of the ☽'s distance inside the 12th is 11.6754, which we call 1.6754, by rejecting 10 in the index.*

CHAPTER X.

TO DIRECT THE SUN OR MOON TO ANY ASPECT IN MUNDO (EXCEPT THE PARALLELS) BY DIRECT MOTION.

WHEN the ☉ or ☽ are supposed to remain fixed in the place they were at birth, and the planets ♅, ♄, ♃, ♂, ♀, or ☿, are moved on to form the aspect according to the regular motion of the heavens, the direction is called *Direct Direction*.

Rule 1.—As the semi-arc of the ☉ or ☽ is to its distance from a certain house, so is the semi-arc of the planet directed to the *second* distance of that planet.

Rule 2.—Add or subtract it from the planet's apparent (or primary) distance, according as it passes or falls short of the cusp; the result is the ARC OF DIRECTION.

Example 1.—Direct the ☉ to ☌ ♄ by direct direction.

☉'s semi-arc 57° 53' log. (arith. comp.) 9.5073 : ☉'s meridian distance 16° 47', log. 1.0304 :: semi-arc of ♄ 64° 24', log. 4464 : *second* distance of ♄, past the M. C. 18° 40', log. 9841.

As ♄ passes the cusp of the 10th, add his meridian distance to form the ☌; thus meridian distance 37° 55' + 18° 40' = the arc of ☉ ☌ ♄ D. D. 56° 35'.†

* These proportional logarithms are found in books on Navigation, &c.; they are given in *Cooper's* Placidus.

† Placidus works these directions sometimes by means of poles, &c.; but he errs against his own rule in Canon xxxvii, which is the correct method.

N.B. having worked one direction, others may generally be had from it by the proportional part of the semi-arc of the planet directed :—

Thus, the arc of the ☉ ☌ ♄ D. D. 56° 35' — half of ♄'s semi-arc 32° 12' = arc of ☉ to semiquartile of ♄ D. D. 24° 23' — 1-6th of ♄ semi-arc 10° 44' = arc of ☉ ✶ ♄ D. D. 13° 39'.

Example 2.—Find the arc of ☽ ☐ ♄ D. D.

1. Semi-arc of ☽ 93° 9' log. A. C. 9.7139 : distance of the ☽ from the 1st house, 7° 2' log. 1.4081 : : semi-arc of Saturn 64° 24' log. .4464 : *second* distance of Saturn to the 10th, 4° 52' log. 1.5684.

2. The meridian distance of Saturn 37° 55' — his *second* distance 4° 52' = arc of ☽ ☐ ♄ D. D. 33° 3' — 1-3d of Saturn's arc 21° 28' = arc of ☽ ✶ Saturn D. D. 11° 35' — 1-6th of ♄'s arc 10° 44' = arc of ☽ semiq. Saturn, D. D. 0° 51'.

N.B. As this latter arc is within one degree, it came into operation in the first year of life; and will act all through life to the injury of the native, it being a radical position, by which ♄ vitiates the ☽. Its effects are mitigated by the ✶ of ♄ to ☽ in zodiac.

CHAPTER XI.

TO DIRECT THE SUN OR MOON TO MUNDANE PARALLELS CONVERSE.

These have been already described in Chap. XIII. Book I. (which see.)

Rule 1.—The semi-arc of the planet to whose parallel Sun or ☽ is directed : its meridian distance : : ☉ or ☽'s semi-arc : *second* distance of ☉ or ☽ from the meridian.

Rule 2.—The *difference* between ☉ or ☽'s meridian distance and *second* distance is the ARC OF DIRECTION ; or if it pass the meridian to form the parallel, the *sum* must be taken.

Example 1.—Required the arc of ☉ to parallel ♄ converse.

Semi-arc of ♄ 64° 24' : meridian distance of ♄ 37° 55' : : semi-arc of ☉ 57° 53' : second distance of ☉ 34° 5' — ☉'s meridian distance 16° 47' = arc of ☉ par. ♄ converse 17° 18'.

Example 2.—Required the arc of ☽ parallel ♂ converse.

Semi-arc of ♂ 79° 19' : meridian distance of ♂ 74° 40' : : semi-arc (diurnal) of ☽ 86° 51' : *second* distance of ☽ 81° 46'.

As the aspect falls above the Earth, the ☽'s *diurnal* meridian distance (= 180º — her meridian distance) must be taken.

The ☽'s diurnal meridian distance 93º 53' — her second distance 81º 46 = arc of ☽ parallel ♂ converse 12º 7'.

CHAPTER XII.

TO DIRECT THE SUN OR MOON TO MUNDANE PARALLELS BY DIRECT DIRECTION.

THIS is reversing the operation of the converse parallels.

Rule 1. — Semi-arc of ☉ or ☽ : its meridian distance : : the planet's semi-arc : its *second* distance.

Rule 2.—The *difference* between the planet's meridian distance and second distance, or if it pass the meridian to form the parallel, their *sum*, will be the ARC OF DIRECTION.

Example.—Find the arc of ☉ parallel ♄ D. D.

Semi-arc of ☉, 57º 53' log. A. C. 9.5073 : ☉'s meridian distance, 16º 47' log. 1.0304 : : the semi-arc of ♄ 64º 24' log. .4464 : *second* distance of ♄ 18º 40' log. .9841.

The meridian distance of ♄ 37º 55' — the *second* distance of ♄ 18º 40' = 19º 15' arc of ☉ parallel ♄ D. D.

CHAPTER XIII.

TO DIRECT THE SUN OR MOON TO RAPT PARALLELS;

Or to Parallel Distances from the Meridian by Rapt Motion.

THIS name of rapt is an old term, meaning *carried away;* and it signifies those parallels which are formed by both the significator (as ☉ or ☽ are termed) and the promittor (as the planets ♅, ♄, ♃, ♂, ♀, and ☿, are termed) being carried away by the motion of the Earth on its axis from the places they were in at birth, till they come to equal or parallel distances from the meridian.

Rule 1.—Take half the sum of the semi-arc of the ☉ or ☽ + that of the planet.

Rule 2.—Take half the difference between the A. R. of the ☉ or ☽ and that of the planet.

Rule 3.—Take half the semi-arc of the body which will be applying towards or approaching the meridian when the parallel is formed.

Rule 4.—Half the sum of the semi-arcs: half the semi-arc of the body applying to the meridian : : half the difference of A. R. : half the *second* distance of the body applying to the meridian; which double. The apparent distance of the body from the meridian — the *second* distance = ARC OF DIRECTION.

Example.—Bring the ☉ to the rapt parallel of ♄ in Ada's nativity.

To semi-arc of ♄ 64° 24′, ½ of it is 32° 12′   A.R. of ♄ .... 311° 17′
Add semi-arc of ☉ 57 53   A.R of ☉   256 35

         2)122 17   2) 54 42

      Half   61 8½ p. log. (A.C) .... 9.5311   Half 27 21
: ½ of ♄'s semi-arc 32 12 7474
:: ½ of the diff. A.R. 27 21 prop. log. 8153

: ½ the *second* distance of ♄ ...... 14° 24′=1.0968
                              ×   2

     Second distance of ♄ 28 48

The meridian distance of ♄, 37° 55′,—*second* distance of ♄ from the meridian, 28° 48′, leaves the *arc of direction* of ☉ rapt parallel ♄, 9° 7′.

N.B. These rapt parallels are most powerful directions, and never fail to produce important effects. This direction it was which caused the death of the native's noble and talented father; as it will be seen, by the rules for turning arcs of direction into time, that it came up exactly at the period of Lord Byron's death. *All parallels act like conjunctions; good with good planets, and evil with evil planets.*

Example 2.—Required the arc for the rapt parallel of ☽ to ♂. The body of ♂ is nearer the ascendant than that of ☽; and he therefore rises first, and will form a parallel distance to the M. C. according to his semi-arc (diurnal, as he will be above the Earth), with that formed by the Moon to the meridian under the Earth, according to her semi-arc. But as the opposition of the Moon will be at an equal distance from the 10th or diurnal meridian as her body is from the 4th or nocturnal meridian; and as the rule requires the arcs used to be both diurnal or both nocturnal, we take the ☍ of ☽ instead of the ☽ herself to work with.

Then to the semi-arc (diurnal) of ♂ .. 100° 41′   A.R. ♂ 18° 42′ + 360° 0′
                                                              = 378 42

Add the semi-arc (diurnal) of the ☍ of ☽,
    which is her own semi-arc, nocturnal 93   9   A.R. of ☽'s ☍ 187 15
                                         ─────────   ─────────
                                         2)193 50   2)191 27
                                                         Half..   95 43

Half......................... 96° 55′ = P. log. (A.C.)   9.7311
: Half semi-arc ♂ .... 50 20..............   5534
:: Half diff. A.R................ 95 43   2743

: Half the second distance .... 49° 43′   5568
                                        × 2

The second dist. ♂ to meridian 99 26

180°—meridian distance ♂ 74° 40′ = primary distance of ♂ to *diurnal* meridian, 105° 20′— ♂ second distance 99° 26′ = 5° 54′ arc of ☽ rapt parallel ♂.

Example 3.—Find the rapt parallel of ☉ to ♃. When ♃ sets, he will *apply* to the nocturnal meridian, and soon form a parallel distance with the ☉ to the diurnal meridian. The opposite place of ☉ must be worked with as if he were in the 3d house, as the nocturnal arcs are used.

To semi-arc of ♃ (nocturnal) 104° 26′   A.R. of ♃   210° 27′
Add the semi-arc of ☉'s ☍   57 53   A.R. of ☍ ☉   76   25
                             ─────────   ─────────
                             2)162 19   2)133 52

          Half 81   9½   Half.. ...... 66 56

Half the sum of the semi-arcs 81° 9½'.................... 9.6541
: Half the semi-arc (nocturnal*) of ♃ 52° 13' 5374
:: Half difference of the A.R. 66° 56' 4296

: Half the second distance .... 43° 4' 6211
　　　　　　　　　　　　　　　　　× 2

　　　　♃'s second distance　86 8

♃'s meridian distance, 117° 5'†—his second distance, 86° 8' = arc of ☉ rapt parallel ♃, 30° 57'.

CHAPTER XIV.

OF DIRECTIONS TO THE PART OF FORTUNE IN MUNDO.

THE ⊕ is a *fixed point*, and has no motion of itself. Bodies of planets may be carried to it, or form aspects with it, except the rapt parallel; but it cannot itself move onwards, either in the zodiac or by converse motion in the world. The ⊕, therefore, has nothing to do with the zodiac, and forms no zodiacal aspects; it is capable of direct direction only. (*See* BOOK I. CHAP. XIV.)

To direct ☉, ☽, *or any Planet, to an Aspect of* ⊕.

Rule 1.—Semi-arc of ⊕ : its distance from any house it may be near :: semi-arc of the planet *directed* : that planet's *second* distance to the house which is in aspect with the house to which ⊕ is measured from.

Rule 2.—Add or subtract the second distance from the apparent, according as the planet passes or falls short of the house; the sum or difference is the ARC OF DIRECTION.

---

* As *he* approaches the meridian when the aspect is formed.
† The nocturnal meridian distance of ♃.

438   GRAMMAR OF ASTROLOGY.

Example.—Required the arc of ⊕ to △ ⊙ in Ada's nativity.

Semi-arc ⊕ 93° 9', log. A.C. 9.7139 ; distance of ⊕ from 4th house, 11° 27', log. 1.1965 :: semi-arc of ⊙ 57° 53', log. 4927 : ⊙'s *second* distance *past* the 8th house, where he will be four houses (a △ asp.) from ⊕, 7° 7' log. 1.4031 + ⊙'s distance to 8th house, 21° 48'=arc of ⊕ △ ⊙ 28° 55'.

To direct any Planet to a Parallel of ⊕.

Rule 1.—Semi-arc ⊕: its meridian distance :: the planet's semi-arc : its second distance from the meridian.

Rule 2.—Take from or add this to the planet's meridian distance for the ARC OF DIRECTION.

Example.—Bring ⊕ to parallel of ♄.

Semi-arc of ⊕, 93° 9', log. A.C. 9.7139 : its meridian distance, 11° 27', log. 1.1965 :: ♄ semi-arc, 64° 24', log. 4464 : ♄'s second meridian distance,* 7° 55', log. 1.3568.

The meridian distance of ♄ 37° 55'—second distance of ♄ to the meridian, 7° 55'=arc of ⊕ parallel to ♄, 30° 0'.

CHAPTER XV.

ON TURNING THE ARC OF DIRECTION INTO TIME, TO LEARN AT WHAT AGE ITS EFFECTS WILL BE FELT.

THIS is termed equating the arc of direction. It is a measure of time, and depends on the motion of ⊙ in the zodiac.

Rule.—To the A.R. of ⊙ at birth add the arc of direction. Find in how many days and hours after birth the Sun acquires this A.R., and allow for each day one year of life, and for each two hours one month. To find this time, look in the Ephemeris for the longitude answering to this A.R., and from the day and hour when ⊙ reaches this longitude take the day and hour of birth ; the difference is the number of days

* This distance of ♄ from the M.C. *added* to his meridian distance will give ⊕ ☍ ♄ =45° 50'.

and hours after birth, which are to be turned into years and months, to know the age at which the direction will operate.

Example.—Required the time of life when the direction of ☉ rapt parallel of Saturn in Ada's nativity will be in operation.

The A.R. of ☉ at birth..........................	256° 35'
The arc of ☉ rapt parallel Saturn...................	9 7
A.R. of ☉ when the aspect is complete	265 42

The longitude answering to A.R. 265° 42' is ♐ 26° 4', and the ☉ arrived at this longitude at 7 o'clock on the evening of the 18th of December 1815.

Then from Dec. 1815	18 days, 7 hours
Take the day and hour of birth	10 days, 1 hour
There remain....................	8 days, 6 hours

which, at the rate of 1 year for 1 day, and 1 month for 2 hours, is the age of 8 years and 3 months, which was March 1824. Now, on the 19th of April 1824, Lord Byron (the native's father) died, which shews the time of birth to be correctly noted, as primary directions can rarely be brought up to nearer than a month of the time of the event, especially those of ♄.

CHAPTER XVI.

OF SECONDARY DIRECTIONS.

ALL the directions we have hitherto considered are termed PRIMARY DIRECTIONS; and they are found to operate for several weeks, and sometimes for many months; especially the mutual aspects of ☉ and ☽, which, owing to their apparent magnitude, generally come into operation, and remain so for 6 or 8 weeks, at least, before and after the time the direction is perfect. The directions of ♄ are generally slow and tedious, bringing a continuation of sickness or trouble to the native, according as they may act. Those of Mars are generally soon over, but sharp and sudden in their effects. Parallels in the zodiac sometimes continue a great length of time in operation; as, when they fall near the tropics, the ☉ or ☽ sometimes lie several days nearly in the same declination; and the effect will be to cause a certain chain of events to befall the native, at times, for many years together.

SECONDARY DIRECTIONS are merely the aspects formed by the ☽ after birth, and they are far less powerful than primary directions; and if these are opposed to them in nature at the time, they have little or no effect. But if the primary and secondary directions agree in nature (for instance, if the ☉ were in ☌ or parallel, &c. of ♄ in the primary and the ☽ in parallel of ☉'s declination, or in ill aspect to ♂ or ♄, &c. in the secondary direction the event is generally shown when the influence is most powerful; viz., when the secondary direction is complete. Secondary directions endure only a week or two.

To calculate Secondary Directions.

Rule.—Observe the day and hour after birth when ☽ forms any aspect either with the ascendant or M.C. or her own place at birth, or those of ☉ or any planet, and take the day and hour of birth from it; the difference will be the *arc of direction*. This arc is to be turned into time, at the rate of 1 year for 1 day, and 1 month for 2 hours. The Moon also forms aspects in the heavens after birth, independent of the places in the figure of birth; and these also must be noted, and the *arc of direction* found in the same manner.

Example.—In Ada's nativity the ☾ comes to the parallel declination of ☉ at 8h. 29m. P.M. on the 18th of December, 1815. And from her birth that measures 8 days 7 hours and 29 minutes, equal to 8 years 3 months and 23 days, which is the 2d of April 1824, within a fortnight of the time of the death of Lord Byron. At 9h. 42m. P.M., which measures to 19th of April, 1824, the day of the father's death, she had 23° 17' declination; and on that very day she had also 23° 17' declination at noon!

CHAPTER XVII.

OF REVOLUTIONS, LUNATIONS, TRANSITS, &c.

THE *Revolution of the Sun* is his return to his place at birth. This may readily be estimated to within a trifle, and the figure erected with the same A.R. of M.C. as at birth, and the places of the planets marked in; and according as the ☉, ☽, Ascendant, and M.C., are well aspected by the planets at the time, will the native be influenced during the following year. If the revolution accords with the directions operating, it gives them greater power, as it is an additional influence; if, however, there be no close aspects at the revolution, it has little effect either way.

Example.—In Ada's nativity ☉ returned to the place he was in at her birth exactly at 11h. 30m. A.M. on the 10th of December, 1823; and here follow the places of the planets at that revolution:—

Planet	♅	♄	♃	♂	☉	♀	☿	☽
	♑	♉	♋	♍	♐	♏	♐	♓
Long.	10° 19	18° 20	8° 23	24° '4	17° 40	1° 14	16° '0	14° 12
Dec.	23° 25	15° '0	23° '5	4° 18	22° 54	9° 30	23° 35	2° 15

Observe, that we find ♃ in parallel with ☉; but his benefic nature is vitiated by being in ☍ to ♅; and both ☿ and ♅ having the declination of ☉, do much afflict that luminary, and in a child's natus tend to injure the father.* The Moon is separating from a △ of ♃, and applying to a close □ of ☉ in the radix or figure of birth; she is in □ also to the place of ♅ at birth: and having returned to her own declination, she is rendered more able to do evil; as the Moon upon her own place at any time has more power for good or evil, as she may be aspected, than in any other situation. The ☉ also is in □ to ♂, who is more evil by being in

* In the secondary motion the ☉ had *exactly* gained this evil declination of Herschel, 23° 25'.

sesquiquadrate aspect to the radical place of Saturn; and, lastly, ☽ is farther afflicted by being in close □ to ☿. All these very evil positions, and some others which I have omitted to notice, denoted much trouble to the native that year; accordingly, in four months after she lost her father. When ☉ returned to his place December 1834, the ☽ was on her radical place, and in ✶ to ♃; ♂ and ♀ in parallel, the latter being in aspect to ☽. The lady married during the year.

LUNATIONS.—The new or full Moon immediately preceding any important event will generally shew, by the positions of the luminaries as regards the planet's places in the radix and at the revolution, the nature of the events about to follow.

Example.—The full Moon preceding Lord Byron's death was at 3h. 47m. P.M on the 13th of April, 1824; and we find that ☉ was in 23¼° of ♈, the radical place of ♂, the ☽ being, of course, in 23¼° of ♎, the ☍ to ♂ at birth; ♂ and ♀ had the same declination 3¼°, which is close on that of ☽ at birth, and at the last revolution. The Moon's declination was 13° 45', close to that of ♄ at the revolution; ☉ and ☿ 9°, that of ♂ at birth. On the 26th June, 1835, a new Moon fell on the cusp of the 4th house in ✶ to ♂, who was in △ to the M.C.; and ☉ and ♃ were in parallel on the declination of ☉ at birth.

TRANSITS.—These are the passing of any planet over any important part of the radical figure, or the *revolutional* figure, such as the places of the ☉, ☽, Ascendant, M.C., &c. Unless it be within two or three weeks of the birthday, transits over the radical places have much less effect; but if near the birth-day, they are very important; in subordination, notwithstanding, to the directions at work. On the 19th of May, 1835, there was a *transit* of ♃ over the place of ☉, ♂, in △ to ☽ and ♅, and ♀ in ☌ ♂ at birth. I have no doubt the native was about that time engaged to be married. The transits of ♄ over the ☌ or ☍ of the ☉ are ever very powerful, especially if he be stationary.

On the day Lord Byron died, ☽ having just gone over the □ of the place of ♂ and sesquiquadrate of ♄ at the revolution, is found at noon of the fatal day in ♑ 10° 4', exactly the place of ♅ at the revolution; and in parallel to ☿ and ♅ at that time, and her own declination in the secondary direction 23° 17′.

INGRESSES.—The places ☉, ☽, M.C., and Asc., have arrived at by directional motion in the zodiac are also worthy of notice; as transits over and in aspect to them have important effects. For example, we find that ☉ has arrived at ♐ 26° 20′ by his motion in the zodiac at the time this native lost her father; as may be seen by bringing ☉ to that point by oblique ascension in his pole, as directed in Chap. II. Book II. Now, on the 17th of April, 1824, ☽ passed that point in the zodiac, being at the time in □ to ♂; and on the day when the native's father died the evil ♂ is found to transit the □ of that very point, being in ♍ 26° 10′ R.: his being retrograde added to his evil nature. The ☉ had arrived at the 8th degree of ♑ by direction at the age of 19 years 7 months in declination 23° 13′. And on the 7th of July, 1835, ♃ was in that exact declination when the native was *married!*

Thus, by the primary direction of ☉ rapt parallel ♄, which measures exactly to the time of the father's death; by the evil secondary direction of ☽ parallel ☉; by an evil revolution, in which ☉ was in □ to ♂, and ☽ in □ to ☉, ☿, and ♂, with other ill testimonies; by a very fatal lunation, the full moon on the 13th April, 1824, and by violent ingresses over the □ of ☉'s place in the zodiac by direction, and transits of ☽ over the body of ♅ at the revolution, her exact declination in the secondary direction, and ♅ to that of ☉ at birth, as well as the numerous similar cases in the instance of marriage, do we find an abundant harvest of evidence in this nativity of the wonderful harmony and power of planetary influence. The student may rely, that, when he meets with persons who deny its existence, they have never given it a fair examination, and, in all probability, no examination whatever; yet "NONE SHOULD CONDEMN WHO DO NOT UNDERSTAND!"

PROGRESSES.—These are the positions the ☽ forms in her progress, by allowing one synodical lunation for one year of the native's life: by proportioning the ratio of motion in any subsequent lunation to that at the birth, we arrive at the place of the ☽. Thus we find that 19 lunations after, which was at 10° 57′ A.M. 24th June 1817, the ☉ △ ♃ and ☽ ☌ ♀ of this radix took place. The mode of working this progressive motion of ☽ is this:—

The Moon's place at birth, and motion during the 1st month, influence the 1st year of life; and when she arrives *at the same distance in longitude* from the Sun as at birth, which is at the end of a synodical month, she begins to influence the next year. And so on the ☽ in her progress always influences a year by a month's motion. To find the position of the ☽ at any period of life, observe that she *finishes* 12 lunations, and enters the 13th, just 11 days less than *one* year after birth; and that 24 lunations are finished in 22 days less than 2 years after birth; and 36 lunations (answering to the age of 36 years) in 33 days less than 3 years, &c.

The ☽ at Ada's birth was 3 signs 17° 59′ = 107° 59′ from the Sun. And I find her at the same distance on the 23d June, 1817, at 3 : 46 P.M.: this, therefore, completes the 19th lunation. The 20th lunation is complete 22d July, 8 : 18 P.M. The time between these is exactly 700.53 hours. I find the ☽ ☌ ♀ at 2 : 30 P.M. on the 10th July, being just 406.7 hours after the completion of the 19th progress. Then I say, 700.53 : 365.25 :: 406. 7 : 212, which reach from the birthday 1834 to the 10th July 1835, and on the 7th of that month the native was married. It is worthy of observation, that on the day of marriage the ☽ ingressed upon the place of ♃ in the progress, ♀ also having the declination of both ☉ and ☽.

N.B. To find the hour of the ☾ forming the same aspect with ☉ as at birth, observe the rule given for secondary directions.

Planet's Places when Lord Byron died.

Planet	♅	♄	♃	♂	☉	♀	☿	☾
	♑	♉	♋	♍	♈	♈	♉	♑
Long.	15° 46′	23° 35′	5° 19′	26° 10′	29° 21′	2° 37′	7° 20′	10° 4′
Dec.	22° 55′	16° 52′	23° 30′	3° 40′	11° 15′	0° 24′	14° 28′	23° 17′

CHAPTER XVIII.

TO RECTIFY THE ESTIMATED TIME OF BIRTH TO FIND THE TRUE TIME.

Unless the time of a child's birth be accurately noted by an astrologer, or for astrological purposes, it is very likely to be incorrect; and as an error of half a minute may throw a direction out six weeks, and an error of two minutes cause the direction to be wrong by six months, it becomes important to know how to learn the true time of birth, when we have only what may be termed the estimate time.

To effect this purpose, erect the figure of the heavens for the estimate time, and complete the speculum of the planet's places for that time; then, if the birth be that of a person who has lived a few years, learn some two or three important events which have happened to the native, and the periods at which they occurred, and then calculate the *solar arc* for each of those periods.

To calculate the Solar Arc.

Rule.—Turn the age at which any event happened into

days and hours after birth, by allowing a day for a year, and two hours for a month; add this number of days and hours to the time of birth, and look in the Ephemeris for the longitude the Sun will have arrived at at that period; then find the A.R. corresponding to that longitude, and subtract the ☉ A.R. from it: the difference will be the *solar arc* required.

Example.—In the nativity of Ada we have the estimate time as given by Lord Byron (*see* Chap. VIII. Book I.), which is one hour, P.M., 10th of Dec. 1815; for which, having erected a figure of the heavens, and found the planet's places, &c., we will proceed to rectify, to find the true moment of birth.

The death of the native's father took place on the 19th of April 1824, at which time the native was 8 years 4 months and 9 days old. Call this 8 years 4 months, which will be equal to 8 days 8 hours of time after birth.

	days	hours
Time of birth December 1815, at	10	1
Add the time of the father's death	8	8
Time of the accident	18	9

The ☉'s longitude at 9 hours P.M. on the 18th of Dec. 1815, was ♐ 26° 9′, the A.R. of which is 265° 48′—☉ A.R. at birth, 256° 35′ = *solar arc* for the time of her father's death, 9° 13′.

Having found the *solar arc*, see if any direction fall near, the nature of which corresponds with the nature of the accident, according to the rules "To judge of the Effects of Directions" (Chap. XI. Book I.); and then, if it be a direction to any of the angles or a rapt parallel, you have only to find the difference between the *solar arc* and the ARC OF DIRECTION, to know the error of the estimate time of birth.

Example.—*Solar arc* for the father's death	9°	13′
The arc for ☉ rapt par. ♄	9	7
Error in minutes of a degree	0	6

Then, if we take off 6′ from the A.R of M.C., it will become 273° 16′; and the *true* time of birth is shewn to have been 24 seconds earlier than the given time.

This error, being so trivial, will cause only about a month error in the predictions made from directions to the angles; and it will have no sensible effect on the other directions, and none at all on those made to ☉ or ☽ in the zodiac.

If, however, you would be correct, add 6′ to the arc of direction for each rapt parallel and for each aspect to the ascendant or M.C. The directions to the parallel's converse and direct should be worked over again, as they may require a correction equal to two months in the native's life.

Should no direction to an angle or rapt parallel apply *nearly* (for it is rare that births, if noted at all, are not correct within 5 minutes), you must see whether any parallel or other mundane aspect applies to the accident; and if you find it does, but that the error exceeds 10′ of a degree (or, if you choose to be very correct, if there be an error of above 2 or 3 minutes of a degree), apply the following

Rule to find the True Time of Birth.

Rule 1.—Reduce the meridian distance of ☉ or ☽, whichever you direct to, into minutes, and call it the *first* position; then add to that meridian distance one degree, reducing that also to minutes, and call it the *second* position; then opposite the second position place the error of the arc of direction, multiply them together, and call the amount A. Work the same direction with the altered meridian distance (taking care to correct by one degree the meridian distance of the planet employed also); find the error of that arc of direction, and place it opposite the first position. Multiply these together, and call the amount B.

Rule 2.—If *both* errors be *greater* or *less* than the *solar*

arc, find the *difference* between the errors, and make it a divisor; find also the difference between A and B, and make it a dividend: the quotient will be the true *meridian distance* of ☉ or ☽ at the moment of birth, the difference between which and the amount of the meridian distance, which was made the first position, is the error of the A.R. of M.C. at the estimate time of birth.

Rule 3.—But if *one* error be *greater* and the *other less* than the *solar arc*, take the *sum* of the errors for a divisor, and the sum of A and B for the dividend; and the quotient is the true meridian distance as above.

Observe.—When you have gained the true meridian distance of ☉ or ☽ by this operation, and found how much you have to add to or diminish the M.C. to ascertain the true A.R. of M.C., turn that correction into *time*, and add it to or deduct it from the estimate time of birth, and you will have the *true time of birth*. And observe also, that all the directions you may have worked to the angles, including rapt parallels, must be corrected by that amount.*

Example.—Suppose the estimate A.R. of M.C. 273° 22′, meridian distance of ☽ 86° 7′, meridian distance of ♀ 63° 5′, and that I find the arc of ☽ to parallel ♀ D.D. to be 22° 22′, while the event which I believe it produced gives a *solar arc* of 22° 38′, the first error is 16′ *too small*.

Add 1° to the first position, and the *second error* will become (as found by working the direction) 2° 20′ or 140′ *too small*.

1st Position 86° 7′ or 5167 × 2d error 140 B = 723380
2d Position 87 7 or 5227 × 1st error 16 A = 83632

$$\overline{}\quad\overline{}$$

124....)639748

Here $\frac{639748'}{124}$ = 5159′ or 85° 59′, the true meridian distance of ☽; which differs 8′ from that of the estimate time, and only 2′ from that of the time as rectified by ☉ rapt parallel ♄. This latter time is, doubtless,

* The other directions must be worked over again, and the poles of ☉ and ☽ and the meridian distances corrected.

the true time of birth, as it gives us the ☽ par. ♀ D.D. 12th May, 1836, at which time the native had a son and heir, which this influence would bring about.

Observe.—The best directions to rectify the estimated time of birth by are those of ♂, as the effects do in general answer very closely to the time of the direction. Whereas in directions to Saturn the event may come on slowly, and the direction may measure some minutes more or less than the solar arc. And I advise to correct by accidents to the person, if they can be known; such as serious falls or hurts, sudden attacks of disease, &c. The measles, scarlatina, or small-pox, are generally caused by ♂, but sometimes by ☉, especially if he be aspected by ♂. It is generally found, that if ☉ or ♂ come to semi-quartile or sesquiquadrate of the ascendant in the early part of life, such complaints fall out at that time. The death of the native's parents, if it have occurred, is also a safe accident to rectify by, as it generally happens upon some powerful directions. But I recommend to take at least two, and, if you can, three events, or "accidents," as they are termed by astrologers, to rectify the given time of the nativity by. And bear in mind, that if you do not at length get the true time of birth *to within half a minute*, you cannot possibly be correct in your predictions of the time at which many events will happen to the native in the course of his existence.

CHAPTER XIX.

A JUDGMENT FOR MARRIAGE IN THE NATIVITY OF LORD BYRON'S DAUGHTER.

It may serve as a useful praxis for the young student, if we examine the directions in this lady's nativity which promise marriage. They are as follow :—

☽ par. ♃ D.D 20° 45'
☽ par. ♃ Con. 21 48
M.C. ✶ ☉ .... 21 54   M.C. ✶ ☉ 21° 54'
☽ par. ♀ D.D. 22 38   A.R. of ☉ 256 35
☽ par. ♀ Con. 23 35
                       ─────────
                       278 29 A.R of ♑ 7° 47', at which ☉ arrives 19^d 18^h after birth, which will be at the age of 19 years 9 months.

Remarks.—The above train of directions will be in operation from the age of 18 and 6 months until that of about 21 years, during which the native will be fortunate, and receive offers of marriage; and the most powerful direction, being M.C. ✶ ☉, *will be the means* of effecting that circumstance.*

Rule to calculate the Time ☽ forms the Aspects.

Rule 1.—Take the amount of the ☽'s motion in 24 hours, from which subtract the amount of the planet's motion (but if the planet be retrograde, add them), and the difference or sum is the ☽'s acceleration.

Rule 2.—Then find how far the ☽ was from the aspect at the noon previous to her forming it; and say, If the ☽'s acceleration give 24 hours, what will the ☽'s distance from the aspect give? The answer is the time after the noon previous, when the aspect will be formed.

* I leave this prediction as it stood in the first edition, a year and a half before the event.

Example.—Required the time ☽ forms ⚹ with ♃ on 29th of December, 1815?

☽'s place at noon, 30th Dec.................... ♑ 6° 38'† ♃ .. ♏ 5° 35'
☽'s place at noon, 29th Dec.................... ♐ 23 58.. ♃.. ♏ 5 26

☽'s motion in the 24 hours .... 12 40 ♃'s motion 9
♃'s during the same 24 hours 9

As ☽'s acceleration .... 12° 31'...... 8.8422
♃'s ⚹ at noon 29th ♑ 5° 26' ⎫ .... to 24 0 ...... .8751
☽'s place ditto .... ♐ 23 58 ⎬
☽'s distance from ♃'s ⚹ 11 28 ⎭ .... so 11 28 ...... 1.1958

                                                         .9131

                                                       D. H. M.
To time of ⚹ being formed 0 21 59
Add the day 29 0 0

                                                        29 21 59
From this take the time of birth........................ 10 1 7

Remains time after birth of ☽ ⚹ ♃ 19 20 52

The ☽ came to ⚹ of the radical place of ♀ on the 1st of July, 1835, in the nativity of the Countess of Lovelace, and the lady's marriage took place on the 7th of that month. This is the calculation :—

Motion of the ☽ in longitude, from the 29th to the 30th of December, 1815 = 12° 40'; the ⚹ ♀ falls in 1° 32' ♑ : the long. ☽ 29th Dec. 23° 58' ♐, which is distant 7° 34'. Then 12° 40' : 24h. :: 7° 34' : 14h. 20m.

                          D. H. M.
This is then 29 14 20
—time of birth 10 1 0

                       19 13 20 = 19 years 6 months 20 days; which, added to the 10th Dec. 1815, brings us to 1st July 1835; being a proof of the influence of Secondary Directions. The M.C. ⚹ ☉ was the primary acting cause.

I shall here give a few directions in this fair lady's nativity, for the student to practise in; and I advise him to bring each up for his own satisfaction.

† To make this subtraction, borrow 30°, and then from 36° 38' take 23° 58'.

DIRECTIONS IN THE NATIVITY OF LORD BYRON'S DAUGHTER.

Remarks.

☽ ☌ ♂ conv. 1 34 ⎫
Asc. △ ☉   2 37 ⎬ These came up in early infancy, and would cause several slight illnesses.
Asc. S. S. Q. ♅ 2 51 ⎭

Asc. ☌ ♂ .. 4 45   This measures to 4 years and 3 months; and from that age to 4 years and 6 months rendered the native subject to the measles, scarlet fever, small-pox, &c. I think it probable that the native may have taken the latter disease.

Asc. S. ☐ ♄   5 49 ⎫
☽ rapt par. ♂ 6 0 ⎭ These measure to the age of 5½ years, at which time she may have suffered illness. But the native's mother is denoted by ☽, and no doubt she had much trouble under these aspects; for, in the nativity of children, the influence of directions, which do not affect the health, falls on the parents or guardians, family, &c.

☉ ☐ ♄ conv. 7 2 ⎫
Asc. ☌ ☽ . 7 8 ⎭ These came into operation at six years old, when I have no doubt the native suffered in her health seriously. The influence lasted great part of the 7th year. And the family (particularly the *father*, who is always signified by the Sun) were afflicted by domestic disputes, &c. &c.*

☉ rapt par. ♄ 9 13   This caused the *death* of the na-

* I have since learned that about this age she had a tendency of blood to the head, and was seriously ill thereby.

☉ ⚹ ♃ D.D. 9 21 ⎫   tive's father, at 8 years and 4 months of her age.
☉ ☌ ♅ conv. 9 32 ⎬   I judge that these caused the native benefit by her father's *will* being in her favour.

☉ ⚹ ♀ D.D. 11 14 ⎫   These are favourable to the family affairs; but I think the latter, in her 11th year, caused affliction to the mother of the native.
☽ par. ♂ zod. 11 41 ⎭

Asc. S.S.Q. ☉ 12 16 ⎫   These, in the 12th year, I think, caused pecuniary losses and vexations; not very material: the worst at *near* 12 years old; also ill health.
Asc. ☍ ♃ . 12 45 ⎭

Asc. ☐ ♄ zod. 14 6 ⎫   At about 12 years and 9 months appear to have brought illness, or some blow or bruise: and also much trouble in the family, with the death of some relation, when about 13 years old, or at 13 and 2 months.
☽ ☐ ♄ zod. 14 48 ⎭

Asc. ☍ ♀   14 44 ⎫   And all the early part of the 14th year the native appears to have suffered in her health by the effect of these directions, which cause *weaknesses* incident to young females, coughs, &c.
☉ ☌ ☿ conv. 14 48 ⎭

☉ ⚹ ♃ zod. 15 36   But this good direction, at about 14, did greatly improve the native's health and spirits.

Asc. ⚹ ♄   16 33   And at 15 years of age she became very grave, studious, and thoughtful in her demeanour, and was benefitted by elderly friends, or received a legacy, &c.

☉ par. ♄ conv. 17 29   But by this ill aspect, at 15 and 6

months, and for a few weeks after, especially about July 1831, the native appears to have affliction. I think she may have lost a relation by death; and her own health was not by any means good.

☉ p. ♄ D.D. 19 28 ⎫
☉ □ ☽ zod. 19 22 ⎬ These three very evil directions came up about the end of May 1833;
☽ rapt par. ☿ 19 45 ⎭ but they remained in operation for some time during the spring and summer of 1833. Indeed, about *April* they appear to have brought trouble, as ☽ came to the parallel of ♄ in the second motion at that time; and I fear that the native had *considerable* illness and vexation. She was subject to some complaint in the eyes, probably from taking cold; and to much trouble to a *near friend*, probably the death of such an one.

☉ △ ♄ conv. 26 20

The train following have been already spoken of as likely to bring about the native's marriage; and therefore I shall name no others but

☉ rapt par. ♀ 27 35 ⎫ these, which I leave the student to
☉ rapt par. ☽ 27 35 ⎬ equate. They will have a powerful
☉ rapt par. ♂ 27 56 ⎪ effect, and, indeed, are dangerous;
Asc. ☍ ☿   29 10 ⎭ yet the aspect of ♀ to the hyleg gives hopes, as ♀ is strong by being in ☌ ♃. These directions will affect the native's husband.

GRAMMAR OF ASTROLOGY. 455

A GLOSSARY OF ASTROLOGICAL TERMS APPLICABLE TO
NATIVITIES.

AFFLICTION.—Any planet being ill aspected, by another, or being in an unfortunate situation, is said to be *afflicted*.

AIRY SIGNS.—♊, ♎, and ♒.

AMBIENT.—The heavens, when spoken of in a general manner.

ANGLE.—The 1st, 4th, 7th, and 10th houses. When planets are therein, they are more powerful than in any other situation. Their order of strength is 10th, 1st, 7th, 4th.

APPLICATION.—To apply. These terms mean the approach of any planet to the body or aspect of another, or to the cusp of any house.

ASCENSION, RIGHT.—The distance any body or point in the heavens is from the beginning of the ecliptic, or first point of *Aries* in a right sphere. It is measured upon the equator in degrees and minutes of a degree, or hours, minutes, and seconds. It is thus abbreviated A.R.

ASCENSION, OBLIQUE.—If a star be not on the equator, it will, when it rises, form an angle with that part of the equator which is rising at the same time, and this is called its

ASCENSIONAL DIFFERENCE.—This, added to its right ascension (A.R.) if it have *south* declination, but subtracted therefrom if it have *north* declination, gives its oblique ascension.

ASCENDANT.—The *first* house, or that space between the eastern horizon and one-third of the distance towards the meridian under the Earth.

BENEFICS.—The good planets ♃ and ♀.,

CADENT.—A planet which has passed any angle, and remains within one-third of its semi-arc of the cusp of that angle. The whole space of the 3d, 6th, 9th, and 12th houses

CIRCLES OF POSITION.—An astronomical term used in calculating the polar elevation of any planet. They are small circles bearing the same relation to the meridian circle which the parallels of latitude do to the equator.

COMBUST.—Being within about 8½ degrees of the ☉, when the planet loses part of its power (owing to the burning qualities of ☉), which is transferred to that luminary. If the planet have great latitude, the ☉ has not much power on it beyond the distance of 7 degrees.

CONVERSE MOTION is that which is caused by the diurnal rotation of the Earth on its axis, which makes the ☉, ☽, &c., appear to rise, approach the meridian, set, &c. It applies particularly to the ☉ and ☽, when they are carried towards the promittors or their aspects.

CUSP.—The beginning of any house. Thus the eastern horizon is the cusp of the 1st house; and the meridian, where the ☉ is at noon, is the beginning, or cusp of the 10th house.

DECLINATION.—The distance any body is north or south of the equator. The ☉ never has more than 23° 28′ of declination, which is when he is in one of the tropics, and is caused by the pole of the Earth being inclined from the plane of the Earth's orbit.

DESCENSION.—The going down of any body from the meridian above to that below the Earth; for though the ☉ is lost sight of at sunset, he still *descends* till he reaches the meridian at midnight.

DESCENSION, OBLIQUE.—The reverse of oblique Ascension (*which see.*)

DESCENDANT.—The 7th house, or that space from the western horizon to one-third of the distance towards the meridian above the Earth.

DIRECTION.—The measuring the space between the bodies or

aspects of any two planets, or that between any two parts of the heavens, to ascertain at what period of life the promised effect will appear. This distance is a certain number of degrees of the A.R. of the Sun, which, when he has passed over, the direction is complete. It is called the *Arc of Direction*.

DIRECTION, SECONDARY.—The aspects formed by the moon in the days immediately succeeding the birth. Each day between the birth and the time the aspect is formed is equal to one exact year of life; thus, if the ☽ form a good aspect with ♃, exactly 21 days after birth, the native will feel its effects just about his 21st birthday.

DIRECT MOTION.—This is in reality converse motion, but is so called to distinguish the case of the promittors being carried towards the bodies or aspects of the Sun or Moon, which directions are considered somewhat less powerful than those by *converse motion*.

DIURNAL ARC.—Is the length of time that part of the heavens in which any planet is at birth is above the Earth; and it is usually measured in degrees.

EARTHY SIGNS.— ♉, ♍, and ♑.

EQUATION OF TIME.—Owing to the irregular motion of the Earth round the Sun, this latter body does not always come to the meridian exactly 24 hours after its last passage over that point; but as all calculations in the *old* Ephemeres of the places of the planets are made for the time the Sun was on the meridian (or *apparent noon*), the watch sometimes was several minutes before or after noon at that moment. This difference between the *apparent* noon, or that shewn by the Sun, being on the meridian, and the *mean* noon, or that shewn by a correct watch, is the *Equation of Time*, which is the angular distance in time between the mean and the true Sun. The amount to be added to, or taken from, the time shewn by the watch is given for every sixth day in my Ephemeris. If the Ephemeris says, "clock before Sun," then take the time mentioned from the time of birth; but if it say, "clock after Sun," then add the time mentioned (which is the equation of time) to the time of birth, as shewn by the watch.—*Example.* The Ephemeris gives the equation of time for November 1, 1840, "clock slow 16m. 17s.": hence, if the time of birth by a watch were the 1st of November, 1840, at 6 o'clock P.M. the *apparent* time of birth would be 6h. 16m. 17s. P.M., to which time all the planets' places, &c., and the figure of the heavens, must be calculated. But this rule applies only to Ephemeres which are calculated to *apparent* time. In my Ephemeris they are calculated to *mean* time, and do not require this correction.

FIERY SIGNS.— ♈, ♌, and ♐.

FIGURE OF THE HEAVENS.—A map or picture of the heavens as they exist at the moment any one is born; shewing the points of the zodiac rising, setting, and on the meridian; also those on the cusp of each house, and the situations of the planets.

HOUSES.—The divisions of the heavens which form (✶, ▢, or △) *aspects* with the meridian or ascendant; or, in other words, those spaces which shew the *one-third part* of any planet's semi-arc, either above or below the horizon. They are also portions of oblique ascension, consisting of 30 degrees each, or *one-twelfth* part of the whole circle of 360 degrees, being thus each equal to one sign of the zodiac; and, like them, they are twelve in number, and are reckoned from the eastern horizon towards the left hand, in the order of the signs, the ascendant being the 1st house. (*See figure* 1.)

HYLEG.—That body or point which is the giver of life.

HYLEGIACAL PLACES.—The 1st house, from 5° above to 25° below its cusp; the 7th house, from 5° below to 25° above its cusp; the 9th house, from 5° outside its cusp to half way between the mid-heaven and the ascendant.

INGRESS.—A transit over the place the ☉, ☽, M. C., or asc. has arrived at in the zodiac.

LATITUDE, on the *earth*, is the distance of any *place* north or south of the equatorial line; in the *heavens*, it is the distance of any body north or south of the ecliptical line.

LONGITUDE, on the *earth*, is the distance of any *place* east or west of Greenwich; in the *heavens*, is the distance of any body from the first point of the zodiac ♈, 0° 0', measured on the ecliptic.

LIGHTS OF LUMINARIES.—The ☉ or ☽.

LUNATION.—The ☌, ☐, or ☍ of ☉ and ☽; also the length of time in which ☽ appears to move round the Earth;* the time from new Moon to new Moon.

MALEFICS.—♅, ♄, and ♂.

M. C. OR MEDIUM CŒLI, OR MID-HEAVEN.—The meridian above the Earth.

MERIDIAN.—That point which is always *south* (where ☉ is at noon) is the meridian above the Earth; and that point which is always *north* (where ☉ is at midnight) is the meridian below the Earth.

MERIDIAN DISTANCE, the distance any body is by A. R. from the meridian.

MODERATOR.—The ☉, ☽, Asc., M. C., or ⊕, because each acts in a mode peculiar to itself.

NOCTURNAL ARC.—The length of time any point in the Heavens is below the Earth, from its setting till it rises again. It is usually turned into degrees.

NODE.—That part of the ecliptic where a planet passes out of north into south latitude is its south node; that where it goes into north latitude is its north node.

* The term "appears" is used, because, in reality, the ☽ does not move round the Earth.

ORIENTAL, OCCIDENTAL.—From the 4th house eastward to the 10th is oriental; and from the 10th westward to the 4th is occidental. But ☉ or ☽ are *oriental* between the 1st and 10th and its opposite quarter, and are *occidental* between the 10th and 7th and its opposite quarter.

PARALLELS, in the *zodiac*, are equal distances from the equator, or having the same declination, whether of the same name or the opposite. In the *world*, they are equal distances from the meridian, in proportion to the *semi-arcs* of the planets which form them.

POLAR ELEVATION OR POLE.—The pole of a country is its latitude; that of a body in the heavens is a certain elevation from the meridian towards the horizon. The word "pole" has caused some confusion; it is merely an abbreviation for "polar elevation."

PROMITTOR.—The planets ♅, ♄, ♃, ♂, ♀, and ☿. If ☉ or ☽ are directed to each other, the one directed to may be termed a promittor; so if ⊕, Asc., or M. C., be directed to ☉ or ☽, these become promittors, because they promise the event.

RADICAL; RADIX.—The figure at birth is the *radix* or root from which every thing is judged; and the term radical refers to it.

RAPT PARALLEL.—Parallels formed by the motion of the Earth on its axis, where both bodies are *rapt* or carried away by the same until they come to equal distances from the meridian.

RECTIFICATION.—The correcting the supposed time of birth, to find the *true* time.

RETROGRADE.—The backward motion which the planets appear to have sometimes, in consequence of the position and motion of the Earth.

REVOLUTION.—The moving round the ☉ by the Earth, which

makes the ☉ appear to revolve and return to his place at birth once a year; very near the time of birth.

SEMI-ARC.—The half the arc a planet would form above the Earth if it remained *fixed* in the zodiac from the time of its rising until that of its setting, is called its semi-arc *diurnal*. The half of the arc it would, in like circumstances, form under the Earth from its setting until its rising, is called its semi-arc *nocturnal*. If a planet were to be on the mid-heaven, and not to move out of its place in the zodiac, it would set, and then descend to the north meridian in exactly 12 sidereal hours, because the Earth is 12 such hours in turning half round; consequently whatever time the planet took in going from the mid-heaven to the horizon, if that time be taken from 12 hours, it would shew the time it takes to go from the horizon to the meridian below the Earth. Hence, if we know the length of a semi-arc, by deducting it from 180° (which are half the circle), we have the other semi-arc of that part of the heavens.— N.B. The spot a planet was in at birth is to be considered as the planet itself, because its influence is fixed in that spot during the life of the native, however the planet itself may move on in the zodiac, &c.

SEPARATION.—When an aspect is past, the planets, &c. are said to be separating from that aspect; and observe, that in a nativity the influence of any aspect to the moderators is *more* powerful if it be a few (4 or 5) degrees past, than if it be not yet formed.

SIDEREAL TIME is the angular distance of the first point of Aries, or the true vernal equinox. It is of course the true right ascension on the meridian at mean noon, or that shewn by a good clock.

SIGNIFICATOR.—That body or point which is directed, as it signifies the nature of the direction's influence. This is a term that has been grossly abused in the science, and might, perhaps, be dispensed with.

SUCCEEDENT.—Those houses which lie between the angular and cadent houses, viz. 2d, 5th, 8th, and 11th, and planets in them.

SUPERIORS and INFERIORS. ♅, ♄, ♃, and ♂, are called the former, being beyond the Earth; and ♀ and ☿ are called the latter, being between the Earth and the Sun. The former are far more powerful and durable, in general, in their effects.

TRANSITS.—These are the passing over the place of any moderator or planet, or their aspects, either in the radix or revolution, &c. by any other body.

WATERY SIGNS.—♋, ♏, and ♓.

A Description of the Twelve Houses.

1st.—This influences the person, health, and character of the native. Good planets shew a good constitution and benevolent disposition; evil planets the reverse.

2d.—Influences *in some degree* the property of the native. If good planets be there, they assist to give wealth, according to their nature; evil planets the reverse.

3d.—This influences the native's journies, and his brethren or near relations.

4th.—This influences the native's father, and his property in land or houses, his inheritance, &c.

5th.—This affects his children, and the good or evil he may receive thereby.

6th.—This will shew something of the nature of the diseases he may be subject to.

7th.—This has influence on the native's fate in marriage.

8th.—This points out, in part, the quality of his death.

9th.—This has something to do with his distant voyages, and his pursuits in science, law, &c.

10th.—This has *much* influence on his honour or credit, and on his trade, profession, or employment.

11th.—This house will shew the character of his friends, whether true or false.

12th.—This is the house of private enemies, and according to the quality of planets therein will the native meet with persons to do him secret mischief.

Observation.—The student must be cautious not to rely too much on the effects of the houses, as that has been one of the great follies of the Arabian and old English writers on the science. When a direction is complete, the house in which the body directed falls will help to point out the character of the circumstances it will produce; thus, if ☉ or ☽ come to an ill aspect with ☿ in the 9th, or with ♅ (he being in evil aspect to ☿ at birth), it may very probably produce a lawsuit. If directions fall in the ascendant, they generally affect health, or the personal affairs of the native.

GRAMMAR OF ASTROLOGY.

Fig. 1.

Fig. 2.

A Table to turn Time into Degrees and Minutes, or to turn Degrees and Minutes into Time.

Deg. Min.	H. M. M. S.	Deg. Min.	H. M. M. S.	Deg. Min.	H. M. M. S.	Deg. Min.	H. M. M. S.	Deg. Min.	H. M. M. S.	Deg. Min.	H. M. M. S.
1	0. 4	31	2. 4	61	4. 4	91	6. 4	121	8. 4	151	10. 4
2	0. 8	32	2. 8	62	4. 8	92	6. 8	122	8. 8	152	10. 8
3	0.12	33	2.12	63	4.12	93	6.12	123	8.12	153	10.12
4	0.16	34	2.16	64	4.16	94	6.16	124	8.16	154	10.16
5	0.20	35	2.20	65	4.20	95	6.20	125	8.20	155	10.20
6	0.24	36	2.24	66	4.24	96	6.24	126	8.24	156	10.24
7	0.28	37	2.28	67	4.28	97	6.28	127	8.28	157	10.28
8	0.32	38	2.32	68	4.32	98	6.32	128	8.32	158	10.32
9	0.36	39	2.36	69	4.36	99	6.36	129	8.36	159	10.36
10	0.40	40	2.40	70	4.40	100	6.40	130	8.40	160	10.40
11	0.44	41	2.44	71	4.44	101	6.44	131	8.44	161	10.44
12	0.48	42	2.48	72	4.48	102	6.48	132	8.48	162	10.48
13	0.52	43	2.52	73	4.52	103	6.52	133	8.52	163	10.52
14	0.56	44	2.56	74	4.56	104	6.56	134	8.56	164	10.56
15	1. 0	45	3. 0	75	5. 0	105	7. 0	135	9. 0	165	11. 0
16	1. 4	46	3. 4	76	5. 4	106	7. 4	136	9. 4	166	11. 4
17	1. 8	47	3. 8	77	5. 8	107	7. 8	137	9. 8	167	11. 8
18	1.12	48	3.12	78	5.12	108	7.12	138	9.12	168	11.12
19	1.16	49	3.16	79	5.16	109	7.16	139	9.16	169	11.16
20	1.20	50	3.20	80	5.20	110	7.20	140	9.20	170	11.20
21	1.24	51	3.24	81	5.24	111	7.24	141	9.24	171	11.24
22	1.28	52	3.28	82	5.28	112	7.28	142	9.28	172	11.28
23	1.32	53	3.32	83	5.32	113	7.32	143	9.32	173	11.32
24	1.36	54	3.36	84	5.36	114	7.36	144	9.36	174	11.36
25	1.40	55	3.40	85	5.40	115	7.40	145	9.40	175	11.40
26	1.44	56	3.44	86	5.44	116	7.44	146	9.44	176	11.44
27	1.48	57	3.48	87	5.48	117	7.48	147	9.48	177	11.48
28	1.52	58	3.52	88	5.52	118	7.52	148	9.52	178	11.52
29	1.56	59	3.56	89	5.56	119	7.56	149	9.56	179	11.56
30	2. 0	60	4. 0	90	6. 0	120	8. 0	150	10.0	180	12. 0

Explanation of the Table to turn Degrees and Minutes into Time, or the Reverse.

Rule to turn Degrees into Time.—Look in the column marked deg. min. for the number of degrees required, and opposite to them, in the next column to the right hand, will be the *hours* and *minutes.*

Rule to turn Minutes of a Degree into Time.—Look in the column marked deg. min. for the number of minutes required, and opposite to them, in the next column to the right hand, will be the *minutes* and *seconds* of time.—N.B. If the degrees are above 180, take that number from them, and find the time for the remainder; then to that time add 12 hours.

Example.—What is the time answering to 49 degrees and 27 minutes? The number opposite 49 degrees is—

	3^h	16^m	0^s
The number opposite 27 minutes is .		1	48
Answer .	3	17	48

Rule to turn Time into Degrees, &c.—Look opposite the required *hours* and *minutes* for the *degrees* in the column before it; and if the time be *minutes* and *seconds*, that column will shew *minutes* of a degree.

A Table of the Poles of the Houses for every half Degree of Latitude in Great Britain.

Ascendant, or 7th House.	3rd, 5th, 9th, or 11th House.	2nd, 6th, 8th, or 12th House.
50 : 0	22 : 33	39 : 14
50 : 30	22 : 58	39 : 46
51 : 0	23 : 21	40 : 18
*51 : 32	23 : 48	40 : 53
52 : 0	24 : 12	41 : 24
52 : 30	24 : 44	42 : 4
53 : 0	25 : 6	42 : 32
53 : 30	25 : 32	43 : 5
54 : 0	26 : 1	43 : 39
54 : 30	26 : 30	44 : 13
55 : 0	26 : 59	44 : 48
55 : 30	27 : 29	45 : 24
56 : 0	28 : 1	45 : 59
56 : 30	28 : 33	46 : 36
57 : 0	29 : 6	47 : 13
57 : 30	29 : 40	47 : 50
58 : 0	30 : 15	48 : 27

Explanation of the Table of the Poles of Houses.

This table will serve for any place in Great Britain, for which it may be desired to erect a figure of the heavens. The 1st column shews the pole of the 1st and 7th houses, which is always the latitude of the country; the 2d column shews the pole of the 3d, 5th, 9th, or 11th houses; and the 3d column the pole of the 2d, 6th, 8th, or 12th houses. If the latitude of the place fall any where between an even degree and half degree, a proportion may be readily calculated for

* The Latitude or Pole of London.

the difference; thus, if the latitude be that of Liverpool, 53° 25′, and it be required to find the pole of the 12th house, say, as 30 miles are to the difference between the poles of the 12th, for 53 degrees and 53° 30′, which is 33 minutes, so is the difference of latitude 25 to the difference of pole 27½ minutes, to be added to the pole of the 12th for 53 degrees. Hence the pole of the 12th at Liverpool is 42° 59½′, which is correct with that found by trigonometry to within half a minute, its true pole being 42° 59′.

RULES TO CALCULATE THE LONGITUDE OF THE CUSPS OF THE HOUSES,

For persons not possessing a table of houses; or if the birth be far distant in latitude from the place for which the table of houses is calculated.

Rule 1.—The oblique ascension of the house is found by adding 30° to the A. R. of the M. C. for each house distant; thus, 30° for the 11th, 60° for the 12th, 90° for the ascendant, 120° for the 2d, and 150° for the the 3d.

Rule 2.—Find the distance of the cusp of the house from ♈ or ♎; the former by taking its oblique ascension from 360 if above 270°, or the latter by taking it from 180° if above 90°.

Rule 3.—Add the *log. cosine* of the oblique ascension of the cusp of the house (reduced as by Rule 2) to the *log. cotangent* of the pole of the house: the sum is the *log. cotangent* of angle A.

Rule 4.—If the oblique ascension be *less* than 90° from *Aries*, add 23° 28′ to angle A; if it be *less* than 90° from *Libra*, take the difference between 23° 28′ and angle A: the result call angle B.

Rule 5.—Add together the arithmetical complement of the *log. cosine* of B, the *log. cosine* of A, and the *log. tangent* of the oblique ascension of the cusp of the house: the sum will be the *log. tangent* of its longitude from Aries or Libra, according as it was nearest to either by oblique ascension.

N.B. If angle B exceed 90,° take the log. *sine* of the excess above 90° instead of the log. cosine, and find its arithmetical complement. And in this case the longitude must be reckoned from the opposite equinox to that of the oblique ascension; if the oblique ascension was measured from ♈, reckon it from ♎; and if the oblique ascension was measured from ♎, reckon the longitude from ♈.

Example.—If the A. R. of the M. C. at Liverpool be 273° 19', what degree of the zodiac is ascending?

A. R. of M. C.	273°	19'
Add 90° for 3 houses	90	0
	363	19
A. R. of ♈ 0° 0'	360	0
Oblique ascension of ascendant	3	19
Log. cosine of 3° 19'		9.99927
Log. co-tangent of pole of Liverpool 53° 25'		9.87053
Log. co-tangent angle A, which is 53° 28'		9.86980
Angle A	53°	28'
Add (the oblique asc. being nearest ♈)	23	28
The sum is angle B	76	56
Log. cosine Angle B (A comp.)		0.64573
Log. cosine angle A		9.77473
Log. tangent oblique asc. from ♈ = 3° 19'		8.76306
Log. tangent of longitude from ♈ = 8° 41		9.18352

It will be seen that the longitude of the ascendant differs slightly from that of London; which makes no difference, except in bringing the ☽ to the ascendant by second motion, as it is the A. R. of the M. C., or oblique ascension of the ascendant, and not the longitude, which is used in working directions.*

APPENDIX.

LOGARITHMS.

THE invention of logarithms is due to Lord Napier, Baron of Merchiston, in Scotland, a very celebrated *Astrologer* of the 16th century. The first table of logarithms was published by the inventor at Edinburgh, in 1614. There have been numerous others published since, of which the best I have seen are those by *Dr. Georgio Frederico Ursino*, in 1827. But there is a neat edition published in 1839 by the Society for the Diffusion of Useful Knowledge, which is low priced and correct.†

Logarithms were invented to facilitate complex computations in numbers, which Lord Napier had much trouble with in his astrological researches. They perform *multiplication* by *addition*, for the sum of the logarithm of any two numbers is the logarithm of their product; and *division* by *subtraction*, for the logarithm of the dividend *minus* the logarithm of the divisor is *equal* to the logarithm of the quotient. Also the logarithm multiplied by the index of the power raises the power; and the logarithm of the number divided by the index of the root extracts the root, &c.

Logarithms are a series of numbers in *arithmetical* progression, which answer to another series of numbers in geometrical progression.

---

* The tables of houses for London and Liverpool, which will be found in my "Tables for Calculating Nativities," will render it unnecessary to refer to this formula in any part of England.

† Taylor and Walton, London.

The most convenient series is the following:

0	1	2	3	4	5 &c. index
1	10	100	1000	10000	100000 logarithm

Wherein the index is seen to be always *one less than the number of figures* the integer contains.

To find the Logarithm of any Number.

Look for the number in the column headed "Num.[*]" and the log. will be found opposite.

To find the Number to any Logarithm.

The logarithm must be sought for, and the number will be found on the left hand.

To find the Logarithm, Sine, Tangent, &c.

Look for the *degree* at the top of the page, and the *minute* on the *left* hand side; or the *degree* at bottom, and the *minute* on the *right* hand.

To multiply by Logarithms.

Rule.—Add the logarithms of the multiplier and multiplicand, and the sum is the logarithm of the product.

```
Multiply   98   Logarithm = 1.99123
By         76   Logarithm = 1.88081
                           ─────────
Product  7448   Logarithm = 3.87204
```

To divide by Logarithms.

Rule.—Subtract the logarithm of the divisor from that of the dividend, and there remains the logarithm of the quotient.

```
Divide   7448   Logarithm = 3.87204
By         76   Logarithm = 1.88081
                           ─────────
Quotient   98   Logarithm = 1.99123
```

[*] In Taylor and Walton's Tables of Logarithms, which require, however, close attention to the rule of the index being one less than the figures of the integer.

The Rule of Three by Logarithms.

Rule.—Add the logarithms of the three terms to find that of the 4th.* If in 712 hours the ☽ progress 230.15 days, what progress will she make in 708.5 hours?

	712 hours	Logarithm (Arith. Comp.)	7.14752
	230.15	Logarithm	2.36202
::	708.5	Logarithm	2.85034
:	229.2	Logarithm	2.35988

Where the index exceeds 10, reject that amount.

To work Problems in Spherical Trigonometry by Logarithms.

This is the same as the rule of three; but the logarithms of the terms are those of *sines, tangents,* &c. The logarithm of the 1st term (unless it be radius, in which case we always take the logarithm of the sine of $90° = 10.00000$) must be taken from 9.99990 to find its *arithmetical complement,* for the sake of working by addition. The tens in the index must be rejected. And if we want the logarithm for any number of degrees above 90°, subtract the given degrees from 180°, and take the logarithm of the remainder. If 90° be subtracted from the given *sine,* the log. *cosine* may be taken.

Useful Notes.

		Logarithm
360 degrees in seconds .... =	1296000	6.11260
24 hours in seconds .... =	86400	4.93651
Sidereal day in seconds .... =	86164	4.93533
Sidereal revolution of the earth in mean solar days	365.25636	2.56260
Earth's equatorial radius in English feet....................	209.21665	7.32060
Earth's polar rad. in ditto	208.52394	7.31916

* Take the arithmetical complement of the 1st term.

		Logarithm
Degree in latitude 52° 50′ in English feet	365000	5.56229
Ditto on the equator	362732	5.55959
Length (in English inches) of the pendulum which vibrates seconds in lat. of Greenwich	39.1393	.59261

OBSERVATIONS ON THE EFFECTS OF DIRECTIONS.

We are to judge whether a direction be good or evil by the nature of the aspect and planet. The extent and character of its effects are to be learned by the degree of angular power of the planet, the sign it is in, and its freedom from affliction; also the opposing influences are to be well considered. Nor can any safe judgment be formed unless *all* the directions in operation within six months of the time, and the transits and ingresses, be considered. A good direction gives prosperity from such things or persons as the planet signifies, and also as the house of which he is lord intimates. In the same manner judge of an evil direction. Take also into consideration the house the moderator is in or rules over, and also the house wherein the direction falls when complete. Directions in children's nativities act upon and through their parents, guardians, &c.

The *Horoscope* or ascendant signifies all matters which affect the person, such as sickness or health, birth or death of children, &c.; also the affections of the mind.

The *Moon's* directions affect both mind and body, also wealth and character, as regards public estimation.

The *Sun* concerns the health, honour, preferment, favour of the great, the father and his affairs.

The *M. C.* denotes honours, character, employment, credit, trade, &c.; also the parents.

The *Pars fortunæ* has influence over money matters, and, in some measure family affairs.

Specific Rules.

Asc. ☌ ☐ ☍, &c. ♄. According to the sign ♄ is in will the native suffer sickness, especially if the ascendant be hyleg), family affliction, or mischief by elderly persons or saturnine affairs, accidents, falls, bruises, &c. The mind becomes dull and heavy, the body suffers *lingering* diseases, especially coughs and colds, phlegmatic complaints, and low fevers. If both ♄ and the ascendant be in watery signs, danger by water; if in ♍, danger of suffocation, or being smothered. On this direction old diseases return.

Asc. ⚹ △ &c. ♄. Benefits by land or houses, inheritances, agricultural pursuits, buildings, &c. legacies, gifts, and favours of old persons. The native becomes grave and studious, and also laborious.

Asc. ☌ ⚹ △ &c. ♃. Health in general, though, if ♃ be afflicted, blood abounds, and pleurisy, &c. occurs on the conjunction. Gifts, patronage, new friends, children, preferment, and general prosperity.

Asc. ☐ ☍ &c. ♃. The body is distempered, blood abounds, danger of pleurisy, or liver complaints, especially if ♃ be in ♌ or ♒. In children measles, and, if ♃ be affected by ♂ the small pox. Losses of money; deceptions and injuries by churchmen and magistrates. The native is careless and improvident; false friends betray.

Asc. ☌ ☐ ☍ &c. ♂. Sickness of the nature of ♂ and the sign he is in, considered with that of the ascendant. Also accidents, cuts, burns, stabs, &c. The native suffers by *hot* diseases, and rarely escapes *loss of blood*. He becomes quarrelsome and venturesome, rushes into disputes and dangers, and suffers accordingly. If he be a gentleman, he may be called out in a duel; if a mechanic, he fights; if a female, she quarrels with her husband, &c. Persons under ♂ influence at birth become violent and furious. If ♂ be in an earthy sign, he threatens great evil; to kill or be killed, &c. in an airy sign inflammation of the blood, falls, &c.; in a fiery sign, violent fevers, burns, stabs, &c.; in a watery sign, bloody flux, danger of drowning, &c.

Asc. ✶ △ &c. ♂. The native becomes martial in his ideas, delights in horse exercise, military affairs, &c. He becomes angry and impatient, inventive and diligent, receives favours from military persons, preferments, &c. or studies chemistry, &c. Females frequently marry under these directions, or have a son born.

Asc. ☌ ☉. The native becomes publicly employed, or receives favours from public characters; his reputation advances. Yet troubles and anxieties attend. Hot diseases in the head, and especially the eyes. In watery signs, flow of humours.

Asc. ✶ △, &c. ☉. Health of body, peace of mind, new friends and eminent. Also preferment and creditable employment, honourable journies, &c. Affairs generally successful. A female may expect marriage, or a son born.

Asc. ☐ ☍, &c. ☉. Troubles and diseases. Envy or ill-treatment from a person in power, quarrels, lawsuits, prosecutions, &c. Also decay of estate, deceit, and disrespect to the native. Danger of imprisonment and shipwreck. Complaints in the eyes, acute diseases, fever, &c. Death or danger to the native's father.

Asc. ☌ ✶ △, &c. ♀. Pleasure and content. He is beloved of women, marries, or has a daughter born or married. He purchases furniture, clothes, &c. and is greatly given to luxury and pleasures, especially under the conjunction, where, if ♀ be afflicted, he may suffer diseases accordingly.

Asc. ☐ ☍, &c. ♀. Disease by surfeit or excess. Inclined to be wild, intemperate, and extravagant. He runs into vicious pursuits, and is scandalized. Many troubles by women, vexations in love matters, &c. jealousy and conjugal quarrels.

Asc. ☌ ☿. This incites a desire to study, poetry, and mathematics. He takes a degree at the University, or enters some school or college, if a youth. It denotes a busy time with accounts, writings, law papers, &c. also journies and changes in situation. The whole good or evil according to the strength of ☿ in the radix.

Asc. ✶ △, &c. ☿. This is of the same character with the ☌; but no evil arises therefrom, even if ☿ be afflicted. It gives changes of residence.

Asc. ☐ ☍, &c. ☿. This brings expenses by literary things and persons. A very unsettled time; disputes, quarrels, lawsuits, annoyances by young persons, &c. He may be arrested or questioned for some mistake or fraud in accounts, or be libelled, or write some foolish book or libel, &c. It also causes cutaneous diseases, coughs, affections of the breath, &c. Much depends on the aspects to ☿.

Asc. ☌ ☽. Sudden benefits or reverses, *changes*, journies, preferment, losses by the populace, death of the native's mother, &c. all depending on the strength of the ☽ on the radix. It brings marriage to males and sea voyages to all. It causes *lunar* diseases, especially if the ascendant be hyleg.

Asc. ✶ △, &c. ☽. Content of mind and body, much active business and employment, a journey or sea voyage. It gives benefits by females, new female friends, marriage, or the birth of a daughter, public esteem and prosperity.

Asc. ☐ ☍, &c. ☽. Disputes and controversies especially with females and vulgar persons; misfortunes at sea, loss of office, many public affronts and open enemies. Also lunar diseases, corrupt humours, cancers, &c. A general tendency to gluttony and intemperance, and the consequent distempers, according to the sign the ☽ is in at birth.

Midheaven ☌ ☐ ☍, &c. ♄. The anger of magistrates and employers is felt; loss of office and trade, disgrace and ruin may occur. Death of parents, &c. He is apt to act discreditably; his servants do the same. Conspiracies against him, private enmity, &c. Accusations, robberies. To a king it denotes tumults and discontent, breach of treaties, &c. And it rarely happens without lowering the native in rank and station. His parents suffer also by death or severe misfortunes.

Midheaven ☌ ♃. Preferment, employment, and numerous benefits by the favour of some person of rank. It raises in life according to the situation of the native. Queen Victoria came to the throne under this direction. It gives increase of wealth; but much depends on how the M.C. is aspected. In a married female's nativity, it benefits her husband; in children, their parents.

Midheaven ⚹ △, &c. ♃. This acts like the ☌, but generally with less power. The △ by ♃ coming to the cusp of the 2d house gives great increase of wealth.

Midheaven ☐ ☍, &c. ♃. Trouble by law and magistrates, the clergy, &c.; losses in commerce and trade; accusations, &c. against the native, which rarely prevail. He suffers by persons pretending to religion. To a king it causes great disputes about law and privileges, &c. quarrels with the nobility, &c.

Midheaven ☌ ☐ ☍, &c. ♂. Great mischances to life and fortunes. The wrath of powerful men fall on the native. He suffers wrong or injury in various ways, imprisonment, disgrace, &c. loss by fire, theft, &c. To a king it denotes war and bloodshed, violent conduct, &c. To a soldier it gives military authority, but danger. It often shews a violent death, where the radix prenotes the same. It kills or afflicts parents, &c.

APPENDIX. 479

Midheaven ✶ △, &c. ♂. The native takes to military actions, fencing, shooting, riding, &c. and he may enter the army or receive promotion. To tradesmen it denotes good business. To kings, war or some increase of the army. The insurrection in Canada broke out exactly as the M. C. came to ✶ ♂ *in zodiaco* in Queen Victoria's nativity.

Midheaven ☌ ☉. This elevates the native to dignity and honour; makes him hold some public office, having command or control. It gives fame and reputation, and also benefits the native's parents. Lord Brougham became Lord Chancellor and a peer of the realm under this direction.

Midheaven ✶ △, &c. ☉. Preferment, success, gifts, honours, &c. by means of persons of rank and power.* It makes the native esteem himself higher, and lays the foundation for his farther advance in life. In a female's nativity it brings marriage, or, if married, the birth of a son. To a king it brings victory, peace, and popularity.

Midheaven □ ☍, &c. ☉. This causes sudden disgrace and loss of office, employment, &c. It causes imprisonment, the sentence of a judge, &c. To a tradesman, &c. it will bring losses and bankruptcy. It afflicts the parents, frequently by means of fire or public calamities. To a king it brings loss of popularity, and many national evils and sufferings.

Midheaven ☌ ✶ △, &c. ♀. Mirth and pleasure, gaiety, &c. to the native, who mixes in female society, falls in love, and may marry, if of proper age, &c. Also the birth of children and their marriage when of age. Prosperity in the family, new female friends, benefits by females, and general success; the going into new houses, buying furniture, &c.

Midheaven □ ☍, &c. ♀. Scandal and disgrace by means of

* The Duke of Wellington received his dukedom under M. C. □ ☉.

females, unfortunate wooings, jealousy, contention, and delusion by women. It shews loss of estate and squandering of property; also a separation, &c. from a wife, and sometimes the death or misfortune of a wife or sister, mother, &c. If marriage occur, it is rash and unhappy. To a king scandal about mistresses, &c.

Midheaven ☌ ⁎ △, &c. ☿. Preferment and credit by learning or literary productions. Much active business, especially with accounts, lawyers, booksellers, merchandize, &c.: also the study of languages, public speaking, &c. Youths go out in the world, young men set up in business, take degrees, &c. It brings new employments, journies, profit by writings, &c. But if ☿ be weak or afflicted, the conjunction may give scandal, libels, informations, &c. against the native.

Midheaven ☌ ☽. This, says Lilly, "argues an unquiet and busy time, afflicted with variety of matter and action, both in body and mind; a troublesome and queasy time, now well, now ill, full of business; sometimes getting, otherwise losing." All depends on the strength of ☽ at birth. If she be strong, it benefits greatly, bringing some new occupation of a public nature; office, trade, or dignity, &c.; also journies and sea voyages, the latter especially, if ☽ be in watery signs. In a male nativity it promises marriage or female connexion and benefits by females.

Midheaven ⁎ △, &c. ☽. Increase of fortune, fame, and estimation, especially among the people: gifts and benefits by ladies. Prosperity in the native's office of employment. A long sea voyage, &c., and sometimes public command, &c., according to the native's rank in life. Changes and general prosperity. With a male, marriage. Birth of children, male or female, as the ☽ may be aspected. Family advancement, &c.

Midheaven □, ☍, &c. ☽. Public disesteem, loss of office and good name; expense and waste of property by low or bad women; danger to the wife, mother, daughter, &c. Quarrels in the family, separations, &c. Punishment by the law, sentence by a judge, &c. for offences. The greatness of the evil depends on the ☽'s aspects and the sign she occupies; fixed signs make it durable.

The ☉ ☌, □, ☍, &c. ♄. If the ☉ be hyleg, danger of severe and fatal illness. Much weakness of body, colds, melancholy, chronic diseases, especially in the head, heart, back, and stomach, or other parts, according to the sign ♄ is in at birth; the eyes are likely to suffer. Danger of falls from buildings, of being crushed, &c. Also the native's father suffers, and may die. Much trouble by saturnine persons, especially such as are in power, noblemen, landlords, &c. Dangers in travelling, loss by storms, shipwreck, &c. Separation of the native's parents, destruction to his fame and credit, loss of business and good name, &c. He is robbed and cheated by servants, tenants, &c. and is full of heavy thoughts, and suffers much vexation, and may be tempted to commit suicide. Envy and malice are active against the native. If an eclipse happen at the time on the place of the ☌, the effect is violent, and generally of a public nature. To a king, defeat, &c.

The ☉ ✶, △, &c. ♄. Some marks of esteem from an aged gentleman or person in power, &c. The native is preferred, and manages his affairs prosperously, receiving, honour, gifts, legacies, &c. It inclines to gravity and severity, laborious studies or works. It imports wealth by husbandry, architecture, or some inheritance. The native succeeds with elderly persons and in all matters under the influence of Saturn.*

* For these see page 37 of " Lilly's Introduction."

The ☉ ☌, ✶, △, &c. ♃. Health of body, peace of mind, increase of wealth and enjoyment of the goods of fortune; preferment, office, dignity, employment, &c., according to the native's situation in life. Church preferment, benefit by lawyers, magistrates, merchants, &c. To a king it denotes peace and tranquillity, commerce flourishing; yet the clergy grasping at power, &c. The native may have a son born, or preferred, &c.

The ☉ ☐ ☍, &c. ♃. The native suffers by lawyers, magistrates, clergymen, and professors of religion, who cause him expenses; yet he usually overcomes, and recovers all. To a king it shews a discontented clergy and nobility, breach of the laws and privileges of the realm, mercantile sufferings, injury to bankers, &c.

The ☉ ☌, ☐, ☍, &c. ♂. Acute diseases, fevers, accidents by fire, iron, or hot water, &c. also bites of dogs, kicks by horses, &c., according to the sign ♂ is in. In a martial nativity, the ☌ gives preferment. In watery signs these directions denote fluxes, and in all cases some loss of blood. The native is rash and violent, he does nothing prudently; let him, therefore, beware of disputes with superiors and men of rank, and let him avoid any new work, for he will have no success. Let him shun quarrels and the company of soldiers, especially if ☉ be hyleg; also let him beware of fevers and inflammation, and live temperately.

The ☉ ✶ △, &c. ♂. These bring martial friends and preferment; also an inclination to shoot, hunt, ride, &c. more than formerly. Soldiers act daringly and meet promotion. It causes a journey, and "much trotting and trudging from one place to another."

The ☉ ☌, ✶, △, &c. ♀. Stirs up a desire for music, plays, and merriment; also all kinds of ♀ pleasures. The native makes love, and spends his time and money among the ladies. If ♀ be weak, the ♂ causes unlawful affections. The body is now healthy, and mind cheerful; all things succeed, the estate is increased, female children born, and the native respected. In female nativities, marriage.

The ☉ □, ☍, &c. ♀. A barren time, no issue. The native given to impure conduct and sordid actions. He incurs discredit and scandal. If ☉ be hyleg, he suffers ♀ diseases according to the sign ♀ is in at birth. He has differences with females, is refused marriage, quarrels with his wife, his daughter elopes, &c.

The ☉ ☌, ✶, △, &c. ☿. Much active business and inclination to literary things and persons. Gain by literature, or dealing in books, new employments, &c. Occupied with accounts and writings. He gains fame thereby, or by some invention, if ☿ be strong. It brings an inclination to travel, and benefits by young persons. Also the ☌ brings controversies and disputes, lawsuits, &c., or prejudice by false witnesses or lies being spoken, &c. of the native; and if ☉ be hyleg, serious diseases, hurts, &c. according as ☿ is aspected. He is generally changeable in his fancy, and unsettled in his studies.

The ☉ □, ☍, &c. ☿. Accusations and suits against the native, or he may be guilty of some deceit or knavery, and be thereby much disgraced. He suffers by forgery and fraud, bad bills, &c. and unsuccessful journies; and is greatly annoyed by lawyers and young persons. His mind is afflicted, and he loses his employment, &c., probably by decision of a court against him. Young persons run away from their employers, are rusticated from college, &c. It gives an averseness from learning, and the native is often unjustly aspersed. His health suffers according to the sign ☿ is in, and the planets which aspect him.

The ☉ ☌ ☽. This impairs the health, brings humours, &c.

in the body, pains in the head, weak eyes, blindness, &c. The native is unsettled, travels, removes, wastes his property by idle courses and improvidence. The ☽ being strong, it gives preferment, and may give marriage; but the wife will be proud and imperious, striving for mastery.

The ☉ ✶, △, &c. ☽. Favour and friendship of powerful persons, rich ladies, &c. who employ the native, or benefit him by preferment, &c. It gives journies of a profitable and honourable kind, and public employments. He is much occupied with females, and may marry a rich wife if ☽ be strong. It increases his friends, and may give the birth of children or their settlement in life to the native's content.

The ☉ □, ☍, &c. ☽. An unhappy time, full of losses and crosses; many powerful men are provoked against the native. He wrangles with his wife, and may separate; quarrels in the family occur. His parents separate, his children die or act amiss. The native lives intemperately, mixes with low company, loose women, &c.; and has ill health. If ☽ be hyleg, he suffers grievous diseases, according to the sign the ☉ is in. It produces fevers, sore eyes, and blindness, the small-pox, measles, worms, &c. It lowers the native's credit and character, and renders him unpopular.

The ☽ ☌ □, ☍, &c. ♄. Many chronic, cold, and moist diseases arise, with humours abounding, and general ill health. If ☽ be hyleg, it gives agues and low fevers, palsy, dropsy, coughs, and influenza, gout, and apoplexy, &c. all *lingering* diseases, according to the nature of ♄, and the sign he occupies. These directions bring mental troubles and afflictions, fears and anxieties; also loss of property and aspersions of character by low vulgar people and the mob. He quarrels with female relations, loses by the sea or seamen, becomes bankrupt or insolvent, &c. It gives death of wife or children, mother, &c.

The ☽ ✶, △, &c. ♄. Gifts and rewards from elderly persons, especially females, Respect from the lower classes, much popularity, &c., friendship of saturnine persons, benefits by dealing in saturnine commodities, as lead, wool, &c., and by buildings, farming, &c.: also legacies.

The ☽ ☌, ✶, △, &c. ♃. Health, honour, and wealth, occur according to the situation in life of the native. Prosperity and success in journies and speculations; injury to his enemies. Office, employment, command, new business, &c. University degrees or law preferments, &c. Many friends. To kings, peace, flourishing revenues, &c.

The ☽ ☐, ☍, &c. ♃. Difficulties in his employment; lawyers, and religious people, magistrates, &c. annoy him; losses of property by waste and extravagance. By his own virtue and exertions he may, however, overcome all attempts against him, and those who were his enemies will become his friends. He may be likely to quarrel with his landlord or some petty lawyer or churchman, or about church matters; yet no lasting evil need be apprehended. The blood becomes corrupt, and hence diseases of the liver, &c.

The ☽ ☌, ☐, ☍, &c. ♂. Abundance of sorrows, accidents, and misfortunes. Imprisonment, loss of property, thefts, squandering on the part of his wife, &c. Active enemies rise against him, and he suffers strange anxieties. He has diseases according to the sign ♂ is in, and accidents. He is in danger of death, if ☽ be hyleg, by fire, cuts, wounds, bites, kicks, or gunshot, &c., and, if ♀ throw an ill aspect, by poison or treachery of females. He is choleric and quarrelsome, very much inclined to bear arms, or associate with martial men; and he becomes addicted to vices according to the sign ♂ is in: if in the house of ♄, he is dogged; if that of ♃, he becomes hypocritical; that of ☉, proud and haughty; his own house, very quarrelsome; that of ♀, loose; that of ☿, fraudulent; that of ☽, he is unsettled, &c. If ♂ be aspected by ♄ or ☉, and he in ♌, especially near *aselli*, he may die of pestilence or fire. He receives disdain and insults by women. If he have a good wife, she may die. It causes injuries to the face or eyes, also the small-pox, stone, gravel, and gonorrhea, &c. If he marry under the ♂, it is very unfortunate. To a king, war and bloodshed, losses, &c.

The ☽ ✶, △, &c. ♂. It gives a desire to martial and manly exercises, as riding, shooting, &c., and the native takes delight in horses, the company of military men, &c., and warlike affairs. Preferment and profit, birth of a son; or, if single, he may marry. Yet he may expect losses by women, and by dealing in horses, unless ♂ be well aspected. If ♂ be weak, and the nativity denote it, he takes to drinking, gaming, or loose conduct. To a king it denotes increase of the army, and if at war, great battles, victories, &c.

The ☽ ☌ ☉. It causes fevers and affections to the eyes, &c. and, if the ☽ be hyleg, it may cause death. Much trouble of mind, many mutations in his affairs and expectations, reverses, &c. In many cases it denotes marriage. To merchants, &c. good trade, yet some slur on their credit. It causes generally some great change in the life and affairs of the native; if ☉ be strong and fortunate, beneficial; if otherwise, the reverse.

The ☽ ✶, △, &c. ☉. Profitable and honourable friends, especially among females of rank, &c.; he becomes popular, receives some office or employment. Journies or voyages beyond sea, especially if it fall in the 9th house and in a watery sign; much gain thereby. The native should exert himself under this influence to rise in life. He is strongly inclined to marry, and if he do, it is prosperous. If married, he may expect a child, unless ☉ be afflicted. To merchants, &c. it brings prosperous trade. To a king renewal of leagues, victory, honourable peace, &c.

The ☾, □ ☍, &c. ☉. Extreme danger and affliction of body and mind. It converts the love of some female to hatred. It causes injury by popular tumults, &c., and the dissembling friendship of some man of rank, by which the native suffers. If the aspect fall near nebulous stars, there is danger of hurts or disease to the eyes. It produces fevers, coughs, colics, fluxes, &c. "according to the nature of the sign and house the significator and promittor are in" says Lilly. To a nobleman it shews popular dislike; to a farmer an ill landlord, who wrongs him; to a poor man danger of the treadmill, &c. It brings contentions and quarrels, and oppressions from men in power; and is an ill time to speculate. It generally endures five or six months.

The ☾ ☌, ⚹, △, &c. ♀. A pleasant and happy period. The native inclines to be merry and jocund, fond of entertainment, and addicted to pleasure, &c., which will be legitimate or otherwise, as ♀ is well or ill aspected. He receives gifts and favours from females; is inclined to lovemaking and marriage, and free from all care. To the married it denotes children, chiefly females, and also the marriage and settlement of children. To merchants good success, to farmers profit by ♀ matters, small cattle, poultry, &c. Generally happy marriage, obedient children, domestic felicity, and prosperity by means of females. To kings peace and new allies, &c.

The ☾ □, ☍, &c. ♀. Much trouble by wandering affections, illicit amours, &c., scandal and infamy in consequence. Many crosses and controversies through women. Waste of estate by improvidence and intemperance. If the native marry under these directions, it is unhappy, and to one whom he loves not, and who will not be obedient and affectionate. It produces ♀ diseases; and, in children, if ♀ be in a watery sign and afflicted, measles, small-pox, &c.; in women irregular and abundant courses, diseases of the *matrix*, &c.

The ☽ ☌ ☿. This direction brings journies or voyages, the latter if ☿ be in ♋. It engages him in causes and controversies sometimes; brings him much active business; he is very energetic, and given to study, writing, public speaking, &c. To a merchant much business, journies, &c.; to a factor many accounts. * To a king foreign news, active exertions among his allies; he sends ambassadors, &c.

The ☽ ✶, △, &c. ☿. Good speed and success to the native in his employments. He is inclined to read, write, and pursue accounts, mathematical studies, &c. It gives a delight in music or mechanical devices, a propensity to travel and make changes in his abode. He has the friendship of some lady of rank, &c., or receives an employment, literary or as a messenger, traveller, ambassador, &c. He has pleasure in his children, may have a child born, or married, apprenticed, &c. He succeeds in law, or with young people.

The ☽ ☐, ☍, &c. ☿. An averseness from study, &c. is felt. He is frowned on by the vulgar, suffers by popular tumult, &c., questioned for some fraud or forgery, imprisoned, banished, sentenced to death, &c., according as ☿ is aspected at birth. Many scandals, libels, false charges,

---

* All depends on how ☿ is aspected; as, if afflicted, he gives trouble by fraud, theft, &c.; also sickness and accidents, according to the sign.

swindling and fraudulent attempts by cunning attorneys, &c. against the native. Injuries by law and lawyers, thefts, &c. He is annoyed by his children, who are unfortunate and impudent; and by young persons generally. He may lose a child. There is sometimes danger of delirium and madness.

The ☉ to his own S ⚹ or ⚹ produces peace and felicity, profit, and renown, &c., the ⚹ chiefly. But it should fall in a good house. To his own parallel, preferment, &c.

The ☉ to his own S □ or □. Abundance of sorrow and misery, and many maladies, according to the sign the ☉ is in, and in which the aspect falls. The □ produces a desire to be dissolved, that he may be at rest.

The ☽ to her S ⚹ or ⚹. Changes in life, journies, &c. and the friendship of females, benefits, &c. by them. To her own parallel, changes.

The ☽ to her own S □ or □. Troubles, losses, changes, and the enmity of women and the populace.

The Part of Fortune.

The ⊕ ☌ □, ☍, &c. ♄. Consumption of estate by theft, gaming, and saturnine persons; sometimes almost imperceptibly.

The ⊕ ⚹, △, &c. ♄. Increase of property by aged persons, legacies, &c., and by buildings, agriculture, sea affairs, cattle, &c.

The ⊕ ☌, ⚹, △, &c. ♃. Gifts, rewards, patronage, jovial persons, success in business, office, &c.

The ⊕ □, ☍, &c. ♃. Losses by gentlemen or churchmen, lawsuits, &c. Some falling off in trade or income, disappointment in receiving money. To a king disputes about taxes, judges, &c. This direction occurred with Queen Victoria when the Commons cut off £20,000 a year from her intended husband, the Chief Justice of the Queen's Bench held the Parliament at bay and the Sheriffs were imprisoned.

The $\oplus$ ✶, △, &c. ♂. Wealth by martial persons, or by buying arms, horses, &c., also by traffic in small cattle, and by going to sea.

The $\oplus$ □, ☍, &c. ♂. Loss by thieving servants, or robbery of thieves or soldiers, firing of houses, &c., or by idle courses, quarrels, lawsuits, &c.

The $\oplus$ ☌ ☉. Honourable disbursements; the native more liberal than formerly; waste of estate and prodigality.

The $\oplus$ ✶, △ ☉. Profit and advantage by persons, of rank, &c.; many friends above his own rank in life; profit but expenditure; not much saving.

The $\oplus$ □ ☍ ☉. Damage by lawsuits, waste of property, by the envy of great persons, false and scandalous accusations, loss of office, &c.

The $\oplus$ ☌, ✶, △ ♀. Great gifts and benefits from ladies of rank; freedom of expenditure on ornaments, attire, &c.; merchants gain rapidly.

The $\oplus$ □ ☍ ♀. Expenses by women, love-making, jealousies, &c.; much consumption of property by extravagance and folly.

The $\oplus$ ☌, ✶, △ ☿. Gain by bargains, contracts, accounts, learning, the law, &c. Also by degrees at the university, by inventions, writings, &c., and by his own exertions and industry. Also profit by some inheritance, or by journies or sea voyages.

The $\oplus$ □ ☍, &c. ☿. The native is cheated in accounts, or by lawyers or literary men, youths, &c. He loses by in-

APPENDIX. 491

genious conceptions, false witnesses, &c. His credit is questioned, and he may act foolishly, and be sued at law, or lose by his children.

The ⊕ ☌, ✶, △, &c. ☽. Friendship and gain by females; much action for and with the common people, by whom the native profits. He may undertake long journeys or voyages, and he will have full employment.

The ⊕ ☐, ☍, &c. ☽. Losses by bargains, contracts, &c. by trade with the lower classes; by sea voyages or sailors. Hatred and loss by some respectable female; many lawsuits and heavy debts, &c.

N.B. Directions to ♅ have effect similar to ☿ and ♄ combined; but events occur suddenly or in a manner quite unexpected. The ☉ or ☽ to ♅ causes deaths of relations* and strange conduct, much trouble by the press and public bodies. His ✶ or △ unlooked for benefits. The hyleg afflicted by direction to ♅ gives sudden dangers and extraordinary accidents.

Final Observation.—Let the student bear in mind, that the *primary* direction usually shews the *general* nature of the event, and the secondary direction its *especial* character, according as the planet is situated in any angle or house of the radical figure. And the effects on the health will be ascertained by attention to the "TABLE OF DISEASES SIGNIFIED BY THE PLANETS IN THE DIFFERENT SIGNS OF THE ZODIAC," for which see *ante,* page 180 of the *Introduction.*

* ☉ par. ♅ zod. in Queen Victoria's nativity in September, caused the death of her aunt, the Princess Augusta, as predicted, page 45 of my Almanac, 1840.

The student should understand that, when a direction threatens sickness, the planet importing it will cause such diseases as are herein mentioned, according to the sign he is in.

THE END OF THE GRAMMAR OF ASTROLOGY.

TABLES

TO BE USED IN

CALCULATING NATIVITIES;

COMPRISING

TABLES OF DECLINATION, RIGHT ASCENSION,
ASCENSIONAL DIFFERENCE, AND
POLAR ELEVATION;

ALSO,

TABLES OF HOUSES

FOR

LONDON AND LIVERPOOL.

Computed by
ZADKIEL,
Author of the " Grammar of Astrology."

PREFACE.

The following Tables are calculated according to the present obliquity of the ecliptic, 23° 28', and are adapted for persons who may desire to calculate a nativity upon the modern and improved rules of Astrology, as set forth in the latest elementary work on Genethliacal Science, the GRAMMAR OF ASTROLOGY.

The Table of Houses for the latitude of *London*, 51° 32' N., contains the Right Ascension of every degree of the zodiac in *hours*, *minutes*, and *seconds*. The Tables of Houses for the latitude of *Liverpool*, 53° 23' N., contains the Right Ascension of every degree of the zodiac in *degrees* and *minutes* of a degree; therefore, by referring from one to the other of these Tables, the student will at once perceive what is the Right Ascension in degrees and minutes of any amount of time within 24 hours, and *vice versâ*. The former of these Tables will answer for any part of Great Britain which is south of the latitude of 52 degrees and a half; and the latter Table will answer equally well for any place between Liverpool and the borders of Scotland. The importance of this Table, which has cost the Author great labour, as it required the taking out 12,600 logarithms, will be instantly perceived, when it is considered that the longitude of the ascendant at Liverpool is sometimes *three degrees* different from the longitude of the ascendant at London. The errors that arose from erecting figures of the heavens for the northern parts of the kingdom, by means of the Table of Houses for London, must have been very great. Even in horary questions it is very important to have the longitude of the ascending degree correct; and in nativities an error of three degrees would throw out a *secondary direction* of the Moon to any aspect of the ascendant not less than *three months;* and so create error and confusion in the judgment of events. As, for example, if the primary directions were such as to denote danger of drowning, and the moon came to an opposition of the ascendant in the secondary direction, it might be judged that the greatest danger would be during the week when the Moon came exactly to the opposite degree

PREFACE. v

and minute of those which were ascending at birth; but if the ascendant were wrong, even by *one* degree, this time could not be ascertained to within a month. To persons who can erect a figure by trigonometry, it is of less importance; but this is seldom done for horary questions.

The Table of Right Ascensions contains only twelve pages instead of twenty-four, as usual, but the extra expense of twelve additional pages is avoided by this means; and it only requires to pay strict attention to the direction at the head of each page, and either add or subtract 180°, as may be required; thus, if the Right Ascension of 10 degrees of *Scorpio* with 3 degrees of *South* latitude be required, learn by the table what is the Right Ascension of the *opposite* point of the zodiac, viz. 10 degrees of *Taurus* with 3 degrees of opposite latitude, and then add 180 degrees, and you have the Right Ascension required.

Thus, Right Ascension of 10° *Taurus* with 3° *North* latitude .... 36° 35'
To which add half the circle.......... 180   0
And you have the Right Asc. of 10° *Scorpio* with 3° *South* latitude 216 35

Again, if you require the Right Asc. of 5 deg. of *Aries* with 2° *South* latitude, find that of the opposite point, viz. 5 deg. of *Libra* with 2° *North* latitude; which is 185° 22′ by the Table; and by taking away the half circle, 180°, you have 5° 22′ for the Right Ascension you require.

The latitudes in these Tables are carried only to 7 degrees, which is the utmost any planet reaches, except Venus. When those rare occasions happen in which Venus is found with latitude exceeding 7 degrees, it will be very easy to see what difference of Right Asc. or Declination one degree of latitude creates opposite the longitude of Venus, and then compute the difference of her Right Asc. &c. As, for example, if Venus be in 20 degrees of *Virgo*, with 8 degrees and a half of *North* latitude, and I require her Right Asc., the difference of Right Asc. between 6 degrees and 7 degrees of *North* latitude, opposite 20 degrees of *Virgo*, is just 24 minutes of a degree; therefore to the Right Asc. under the 7th degree, which is 173° 37′, I add 24 min., and it gives 174° 1′ for the Right Asc. of Venus, with 8 degrees of North lat. opposite 20 *Virgo*; and for the half degree I add 12 min. more, and it gives 174° 13′, the Right Asc. of Venus in 20° *Virgo* and 8° 30′ *North* latitude; and by adding 180° to this, we have 354° 13′ for the Right Asc. of Venus if she had been in 20° *Pisces* with 8° 30′ of *South* latitude.

On some rare occasions the Moon's declination will exceed 28° the limits of our Table of Ascensional Difference; but the difference between 27° and 28° being found, and the proportion allowed for the next degree, it will give the Asc. Diff. of the Moon sufficiently near. For example, the Moon's declination at noon on the 17th February, 1806, was 28° 12′; required her Asc. Diff. in latitude 55°? The difference between 27° and 28° of declination is 2° 43′ of Asc. Diff. in that high latitude; then say, if one degree gives 2° 43′ = 163 minutes, what will 12 minutes give? Answer, 33 minutes: which, added, to 49° 24′, the Asc. Diff. for 28° declination, gives the Asc. Diff. required, viz. 49° 57′.

The great interest evinced in the examination of Astrology in the present age, as shewn by the ready sale of a large edition of the "Grammar of Astrology," has induced the Author to put forth these Tables; by which means still farther facility is offered to those persons whose sense of the value of experience will induce them to place more reliance on one fact than on a hundred crude arguments, or a thousand idle assertions. Feeling that the question of the truth or falsehood of Astrology has never been discussed in the present day by such arguments as science would acknowledge, the Author has no hesitation in declaring, that ignorance of its principles and practice is the chief foundation of the prejudice which exists against the science; and he trusts that these Tables will assist to overcome much of that ignorance, and thereby overthrow one obstacle in the path of truth.

Liverpool,
July 17, 1834.

TABLE OF HOUSES FOR LONDON.

Lat, 51° 32'.

Right Ascen. of Meridian.			10 Aries.	11 Taurus.	12 Gemini.	Ascend. Cancer.		2 Leo.	3 Virgo.
H.	M.	S.	°	°	°	°	′	°	°
0	0	0	0	9	22	26	36	12	3
0	3	40	1	10	23	27	17	13	3
0	7	20	2	11	24	27	56	14	4
0	11	0	3	12	25	28	42	15	5
0	14	41	4	13	25	29	17	15	6
0	18	21	5	14	26	29	55	16	7
0	22	2	6	15	27	0 ♌ 34		17	8
0	25	42	7	16	28	1	14	18	8
0	29	23	8	17	29	1	55	18	9
0	33	4	9	18	♋	2	33	19	10
0	36	45	10	19	1	3	14	20	11
0	40	26	11	20	1	3	54	20	12
0	44	8	12	22	2	4	33	21	13
0	47	50	13	23	3	5	12	22	14
0	51	32	14	24	4	5	52	23	15
0	55	14	15	25	5	6	30	23	15
0	58	5	16	26	6	7	9	24	16
1	2	40	17	27	6	7	50	25	17
1	6	23	18	28	7	8	30	26	18
1	10	7	19	29	8	9	9	26	19
1	13	51	20	♊	9	9	48	27	19
1	17	35	21	1	10	10	29	28	20
1	21	20	22	2	10	11	7	28	21
1	25	6	23	3	11	11	48	29	22
1	28	52	24	4	12	12	28	♍	23
1	32	38	25	5	13	13	8	1	24
1	36	25	26	6	14	13	48	1	25
1	40	12	27	7	14	14	28	2	25
1	44	0	28	7	15	15	8	3	26
1	47	48	29	8	16	15	47	4	27
1	51	37	30	9	17	16	27	4	28

TABLE OF HOUSES FOR LONDON.

Lat. 51° 32'.

Right Ascen. of Meridian.	10 Taurus Aries.	11 Gemini.	12 Cancer.	Ascend. Leo.	2 Virgo.	3 Virgo.
H. M. S.				° ′		
1 51 37	0	0	17	16 28	4	28
1 55 27	1	10	18	17 8	5	29
1 59 17	2	11	19	17 48	6	♎
2 3 8	3	12	19	18 27	7	1
2 6 59	4	13	20	19 9	8	2
2 10 51	5	14	21	19 49	9	2
2 14 44	6	15	22	20 29	9	3
2 18 37	7	16	22	21 10	10	4
2 22 31	8	17	23	21 52	11	5
2 26 25	9	18	24	22 32	11	6
2 30 20	10	19	25	23 14	12	7
2 34 16	11	20	25	23 55	13	8
2 38 13	12	21	26	24 36	14	9
2 42 10	13	22	27	25 17	15	10
2 46 8	14	23	28	25 58	15	11
2 50 7	15	24	29	26 40	16	12
2 54 7	16	25	29	27 22	17	12
2 58 7	17	26	♌	28 4	18	13
3 2 8	18	26	1	28 45	18	14
3 6 9	19	27	2	29 28	19	15
3 10 12	20	28	3	0♍12	20	16
3 14 15	21	29	3	0 54	21	17
3 18 19	22	♋	4	1 36	22	18
3 22 23	23	1	5	2 20	22	19
3 26 29	24	2	6	3 1	23	20
3 30 35	25	3	7	3 45	24	21
3 34 41	26	4	7	4 28	25	22
3 38 49	27	5	8	5 11	26	23
3 42 57	28	6	9	5 54	27	24
3 47 6	29	7	10	6 29	27	25
3 51 15	30	8	11	7 21	28	25

TABLE OF HOUSES FOR LONDON.

Lat. 51° 32′.

Right Ascen. of Meridian.	10	11	12	Ascend.	2	3
	Gemini.	*Cancer.*	*Leo.*	*Virgo.*	*Virgo.*	*Libra.*
H. M. s.	0	0	0	0 ′	0	0
3 51 15	0	8	11	7 21	28	25
3 55 25	1	9	12	8 5	29	26
3 59 36	2	10	12	8 49	♎	27
4 3 48	3	10	13	9 33	1	28
4 8 0	4	11	14	10 16	2	29
4 12 13	5	12	15	11 2	2	♏
4 16 26	6	13	16	11 46	3	1
4 20 40	7	14	17	12 30	4	2
4 24 55	8	15	17	13 15	5	3
4 29 10	9	16	18	14 0	6	4
4 33 26	10	17	19	14 45	7	5
4 37 42	11	18	20	15 30	8	6
4 41 59	12	19	21	16 15	8	7
4 46 16	13	20	21	17 0	9	8
4 50 34	14	21	22	17 45	10	9
4 54 52	15	22	23	18 30	11	10
4 59 10	16	23	24	19 16	12	11
5 3 29	17	24	25	20 4	13	12
5 7 49	18	25	26	20 49	14	13
5 12 9	19	25	27	21 35	14	14
5 16 29	20	26	28	22 20	15	14
5 20 49	21	27	28	23 6	16	15
5 25 9	22	28	29	23 51	17	16
5 29 30	23	29	♍	24 37	18	17
5 33 51	24	♌	1	25 25	19	18
5 38 12	25	1	2	26 9	20	19
5 42 34	26	2	3	26 55	21	20
5 46 55	27	3	4	27 41	21	21·
5 51 17	28	4	4	28 27	22	22
5 55 38	29	5	5	29 13	23	23
6 0 0	30	6	6	30 0	24	24

12

TABLE OF HOUSES FOR LONDON.

Lat. 51° 32′.

Right Ascen. of Meridian.			10	11	12	Ascend.		2	3
			Cancer.	Leo.	Virgo.	Libra.		Libra.	Scorpio.
H.	M.	s.	°	°	°	°		°	°
6	0	0	0	6	6	0	0	24	24
6	4	22	1	7	7	0	47	25	25
6	8	43	2	8	8	1	33	26	26
6	13	5	3	9	9	2	19	27	27
6	17	26	4	10	10	3	5	27	28
6	21	48	5	11	10	3	51	28	29
6	26	9	6	12	11	4	27	29	♐
6	30	30	7	13	12	5	23	♏	1
6	34	51	8	14	13	6	9	1	2
6	39	11	9	15	14	6	55	2	3
6	43	31	10	16	15	7	40	2	4
6	47	51	11	16	16	8	26	3	4
6	52	11	12	17	16	9	12	4	5
6	56	31	13	18	17	9	58	5	6
7	0	50	14	19	18	10	41	6	7
7	5	8	15	20	19	11	28	7	8
7	9	26	16	21	20	12	14	8	9
7	13	44	17	22	21	12	59	8	10
7	18	1	18	23	22	13	46	9	11
7	22	18	19	24	22	14	30	10	12
7	26	34	20	25	23	15	15	11	13
7	30	50	21	26	24	15	59	12	14
7	35	5	22	27	25	16	45	13	15
7	39	20	23	28	26	17	30	13	16
7	43	34	24	29	27	18	15	14	17
7	47	47	25	♍	28	18	59	15	18
7	52	0	26	1	28	19	43	16	19
7	56	12	27	2	29	20	27	17	20
8	0	24	28	3	♎	21	11	18	20
8	4	35	29	4	1	21	56	18	21
8	8	45	30	5	2	22	40	19	22

TABLE OF HOUSES FOR LONDON.

Lat. 51° 32′.

Right Ascen. of Meridian.	10	11	12	Ascend.	2	3
	Leo.	Virgo.	Libra.	Libra.	Scorpio.	Sagitt.
H. M. S.	°	°	°	° ′	°	°
8 8 45	0	5	2	22 40	19	22
8 12 54	1	5	3	23 24	20	23
8 17 3	2	6	3	24 7	21	24
8 21 11	3	7	4	24 50	22	25
8 25 19	4	8	5	25 34	23	26
8 29 26	5	9	6	26 18	23	27
8 33 31	6	10	7	27 0	24	28
8 37 37	7	11	8	27 44	25	29
8 41 41	8	12	8	28 25	26	♑
8 45 45	9	13	9	29 8	27	1
8 49 48	10	14	10	29 50	27	2
8 53 51	11	15	11	0♏32	28	3
8 57 52	12	16	12	1 15	29	4
9 1 53	13	17	12	1 58	♐	4
9 5 53	14	18	13	2 39	1	5
9 9 53	15	18	14	3 21	2	6
9 13 52	16	19	15	4 3	2	7
9 17 50	17	20	16	4 44	3	8
9 21 47	18	21	16	5 24	4	9
9 25 44	19	22	17	6 7	5	10
9 29 40	20	23	18	6 48	5	11
9 33 35	21	24	19	7 29	6	12
9 37 29	22	25	19	8 9	7	13
9 41 23	23	26	20	8 50	8	14
9 45 16	24	27	21	9 31	9	15
9 49 9	25	28	22	10 11	9	16
9 53 1	26	28	23	10 51	10	17
9 56 52	27	29	23	11 32	11	18
10 0 43	28	♎	24	12 12	12	19
10 4 33	29	1	25	12 53	12	20
10 8 23	30	2	26	13 33	13	20

TABLE OF HOUSES FOR LONDON.

Lat. 51° 32'.

Right Ascen. of Meridian.			10	11	12	Ascend.		2	3
			Virgo.	Libra.	Libra.	Scorpio.		Sagitt.	Capric.
H.	M.	S.	°	°	°	°	'	°	°
10	8	23	0	2	26	13	33	13	20
10	12	12	1	3	26	14	13	14	21
10	16	0	2	4	27	14	43	15	22
10	19	48	3	5	28	15	33	16	23
10	23	35	4	5	29	16	13	16	24
10	27	22	5	6	29	16	52	17	25
10	31	8	6	7	♏	17	32	18	26
10	34	54	7	8	1	18	13	19	27
10	38	40	8	9	2	18	51	20	28
10	42	25	9	10	2	19	31	20	29
10	46	9	10	11	3	20	11	21	♒
10	49	53	11	11	4	20	52	22	1
10	53	37	12	12	4	21	30	23	2
10	27	20	13	13	5	22	9	24	3
11	1	3	14	14	6	22	49	24	4
11	4	46	15	15	7	23	28	25	5
11	8	28	16	16	7	24	8	26	6
11	12	10	17	17	8	24	47	27	8
11	15	52	18	17	9	25	27	28	9
11	19	34	19	18	10	26	5	29	10
11	23	15	20	19	10	26	45	30	11
11	26	56	21	20	11	27	26	♑	12
11	30	37	22	21	12	28	5	1	13
11	34	18	23	22	13	28	44	2	14
11	37	58	24	23	13	29	24	3	15
11	41	39	25	23	14	0 ♐	3	4	16
11	45	19	26	24	15	0	43	5	17
11	49	0	27	25	15	1	23	5	18
11	52	40	28	26	16	2	4	6	19
11	56	20	29	26	17	2	43	7	20
12	0	0	30	27	17	3	23	8	21

TABLE OF HOUSES FOR LONDON

Lat. 51° 32'.

Right Ascen. of Meridian.	10	11	12	Ascend.		2	3
	Libra.	Libra.	Scorpio.	Sagitt.		Capric.	Aquar.
H. M. S.	°	°	°	°	′	°	°
12 0 0	0	27	17	3	23	8	21
12 3 40	1	28	18	4	4	9	22
12 7 20	2	29	19	4	45	10	24
12 11 0	3	♏	20	5	25	11	25
12 14 41	4	1	20	6	7	12	26
12 18 21	5	1	21	6	48	13	27
12 22 2	6	2	22	7	29	14	28
12 25 42	7	3	23	8	10	15	29
12 29 23	8	4	23	8	51	16	♓
12 33 4	9	5	24	9	33	17	2
12 36 45	10	6	25	10	15	18	3
12 40 26	11	6	25	10	57	19	4
12 44 8	12	7	26	11	40	20	5
12 47 50	13	8	27	12	22	21	6
12 51 32	14	9	28	13	4	22	7
12 55 14	15	10	28	13	47	23	9
12 58 57	16	11	29	14	30	24	10
13 2 40	17	11	♐	15	15	25	11
13 6 23	18	12	1	15	59	26	12
13 10 7	19	13	1	16	44	27	13
13 13 51	20	14	2	17	28	28	15
13 17 35	21	15	3	18	13	29	16
13 21 20	22	16	4	19	0	♏	17
13 25 6	23	16	4	19	44	1	18
13 28 52	24	17	5	20	31	2	20
13 32 38	25	18	6	21	19	4	21
13 36 25	26	19	7	22	6	5	22
13 40 12	27	20	7	22	54	6	23
13 44 0	28	21	8	23	42	7	25
13 47 48	29	21	9	24	31	8	26
13 51 37	30	22	10	25	20	10	27

16

TABLE OF HOUSES FOR LONDON.

Lat. 51° 32'.

Right Ascen. of Meridian.	10	11	12	Ascend.	2	3
	Scorpio.	Scorpio.	Sagitt.	Sagitt.	Aquar.	Pisces.
H. M. S.	°	°	°	° ′	°	°
13 51 37	0	22	10	25 20	10	27
13 55 27	1	23	11	26 10	11	28
13 59 17	2	24	11	27 2	12	♈
14 3 8	3	25	12	27 53	14	1
14 6 59	4	26	13	28 45	15	2
14 10 51	5	26	14	29 36	16	4
14 14 44	6	27	15	0♑29	18	5
14 18 37	7	28	15	1 23	19	6
14 22 31	8	29	16	2 18	20	8
14 26 25	9	♐	17	3 16	22	9
14 30 20	10	1	18	4 11	23	10
14 34 16	11	2	19	5 9	25	11
14 38 13	12	2	20	6 7	26	13
14 42 10	13	3	20	7 6	28	14
14 46 8	14	4	21	8 6	29	15
14 50 7	15	5	22	9 8	♓	17
14 54 7	16	6	23	10 11	3	18
14 58 7	17	7	24	11 15	4	19
15 2 8	18	8	25	12 20	6	21
15 6 9	19	9	26	13 27	8	22
15 10 12	20	9	27	14 35	9	23
15 14 15	21	10	27	15 43	11	24
15 18 19	22	11	28	16 52	13	26
15 22 23	23	12	29	18 3	14	27
15 26 29	24	13	♑	19 16	16	28
15 30 35	25	14	1	20 32	17	29
15 34 41	26	15	2	21 48	19	♉
15 38 49	27	16	3	23 8	21	2
15 42 57	28	17	4	24 29	22	3
15 47 6	29	18	5	25 51	24	5
15 51 15	30	18	6	27 15	26	6

17

TABLE OF HOUSES FOR LONDON.

Lat. 51° 32'.

Right Ascen. of Meridian.	10	11	12	Ascend.	2	3
	Sagitt.	Sagitt.	Capric.	Capricorn.	Pisces.	Taurus.
H. M. S.	°	°	°	° ′	°	°
15 51 15	0	18	6	27 15	26	6
15 55 25	1	19	7	28 42	28	7
15 59 36	2	20	8	0≈11	♈	9
16 3 48	3	21	9	1 42	1	10
16 7 0	4	22	10	3 16	3	11
16 12 13	5	23	11	4 53	5	12
16 16 26	6	24	12	6 32	7	14
16 20 40	7	25	13	8 13	9	15
16 24 55	8	26	14	9 57	11	16
16 29 10	9	27	16	11 44	12	17
16 33 26	10	28	17	12 34	14	18
16 37 42	11	29	18	15 24	16	20
16 41 59	12	♑	19	17 20	18	21
16 46 16	13	1	20	19 18	20	22
16 50 34	14	2	21	21 22	21	23
16 54 52	15	3	22	23 27	23	25
16 59 10	16	4	24	25 35	25	26
17 3 29	17	5	25	27 46	27	27
17 7 49	18	6	26	30 0	28	28
17 12 9	19	7	27	2 ✕ 19	♉	29
17 16 29	20	8	29	4 40	2	♊
17 20 49	21	9	≈	7 2	3	1
17 25 9	22	10	1	9 26	5	2
17 29 30	23	11	3	11 54	7	3
17 33 51	24	12	4	14 24	8	5
17 38 12	25	13	5	17 0	10	6
17 42 34	26	14	7	19 33	11	7
17 46 55	27	15	8	22 6	13	8
17 51 17	28	16	10	24 40	14	9
17 55 38	29	17	11	27 30	16	10
18 0 0	30	18	13	30 0	17	11

B

18

TABLE OF HOUSES FOR LONDON.
Lat. 51° 32'.

Right Ascen. of Meridian.	10	11	12	Ascend.	2	3
	Capric.	Capric.	Aquar.	Aries.	Taurus.	Gemini.
H. M. S.	°	°	°	°	°	°
18 0 0	0	18	13	0 0	17	11
18 4 22	1	20	14	2 37	19	13
18 8 43	2	21	16	5 19	20	14
18 13 5	3	22	17	7 55	22	15
18 17 26	4	23	19	10 29	23	16
18 21 48	5	24	20	13 2	25	17
18 26 9	6	25	22	15 36	26	18
18 30 30	7	26	23	18 6	28	19
18 34 51	8	27	25	20 34	29	20
18 39 11	9	29	27	22 59	II	21
18 43 31	10	♒	28	25 22	1	22
18 47 51	11	1	♓	27 42	2	23
18 52 11	12	2	2	29 58	4	24
18 56 31	13	3	3	2 ♉ 13	5	25
19 0 50	14	4	5	4 24	6	26
19 5 8	15	6	7	6 30	8	27
19 9 20	16	7	9	8 36	9	28
19 13 44	17	8	10	10 40	10	29
19 18 1	18	9	12	12 39	11	♋
19 22 18	19	10	14	14 37	12	1
19 26 34	20	12	16	16 28	13	2
19 30 50	21	13	18	18 17	14	3
19 35 5	22	14	19	20 3	16	4
19 39 20	23	15	21	21 48	17	5
19 43 34	24	16	23	23 29	18	6
19 47 47	25	18	25	25 9	19	7
19 52 0	26	19	27	26 45	20	8
19 56 12	27	20	28	28 18	21	9
20 0 24	28	21	♈	29 49	22	10
20 4 35	29	23	2	1 II 19	23	11
20 8 45	30	24	4	2 45	24	12

TABLE OF HOUSES FOR LONDON.

Lat. 51° 32'.

Right Ascen. of Meridian.	10	11	12	Ascend.	2	3
	Aquar.	Aquar.	Aries.	Gemini.	Gemini.	Cancer.
H. M. S.	0	0	0	0 0	0	0
20 8 45	0	24	4	2 45	24	12
20 12 54	1	25	6	4 9	25	12
20 17 3	2	27	7	5 32	26	13
20 21 11	3	28	9	6 53	27	14
20 25 19	4	29	11	8 12	28	15
20 29 26	5	♓	13	9 27	29	16
20 33 31	6	2	14	10 43	♋	17
20 37 37	7	3	16	11 57	1	18
20 41 41	8	4	18	13 8	2	19
20 45 45	9	6	19	14 18	3	20
20 49 38	10	7	21	15 25	3	21
20 53 51	11	8	23	16 33	4	21
20 57 52	12	9	24	17 39	5	22
21 1 53	13	11	26	18 44	6	23
21 5 53	14	12	28	19 48	7	24
21 9 53	15	13	29	20 51	8	25
21 13 52	16	15	♉	21 53	9	26
21 17 50	17	16	2	22 53	10	27
21 21 47	18	17	4	23 52	10	28
21 25 44	19	19	5	24 51	11	28
21 29 40	20	20	7	25 48	12	29
21 33 35	21	22	8	26 44	13	♌
21 37 29	22	23	10	27 40	14	1
21 41 23	23	24	11	28 34	15	2
21 45 16	24	25	13	29 29	15	3
21 49 9	25	26	14	0♋22	16	4
21 53 1	26	28	15	1 15	17	4
21 56 52	27	29	16	2 7	18	5
22 0 43	28	♈	18	2 57	19	6
22 4 33	29	2	19	3 49	19	7
22 8 23	30	3	20	4 38	20	8

TABLE OF HOUSES FOR LONDON.

Lat. 51° 32'.

Right Ascen. of Meridian.	10	11	12	Ascend.	2	3
	Pisces.	Aries.	Taurus.	Cancer.	Cancer.	Leo.
H. M. S.	0	0	0	0 ′	0	0
22 8 23	0	3	20	4 38	20	8
22 12 12	1	4	21	5 28	21	8
22 16 0	2	6	23	6 16	22	9
22 19 48	3	7	24	7 5	23	10
22 23 35	4	8	25	7 53	23	11
22 27 22	5	9	26	8 42	24	12
22 31 8	6	10	28	9 29	25	13
22 34 54	7	12	29	10 16	26	14
22 38 40	8	13	♊	11 1	26	14
22 42 25	9	14	1	11 46	27	15
22 46 9	10	15	2	12 31	28	16
22 49 53	11	17	3	13 16	29	17
22 53 37	12	18	4	14 1	29	18
22 57 20	13	19	5	14 48	♌	19
23 1 3	14	20	6	15 29	1	19
23 4 46	15	21	7	16 11	2	20
23 8 28	16	23	8	16 55	2	21
23 12 10	17	24	9	17 38	3	22
23 15 52	18	25	10	18 20	4	23
23 19 34	19	26	11	19 3	5	24
23 23 15	20	27	12	19 46	5	24
23 26 56	21	29	13	20 26	6	25
23 30 37	22	♉	14	21 8	7	26
23 34 18	23	1	15	21 50	7	27
23 37 58	24	2	16	22 31	8	28
23 41 39	25	3	17	23 12	9	28
23 45 19	26	4	18	23 53	9	29
23 49 0	27	5	19	24 33	10	♍
23 51 40	28	6	20	25 15	11	1
23 56 20	29	8	21	25 56	12	2
24 0 0	30	9	22	26 36	12	3

DECLINATION.

CANCER.	\multicolumn{16}{c	}{Degrees of North Latitude.}	GEMINI.
	\multicolumn{2}{c	}{0°}	\multicolumn{2}{c	}{1°}	\multicolumn{2}{c	}{2°}	\multicolumn{2}{c	}{3°}	\multicolumn{2}{c	}{4°}	\multicolumn{2}{c	}{5°}	\multicolumn{2}{c	}{6°}	\multicolumn{2}{c	}{7°}	
D.	D.	M.	D.	M	D.	M.	D.	M.	D.	M.	D.	M.	D.	M.	D.	M.	°
0	23	28	24	28	25	28	26	28	27	28	28	28	29	28	30	28	30
1	23	28	24	28	25	28	26	28	27	28	28	28	29	28	30	28	29
2	23	27	24	27	25	27	26	27	27	27	28	27	29	27	30	27	28
3	23	26	24	26	25	26	26	26	27	26	28	26	29	26	30	26	27
4	23	24	24	24	25	24	26	24	27	24	28	24	29	24	30	24	26
5	23	22	24	22	25	22	26	22	27	22	28	22	29	22	30	22	25
6	23	20	24	19	25	19	26	19	27	19	28	19	29	19	30	19	24
7	23	17	24	16	25	16	26	16	27	16	28	16	29	16	30	16	23
8	23	13	24	13	25	13	26	13	27	13	28	13	29	13	30	13	22
9	23	10	24	9	25	9	26	9	27	9	28	9	29	9	30	9	21
10	23	5	24	5	25	5	26	5	27	5	28	5	29	5	30	5	20
11	23	1	24	1	25	1	26	1	27	0	28	0	29	0	30	0	19
12	22	56	23	56	24	56	25	56	26	56	27	56	28	56	29	55	18
13	22	50	23	50	24	50	25	50	26	50	27	50	28	50	29	48	17
14	22	44	23	44	24	43	25	43	26	43	27	42	28	42	29	41	16
15	22	37	23	37	24	36	25	36	26	36	27	35	28	35	29	34	15
16	22	30	23	30	24	29	25	29	26	29	27	28	28	28	29	27	14
17	22	23	23	23	24	22	25	22	26	21	27	20	28	19	29	18	13
18	22	15	23	15	24	14	25	14	26	13	27	12	28	11	29	10	12
19	22	7	23	7	24	6	25	6	26	5	27	4	28	3	29	2	11
20	21	58	22	58	23	57	24	56	25	55	26	54	27	53	28	52	10
21	21	49	22	49	23	48	24	47	25	46	26	45	27	44	28	43	9
22	21	40	22	40	23	39	24	38	25	37	26	36	27	35	28	35	8
23	21	30	22	30	23	29	24	28	25	27	26	26	27	25	28	25	7
24	21	20	22	19	23	18	24	17	25	16	26	15	27	14	28	13	6
25	21	9	22	8	23	7	24	6	25	5	26	4	27	3	28	2	5
26	20	58	21	56	22	55	23	54	24	53	25	52	26	51	27	50	4
27	20	47	21	44	22	43	23	42	24	41	25	40	26	39	27	38	3
28	20	35	21	32	22	31	23	30	24	29	25	28	26	26	27	25	2
29	20	23	21	30	22	19	23	18	24	17	25	16	26	14	27	13	1
30	20	10	21	8	22	6	23	5	24	4	25	2	26	0	26	59	0

DECLINATION.

LEO.	Degrees of North Latitude.														TAURUS.
	0°		1°		2°		3°		4°		5°		6°		7°	
D	D.	M.	D.	M.	D.	M.	D.	M.	D.	M	D.	M.	D.	M.	D.	M.	D.
0	20	10	21	8	22	6	23	5	24	4	25	2	26	0	26	59	30
1	19	57	20	56	21	54	22	53	23	51	24	50	25	48	26	46	29
2	19	44	20	42	21	41	22	39	23	37	24	36	25	34	26	32	28
3	19	31	20	28	21	27	22	25	23	23	24	22	25	20	26	18	27
4	19	17	20	14	21	13	22	11	23	9	24	8	25	6	26	4	26
5	19	2	20	0	20	59	21	57	22	55	23	53	24	51	25	49	25
6	18	48	19	46	20	44	21	42	22	40	23	38	24	36	25	34	24
7	18	33	19	31	20	29	21	27	22	25	23	23	24	21	25	19	23
8	18	17	19	15	20	13	21	11	22	9	23	7	24	5	25	3	22
9	18	2	18	59	19	57	20	55	21	53	22	51	23	49	24	46	21
10	17	46	18	43	19	41	20	38	21	36	22	34	23	31	24	28	20
11	17	29	18	26	19	24	20	22	21	19	22	17	23	14	24	11	19
12	17	13	18	9	19	7	20	5	21	2	22	0	22	57	23	54	18
13	16	56	17	52	18	50	19	47	20	44	21	42	22	39	23	36	17
14	16	39	17	35	18	33	19	30	20	27	21	25	22	22	23	19	16
15	16	21	17	18	18	15	19	12	20	9	21	7	22	4	23	1	15
16	16	3	17	0	17	57	18	54	19	51	20	49	21	46	22	43	14
17	15	45	16	42	17	39	18	36	19	33	20	30	21	27	22	24	13
18	15	27	16	23	17	20	18	17	19	14	20	11	21	8	22	5	12
19	15	9	16	4	17	1	17	58	18	55	19	52	20	49	21	46	11
20	14	50	15	45	16	41	17	38	18	35	19	32	20	29	21	26	10
21	14	31	15	26	16	22	17	19	18	16	19	13	20	10	21	7	9
22	14	11	15	7	16	3	17	0	17	56	18	53	19	50	20	47	8
23	13	52	14	47	15	43	16	40	17	36	18	33	19	29	20	26	7
24	13	32	14	27	15	23	16	19	17	15	18	12	19	8	20	5	6
25	13	12	14	7	15	3	16	0	16	56	17	53	18	49	19	45	5
26	12	52	13	47	14	43	15	39	16	35	17	32	18	28	19	24	4
27	12	32	13	27	14	23	15	19	16	15	17	12	18	8	19	4	3
28	12	11	13	6	14	2	14	58	15	54	16	51	17	47	18	43	2
29	11	50	12	45	13	41	14	37	15	33	16	30	17	26	18	22	1
30	11	29	12	24	13	20	14	16	15	12	16	8	17	4	18	0	0

DECLINATION.

VIRGO.	\multicolumn{16}{c	}{Degrees of North Latitude.}	ARIES.
	\multicolumn{2}{c	}{0°}	\multicolumn{2}{c	}{1°}	\multicolumn{2}{c	}{2°}	\multicolumn{2}{c	}{3°}	\multicolumn{2}{c	}{4°}	\multicolumn{2}{c	}{5°}	\multicolumn{2}{c	}{6°}	\multicolumn{2}{c	}{7°}	0
D.	D.	M.	D.	M.	D.	M.	D.	M.	D.	M.	D.	M.	D.	M.	D.	M.	
0	11	29	12	24	13	20	14	16	15	12	16	8	17	4	18	0	30
1	11	8	12	4	13	0	13	56	14	51	15	47	16	43	17	39	29
2	10	46	11	42	12	38	13	33	14	29	15	25	16	21	17	17	28
3	10	25	11	21	12	17	13	12	14	8	15	4	16	0	16	56	27
4	10	3	10	59	11	55	12	51	13	47	14	43	15	39	16	35	26
5	9	41	10	39	11	35	12	30	13	26	14	22	15	18	16	14	25
6	9	19	10	15	11	11	12	6	13	2	13	58	14	54	15	50	24
7	8	57	9	53	10	49	11	44	12	40	13	35	14	31	15	26	23
8	8	35	9	31	10	27	11	22	12	18	13	13	14	9	15	4	22
9	8	12	9	8	10	4	10	59	11	54	12	49	13	44	14	39	21
10	7	50	8	46	9	41	10	36	11	31	12	26	13	21	14	16	20
11	7	27	8	22	9	17	10	12	11	7	12	2	12	57	13	52	19
12	7	5	8	0	8	55	9	50	10	45	11	40	12	35	13	30	18
13	6	41	7	36	8	31	9	26	10	21	11	16	12	11	13	6	17
14	6	18	7	13	8	8	9	3	9	58	10	53	11	48	12	43	16
15	5	55	6	51	7	46	8	41	9	36	10	31	11	26	12	21	15
16	5	32	6	28	7	23	8	18	9	13	10	8	11	3	11	58	14
17	5	8	6	4	6	59	7	54	8	49	9	44	10	39	11	34	13
18	4	45	5	41	6	36	7	31	8	26	9	21	10	16	11	11	12
19	4	21	5	17	6	12	7	7	8	2	8	57	9	52	10	47	11
20	3	58	4	54	5	49	6	44	7	39	8	34	9	29	10	24	10
21	3	34	4	30	5	25	6	20	7	15	8	10	9	5	10	0	9
22	3	11	4	7	5	2	5	57	6	52	7	47	8	42	9	37	8
23	2	47	3	43	4	38	5	33	6	28	7	23	8	18	9	13	7
24	2	23	3	19	4	14	5	9	6	4	6	59	7	54	8	49	6
25	2	0	2	55	3	50	4	45	5	40	6	35	7	30	8	25	5
26	1	36	2	31	3	26	4	21	5	16	6	11	7	6	8	1	4
27	1	12	2	7	3	2	3	57	4	52	5	47	6	42	7	37	3
28	0	48	1	48	2	43	3	38	4	33	5	23	6	18	7	13	2
29	0	24	1	19	2	14	3	9	4	4	4	59	5	54	6	49	1
30	0	0	0	55	1	50	2	45	3	40	4	35	5	30	6	25	0

DECLINATION.

<table>
<tr><th rowspan="2">LIBRA.</th><th colspan="8">DEGREES OF NORTH LATITUDE.</th><th rowspan="2">PISCES.</th></tr>
<tr><th>0°
0</th><th>0°
1</th><th>0°
2</th><th>0°
3</th><th>0°
4</th><th>0°
5</th><th>0°
6</th><th>0°
7</th></tr>
<tr><td>D</td><td>D. M.</td><td>D. M.</td><td>D. M.</td><td>D. M.</td><td>D. M.</td><td>D. M.</td><td>D. M.</td><td>D. M.</td><td>D.</td></tr>
<tr><td>0</td><td>0 0</td><td>0 55</td><td>1 50</td><td>2 45</td><td>3 40</td><td>4 35</td><td>5 30</td><td>6 25</td><td>30</td></tr>
<tr><td>1</td><td>0 24</td><td>0 31</td><td>1 27</td><td>2 21</td><td>3 16</td><td>4 11</td><td>5 6</td><td>6 1</td><td>29</td></tr>
<tr><td>2</td><td>0 48</td><td>0 7</td><td>1 3</td><td>1 57</td><td>2 52</td><td>3 47</td><td>4 42</td><td>5 37</td><td>28</td></tr>
<tr><td>3</td><td>1 12</td><td>0 17</td><td>0 39</td><td>1 34</td><td>2 29</td><td>3 24</td><td>4 19</td><td>5 14</td><td>27</td></tr>
<tr><td>4</td><td>1 36</td><td>0 41</td><td>0 15</td><td>1 10</td><td>2 5</td><td>3 0</td><td>3 55</td><td>4 50</td><td>26</td></tr>
<tr><td>5</td><td>2 0</td><td>1 5</td><td>0 10</td><td>0 46</td><td>1 41</td><td>2 36</td><td>3 31</td><td>4 26</td><td>25</td></tr>
<tr><td>6</td><td>2 23</td><td>1 28</td><td>0 33</td><td>0 22</td><td>1 17</td><td>2 12</td><td>3 7</td><td>4 2</td><td>24</td></tr>
<tr><td>7</td><td>2 47</td><td>1 52</td><td>0 57</td><td>0 2</td><td>0 53</td><td>1 48</td><td>2 43</td><td>3 34</td><td>23</td></tr>
<tr><td>8</td><td>3 11</td><td>2 15</td><td>1 21</td><td>0 26</td><td>0 29</td><td>1 25</td><td>2 20</td><td>3 15</td><td>22</td></tr>
<tr><td>9</td><td>3 34</td><td>2 36</td><td>1 44</td><td>0 49</td><td>0 6</td><td>1 2</td><td>1 57</td><td>2 52</td><td>21</td></tr>
<tr><td>10</td><td>3 58</td><td>3 3</td><td>2 8</td><td>1 13</td><td>0 18</td><td>0 38</td><td>1 33</td><td>2 28</td><td>20</td></tr>
<tr><td>11</td><td>4 21</td><td>3 26</td><td>2 31</td><td>1 36</td><td>0 41</td><td>0 14</td><td>1 9</td><td>2 4</td><td>19</td></tr>
<tr><td>12</td><td>4 45</td><td>3 50</td><td>2 55</td><td>2 0</td><td>1 5</td><td>0 10</td><td>0 46</td><td>1 41</td><td>18</td></tr>
<tr><td>13</td><td>5 8</td><td>4 13</td><td>3 18</td><td>2 23</td><td>1 28</td><td>0 33</td><td>0 24</td><td>1 18</td><td>17</td></tr>
<tr><td>14</td><td>5 32</td><td>4 37</td><td>3 42</td><td>2 46</td><td>1 51</td><td>0 56</td><td>0 0</td><td>0 55</td><td>16</td></tr>
<tr><td>15</td><td>5 55</td><td>5 0</td><td>4 5</td><td>3 9</td><td>2 14</td><td>1 18</td><td>0 23</td><td>0 32</td><td>15</td></tr>
<tr><td>16</td><td>6 18</td><td>5 23</td><td>4 27</td><td>3 31</td><td>2 36</td><td>1 40</td><td>0 45</td><td>0 9</td><td>14</td></tr>
<tr><td>17</td><td>6 41</td><td>5 45</td><td>4 50</td><td>3 54</td><td>2 59</td><td>2 3</td><td>1 8</td><td>0 13</td><td>13</td></tr>
<tr><td>18</td><td>7 5</td><td>6 9</td><td>5 14</td><td>4 18</td><td>3 23</td><td>2 27</td><td>1 32</td><td>0 36</td><td>12</td></tr>
<tr><td>19</td><td>7 27</td><td>6 31</td><td>5 36</td><td>4 40</td><td>3 45</td><td>2 49</td><td>1 54</td><td>0 58</td><td>11</td></tr>
<tr><td>20</td><td>7 50</td><td>6 54</td><td>5 58</td><td>5 2</td><td>4 6</td><td>3 10</td><td>2 15</td><td>1 19</td><td>10</td></tr>
<tr><td>21</td><td>8 12</td><td>7 16</td><td>6 20</td><td>5 24</td><td>4 28</td><td>3 32</td><td>2 37</td><td>1 41</td><td>9</td></tr>
<tr><td>22</td><td>8 35</td><td>7 39</td><td>6 43</td><td>5 47</td><td>4 51</td><td>3 56</td><td>3 0</td><td>2 4</td><td>8</td></tr>
<tr><td>23</td><td>8 57</td><td>8 1</td><td>7 5</td><td>6 9</td><td>5 13</td><td>4 18</td><td>3 22</td><td>2 26</td><td>7</td></tr>
<tr><td>24</td><td>9 19</td><td>8 23</td><td>7 27</td><td>6 31</td><td>5 35</td><td>4 40</td><td>3 45</td><td>2 49</td><td>6</td></tr>
<tr><td>25</td><td>9 41</td><td>8 45</td><td>7 49</td><td>6 53</td><td>5 58</td><td>5 2</td><td>4 6</td><td>3 10</td><td>5</td></tr>
<tr><td>26</td><td>10 3</td><td>9 7</td><td>8 11</td><td>7 15</td><td>6 19</td><td>5 24</td><td>4 28</td><td>3 32</td><td>4</td></tr>
<tr><td>27</td><td>10 25</td><td>9 30</td><td>8 34</td><td>7 38</td><td>6 42</td><td>5 46</td><td>4 50</td><td>3 54</td><td>3</td></tr>
<tr><td>28</td><td>10 46</td><td>9 51</td><td>8 55</td><td>8 1</td><td>7 4</td><td>6 8</td><td>5 12</td><td>4 16</td><td>2</td></tr>
<tr><td>29</td><td>11 8</td><td>10 13</td><td>9 17</td><td>8 21</td><td>7 24</td><td>6 28</td><td>5 32</td><td>4 36</td><td>1</td></tr>
<tr><td>30</td><td>11 29</td><td>10 33</td><td>9 37</td><td>8 41</td><td>7 44</td><td>6 48</td><td>5 52</td><td>4 56</td><td>0</td></tr>
</table>

25

DECLINATION.

SCORPIO.	Degrees of North Latitude.														AQUARIUS
	0°0'		0°1'		0°2'		0°3'		0°4'		0°5'		0°6'		0°7'	
D.	D.	M.	D.	M	D.	M.	D.	M.	D.	M.	D.	M.	D.	M.	D.	M.	°
0	11	29	10	33	9	37	8	41	7	45	6	49	5	53	4	57	30
1	11	50	10	54	9	58	9	2	8	6	7	10	6	14	5	18	29
2	12	11	11	15	10	18	9	22	8	26	7	29	6	32	5	36	28
3	12	32	11	36	10	39	9	43	8	47	7	50	6	54	5	58	27
4	12	52	11	56	10	58	10	1	9	5	8	8	7	12	6	16	26
5	13	12	12	16	11	19	10	22	9	26	8	29	7	33	6	37	25
6	13	32	12	36	11	39	10	42	9	46	8	49	7	52	6	55	24
7	13	52	12	56	11	59	11	2	10	5	9	8	8	11	7	14	23
8	14	11	13	14	12	17	11	20	10	23	9	26	8	29	7	32	22
9	14	31	13	34	12	37	11	40	10	43	9	46	8	49	7	52	21
10	14	50	13	53	12	56	11	59	11	2	10	5	9	8	8	11	20
11	15	9	14	12	13	15	12	18	11	21	10	23	9	26	8	29	19
12	15	27	14	30	13	33	12	36	11	39	10	41	9	44	8	47	18
13	15	45	14	47	13	50	12	53	11	56	10	58	10	1	9	4	17
14	16	3	15	5	14	8	13	11	12	14	11	16	10	19	9	22	16
15	16	21	15	23	14	26	13	29	12	32	11	34	10	37	9	40	15
16	16	39	15	44	14	44	13	46	12	49	11	51	10	54	9	57	14
17	16	56	15	58	15	1	14	3	13	6	12	8	11	11	10	14	13
18	17	13	16	15	15	18	14	20	13	22	12	24	11	27	10	30	12
19	17	29	16	31	15	33	14	35	13	37	12	39	11	42	10	45	11
20	17	46	16	48	15	50	14	52	13	54	12	56	11	59	11	1	10
21	18	2	17	4	16	6	15	8	14	10	13	12	12	15	11	17	9
22	18	17	17	19	16	21	15	23	14	25	13	26	12	28	11	30	8
23	18	33	17	35	16	36	15	38	14	40	13	41	12	43	11	45	7
24	18	48	17	50	16	52	15	54	14	56	13	57	12	59	12	0	6
25	19	2	18	4	17	6	16	8	15	10	14	11	13	15	12	14	5
26	19	17	18	19	17	20	16	22	15	24	14	25	13	27	12	29	4
27	19	31	18	33	17	34	16	36	15	37	14	39	13	40	12	42	3
28	19	44	18	45	17	47	16	48	15	49	14	51	13	52	12	54	2
29	19	57	18	58	17	59	17	1	16	2	15	4	14	5	13	7	1
30	20	10	19	11	18	12	17	14	16	15	15	16	14	17	13	18	0

DECLINATION.

SAGITTARY.	Degrees of North Latitude.															CAPRICORN
	0°/0		0°/1		0°/2		0°/3		0°/4		0°/5		0°/6		0°/7		
D.	D.	M.	D.	M.	D.	M.	D.	M.	D.	M.	D.	M.	D.	M.	D.	M.	D.
0	20	10	19	11	18	12	17	14	16	15	15	16	14	17	13	18	30
1	20	23	19	24	18	25	17	26	16	27	15	29	14	30	13	31	29
2	20	35	19	36	18	37	17	38	16	39	15	41	14	42	13	43	28
3	20	47	19	48	18	49	17	50	16	52	15	53	14	54	13	55	27
4	20	58	19	59	19	0	18	1	17	2	16	3	15	5	14	6	26
5	21	9	20	10	19	11	18	12	17	12	16	14	15	15	14	16	25
6	21	20	20	21	19	22	18	23	17	24	16	25	15	25	14	26	24
7	21	30	20	31	19	32	18	33	17	34	16	34	15	35	14	36	23
8	21	40	20	41	19	42	18	43	17	44	16	43	15	44	14	44	22
9	21	49	20	50	19	51	18	52	17	53	16	53	15	54	14	54	21
10	21	58	20	59	20	0	19	1	18	2	17	2	16	2	15	3	20
11	22	7	21	8	20	9	19	10	18	11	17	11	16	11	15	12	19
12	22	15	21	16	20	17	19	18	18	19	17	19	16	19	15	20	18
13	22	23	21	24	20	25	19	25	18	26	17	26	16	26	15	27	17
14	22	30	21	31	20	32	19	32	18	33	17	33	16	33	15	34	16
15	22	37	21	37	20	37	19	37	18	38	17	38	16	38	15	39	15
16	22	44	21	44	20	44	19	40	18	45	17	45	16	45	15	46	14
17	22	50	21	50	20	50	19	50	18	51	17	51	16	51	15	52	13
18	22	56	21	56	20	56	19	56	18	57	17	57	16	57	15	58	12
19	23	1	22	1	21	1	20	1	19	2	18	2	17	2	16	2	11
20	23	5	22	5	21	5	20	5	19	5	18	5	17	5	16	5	10
21	23	10	22	9	21	9	20	9	19	9	18	9	17	9	16	9	9
22	23	13	22	13	21	13	20	13	19	13	18	13	17	13	16	13	8
23	23	17	22	16	21	16	20	16	19	16	18	16	17	16	16	16	7
24	23	20	22	19	21	19	20	19	19	19	18	19	17	19	16	19	6
25	23	22	22	22	21	22	20	22	19	22	18	22	17	22	16	22	5
26	23	24	22	25	21	25	20	25	19	25	18	25	17	25	16	25	4
27	23	26	22	26	21	26	20	26	19	26	18	26	17	26	16	26	3
28	23	27	22	27	21	27	20	27	19	27	18	27	17	27	16	27	2
29	23	28	22	28	21	28	20	28	19	28	18	28	17	28	16	28	1
30	23	28	22	28	21	28	20	28	19	28	18	28	17	28	16	28	0

DECLINATION.

CANCER.	Degrees of South Latitude.															GEMINI.
	0 0		0 1		0 2		0 3		0 4		0 5		0 6		0 7		
D.	D.	M.	D.	M.	D.	M.	D.	M.	D.	M.	D.	M.	D.	M.	D.	M.	D.
0	23	28	22	28	21	28	20	28	19	28	18	28	17	28	16	28	30
1	23	28	22	28	21	28	20	28	19	28	18	28	17	28	16	28	29
2	23	27	22	27	21	27	20	27	19	27	18	27	17	27	16	27	28
3	23	26	22	26	21	26	20	26	19	26	18	26	17	26	16	26	27
4	23	24	22	25	21	25	20	25	19	25	18	25	17	25	16	25	26
5	23	22	22	22	21	22	20	22	19	22	18	22	17	22	16	22	25
6	23	20	22	19	21	19	20	19	19	19	18	19	17	19	16	19	24
7	23	17	22	16	21	16	20	16	19	16	18	16	17	16	16	16	23
8	23	13	22	13	21	13	20	13	19	13	18	13	17	13	16	13	22
9	23	10	22	9	21	9	20	9	19	9	18	9	17	9	16	9	21
10	23	5	22	5	21	5	20	5	19	5	18	5	17	5	16	5	20
11	23	1	22	1	21	1	20	1	19	2	18	2	17	2	16	2	19
12	22	56	21	56	20	56	19	56	18	57	17	57	16	57	15	58	18
13	22	50	21	50	20	50	19	50	18	51	17	51	16	51	15	52	17
14	22	44	21	44	20	44	19	44	18	45	17	45	16	45	15	46	16
15	22	37	21	37	20	37	19	37	18	38	17	38	16	38	15	39	15
16	22	30	21	31	20	32	19	32	18	33	17	33	16	33	15	34	14
17	22	23	21	24	20	25	19	25	18	26	17	26	16	26	15	27	13
18	22	15	21	16	20	17	19	18	18	19	17	19	16	19	15	20	12
19	23	7	21	8	20	9	19	10	18	11	17	11	16	11	15	12	11
20	21	58	20	59	20	0	19	1	18	2	17	2	16	2	15	3	10
21	21	49	20	50	19	51	18	52	17	53	16	53	15	54	14	54	9
22	21	40	20	41	19	42	18	43	17	44	16	43	15	44	14	44	8
23	21	30	20	31	19	32	18	33	17	34	16	34	15	35	14	36	7
24	21	20	20	21	19	22	18	23	17	24	16	25	15	25	14	26	6
25	21	9	20	10	19	11	18	12	17	12	16	14	15	15	14	16	5
26	20	58	19	59	19	0	18	1	17	2	16	3	15	5	14	6	4
27	20	47	19	48	18	49	17	50	16	52	15	53	14	54	13	55	3
28	20	35	19	36	18	37	17	38	16	39	15	41	14	42	13	43	2
29	20	23	19	24	18	25	17	26	16	27	15	29	14	30	13	31	1
30	20	10	19	11	18	12	17	14	16	15	15	16	14	17	13	18	0

28

DECLINATION.

LEO.	Degrees of South Latitude.														TAURUS.
	0°		1°		2°		3°		4°		5°		6°		7°	
D.	D.	M.	D.	M.	D.	M.	D.	M.	D.	M.	D.	M.	D.	M.	D.	M.	°
0	20	10	19	11	18	12	17	14	16	15	15	16	14	17	13	18	30
1	19	57	18	58	17	59	17	1	16	2	15	14	14	5	13	7	29
2	19	44	18	45	17	47	16	48	15	49	14	51	13	52	12	54	28
3	19	31	18	33	17	34	16	36	15	37	14	39	13	40	12	42	27
4	19	17	18	19	17	20	16	22	15	24	14	25	13	27	12	29	26
5	19	2	18	4	17	6	16	8	15	10	14	11	13	13	12	14	25
6	18	48	17	50	16	52	15	54	14	56	13	57	12	59	12	0	24
7	18	33	17	35	16	36	15	38	14	40	13	41	12	43	11	45	23
8	18	17	17	19	16	21	15	23	14	25	13	26	12	28	11	30	22
9	18	2	17	4	16	6	15	8	14	10	13	12	12	15	11	17	21
10	17	46	16	48	15	50	14	52	13	54	12	56	11	59	11	1	20
11	17	29	16	31	15	33	14	35	13	37	12	39	11	42	10	45	19
12	17	13	16	15	15	18	14	20	13	22	12	24	11	27	10	30	18
13	16	56	15	58	15	1	14	3	13	6	12	8	11	11	10	14	17
14	16	39	15	44	14	44	13	46	12	49	11	51	10	54	9	57	16
15	16	21	15	23	14	26	13	29	12	32	11	34	10	37	9	40	15
16	16	3	15	5	14	8	13	11	12	14	11	16	10	19	9	22	14
17	15	45	14	47	13	50	12	53	11	56	10	58	10	1	9	4	13
18	15	27	14	30	13	33	12	36	11	39	10	41	9	44	8	47	12
19	15	9	14	12	13	15	12	18	11	21	10	23	9	26	8	29	11
20	14	50	13	53	12	56	11	59	11	2	10	5	9	8	8	11	10
21	14	31	13	34	12	37	11	40	10	43	9	46	8	49	7	52	9
22	14	11	13	14	12	17	11	20	10	23	9	26	8	29	7	32	8
23	13	52	12	56	11	59	11	2	10	5	9	8	8	11	7	14	7
24	13	32	12	36	11	39	10	42	9	46	8	49	7	52	6	55	6
25	13	12	12	16	11	19	10	22	9	26	8	29	7	33	6	37	5
26	12	52	11	56	10	58	10	1	9	5	8	8	7	12	6	16	4
27	12	32	11	36	10	39	9	43	8	47	7	50	6	54	5	58	3
28	12	11	11	15	10	18	9	22	8	26	7	29	6	32	5	36	2
29	11	50	10	54	9	58	9	2	8	6	7	10	6	14	5	18	1
30	11	29	10	33	9	37	8	41	7	45	6	49	5	53	4	57	0

29

DECLINATION.

VIRGO.	\multicolumn{8}{c	}{Degrees of South Latitude.}	ARIES.
	0°0	0°1	0°2	0°3	0°4	0°5	0°6	0°7	
D.	D. M.	D. M.	D. M.	D. M.	D. M.	D. M.	D. M.	D. M.	D.
0	11 29	10 33	9 37	8 41	7 45	6 49	4 53	5 57	30
1	11 8	10 13	9 17	8 21	7 24	6 28	5 32	4 36	29
2	10 46	9 51	8 55	8 0	7 4	6 8	5 12	4 16	28
3	10 25	9 30	8 34	7 38	6 42	5 46	4 50	3 54	27
4	10 3	9 7	8 11	7 15	6 19	5 24	4 28	3 32	26
5	9 41	8 45	7 49	6 53	6 57	5 2	4 6	3 10	25
6	9 19	8 23	7 27	6 31	5 35	4 40	3 45	2 49	24
7	8 57	8 1	7 5	6 9	5 13	4 18	3 22	2 26	23
8	8 35	7 39	6 43	5 47	4 51	3 56	3 0	2 4	22
9	8 12	7 16	6 20	5 24	4 28	3 32	2 37	1 41	21
10	7 50	6 54	5 58	5 2	4 6	3 10	2 15	1 19	20
11	7 27	6 31	5 36	4 40	3 45	2 49	1 54	0 58	19
12	7 5	6 9	5 14	4 18	3 23	2 27	1 32	0 36	18
13	6 41	5 45	4 50	3 54	2 59	2 3	1 8	0 13	17
14	6 18	5 22	4 27	3 31	2 36	1 40	0 45	0 9	16
15	5 55	5 0	4 5	3 9	2 14	1 18	0 23	0 32	15
16	5 32	4 37	3 42	2 46	1 51	0 56	0 0	0 55	14
17	5 8	4 13	3 18	2 23	1 28	0 33	0 24	1 19	13
18	4 45	3 50	2 55	2 0	1 5	0 14	0 46	1 41	12
19	4 21	3 26	2 31	1 36	0 41	0 14	1 9	2 4	11
20	3 58	3 3	2 8	1 13	0 18	0 38	1 33	2 28	10
21	3 34	2 39	1 44	0 49	0 6	1 2	1 57	2 52	9
22	3 11	2 16	1 21	0 26	0 29	1 25	2 20	3 15	8
23	2 47	1 52	0 57	0 2	0 53	1 48	2 43	3 38	7
24	2 23	1 28	0 33	0 22	1 17	2 12	3 7	4 2	6
25	2 0	1 5	0 10	0 46	1 41	2 36	3 31	4 26	5
26	1 36	0 41	0 15	1 10	2 5	3 0	3 55	4 50	4
27	1 12	0 17	0 39	1 34	2 29	3 24	4 19	5 14	3
28	0 48	0 7	1 3	1 57	2 52	3 47	4 42	5 37	2
29	0 24	0 31	1 27	2 21	3 16	4 11	5 6	6 1	1
30	0 0	0 55	1 50	2 45	3 40	4 35	5 30	6 25	0

NORTH. / SOUTH. / NORTH.

DECLINATION.

LIBRA	\multicolumn{14}{c	}{Degrees of South Latitude.}	PISCES
	\multicolumn{2}{c	}{0°0′}	\multicolumn{2}{c	}{0°1′}	\multicolumn{2}{c	}{0°2′}	\multicolumn{2}{c	}{0°3′}	\multicolumn{2}{c	}{0°4′}	\multicolumn{2}{c	}{0°5′}	\multicolumn{2}{c	}{0°6′}	\multicolumn{2}{c	}{0°7′}	
D.	D.	M.	D.	M.	D.	M.	D.	M.	D.	M.	D.	M.	D.	M.	D.	M.	D.
0	0	0	0	55	1	50	2	45	3	40	4	35	5	30	6	25	30
1	0	24	1	19	2	14	3	9	4	4	4	59	5	55	6	49	29
2	0	48	1	48	2	43	3	38	4	33	5	23	6	18	7	13	28
3	1	12	2	7	3	2	3	57	4	52	5	47	6	42	7	37	27
4	1	36	2	31	3	26	4	21	5	16	6	11	7	6	8	1	26
5	2	0	2	55	3	50	4	45	5	40	6	35	7	30	8	25	25
6	2	23	3	19	4	14	5	9	6	4	6	59	7	54	8	49	24
7	2	47	3	43	4	38	5	33	6	28	7	23	8	18	9	13	23
8	3	11	4	7	5	2	5	57	6	52	7	47	8	42	9	37	22
9	3	34	4	30	5	25	6	20	7	15	8	10	9	5	10	0	21
10	3	58	4	54	5	49	6	44	7	39	8	34	9	29	10	24	20
11	4	21	5	17	6	12	7	7	8	2	8	57	9	52	10	47	19
12	4	45	5	41	6	36	7	31	8	26	9	21	10	16	11	11	18
13	5	8	6	4	6	59	7	54	8	49	9	44	10	39	11	34	17
14	5	32	6	28	7	23	8	18	9	13	10	8	11	3	11	58	16
15	5	55	6	51	7	46	8	41	9	30	10	31	11	26	12	21	15
16	6	18	7	13	8	8	9	3	9	58	10	53	11	48	12	43	14
17	6	41	7	36	8	31	9	26	10	21	11	16	12	11	13	6	13
18	7	5	8	0	8	55	9	50	10	45	11	40	12	35	13	30	12
19	7	27	8	22	9	17	10	12	11	7	12	2	12	57	13	52	11
20	7	50	8	46	9	41	10	36	11	31	12	26	13	21	14	16	10
21	8	12	9	8	10	4	10	59	11	54	12	49	13	44	14	39	9
22	8	35	9	31	10	27	11	22	12	18	13	13	14	9	15	4	8
23	8	57	9	53	10	49	11	44	12	40	13	35	14	31	15	26	7
24	9	19	10	15	11	11	12	6	13	2	13	58	14	54	15	50	6
25	9	41	10	39	11	35	12	30	13	26	14	22	15	18	16	14	5
26	10	3	10	59	11	55	12	51	13	47	14	43	15	39	16	35	4
27	10	25	11	21	12	17	13	12	14	8	15	4	16	0	16	56	3
28	10	46	11	42	12	38	13	33	14	29	15	25	16	21	17	17	2
29	11	8	12	4	13	0	13	56	14	51	15	47	16	43	17	39	1
30	11	29	12	24	13	20	14	16	15	12	16	8	17	4	18	0	0

DECLINATION.

SCORPIO.	\multicolumn{14}{c}{Degrees of South Latitude.}	AQUARIUS
	\multicolumn{2}{c}{0°0'}	\multicolumn{2}{c}{0°1'}	\multicolumn{2}{c}{0°2'}	\multicolumn{2}{c}{0°3'}	\multicolumn{2}{c}{0°4'}	\multicolumn{2}{c}{0°5'}	\multicolumn{2}{c}{0°6'}	\multicolumn{2}{c}{0°7'}	
D.	D.	M.	D.	M.	D.	M.	D.	M.	D.	M.	D.	M.	D.	M.	D.	M.	D.
0	11	29	12	24	13	20	14	16	15	12	16	8	17	4	18	0	30
1	11	50	12	45	13	41	14	37	15	33	16	30	17	26	18	22	29
2	12	11	13	6	14	2	14	58	15	54	16	51	17	47	18	43	28
3	12	32	13	27	14	23	15	19	16	15	17	12	18	8	19	4	27
4	12	52	13	47	14	43	15	39	16	35	17	32	18	28	19	24	26
5	13	12	14	7	15	3	16	0	16	56	17	53	18	49	19	45	25
6	13	32	14	27	15	23	16	19	17	15	18	12	19	8	20	5	24
7	13	52	14	47	15	43	16	40	17	36	18	33	19	29	20	26	23
8	14	11	15	7	16	3	17	0	17	56	18	53	19	50	20	47	22
9	14	31	15	26	16	22	17	19	18	16	19	13	20	10	21	7	21
10	14	50	15	45	16	41	17	38	18	35	19	32	20	29	21	26	20
11	15	9	16	4	17	1	17	58	18	55	19	52	20	49	21	46	19
12	15	27	16	23	17	20	18	17	19	14	20	11	21	8	22	5	18
13	15	45	16	42	17	39	18	36	19	33	20	30	21	27	22	24	17
14	16	3	17	0	17	57	18	54	19	51	20	49	21	46	22	43	16
15	16	21	17	18	18	15	19	12	20	9	21	7	22	4	23	1	15
16	16	39	17	35	18	33	19	30	20	27	21	25	22	22	23	19	14
17	16	56	17	52	18	50	19	47	20	44	21	42	22	39	23	36	13
18	17	13	18	9	19	7	20	5	21	2	22	0	22	57	23	54	12
19	17	29	18	26	19	24	20	22	21	19	22	17	23	14	24	11	11
20	17	46	18	43	19	41	20	38	21	36	22	34	23	31	24	28	10
21	18	2	18	59	19	57	20	55	21	53	22	51	23	49	24	46	9
22	18	17	19	15	20	13	21	1	22	9	23	7	24	5	25	3	8
23	18	33	19	31	20	29	21	27	22	25	23	23	24	21	25	19	7
24	18	48	19	46	20	44	21	42	22	40	23	38	24	36	25	34	6
25	19	2	20	0	20	59	21	57	22	55	23	53	24	51	25	49	5
26	19	17	20	14	21	13	22	11	23	9	24	8	25	6	26	4	4
27	19	31	20	28	21	27	22	25	23	23	24	22	25	20	26	18	3
28	19	44	20	42	21	41	22	39	23	37	24	37	25	34	26	32	2
29	19	57	20	56	21	54	22	53	23	51	24	50	25	48	26	46	1
30	20	10	21	8	22	6	23	5	24	4	25	2	26	0	26	59	0

DECLINATION.

SAGITTARY	Degrees of South Latitude.															CAPRICORN
	0° 0'		0° 1'		0° 2'		0° 3'		0° 4'		0° 5'		0° 6'		0° 7'		
D.	D.	M.	D.	M.	D.	M.	D.	M.	D.	M.	D.	M.	D.	M.	D.	M.	D.
0	20	10	21	8	22	6	23	5	24	4	25	2	26	0	26	59	30
1	20	23	21	20	22	19	23	18	24	17	25	16	26	14	27	13	29
2	20	35	21	32	22	31	23	30	24	29	25	28	26	26	27	25	28
3	20	47	21	44	22	43	23	42	24	41	25	40	26	39	27	38	27
4	20	58	21	56	22	55	23	54	24	53	25	52	26	51	27	50	26
5	21	9	22	8	22	7	24	6	25	5	26	4	27	3	28	2	25
6	21	20	22	19	23	18	24	17	25	16	26	15	27	14	28	13	24
7	21	30	22	30	23	29	24	28	25	27	26	26	27	25	28	25	23
8	21	40	22	40	23	39	24	38	25	57	26	36	27	35	28	35	22
9	21	49	22	49	23	48	24	47	25	46	26	45	27	44	28	43	21
10	21	58	22	58	23	57	24	56	25	55	26	54	27	53	28	52	20
11	22	7	23	7	24	6	25	6	26	5	27	4	28	3	29	2	19
12	22	15	23	50	24	14	25	14	26	13	27	12	28	11	29	10	18
13	22	23	23	23	24	22	25	22	26	21	27	20	28	19	29	18	17
14	22	30	23	30	24	29	25	29	26	29	27	28	28	28	29	27	16
15	22	37	23	37	24	36	25	36	26	36	27	35	28	35	29	34	15
16	22	44	23	44	24	43	25	43	26	43	27	42	28	42	29	41	14
17	22	50	23	50	24	50	25	50	26	50	27	50	28	50	29	48	13
18	22	56	23	56	24	56	25	56	26	56	27	56	28	56	29	55	12
19	23	1	24	1	25	1	26	1	27	0	28	0	29	0	30	0	11
20	23	5	24	5	25	5	26	5	27	5	28	5	29	5	30	5	10
21	23	10	24	9	25	9	26	9	27	9	28	9	29	9	30	9	9
22	23	13	24	13	25	13	26	13	27	13	28	13	29	13	30	13	8
23	23	17	24	16	25	16	26	16	27	16	28	16	29	16	30	16	7
24	23	20	24	19	25	19	26	19	27	19	28	19	29	19	30	19	6
25	23	22	24	22	25	22	26	22	27	22	28	22	29	22	30	22	5
26	23	24	24	24	25	24	26	24	27	24	28	24	29	24	30	24	4
27	23	26	24	26	25	26	26	26	27	26	28	26	29	26	30	26	3
28	23	27	24	27	25	27	26	27	27	27	28	27	29	27	30	27	2
29	23	28	24	28	25	28	26	28	27	28	28	28	29	28	30	28	1
30	23	28	24	28	25	28	26	28	27	28	28	28	29	28	30	28	0

38

RIGHT ASCENSION.

(N.B. For *Libra* add 180°: when the amount exceeds 360° subtract that sum.)

Aries, with *North* Latitude.—*Libra* with *South* Latitude.

	0° 0		0° 1		0° 2		0° 3		0° 4		0° 5		0° 6		0° 7	
D.	D.	M.	D.	M.	D.	M.	D.	M.	D.	M.	D.	M.	D.	M.	D.	M.
0	0	0	359	37	359	13	358	49	358	25	358	1	357	37	357	13
1	0	55	0	0	0	8	359	44	359	20	358	58	358	32	358	8
2	1	50	1	27	1	3	0	39	0	15	359	51	359	27	359	3
3	2	45	2	22	1	58	1	34	1	10	0	46	0	22	359	58
4	3	40	3	17	2	53	2	29	2	5	1	41	1	17	0	53
5	4	35	4	12	3	48	3	24	3	0	2	36	2	12	1	48
6	5	30	5	7	4	43	4	19	3	55	3	31	3	7	2	43
7	6	25	6	2	5	38	5	14	4	50	4	26	4	2	3	38
8	7	21	6	57	6	33	6	9	5	45	5	21	4	57	4	32
9	8	16	7	52	7	28	7	4	6	40	6	16	5	52	5	28
10	9	11	8	47	8	23	7	59	7	35	7	11	6	47	6	23
11	10	6	9	42	9	18	8	55	8	31	8	7	7	43	7	19
12	11	2	10	38	10	14	9	51	9	27	9	3	8	39	8	15
13	11	57	11	33	11	9	10	46	10	22	9	58	9	34	9	10
14	12	53	12	29	12	5	11	42	11	18	10	54	10	30	10	6
15	13	48	13	25	13	1	12	38	12	14	11	50	11	26	11	2
16	14	44	14	20	13	57	13	34	13	10	11	46	12	22	11	58
17	15	40	15	16	14	53	14	30	14	6	13	42	13	18	12	54
18	16	31	16	12	15	49	15	26	15	2	14	39	14	15	13	51
19	17	35	17	8	16	45	16	22	15	58	15	35	15	11	14	47
20	18	27	18	4	17	41	17	18	16	54	16	31	16	7	15	44
21	19	23	19	0	18	37	18	14	17	51	17	28	17	4	16	41
22	20	20	19	56	19	33	19	11	18	48	18	25	18	1	17	38
23	21	16	20	53	20	30	20	6	19	45	19	22	18	58	18	35
24	22	12	21	50	21	27	21	5	20	42	20	19	19	55	19	32
25	23	9	22	47	22	24	22	2	21	39	21	16	20	52	20	29
26	24	6	23	44	23	21	22	59	22	36	22	13	21	50	21	27
27	25	2	24	41	24	19	23	57	23	34	23	11	22	48	22	25
28	25	59	25	38	25	16	24	54	24	31	24	9	23	46	23	23
29	26	57	26	35	26	13	25	51	25	29	25	7	24	44	24	21
30	27	54	27	33	27	11	26	49	26	27	26	5	25	42	25	19

RIGHT ASCENSION.

(N.B. For *Scorpio* add 180°.

Taurus with *North* Latitude.—*Scorpio* with *South* Latitude.															
	0°		1°		2°		3°		4°		5°		6°		7°
D.	D.	M.	D.	M.	D.	M.	D.	M.	D.	M.	D.	M.	D.	M.	D.	M.
0	27	54	27	33	27	11	26	49	26	27	26	5	25	42	25	19
1	28	51	28	30	28	8	27	47	27	25	27	3	26	40	26	17
2	29	49	29	27	29	6	28	45	28	23	28	1	27	38	27	16
3	30	46	30	25	30	4	29	43	29	21	28	59	28	37	28	15
4	31	44	31	23	31	2	30	41	30	19	29	58	29	36	29	14
5	32	42	32	21	32	0	31	39	31	18	30	57	30	35	30	13
6	33	40	33	20	32	59	32	38	32	17	31	56	31	34	31	12
7	34	38	34	18	33	58	33	37	33	16	32	55	32	33	32	12
8	35	37	35	17	34	57	34	36	34	15	33	54	33	33	33	12
9	36	36	36	16	35	56	35	36	35	15	34	54	34	33	34	12
10	37	34	37	15	36	55	36	35	36	15	35	54	35	33	35	12
11	38	33	38	14	37	54	37	35	37	15	36	54	36	33	36	13
12	39	33	39	14	38	54	38	35	38	15	37	55	37	34	37	14
13	40	32	40	13	39	54	39	35	39	15	38	56	38	35	38	15
14	41	31	41	13	40	54	40	35	40	16	39	57	39	36	39	16
15	42	31	42	13	41	54	41	36	41	17	40	58	40	38	40	18
16	43	31	43	13	42	54	42	36	42	18	41	59	41	39	41	19
17	44	31	44	13	43	55	43	37	43	19	43	0	42	40	42	21
18	45	31	45	14	44	56	44	38	44	20	44	1	43	42	43	23
19	46	32	46	14	45	57	45	39	45	21	45	3	44	44	44	25
20	47	32	47	15	46	58	46	40	46	23	46	5	45	46	45	28
21	48	33	48	16	47	59	47	42	47	25	47	7	46	49	46	31
22	49	34	49	17	49	0	48	44	48	27	48	9	47	52	47	34
23	50	35	50	18	50	2	49	46	49	29	49	12	48	55	48	37
24	51	36	51	20	51	4	50	48	50	32	50	15	49	58	49	41
25	52	38	52	22	52	6	51	51	51	35	51	18	51	2	50	45
26	53	40	53	24	53	9	52	54	52	38	52	22	52	6	51	49
27	54	42	54	27	54	12	53	57	53	42	53	25	53	10	52	54
28	55	44	55	29	55	15	55	0	54	45	54	30	54	14	53	58
29	56	46	56	32	56	18	56	3	55	49	55	34	55	18	55	3
30	57	48	57	35	57	21	57	7	56	53	56	38	56	23	56	8

35

RIGHT ASCENSION.

(N.B. For *Sagittary* add 180°.)

Gemini with *North* Latitude.—*Sagittary* with *South* Latitude.																
	0°0		0°1		0°2		0°3		0°4		0°5		0°6		0°7	
D.	D.	M.	D.	M.	D.	M.	D.	M.	D.	M.	D.	M.	D.	M.	D.	M.
0	57	48	57	35	57	21	57	7	56	53	56	38	56	23	56	8
1	58	51	58	38	58	24	58	10	57	57	57	42	57	28	57	13
2	59	53	59	41	59	27	59	14	59	1	58	47	58	33	58	19
3	60	56	60	44	60	31	60	18	60	5	59	52	59	38	59	25
4	61	59	61	47	61	35	61	22	61	10	60	57	60	44	60	31
5	63	3	62	51	62	39	62	27	62	15	62	2	61	50	61	37
6	64	6	63	55	63	43	63	32	63	20	63	8	62	56	62	44
7	65	9	64	59	64	47	64	37	64	25	64	13	64	2	63	50
8	66	13	66	3	65	52	65	42	65	30	65	19	65	8	64	56
9	67	17	67	7	66	57	66	47	66	36	66	25	66	14	66	3
10	68	21	68	11	68	2	67	52	67	42	67	31	67	21	67	10
11	69	25	69	16	69	7	68	57	68	48	68	38	68	28	68	18
12	70	29	70	21	70	12	70	3	69	54	69	45	69	35	69	26
13	71	34	71	26	71	17	71	9	71	0	70	51	70	42	70	33
14	72	38	72	31	72	22	72	15	72	6	71	58	71	49	71	41
15	73	43	73	36	73	28	73	21	73	13	73	5	72	57	72	49
16	74	47	74	41	74	33	74	27	74	19	74	12	74	4	73	57
17	75	52	75	46	75	39	75	33	75	26	75	19	75	12	75	5
18	76	57	76	51	76	45	76	39	76	33	76	27	76	20	76	14
19	78	2	77	56	77	51	77	45	77	40	77	34	77	28	77	22
20	79	7	79	2	78	57	78	52	78	47	78	41	78	36	78	30
21	80	12	80	8	80	3	79	59	79	54	79	49	79	44	79	39
22	81	17	81	13	81	9	81	5	80	1	80	56	80	52	80	48
23	82	22	82	18	82	15	82	11	82	8	82	4	82	0	81	57
24	83	28	83	24	83	21	83	18	83	15	83	11	83	9	83	6
25	84	33	84	30	84	27	84	25	84	22	84	20	84	17	84	15
26	85	38	85	36	85	33	85	32	85	39	85	28	85	25	85	24
27	86	44	86	42	86	40	86	39	86	37	86	36	86	34	86	33
28	87	49	87	48	87	46	87	46	87	44	87	44	87	42	87	42
29	88	55	88	54	88	53	88	53	88	52	88	52	88	51	88	51
30	90	0	90	0	90	0	90	0	90	0	90	0	90	0	90	0

RIGHT ASCENSION.

(N.B. For *Capricorn* add 180°).

Cancer with *North* Latitude.—*Capricorn* with *South* Latitude.

°	0		1		2		3		4		5		6		7	
.	D.	M.	D.	M.	D.	M.	D.	M.	D.	M.	D.	M.	D.	M.	D.	M
0	90	0	90	0	90	0	90	0	90	0	90	0	90	0	90	0
1	91	5	91	6	91	7	91	7	91	7	91	8	91	9	91	9
2	92	11	92	12	92	14	92	14	92	15	92	10	92	18	92	18
3	93	16	93	18	93	20	93	21	93	23	93	24	93	26	93	27
4	94	22	94	24	94	27	94	28	94	30	94	32	94	35	94	36
5	95	27	95	30	95	33	95	35	95	38	95	40	95	43	95	45
6	96	32	96	36	96	39	96	42	96	45	96	48	96	51	96	54
7	97	38	97	42	97	45	97	49	97	52	97	56	98	0	98	3
8	98	43	98	47	98	51	98	55	99	0	99	4	99	8	99	12
9	99	48	99	52	99	57	100	1	100	7	100	12	100	16	100	21
10	100	53	100	58	101	3	101	8	101	14	101	19	101	24	101	30
11	101	58	102	4	102	9	102	15	102	21	102	26	102	32	102	38
12	103	3	103	9	103	15	103	21	103	27	103	33	103	40	103	46
13	104	8	104	14	104	21	104	27	104	34	104	41	104	48	104	55
14	105	13	105	19	105	27	105	33	105	41	105	48	105	56	106	3
15	106	17	106	24	106	33	106	39	106	47	106	55	107	3	107	11
16	107	22	107	29	107	38	107	45	107	53	108	2	108	11	108	19
17	108	26	108	34	108	43	108	53	108	59	109	9	109	18	109	27
18	109	31	109	39	109	48	109	57	110	5	110	15	110	25	110	34
19	110	35	110	44	110	53	111	3	111	12	111	22	111	32	111	42
20	111	39	111	49	111	58	112	8	112	18	112	29	112	35	112	50
21	112	43	112	53	113	3	113	13	113	24	113	35	113	46	113	56
22	113	47	113	57	114	8	114	18	114	30	114	41	114	52	115	4
23	114	51	115	1	115	13	115	23	115	35	115	47	115	58	116	10
24	115	54	116	5	116	17	116	28	116	41	116	52	117	4	117	17
25	116	57	117	9	117	21	117	33	117	46	117	58	118	10	118	23
26	118	1	118	13	118	25	118	38	118	51	119	3	119	16	119	29
27	119	4	119	16	119	29	119	42	119	55	120	8	120	22	120	35
28	120	7	120	19	120	32	120	46	120	59	121	13	121	27	121	41
29	121	9	121	22	121	36	121	50	122	3	122	18	122	32	122	47
30	122	12	122	25	122	39	122	53	123	7	123	22	123	37	123	52

RIGHT ASCENSION.

(N.B. For *Aquarius* add 180°.)

Leo with *North* Latitude.—*Aquarius* with *South* Latitude.

	0°		1°		2°		3°		4°		5°		6°		7°	
D.	D.	M.	D.	M.	D.	M.	D.	M.	D.	M.	D.	M.	D.	M.	D.	M.
0	122	12	122	25	122	39	122	53	123	7	123	22	123	37	123	52
1	123	14	123	28	123	42	123	57	124	11	124	26	124	42	124	57
2	124	16	124	31	124	45	125	0	125	15	125	30	125	46	126	2
3	125	18	125	33	125	48	126	3	126	18	126	34	126	50	127	6
4	126	20	126	36	126	51	127	6	127	22	127	38	127	54	128	11
5	127	22	127	38	127	54	128	9	128	25	128	42	128	58	129	15
6	128	24	128	40	128	56	129	12	129	28	129	45	130	2	130	19
7	129	25	129	42	129	58	130	14	130	31	130	48	131	5	131	23
8	130	26	130	43	131	0	131	16	131	33	131	51	132	8	132	26
9	131	27	131	44	132	1	132	18	132	35	132	53	133	11	133	29
10	132	28	132	45	133	2	133	20	133	37	133	55	134	14	134	22
11	133	28	133	46	134	3	134	21	134	39	134	57	135	16	135	35
12	134	29	134	47	135	4	135	22	135	40	135	59	136	18	136	37
13	135	29	135	47	136	5	136	23	136	41	137	0	137	20	137	39
14	136	29	136	47	137	6	137	24	137	42	138	1	138	21	138	41
15	137	29	137	47	138	6	138	24	138	43	139	2	139	22	139	42
16	138	29	138	47	139	6	139	25	139	44	140	3	140	24	140	44
17	139	28	139	47	140	6	140	25	140	45	141	4	141	25	141	45
18	140	28	140	46	141	6	141	25	141	45	142	5	142	26	142	46
19	141	27	141	46	142	6	142	25	142	45	143	6	143	27	143	47
20	142	26	142	45	143	5	143	25	143	45	144	6	144	27	144	48
21	143	25	143	44	144	4	144	24	144	45	145	6	145	27	145	48
22	144	23	144	43	145	3	145	24	145	45	146	6	146	27	146	48
23	145	22	145	42	146	2	146	23	146	44	147	5	147	27	147	48
24	146	20	146	40	147	1	147	22	147	43	148	4	148	26	148	48
25	147	18	147	39	148	0	148	21	148	42	149	3	149	25	149	47
26	148	16	148	37	148	58	149	19	149	41	150	2	150	24	150	46
27	149	14	149	35	149	56	150	17	150	39	151	1	151	28	151	45
28	150	11	150	33	150	54	151	15	151	37	151	59	152	22	152	44
29	151	9	151	30	151	52	152	18	152	35	152	57	153	20	153	43
30	152	6	152	27	152	49	153	11	153	33	153	55	154	18	154	41

38

RIGHT ASCENSION.

(N.B. For *Pisces* add 180°: if the amount exceeds 360° subtract that sum.)

Virgo with *North* Latitude.—*Pisces* with *South* Latitude.

D.	0°		1°		2°		3°		4°		5°		6°		7°	
	D.	M.	D.	M.	D.	M.	D.	M.	D.	M.	D.	M.	D.	M.	D.	M.
0	152	6	152	27	152	49	153	11	153	33	153	55	154	18	154	41
1	153	4	153	25	153	47	154	9	154	31	154	53	155	16	155	39
2	154	1	154	22	154	44	155	6	155	29	155	51	156	14	156	37
3	154	58	155	19	155	41	156	3	156	26	156	49	157	12	157	35
4	155	54	156	16	156	39	157	1	157	24	157	47	158	10	158	33
5	156	51	157	13	157	36	157	58	158	21	158	44	159	8	159	31
6	157	48	158	10	158	33	158	55	159	18	159	41	160	5	160	28
7	158	44	159	7	159	30	159	51	160	15	160	38	161	2	161	25
8	159	40	160	4	160	27	160	49	161	12	161	35	161	59	162	22
9	160	37	161	0	161	23	161	46	162	9	162	32	162	56	163	19
10	161	33	161	56	162	19	162	42	163	6	163	29	163	53	164	16
11	162	29	162	52	163	15	163	38	164	2	164	25	164	49	165	12
12	163	25	163	50	164	11	164	34	164	58	165	21	165	45	166	9
13	164	20	164	44	165	7	165	30	165	54	166	18	166	42	167	6
14	165	16	165	40	166	3	166	26	166	50	167	14	167	38	168	2
15	166	12	166	35	166	59	167	22	167	46	168	10	168	34	168	58
16	167	7	167	31	167	55	168	18	168	42	169	6	169	30	159	54
17	168	3	168	27	168	51	169	14	169	38	170	2	170	26	170	50
18	168	58	169	23	169	46	170	9	170	33	170	57	171	21	171	45
19	169	54	170	18	170	42	171	5	171	29	171	53	172	17	172	41
20	170	49	171	13	171	37	172	1	172	25	172	49	173	13	173	37
21	171	44	172	8	172	32	172	56	173	20	173	44	174	8	174	32
22	172	39	173	3	173	27	173	51	174	15	174	39	175	3	175	27
23	173	35	173	58	174	22	174	46	175	10	175	34	175	58	176	22
24	174	30	174	53	175	17	175	41	176	5	176	29	176	53	177	17
25	175	25	175	48	176	12	176	36	177	0	177	24	177	48	178	12
26	176	20	176	43	177	7	177	31	177	56	178	19	178	43	179	7
27	177	15	177	38	178	2	178	26	178	50	179	14	179	38	180	2
28	178	10	178	33	178	57	179	21	179	45	180	9	180	33	180	57
29	179	5	179	28	179	52	180	16	180	40	181	4	181	28	181	52
30	180	0	180	23	180	47	181	11	181	35	181	59	182	23	182	47

RIGHT ASCENSION.

(N.B. For *Aries* subtract 180°.)

Libra with *North* Latitude.—*Aries* with *South* Latitude.

D.	0°0 D. M.	0°1 D. M.	0°2 D. M.	0°3 D. M.	0°4 D. M.	0°5 D. M.	0°6 D. M.	0°7 D. M.
0	180 0	180 23	180 47	181 11	181 35	181 59	182 23	182 47
1	180 55	181 18	181 42	182 6	182 30	182 54	183 18	183 42
2	181 50	182 13	182 37	183 1	183 25	183 49	184 13	184 37
3	182 45	183 8	183 32	183 56	184 20	184 44	185 8	185 32
4	183 40	184 3	184 27	184 51	185 15	185 39	186 3	186 27
5	184 35	184 58	185 22	185 46	186 10	186 34	186 58	187 22
6	185 30	185 54	186 18	186 42	187 6	187 30	187 53	188 17
7	186 25	186 49	187 13	187 37	188 1	188 25	188 48	189 12
8	187 21	187 44	188 8	188 32	188 56	189 20	189 43	190 7
9	188 16	188 39	189 3	189 27	189 51	190 15	190 38	191 2
10	189 11	189 34	189 58	190 22	190 46	191 10	191 33	191 57
11	190 6	190 29	190 53	191 17	191 41	192 5	192 28	192 52
12	191 2	191 25	191 48	192 13	192 36	193 0	193 23	193 47
13	191 57	192 20	192 43	193 8	193 31	193 55	194 18	194 41
14	192 53	193 16	193 39	194 3	194 26	194 50	195 13	195 36
15	193 48	194 12	194 35	194 58	195 21	195 45	196 8	196 31
16	194 44	195 7	195 30	195 53	196 16	196 40	197 3	197 26
17	195 40	196 2	196 25	196 48	197 11	197 35	197 58	198 21
18	196 35	196 58	197 21	197 44	198 7	198 30	198 53	199 16
19	197 31	197 54	198 17	198 40	199 2	199 25	199 48	200 11
20	198 27	198 50	199 13	199 36	199 58	200 21	200 43	201 7
21	199 23	199 46	200 9	200 32	200 54	201 16	201 39	202 2
22	200 20	200 42	201 5	201 28	201 50	202 12	202 34	202 57
23	201 16	201 38	202 1	202 24	202 46	203 8	203 30	203 52
24	202 12	202 35	202 57	203 20	203 42	204 4	204 26	204 48
25	203 9	203 31	203 53	204 16	204 38	205 0	205 21	205 43
26	204 6	204 29	204 50	205 12	205 34	205 56	206 17	206 39
27	205 2	205 25	205 47	206 9	206 30	206 52	207 13	207 35
28	205 59	206 22	206 43	207 5	207 26	207 48	208 9	208 30
29	206 57	207 19	207 40	208 1	208 22	208 44	209 5	209 26
30	207 54	208 16	208 37	208 58	209 19	209 40	210 1	210 22

RIGHT ASCENSION.

(N.B. For *Taurus* subtract 180°.)

Scorpio with *North* Latitude.—*Taurus* with *South* Latitude.

	0°		1°		2°		3°		4°		5°		6°		7°	
D.	D.	M.	D.	M.	D.	M.	D.	M.	D.	M.	D.	M.	D.	M.	D.	M.
0	207	54	208	16	208	37	208	58	209	19	209	40	210	1	210	22
1	208	51	209	13	209	34	209	55	210	16	210	37	210	57	211	18
2	209	49	210	10	210	31	210	52	211	13	211	34	211	54	212	14
3	210	46	211	17	211	28	211	49	212	10	212	31	212	51	213	11
4	211	44	212	5	212	25	212	46	213	7	213	27	213	47	214	7
5	212	42	213	3	213	23	213	43	214	4	214	24	214	44	215	4
6	213	40	214	1	214	21	214	41	215	1	215	21	215	41	216	1
7	214	38	214	59	215	19	215	39	215	58	216	18	216	38	216	57
8	215	37	215	57	216	17	216	37	216	56	217	15	217	35	217	54
9	216	36	216	56	217	15	217	35	217	54	218	13	218	32	218	51
10	217	34	217	54	218	13	218	33	218	52	219	11	219	29	219	48
11	218	33	218	53	219	12	219	31	219	50	220	9	220	27	220	45
12	219	33	219	52	220	11	220	30	220	48	221	7	221	25	221	43
13	220	32	220	51	221	10	221	28	221	46	222	5	222	23	222	41
14	221	31	221	50	222	9	222	27	222	45	223	3	223	21	223	39
15	222	31	222	50	223	8	223	26	223	44	224	2	224	19	224	37
16	223	31	223	49	224	7	224	25	224	43	225	0	225	17	225	35
17	224	31	224	49	225	6	225	24	225	42	225	59	226	15	226	33
18	225	31	225	49	226	6	226	23	226	41	226	58	227	14	227	31
19	226	32	226	49	227	6	227	23	227	40	227	57	228	13	228	29
20	227	32	227	49	228	6	228	23	228	39	228	56	229	12	229	28
21	228	33	228	50	229	6	229	23	229	39	229	55	230	11	230	27
22	229	34	229	50	230	6	230	23	230	38	230	54	231	10	231	25
23	230	35	230	51	231	6	231	23	231	38	231	53	232	9	232	24
24	231	36	231	52	232	7	232	23	232	38	232	53	233	8	233	23
25	232	38	232	53	233	8	233	24	233	38	233	53	234	8	234	22
26	233	40	233	55	234	9	234	24	234	38	234	53	235	7	235	21
27	234	41	234	57	235	11	235	25	235	39	235	53	236	7	236	21
28	235	43	235	58	236	12	236	26	236	40	236	54	237	7	237	20
29	236	46	237	0	237	14	237	27	237	41	237	54	238	7	238	20
30	237	48	238	2	238	15	238	29	238	42	238	55	239	7	239	20

41

RIGHT ASCENSION.

(N.B. For *Gemini* subtract 180°.)

Sagittary with *North* Latitude.—*Gemini* with *South* Latitude.

D.	0° D. M.	1° D. M.	2° D. M.	3° D. M.	4° D. M.	5° D. M.	6° D. M.	7° D. M.
0	237 48	238 2	238 15	238 29	238 42	238 55	239 7	239 20
1	238 51	239 4	239 17	239 30	239 43	239 55	240 7	240 20
2	239 53	240 6	240 19	240 31	240 44	240 56	241 8	241 20
3	240 56	241 9	241 21	241 33	241 45	241 57	242 9	242 21
4	241 59	242 11	242 23	242 35	242 46	242 58	243 9	243 21
5	243 3	243 14	243 25	243 37	243 48	243 59	244 10	244 21
6	244 6	244 17	244 28	244 39	244 50	245 1	245 11	245 22
7	245 9	245 20	245 31	245 41	245 52	246 2	246 12	246 22
8	246 13	246 23	246 34	246 44	246 54	247 4	247 13	247 23
9	247 17	247 27	247 37	247 47	247 56	248 6	248 15	248 24
10	248 21	248 30	248 40	248 49	248 58	249 7	249 16	249 25
11	249 25	249 34	249 43	249 52	250 0	250 9	250 17	250 26
12	250 29	250 38	250 46	250 55	251 3	251 11	251 19	251 27
13	251 34	251 42	251 49	251 58	252 5	252 13	252 21	252 28
14	252 38	252 46	252 53	253 1	253 8	253 15	253 23	253 30
15	253 43	253 50	253 57	254 4	254 11	254 18	254 25	254 32
16	254 47	254 54	255 1	255 7	255 14	255 20	255 27	255 33
17	255 52	255 58	256 5	256 11	256 17	256 22	256 29	256 35
18	256 57	257 3	257 9	257 15	257 20	257 25	257 31	257 37
19	258 2	258 7	258 13	258 18	258 23	258 28	258 33	258 38
20	259 7	259 12	259 17	259 21	259 26	259 31	259 35	259 40
21	260 12	260 17	260 21	260 25	260 29	260 34	260 38	260 42
22	261 17	261 21	261 25	261 28	261 32	261 36	261 40	261 44
23	262 22	262 25	262 29	262 32	262 35	262 39	262 42	262 46
24	263 28	263 30	263 33	263 36	263 39	263 42	263 45	263 48
25	264 33	264 35	264 37	264 40	264 42	264 45	264 47	264 50
26	265 38	265 40	265 41	265 44	265 45	265 48	265 49	265 52
27	266 44	266 45	266 46	266 48	266 49	266 51	266 52	266 54
28	267 49	267 50	267 50	267 52	267 52	267 54	267 54	267 56
29	268 55	268 55	268 55	268 56	268 56	268 57	268 57	268 58
30	270 0	270 0	270 0	270 0	270 0	270 0	270 0	270 0

RIGHT ASCENSION.

(N.B. For *Cancer* subtract 180°.)

Capricorn with *North* Latitude.—*Cancer* with *South* Latitude.

	0 0		0 1		0 2		0 3		0 4		0 5		0 6		0 7	
D.	D.	M.	D.	M.	D.	M.	D.	M.	D.	M.	D.	M.	D.	M.	D.	M.
0	270	0	270	0	270	0	270	0	270	0	270	0	270	0	270	0
1	271	5	271	5	271	5	271	4	271	4	271	3	271	3	271	2
2	272	11	272	10	272	10	272	8	272	8	272	6	272	6	272	4
3	273	16	273	15	273	14	273	12	273	11	273	9	273	8	273	6
4	274	22	274	20	274	19	274	16	274	15	274	12	274	11	274	8
5	275	27	275	25	275	23	275	20	275	18	275	15	275	13	275	10
6	276	32	276	30	276	27	276	24	276	21	276	18	276	15	276	12
7	277	38	277	35	277	31	277	28	277	25	277	21	277	18	277	14
8	278	43	278	39	278	35	278	32	278	28	278	24	278	20	278	16
9	279	48	279	43	279	39	279	35	279	31	279	26	279	22	279	18
10	280	53	280	48	280	43	280	39	280	34	280	29	280	25	280	20
11	281	58	281	53	281	47	281	42	281	37	281	32	281	27	281	22
12	283	3	282	57	282	51	282	45	282	40	282	34	282	29	282	23
13	284	8	284	2	283	55	283	49	283	43	283	37	283	31	283	25
14	285	13	285	6	284	59	284	53	284	46	284	40	284	33	284	27
15	286	17	286	10	286	3	284	56	285	49	285	42	285	35	285	28
16	287	22	287	14	287	7	286	59	286	52	286	45	286	37	286	30
17	288	26	288	18	288	11	288	2	287	55	287	47	287	39	287	32
18	289	31	289	22	289	14	289	5	288	57	288	49	288	41	288	33
19	290	35	290	26	290	17	290	8	299	0	289	51	289	43	289	34
20	291	39	291	30	291	20	291	11	299	2	280	53	290	44	290	35
21	292	48	292	33	292	23	292	13	292	4	291	55	291	45	291	36
22	293	47	293	37	293	26	293	16	293	6	292	56	292	47	292	37
23	294	51	294	40	294	29	294	19	294	8	293	58	293	48	293	38
24	295	54	295	43	295	32	295	21	295	10	294	59	294	49	294	38
25	296	57	296	46	296	35	296	23	296	12	296	1	295	50	295	39
26	298	1	297	49	297	37	297	25	297	14	297	2	296	51	296	39
27	299	4	298	51	298	39	298	27	298	15	298	3	297	51	297	39
28	300	7	299	54	299	41	299	29	299	16	299	4	298	52	298	40
29	301	9	300	56	300	43	300	30	300	17	300	5	299	53	299	40
30	302	12	301	58	301	45	301	31	301	18	301	5	300	53	300	40

43

RIGHT ASCENSION.

(N.B. For *Leo* subtract 180°.)

Aquarius with *North* Latitude.—*Leo* with *South* Latitude.

D.	0°		1°		2°		3°		4°		5°		6°		7°	
	D.	M.	D.	M.	D.	M.	D.	M.	D.	M.	D.	M.	D.	M	D.	M.
0	302	12	301	58	301	45	301	31	301	18	301	5	300	53	300	40
1	303	14	303	0	302	47	302	33	302	19	302	6	301	53	301	40
2	304	16	304	2	303	48	303	34	303	20	303	6	302	53	302	40
3	305	18	305	3	304	50	304	35	304	21	304	7	303	53	303	39
4	306	20	306	5	305	51	305	36	305	22	305	7	304	53	304	39
5	307	22	307	7	306	52	306	36	306	22	306	7	305	52	305	38
6	308	24	308	8	307	53	307	37	307	22	307	7	306	52	306	37
7	309	25	309	9	308	54	308	37	308	22	308	7	307	51	307	36
8	310	26	310	10	309	54	309	37	309	22	309	6	308	50	308	35
9	311	27	311	10	310	54	310	37	310	21	310	5	309	49	309	33
10	312	28	312	11	311	54	311	37	311	21	311	4	310	48	310	32
11	313	28	313	11	312	54	312	37	312	20	312	3	311	47	311	31
12	314	29	314	11	313	54	313	37	313	19	313	2	312	46	312	29
13	315	29	315	11	314	54	314	36	314	18	314	1	313	45	313	27
14	316	29	316	11	315	53	315	35	315	17	315	0	314	43	314	25
15	317	29	317	10	316	52	316	34	316	16	315	58	315	41	315	23
16	318	29	318	10	317	51	317	33	317	15	316	57	316	39	316	21
17	319	28	319	9	318	50	318	32	318	14	317	55	317	37	317	19
18	320	27	320	8	319	49	319	30	319	12	318	53	318	35	318	17
19	321	27	321	7	320	48	320	29	320	10	319	51	319	33	319	15
20	322	26	322	6	321	47	321	27	321	8	320	49	320	31	320	12
21	323	25	323	4	322	45	322	25	322	6	321	47	321	28	321	9
22	324	23	324	3	323	43	323	23	323	4	322	45	322	25	322	6
23	325	22	325	1	324	41	324	21	324	1	323	42	323	22	323	3
24	326	20	325	59	325	39	325	19	324	59	324	39	324	19	323	59
25	327	18	326	57	326	37	326	17	325	56	325	36	325	16	325	56
26	328	16	327	55	327	35	327	14	326	53	326	33	326	13	325	53
27	329	14	328	53	328	32	328	11	327	50	327	30	327	10	326	49
28	330	11	329	50	329	29	329	8	328	47	328	27	328	6	327	46
29	331	9	330	47	330	26	330	5	329	44	329	25	329	3	328	42
30	332	6	331	44	331	23	331	2	330	41	330	20	329	59	329	39

44

RIGHT ASCENSION.

(N.B. For *Virgo* subtract 180°.)

Pisces with *North* Latitude.—*Virgo* with *South* Latitude.

	0°		1°		2°		3°		4°		5°		6°		7°	
D.	D.	M.	D.	M.	D.	M.	D.	M.	D.	M.	D.	M.	D.	M.	D.	M.
0	332	6	331	44	331	23	331	2	330	41	330	20	329	59	329	38
1	333	4	332	41	332	20	331	59	331	38	331	16	330	55	330	34
2	334	1	333	38	333	17	332	55	332	34	332	12	331	51	331	30
3	334	58	334	35	334	13	333	51	333	30	333	8	332	47	332	25
4	335	55	335	32	335	10	334	48	334	26	334	4	333	43	333	21
5	336	51	336	29	336	7	335	44	335	22	335	0	334	39	334	17
6	337	48	337	25	337	3	336	40	336	18	335	56	335	34	335	12
7	338	44	338	22	337	59	337	36	337	14	336	52	336	30	336	8
8	339	40	339	18	338	55	338	32	338	10	337	48	337	26	337	3
9	340	37	340	14	339	51	339	28	339	6	338	43	338	21	337	58
10	341	33	341	10	340	47	340	24	340	2	339	39	339	17	338	54
11	342	29	342	6	341	43	341	20	340	58	340	35	340	12	339	49
12	343	25	343	2	342	39	342	16	341	53	341	30	341	7	340	44
13	344	20	343	58	343	35	343	12	342	49	342	25	342	2	341	39
14	345	16	344	53	344	30	344	7	343	44	343	20	342	57	342	34
15	346	12	345	48	345	25	345	2	344	39	344	15	343	52	343	29
16	347	7	346	44	346	21	345	57	345	34	345	10	344	47	344	24
17	348	3	347	40	347	17	346	52	346	29	346	5	345	42	345	19
18	348	58	348	35	348	12	347	47	347	24	347	0	346	37	346	13
19	349	54	349	31	349	7	348	43	348	19	347	55	347	32	347	8
20	350	49	350	26	350	3	349	38	349	14	348	50	348	27	348	3
21	351	44	351	21	350	57	350	33	350	9	349	45	349	22	348	58
22	352	39	352	16	351	52	351	28	351	4	350	40	350	17	349	53
23	353	35	353	11	352	47	352	23	351	59	351	35	351	12	350	48
24	354	30	354	6	353	42	353	18	352	54	352	30	352	7	351	43
25	355	25	355	1	354	36	354	14	353	50	353	26	353	2	352	38
26	356	20	355	57	355	33	355	9	354	45	354	21	353	57	353	33
27	357	15	356	52	356	28	356	4	355	40	355	16	354	52	354	28
28	358	10	357	47	357	23	356	59	356	35	356	11	355	47	355	23
29	359	5	358	42	358	18	357	54	357	30	357	6	356	42	356	18
30	360	0	359	37	359	13	358	49	358	25	358	1	357	37	357	13

TABLES OF ASCENSIONAL DIFFERENCE.

DECLINATION.	LATITUDE OR POLAR ELEVATION.								
	0 1	0 2	0 3	0 4	0 5	0 6	0 7	0 8	0 9
	D. M.	D. M.	D. M.	D. M.	D. M.	D. M.	D. M.	D. M.	D. M.
1	0 1	0 2	0 3	0 4	0 5	0 6	0 7	0 8	0 9
2	0 2	0 4	0 6	0 8	0 10	0 13	0 15	0 7	0 19
3	0 3	0 6	0 9	0 13	0 16	0 19	0 22	0 25	0 29
4	0 4	0 8	0 13	0 17	0 21	0 25	0 30	0 34	0 38
5	0 5	0 10	0 16	0 21	0 26	0 32	0 37	0 42	0 48
6	0 6	0 13	0 19	0 25	0 32	0 38	0 44	0 51	0 57
7	0 7	0 15	0 22	0 30	0 37	0 44	0 52	0 59	1 7
8	0 8	0 17	0 25	0 34	0 42	0 51	0 59	1 8	1 16
9	0 9	0 19	0 29	0 38	0 48	0 57	1 7	1 16	1 26
10	0 11	0 21	0 32	0 42	0 53	1 4	1 14	1 25	1 36
11	0 12	0 23	0 35	0 47	0 58	1 10	1 22	1 34	1 46
12	0 13	0 25	0 38	0 51	1 4	1 17	1 30	1 43	1 56
13	0 14	0 28	0 42	0 56	1 9	1 23	1 37	1 52	2 6
14	0 15	0 30	0 45	1 0	1 15	1 30	1 45	2 1	2 16
15	0 16	0 32	0 48	1 4	1 21	1 37	1 53	2 10	2 2o
6	0 17	0 34	0 52	1 9	1 26	1 44	2 1	2 19	2 36
17	0 18	0 37	0 55	1 14	1 32	1 50	2 9	2 28	2 47
18	0 19	0 39	0 59	1 18	1 38	1 57	2 17	2 37	2 5/
19	0 21	0 41	1 2	1 23	1 44	2 4	2 25	2 46	3 8
20	0 22	0 44	1 6	1 27	1 49	2 12	2 34	2 56	3 18
21	0 23	0 46	1 9	1 32	1 55	2 19	2 41	3 6	3 29
22	0 24	0 49	1 13	1 37	2 2	2 26	2 50	3 15	3 40
23	0 25	0 51	1 17	1 42	2 8	2 33	2 59	3 25	3 51
24	0 27	0 53	1 20	1 47	2 14	2 41	3 9	3 35	4 3
25	0 28	0 56	1 24	1 52	2 20	2 49	3 17	3 45	4 14
26	0 29	0 59	1 28	1 57	2 27	2 56	3 26	3 56	4 26
27	0 31	1 1	1 32	2 3	2 33	3 4	3 35	4 6	4 38
28	0 32	1 4	1 36	2 8	2 40	3 12	3 45	4 17	4 50

TABLES OF ASCENSIONAL DIFFERENCE.

Declination	|	Latitude or Polar Elevation.							
		10°	11°	12°	13°	14°	15°	16°	17°	18°
		D. M.	D. M.	D. M.	D. M.	D. M.	D. M.	D. M	D. M.	D. M.
1	|	0 11	0 12	0 13	0 14	0 15	0 16	0 17	0 18	0 19
2		0 21	0 23	0 25	0 28	0 30	0 32	0 34	0 37	0 39
3		0 32	0 35	0 38	0 42	0 45	0 48	0 52	0 54	0 59
4		0 42	0 47	0 51	0 56	1 0	1 4	1 9	1 14	1 18
5		0 53	0 58	1 4	1 9	1 15	1 21	1 26	1 32	1 38
6	|	1 4	1 10	1 17	1 23	1 30	1 37	1 44	1 50	1 57
7		1 14	1 22	1 30	1 37	1 45	1 53	2 1	2 9	2 17
8		1 25	1 35	1 43	1 52	2 0	2 9	2 19	2 28	2 37
9		1 36	1 46	1 56	2 6	2 16	2 26	2 36	2 47	2 57
10		1 47	1 58	2 9	2 20	2 31	2 42	2 54	3 5	3 17
11	|	1 58	2 10	2 22	2 34	2 47	2 59	3 12	3 24	3 37
12		2 9	2 22	2 35	2 49	3 2	3 16	3 30	3 44	3 58
13		2 20	2 34	2 49	3 3	3 18	3 33	3 48	4 3	4 18
14		2 31	2 47	3 2	3 18	3 34	3 50	4 6	4 22	4 39
15		2 42	2 59	3 16	3 33	3 50	4 7	4 24	4 42	5 0
16	|	2 54	3 12	3 30	3 48	4 6	4 24	4 43	5 2	5 21
17		3 5	3 24	3 44	4 3	4 22	4 42	5 2	5 22	5 42
18		3 17	3 37	3 58	4 18	4 39	5 0	5 21	5 42	6 4
19		3 29	3 50	4 12	4 34	4 55	5 18	5 40	6 3	6 26
20		3 41	4 3	4 26	4 49	5 12	5 36	5 59	6 24	6 48
21	|	3 53	4 17	4 44	5 5	5 30	5 54	6 19	6 45	7 10
22		4 5	4 30	4 56	5 24	5 47	6 13	6 39	7 6	7 33
23		4 18	4 44	5 11	5 37	6 5	6 32	6 59	7 27	7 56
24		4 30	4 58	5 26	5 54	6 23	6 51	7 20	7 49	8 19
25		4 43	5 12	5 41	6 11	6 41	7 11	7 41	8 12	8 43
26	|	4 56	5 26	5 57	6 28	6 59	7 31	8 2	8 35	9 7
27		5 9	5 41	6 13	6 45	7 18	7 51	8 24	8 58	9 32
28		5 23	5 56	6 29	7 3	7 37	8 11	8 46	9 21	9 57

TABLE OF ASCENSIONAL DIFFERENCE.

Declination	Latitude or Polar Elevation.															
	19°		20°		21°		22°		23°		24°		25°		26°		28°	
	D.	M.	D.	M.	D.	M.	D.	M.	D.	M.	D.	M.	D.	M.	D.	M.	D.	M.
1	0	21	0	22	0	23	0	24	0	25	0	27	0	28	0	29	0	31
2	0	42	0	44	0	46	0	49	0	51	0	53	0	56	0	59	1	1
3	1	2	1	6	1	9	1	13	1	17	1	20	1	24	1	28	1	32
4	1	23	1	27	1	32	1	37	1	42	1	47	1	52	1	57	2	3
5	1	44	1	49	1	55	2	2	2	8	2	14	2	20	2	27	2	33
6	2	4	2	12	2	19	2	26	2	33	2	41	2	49	2	56	3	4
7	2	25	2	34	2	42	2	51	2	59	3	8	3	17	3	26	3	35
8	2	46	2	56	3	6	3	15	3	25	3	35	3	45	3	56	4	6
9	3	8	3	18	3	29	3	40	3	51	4	3	4	14	4	26	4	38
10	3	29	3	41	3	53	3	5	4	18	4	30	4	53	4	56	5	9
11	3	50	4	3	4	17	4	30	4	44	4	58	5	12	5	26	5	41
12	4	12	4	26	4	41	4	56	5	11	5	26	5	41	5	57	6	13
13	4	34	4	49	5	55	5	21	5	38	5	54	6	11	6	28	6	45
14	4	56	5	12	5	30	5	47	6	5	6	22	6	41	6	59	7	18
15	5	18	5	36	5	54	6	13	6	32	6	51	7	11	7	31	7	51
16	5	40	5	59	6	19	6	39	6	59	7	20	7	41	8	3	8	24
17	6	22	6	23	6	44	7	6	7	27	7	49	8	12	8	35	8	58
18	6	25	6	47	7	10	7	33	7	56	8	19	8	43	9	7	9	32
19	6	49	7	12	7	36	8	0	8	24	8	49	9	14	9	49	10	6
20	7	12	7	37	8	2	8	27	8	53	9	19	9	40	10	14	10	41
21	7	36	8	2	8	28	8	55	9	23	9	50	10	19	10	47	11	17
22	8	0	8	27	8	55	9	24	9	53	10	22	10	52	11	22	11	53
23	8	24	8	53	9	22	9	53	10	23	10	54	11	25	11	57	12	29
24	8	49	9	19	9	50	10	22	10	54	11	26	11	59	12	33	13	7
25	9	14	9	40	10	19	10	52	11	25	11	59	12	34	13	9	13	45
26	9	40	10	14	10	47	11	22	11	57	12	33	13	9	13	46	14	24
27	10	6	10	41	11	17	11	53	12	26	13	7	13	45	14	23	15	3
28	10	33	11	9	11	47	12	24	13	3	13	42	14	21	15	2	15	43

TABLE OF ASCENSIONAL DIFFERENCE.

DECLINATION.	LATITUDE OR POLAR ELEVATION.																
	28°		29°		30°		31°		32°		33°		34°		35°		36°
	D.	M.	D.	M.	D.	M.	D.	M.	D.	M.	D.	M.	D.	M.	D.	M.	D. M.
1	0	32	0	33	0	35	0	36	0	37	0	39	0	40	0	42	0 44
2	1	4	1	7	1	9	1	12	1	15	1	18	1	21	1	24	1 27
3	1	36	1	40	1	44	1	48	1	53	1	57	2	2	2	6	2 11
4	2	8	2	13	2	19	2	24	2	30	2	36	2	42	2	48	2 55
5	2	40	2	47	2	54	3	1	3	8	3	15	3	23	3	31	3 39
6	3	12	3	20	3	29	3	37	3	46	3	55	4	3	4	13	4 23
7	3	45	3	54	4	4	4	14	4	24	4	34	4	45	4	56	5 7
8	4	17	4	28	4	39	4	51	5	2	5	14	5	26	5	39	5 52
9	4	50	5	2	5	15	5	28	5	41	5	54	6	8	6	22	6 37
10	5	23	5	38	5	51	6	5	6	20	6	35	6	50	7	9	7 22
11	5	56	6	11	6	27	6	42	6	59	7	15	7	32	7	49	8 7
12	6	29	6	46	7	3	7	20	7	38	7	56	8	15	8	34	8 53
13	7	3	7	21	7	40	7	58	8	18	8	37	8	58	9	18	9 39
14	7	37	7	56	8	17	8	37	8	58	9	19	9	41	10	3	10 26
15	8	11	8	32	8	54	9	16	9	38	10	1	10	25	10	49	11 14
16	8	46	9	8	9	32	9	55	10	19	10	44	11	9	11	35	12 2
17	9	21	9	45	10	10	10	35	11	1	11	27	11	54	12	22	12 54
18	9	56	10	23	10	49	11	16	11	43	12	11	12	40	13	9	13 39
19	10	53	11	0	11	28	11	56	12	26	12	55	13	26	13	57	14 29
20	11	9	11	38	12	8	12	38	13	9	13	40	14	13	14	46	15 20
21	11	46	12	17	12	48	13	20	13	53	14	26	15	0	15	36	16 12
22	12	24	12	56	13	29	14	3	14	37	15	13	15	49	16	27	17 5
23	13	3	13	37	14	11	14	47	15	23	16	0	16	38	17	17	17 58
24	13	42	14	17	14	54	15	51	16	9	16	48	17	29	18	10	18 52
25	14	21	14	59	15	37	16	16	16	56	17	38	18	20	19	3	19 48
26	15	2	15	41	16	21	17	2	17	45	18	28	19	12	19	58	20 45
27	15	43	15	24	17	6	17	50	18	34	19	19	20	6	20	54	21 44
28	16	25	17	8	17	53	18	38	19	24	20	12	21	1	21	51	22 44

TABLES OF ASCENSIONAL DIFFERENCE.

Declination	Latitude or Polar Elevation.																	
	37°		38°		39°		40°		41°		42°		43°		44°		45°	
	D.	M.	D.	M.	D.	M.	D.	M.	D.	M.	D.	M.	D.	M.	D.	M.	D.	M.
1	0	45	0	47	0	49	0	50	0	52	0	54	0	56	0	58	1	0
2	1	31	1	34	1	37	1	41	1	44	1	48	1	52	1	56	2	0
3	2	16	2	21	2	26	2	31	2	37	2	42	2	48	2	54	3	0
4	3	1	3	8	3	15	3	22	3	29	3	37	3	44	3	52	4	1
5	3	47	3	55	4	4	4	13	4	22	4	31	4	41	4	51	5	1
6	4	33	4	42	4	53	5	4	5	15	5	26	5	37	5	50	6	2
7	5	19	5	30	5	42	5	55	6	8	6	21	6	34	6	49	7	5
8	6	5	6	18	6	32	6	46	7	1	7	16	7	32	7	48	8	5
9	6	51	7	6	7	22	7	38	7	55	8	12	8	30	8	48	9	7
10	7	38	7	55	8	13	8	30	8	49	9	8	9	28	9	48	10	9
11	8	25	8	44	9	3	9	23	9	44	10	5	10	27	10	49	11	12
12	9	13	9	34	9	55	10	16	10	39	11	2	11	26	11	51	12	16
13	10	1	10	24	10	46	11	10	11	35	12	0	12	26	12	53	13	21
14	10	50	11	14	11	39	12	4	12	31	12	58	13	27	13	56	14	26
15	11	39	12	5	12	32	13	0	13	28	13	58	14	28	14	0	15	32
16	12	29	12	57	13	26	13	55	14	26	14	58	15	31	16	5	16	40
17	13	19	13	49	14	20	14	52	15	25	15	59	16	34	17	10	17	48
18	14	10	14	42	15	15	15	49	16	24	17	1	17	38	18	17	18	58
19	15	2	15	36	16	11	16	48	17	25	18	4	18	44	19	25	20	9
20	15	55	16	31	17	8	17	47	18	27	19	8	19	51	20	35	21	21
21	16	49	17	27	18	7	18	47	19	30	20	13	20	59	21	46	22	34
22	17	44	18	24	19	6	19	49	20	34	21	20	22	8	22	58	23	50
23	18	39	19	22	20	6	20	52	21	39	22	28	23	19	24	12	25	7
24	19	36	20	21	21	8	21	56	22	46	23	38	24	32	25	28	26	26
25	20	34	21	21	22	11	23	1	23	55	24	50	25	47	26	46	27	48
26	21	34	22	24	23	16	24	10	25	5	26	3	27	3	28	6	29	11
27	22	35	23	28	24	22	25	19	26	17	27	18	28	22	29	29	30	38
28	23	37	24	33	25	30	26	30	27	31	28	36	29	44	30	54	32	7

D

TABLE OF ASCENSIONAL DIFFERENCE.

Declination.	Latitude or Polar Elevation.															
	46°		47°		48°		49°		50°		51°		52°		53°		54°
	D.	M.	D.	M.	D.	M.	D.	M.	D.	M.	D.	M.	D.	M.	D.	M.	D.	M.
1	1	2	1	4	1	7	1	9	1	12	1	14	1	17	1	20	1	23
2	2	4	2	9	2	13	2	18	2	23	2	28	2	34	2	39	2	45
3	3	7	3	13	3	20	3	27	3	35	3	43	3	51	3	59	4	8
4	4	9	4	18	4	27	4	37	4	47	4	57	5	8	5	19	5	31
5	5	12	5	23	5	35	5	47	5	59	6	12	6	26	6	40	6	55
6	6	15	6	28	6	42	6	57	7	12	7	27	7	44	8	1	8	19
7	7	18	7	34	7	50	8	7	8	25	8	43	9	2	9	23	9	44
8	8	22	8	40	8	59	9	18	9	38	10	0	10	22	10	45	11	9
9	9	26	9	47	10	8	10	30	10	53	11	17	11	42	12	8	12	35
10	10	31	10	54	11	18	11	42	12	8	12	35	13	2	13	32	14	3
11	11	57	12	1	12	28	12	55	13	24	13	53	14	24	14	57	15	31
12	12	43	13	11	13	39	14	9	14	40	15	13	15	49	16	23	17	0
13	13	50	14	20	14	51	15	24	15	58	16	24	17	11	17	50	18	32
14	14	58	15	30	16	5	16	40	17	17	17	56	18	37	19	19	20	4
15	16	7	16	42	17	19	17	57	18	37	19	19	20	4	20	50	21	38
16	17	16	17	54	18	34	19	16	19	59	20	44	21	32	22	22	23	15
17	18	27	19	8	19	51	20	36	21	22	22	11	23	2	23	56	24	53
18	19	40	20	23	21	9	21	57	22	47	23	39	24	34	25	35	26	34
19	20	53	21	40	22	29	23	18	24	14	25	10	26	9	27	11	28	17
20	22	8	22	58	23	51	24	45	25	42	26	43	27	46	28	53	30	4
21	23	25	24	10	25	14	26	12	27	14	28	18	29	26	30	37	31	54
22	24	44	25	40	26	40	27	42	28	47	29	55	31	8	32	25	33	47
23	26	5	27	5	28	8	29	14	30	23	31	43	32	54	34	17	35	45
24	27	27	28	31	29	38	30	48	32	3	33	32	34	44	36	13	37	48
25	28	52	30	0	31	12	32	26	33	46	35	21	36	39	38	14	39	59
26	30	20	31	32	32	48	34	0	35	32	37	10	38	38	40	20	42	10
27	31	51	33	7	34	28	35	53	37	23	39	0	40	42	42	33	44	32
28	33	25	34	46	36	12	37	43	39	19	41	2	42	53	44	53	47	2

TABLE OF ASCENSIONAL DIFFERENCE.

Declination.	Latitude or Polar Elevation.					
	0° 55	0° 56	0° 57	0° 58	0° 59	0° 60
	D. M.	D. M.	D. M.	D. M.	D. M.	D. M.
1	1 26	1 29	1 32	1 36	1 40	1 44
2	2 52	2 58	3 5	3 12	3 20	3 28
3	4 18	4 27	4 48	4 40	5 0	5 13
4	5 44	5 57	5 11	6 25	6 41	6 57
5	7 11	7 27	7 44	8 3	8 22	8 42
6	8 38	8 58	9 19	9 4	10 4	10 28
7	10 6	10 29	10 54	11 20	11 47	12 17
8	11 35	12 2	12 30	13 0	13 31	14 5
9	13 4	13 35	14 7	14 41	15 17	15 55
10	14 35	15 9	15 45	16 23	17 4	17 47
11	16 7	16 45	17 25	18 8	18 53	19 41
12	17 40	18 22	19 6	19 53	20 43	21 36
13	19 15	20 1	20 50	21 41	22 36	23 34
14	20 52	21 42	22 35	23 3	24 31	25 35
15	22 30	23 24	24 22	25 23	26 29	27 39
16	24 10	25 9	26 12	27 19	29 30	29 47
17	25 53	26 57	28 5	29 18	30 35	31 59
18	27 39	28 48	30 1	31 10	32 44	34 19
19	29 27	30 41	32 1	33 26	34 58	36 37
20	31 19	32 26	34 5	35 37	37 17	39 5
21	33 15	34 41	36 14	37 54	39 42	41 40
22	35 14	36 48	38 28	40 17	42 15	44 25
23	37 19	39 0	40 49	42 47	44 57	47 20
24	39 29	41 18	43 17	45 26	47 49	50 27
25	41 45	43 48	45 54	48 16	50 54	53 52
26	44 9	46 18	48 41	51 19	54 16	57 39
27	46 41	49 4	51 41	53 38	58 1	61 57
28	49 24	52 1	54 58	59 19	62 14	67 4

TABLE OF THE POLES OF THE HOUSES.

From the *Equator* to 60 *Degrees* of *Latitude*.

LAT.	Pole of the 11th, 3rd, 5th, & 9th Houses.		Pole of the 12th, 2nd, 6th, & 8th Houses.		LAT.	Pole of the 11th, 3rd, 5th, & 9th Houses.		Pole of the 12th, 2nd, 6th, & 8th Houses.	
DEG.	DEG.	MIN.	DEG.	MIN.	DEG.	DEG.	MIN.	DEG.	MIN.
1	0	21	0	42	31	11	26	21	56
2	0	41	1	22	32	11	54	22	46
3	1	0	2	0	33	12	23	23	36
4	1	21	2	41	34	12	51	24	25
5	1	41	3	23	35	13	26	24	15
6	2	0	4	0	36	13	51	26	5
7	2	21	4	40	37	14	18	26	55
8	2	41	5	21	38	14	52	27	48
9	3	2	6	2	39	15	24	28	40
10	3	23	6	43	40	15	56	29	32
11	3	43	7	24	41	16	29	30	25
12	4	4	8	5	42	17	5	31	20
13	4	24	8	45	43	17	42	32	18
14	4	45	9	26	44	18	20	33	15
15	5	7	10	10	45	18	58	34	13
16	5	29	10	50	46	19	37	35	10
17	5	49	11	30	47	20	19	36	10
18	6	12	12	14	48	21	3	37	12
19	6	34	12	57	49	21	46	38	12
20	6	57	13	41	50	22	33	39	14
21	7	20	14	24	51	23	21	40	18
22	7	43	15	7	52	24	12	41	24
23	8	5	15	50	53	25	6	42	32
24	8	30	16	36	54	26	1	43	39
25	8	54	17	22	55	26	59	44	48
26	9	17	18	5	56	28	1	45	59
27	9	43	18	52	57	22	6	47	13
28	10	8	19	37	58	30	15	48	27
29	10	32	20	21	59	31	29	49	44
30	10	59	21	9	60	32	48	51	4

TABLE OF HOUSES FOR LIVERPOOL.

Latitude 53° 25′North.

Right Asc. of Meridian.	10th House.	11th House.	12th House.	Ascendant.	2nd House.	3rd House.
DEG. MIN.	Aries.	Taurus.	Gemini.	Cancer.	Leo.	Virgo.
0 0	0	10	24	28 13	14	3
0 55	1	11	25	28 46	14	4
1 50	2	12	26	29 25	15	5
2 45	3	13	27	0 ♌ 14	16	6
3 40	4	14	28	0 49	17	6
4 35	5	15	29	1 25	17	7
5 30	6	16	29	2 7	18	8
6 25	7	17	♋	2 42	19	9
7 21	8	18	1	3 26	19	10
8 16	9	19	2	4 4	20	10
9 11	10	20	3	4 41	21	11
10 6	11	22	4	5 19	22	12
11 2	12	23	4	5 58	22	13
11 57	13	24	5	6 36	23	14
12 53	14	25	6	7 14	24	15
13 48	15	26	7	7 53	24	15
14 44	16	27	8	8 32	25	16
15 40	17	28	8	9 10	26	17
16 35	18	29	9	9 47	26	18
17 31	19	♊	10	10 25	27	19
18 27	20	1	11	11 5	28	20
19 23	21	2	12	11 43	29	20
20 20	22	3	12	12 22	29	21
21 16	23	4	13	13 0	♍	22
22 12	24	5	14	13 39	1	23
23 9	25	6	15	14 18	2	24
24 6	26	7	16	14 56	2	25
25 2	27	8	16	15 35	3	26
25 59	28	9	17	16 14	4	26
26 57	29	10	18	16 53	4	27
27 54	30	11	19	17 32	5	28

TABLE OF HOUSES FOR LIVERPOOL.

Latitude 53° 25' North.

Right Asc. of Meridian.	10th House.	11th House.	12th House.	Ascendant.	2nd House.	3rd House.
Taurus.	Taurus.	Gemini.	Cancer.	Leo.	Virgo.	Virgo.
DEG. MIN.	°	°	°	° ′	°	°
27 54	0	11	19	17 32	5	28
28 51	1	12	20	18 11	6	29
29 49	2	13	21	18 51	7	♎
30 46	3	14	21	19 30	8	1
31 44	4	15	22	20 9	8	1
32 42	5	15	23	20 48	9	2
33 40	6	16	24	21 37	10	3
34 38	7	17	24	22 8	11	4
35 37	8	18	25	22 47	11	5
36 36	9	19	26	23 28	12	6
37 34	10	20	27	24 8	13	7
38 33	11	21	27	24 48	13	8
39 33	12	22	28	25 28	14	9
40 32	13	23	29	26 8	15	10
41 31	14	24	♌	26 48	15	11
42 31	15	25	0	27 29	16	11
43 31	16	26	1	28 10	17	12
44 31	17	27	2	28 51	18	13
45 31	18	28	3	29 ♍ 32	19	14
46 32	19	29	4	0 13	20	15
47 32	20	♋	5	0 54	20	16
48 33	21	0	5	1 36	21	17
49 34	22	1	6	2 17	22	18
50 35	23	2	7	2 59	23	19
51 36	24	3	8	3 41	24	20
52 38	25	4	8	4 23	25	21
53 40	26	5	9	5 5	25	21
54 42	27	6	10	5 47	26	22
55 44	28	7	11	6 30	27	23
56 46	29	8	12	7 12	28	24
57 48	30	9	12	7 54	28	25

TABLE OF HOUSES FOR LIVERPOOL.

Latitude 53° 22' North.

Right Asc. of Meridian.	10th House.	11th House.	12th House.	Ascendant.	2nd House.	3rd House.
DEG. MIN.	Gemini.	Cancer.	Leo.	Virgo.	Virgo.	Libra.
° ′	°	°	°	° ′	°	°
57 48	0	9	12	7 54	28	25
58 51	1	10	13	8 37	29	26
59 53	2	11	14	9 20	♎	27
60 56	3	12	15	10 3	1	28
61 59	4	13	16	10 47	1	29
63 3	5	14	16	11 30	2	♏
64 6	6	15	17	12 13	3	0
65 9	7	15	18	12 56	4	1
66 13	8	16	19	13 40	5	2
67 17	9	17	20	14 24	6	3
68 21	10	18	20	15 8	6	4
69 25	11	19	21	15 52	7	5
70 29	12	20	22	16 36	8	6
71 34	13	21	23	17 19	9	7
72 38	14	22	24	18 4	10	8
73 43	15	23	25	18 49	11	9
74 47	16	24	25	19 33	12	10
75 52	17	25	26	20 17	12	11
76 57	18	26	27	21 1	13	12
78 2	19	27	28	21 46	14	13
79 7	20	27	28	22 31	15	13
80 12	21	28	29	23 16	16	14
81 17	22	29	♍	24 0	17	15
82 22	23	♌	1	24 45	17	16
83 28	24	1	2	25 30	18	17
84 33	25	2	3	26 15	19	18
85 38	26	3	3	27 0	20	20
86 44	27	4	4	27 45	20	20
87 49	28	5	5	28 30	21	21
88 55	29	6	6	29 15	22	22
90 0	30	7	7	30 0	23	23

TABLE OF HOUSES FOR LIVERPOOL.

LATITUDE 53° 25' NORTH.

Right Asc. of Meridian.		10th House.	11th House.	12th House.	Ascendant.		2nd House.	3rd House.
DEG.	MIN.	Cancer.	Leo.	Virgo.	Libra.		Libra.	Scorpio.
90	0	0	7	7	0	0	23	23
91	5	1	8	8	0	45	24	24
92	11	2	9	9	1	30	25	25
93	16	3	10	9	2	15	26	26
94	22	4	11	10	3	0	27	27
95	27	5	11	11	3	45	27	28
96	32	6	12	12	4	30	28	29
97	38	7	13	13	5	15	29	29
98	43	8	14	13	6	0	♏	♐
99	48	9	15	14	6	44	1	1
100	53	10	16	15	7	29	2	2
101	58	11	17	16	8	14	2	3
103	3	12	18	17	8	59	3	4
104	8	13	19	18	9	43	4	5
105	13	14	20	18	10	27	5	6
106	17	15	21	19	11	11	5	7
107	22	16	22	20	11	56	6	8
108	26	17	23	21	12	40	7	9
109	31	18	24	22	13	24	8	10
110	35	19	25	23	14	8	9	11
111	39	20	25	23	14	52	10	12
112	43	21	26	24	15	36	10	13
113	47	22	27	25	16	20	11	14
114	51	23	28	26	17	4	12	14
115	54	24	29	27	17	47	13	15
116	57	25	♍	28	18	30	14	16
118	1	26	1	29	19	13	15	18
119	4	27	2	29	19	57	15	1
120	7	28	3	♎	20	40	16	19
121	9	29	4	1	21	23	17	20
122	12	30	5	2	22	6	18	21

TABLE OF HOUSES FOR LIVERPOOL.

LATITUDE 53° 25' NORTH.

Right Asc. of Meridian.	10th House.	11th House.	12th House.	Ascendant.	2nd House.	3rd House.
DEG. MIN.	Leo.	Virgo.	Libra.	Libra.	Scorpio.	Sagitt.
° ′	°	°	°	° ′	°	°
122 12	0	5	2	22 6	18	21
123 14	1	6	2	22 48	19	22
124 16	2	7	3	23 30	19	23
125 18	3	8	4	24 13	20	24
126 20	4	9	5	24 55	21	25
127 22	5	10	6	25 37	22	26
128 24	6	10	6	26 19	22	27
129 25	7	11	7	27 1	23	28
130 26	8	12	8	27 43	24	28
131 27	9	13	9	28 24	25	29
132 28	10	14	9	29 6	26	♑
133 28	11	15	10	29 47	26	1
134 29	12	16	11	0♏28	27	2
135 29	13	17	12	1 9	28	3
136 29	14	18	13	1 50	29	4
137 29	15	18	13	2 31	29	5
138 29	16	19	14	3 12	♐	6
139 28	17	20	15	3 52	1	7
140 28	18	21	16	4 32	2	8
141 27	19	22	17	5 12	3	9
142 26	20	23	17	5 52	3	10
143 25	21	24	18	6 32	4	11
144 23	22	25	19	7 13	5	12
145 22	23	26	20	7 53	6	13
146 20	24	27	21	8 23	7	14
147 18	25	28	21	9 12	8	15
148 16	26	28	22	9 51	8	16
149 14	27	29	23	10 30	9	17
150 11	28	♎	24	11 9	10	18
151 9	29	1	24	11 48	10	19
152 6	30	2	25	12 28	11	20

TABLE OF HOUSES FOR LIVERPOOL.

Latitude 53° 25' North.

Right Asc. of Meridian.		10th House.	11th House.	12th House.	Ascendant.		2nd House.	3rd House.
DEG.	MIN.	Virgo.	Libra.	Libra.	Scorpio.		Sagitt.	Capric.
°	′	°	°	°	°	′	°	°
152	6	0	2	25	12	28	11	20
153	4	1	3	26	13	6	12	21
154	1	2	3	26	13	45	13	21
154	58	3	4	27	14	25	14	22
155	54	4	5	28	15	4	14	23
156	51	5	7	29	15	42	15	24
157	48	6	7	29	16	21	16	25
158	44	7	8	♏	17	0	17	26
159	40	8	9	1	17	39	18	27
160	37	9	10	2	18	17	19	28
161	33	10	10	2	18	55	19	29
162	29	11	11	3	19	34	20	♏
163	25	12	12	4	20	13	21	1
164	20	13	13	4	20	51	22	2
165	16	14	14	5	21	30	23	4
166	12	15	15	6	22	8	24	5
167	7	16	16	6	22	46	24	6
168	3	17	17	7	23	24	25	7
168	58	18	17	8	24	2	26	8
169	54	19	18	9	24	40	27	9
170	49	20	19	9	25	19	28	10
171	44	21	20	10	25	59	29	11
172	39	22	20	11	26	38	29	12
173	35	23	21	11	27	15	♑	13
174	30	24	22	12	27	53	0	14
175	25	25	23	13	28	32	1	15
176	20	26	24	13	29	11	2	16
177	15	27	25	14	29	53	3	17
178	10	28	25	15	0 ♐	35	4	18
179	5	29	26	15	1	11	5	20
180	0	30	27	16	1	47	6	21

TABLE OF HOUSES FOR LIVERPOOL.

Latitude 53° 25' North.

Right Asc. of Meridian.	10th House.	11th House.	12th House.	Ascendant.		2nd House.	3rd House.
DEG. MIN.	Libra.	Libra.	Scorpio.	Sagittary.		Capric.	Aquar.
180 0	0	27	16	1	47	6	21
180 55	1	28	17	2	33	7	22
181 50	2	29	18	3	11	8	23
182 45	3	♏	18	3	49	9	24
183 40	4	0	19	4	28	10	25
184 35	5	1	20	5	7	10	26
185 30	6	2	20	5	47	11	28
186 25	7	3	21	6	27	12	29
187 21	8	3	22	7	6	12	♓
188 16	9	4	22	7	46	14	1
189 11	10	5	23	8	26	15	2
190 6	11	6	24	9	7	16	3
191 2	12	7	25	9	48	17	5
191 57	13	7	25	10	29	18	6
192 53	14	8	26	11	11	19	7
193 48	15	9	27	11	53	20	8
194 44	16	10	27	12	35	21	10
195 40	17	11	28	13	17	22	10
196 35	18	11	29	14	0	23	12
197 31	19	12	29	14	43	24	13
198 27	20	13	♐	15	27	25	14
199 23	21	14	1	16	11	26	15
200 20	22	15	2	16	54	27	17
201 16	23	15	2	17	38	29	18
202 12	24	16	3	18	25	♒	19
203 9	25	17	4	19	10	1	20
204 6	26	18	5	19	57	2	22
205 2	27	19	6	20	43	3	23
205 59	28	20	6	21	29	4	24
206 57	29	21	7	22	16	6	26
207 54	30	21	8	23	4	7	27

TABLE OF HOUSES FOR LIVERPOOL.

Latitude 53° 25′ North.

Right Asc. of Meridian.	10th House.	11th House.	12th House.	Ascendant.	2nd House.	3rd House.
DEG. MIN.	Scorpio.	Scorpio.	Sagitt.	Sagittary.	Aquar.	Pisces.
207 54	0	21	8	23 4	7	27
208 51	1	22	9	23 53	9	29
209 49	2	23	9	24 42	10	♈
210 46	3	24	10	25 31	11	1
211 44	4	25	11	26 21	13	3
212 42	5	26	12	27 13	14	4
213 40	6	26	13	28 5	16	6
214 38	7	27	13	28 58	17	7
215 37	8	28	14	29 51	19	8
216 36	9	29	15	0♑45	20	9
217 34	10	♐	16	1 40	21	11
218 33	11	1	16	2 36	23	12
219 33	12	1	17	3 32	24	13
220 32	13	2	18	4 30	26	15
221 31	14	3	19	5 28	28	16
222 31	15	4	20	6 28	29	18
223 31	16	5	21	7 28	♓	19
224 31	17	6	22	8 30	2	20
225 31	18	7	23	9 33	4	21
226 32	19	7	23	10 38	6	23
227 32	20	8	24	11 44	8	24
228 33	21	9	25	12 52	9	25
229 34	22	10	26	14 0	11	27
230 35	23	11	27	15 10	13	28
231 36	24	12	28	16 21	15	29
232 38	25	13	29	17 37	17	♉
233 40	26	14	♑	18 53	19	2
234 41	27	15	1	20 10	20	3
235 43	28	15	2	21 28	22	4
236 46	29	16	3	22 50	24	6
237 48	30	17	4	24 13	26	7

TABLE OF HOUSES FOR LIVERPOOL.

LATITUDE 53° 25′ NORTH.

Right Asc. of Meridian.		10th House.	11th House.	12th House.	Ascendant.		2nd House.	3rd House.
DEG.	MIN.	Sagitt.	Sagitt.	Capric.	Capricorn.		Pisces.	Taurus.
°	′	°	°	°	°	′	°	°
237	48	0	17	4	24	13	26	7
238	51	1	18	5	25	39	28	8
239	53	2	19	6	27	9	29	10
240	56	3	20	7	28	40	♈	11
241	59	4	21	7	0♒11		2	12
243	3	5	22	9	1	48	4	13
244	6	6	23	9	3	28	6	14
245	9	7	24	11	5	9	9	16
246	13	8	25	12	6	55	11	17
247	17	9	26	13	8	44	13	18
248	21	10	27	14	10	36	15	20
249	25	11	28	15	12	31	17	21
250	29	12	29	16	14	30	19	22
251	34	13	♑	17	16	31	21	24
252	38	14	1	19	18	39	23	25
253	43	15	2	20	20	49	25	26
254	47	16	3	21	23	2	27	27
255	52	17	4	22	25	20	28	28
256	57	18	5	23	27	41	♉	29
258	2	19	6	25	0♓	7	2	♊
259	7	20	7	26	2	36	3	2
260	12	21	8	27	5	9	5	3
261	17	22	9	29	7	44	7	4
262	22	23	10	♒	10	22	8	5
263	28	24	11	1	13	4	10	6
264	33	25	12	3	15	51	12	7
265	38	26	13	4	18	37	14	8
266	44	27	14	5	21	25	15	9
267	49	28	15	7	24	14	17	10
268	55	29	16	8	27	7	19	11
270	0	30	17	10	30	0	20	13

TABLE OF HOUSES FOR LIVERPOOL.

Latitude 53° 25' North.

Right Asc. of Meridian.		10th House.	11th House.	12th House.	Ascendant.		2nd House.	3rd House.
		Capric.	*Capric.*	*Aquar.*	*Aries.*		*Taurus.*	*Gemini.*
DEG.	MIN.							
270	0	0	17	10	0	0	20	13
271	5	1	18	11	2	53	21	14
272	11	2	19	13	5	46	23	15
273	16	3	20	15	8	35	25	16
274	22	4	21	16	11	23	26	17
275	27	5	23	18	14	9	27	18
276	32	6	24	20	16	56	29	19
277	38	7	25	21	19	38	♊	20
278	43	8	26	23	22	16	1	21
279	48	9	27	24	24	51	2	22
280	53	10	28	26	27	24	4	23
281	58	11	♒	28	29	53	5	24
283	3	12	1	29	2 ♉ 19		7	25
284	8	13	2	♓	4	40	8	26
285	13	14	3	2	6	58	9	27
286	17	15	4	4	9	11	10	28
287	22	16	5	6	11	21	11	29
288	26	17	7	8	13	29	12	♋
289	31	18	8	10	15	30	14	1
290	35	19	9	12	17	29	15	2
291	39	20	10	14	19	24	16	3
292	43	21	12	16	21	16	16	4
293	47	22	13	28	23	5	18	5
294	51	23	14	20	24	51	19	6
295	54	24	15	22	26	32	20	7
296	57	25	17	24	28	12	21	8
298	1	26	18	26	29	49	22	9
299	4	27	19	28	1 ♊ 20		23	10
300	7	28	20	♈	2	51	25	11
301	9	29	21	1	4	21	26	12
302	12	30	23	3	5	47	26	13

TABLE OF HOUSES FOR LIVERPOOL.

Latitude 53° 25' North.

Right Asc. of Meridian.	10th House.	11th House.	12th House.	Ascendant.	2nd House.	3rd House.
DEG. MIN.	Aquar.	Aquar.	Aries.	Gemini.	Gemini.	Cancer.
302 12	0	23	3	5 47	26	13
303 14	1	24	5	7 10	28	14
304 16	2	25	7	8 32	28	14
305 18	3	27	9	9 50	29	15
306 20	4	28	11	11 7	♋	16
307 22	5	29	13	12 23	1	17
308 24	6	♓	15	13 39	2	18
309 25	7	2	17	14 50	3	19
310 26	8	3	18	16 0	4	20
311 27	9	4	20	17 8	5	21
312 28	10	6	22	18 16	6	22
313 28	11	7	24	19 22	7	22
314 29	12	9	26	20 27	7	23
315 29	13	10	27	21 30	8	24
316 29	14	11	29	22 32	9	25
317 29	15	12	♉	23 32	10	26
318 29	16	14	2	24 32	11	27
319 28	17	15	4	25 30	12	27
320 27	18	17	6	26 28	12	28
321 27	19	18	7	27 24	13	29
322 26	20	19	9	28 20	14	♌
323 25	21	21	10	29 15	15	1
324 23	22	22	11	0♋ 9	16	2
325 22	23	23	13	1 2	16	3
326 20	24	25	15	1 55	17	4
327 18	25	26	16	2 47	18	4
328 16	26	28	17	3 39	19	5
329 14	27	29	19	4 29	20	6
330 11	28	♈	21	5 18	21	7
331 9	29	1	21	6 7	21	8
332 6	30	3	23	6 56	22	9

TABLE OF HOUSES FOR LIVERPOOL.

Latitude 53° 25' North.

Right Asc. of Meridian.	10th House.	11th House.	12th House.	Ascendant.	2nd House.	3rd House.
DEG. MIN.	*Pisces.*	*Aries.*	*Taurus.*	*Cancer.*	*Cancer.*	*Leo.*
° ′	°	°	°	° ′	°	°
332 6	0	3	23	6 56	22	9
333 4	1	4	24	7 44	23	10
334 1	2	5	♊25	8 31	23	10
334 58	3	7	26	9 17	24	11
335 55	4	8	27	10 3	25	12
336 51	5	9	29	10 50	26	13
337 48	6	10	♊	11 35	26	13
338 44	7	12	1	12 22	27	14
339 40	8	13	2	13 6	28	15
340 37	9	14	3	13 49	29	16
341 38	10	16	4	14 33	29	17
342 29	11	17	5	15 17	♌	18
343 25	12	18	7	16 0	1	18
344 20	13	20	8	16 43	2	19
345 16	14	21	9	17 25	3	20
346 12	15	22	10	18 7	4	21
347 7	16	23	11	18 49	4	22
348 3	17	24	12	19 31	5	23
348 58	18	26	13	20 12	6	24
349 54	19	27	14	20 53	6	24
350 49	20	28	15	21 34	7	25
351 44	21	29	16	22 14	8	26
352 39	22	♉	17	22 52	8	27
353 35	23	1	18	23 33	9	27
354 30	24	2	19	24 13	10	28
355 25	25	4	20	24 53	11	29
356 20	26	5	21	25 32	11	♍
357 15	27	6	22	26 11	12	1
358 10	28	7	23	26 49	13	2
359 5	29	8	24	27 27	13	2
360 0	30	10	24	28 13	14	3

ABOUT THE AUTHORS

William Lilly was born in 1602 in Diseworth, Leicestershire, where his family were long-established yeomen. He received a basic classical education at the school of Ashby-de-la-Zouch, but maked a point of saying that his master never taught logic.

He began to dabble in astrology, reading all the books on the subject he could fall in with, and occasionally trying his hand at unravelling mysteries by means of his art. The years 1642 and 1643 were devoted to a careful revision of all his previous reading, and in particular, having lighted on Valentine Naibod's *Commentary* on Alcabitius, he "seriously studied him and found him to be the profoundest author he ever met with". And, having thereupon "made some essays", he "found encouragement to proceed further, and ultimately framed to himself that method which he ever afterwards followed."

Lilly's most comprehensive book was published in 1647 and was entitled *Christian Astrology*. It is so large that it came in three separate volumes in modern times, and it remains popular even today and has never gone totally out-of-print. It is considered one of the classic texts for the study of traditional astrology from the Middle Ages, in particular horary astrology, which is mainly concerned with predicting future events or investigating unknown elements of current affairs, based on an astrological chart cast for the time a particular question is asked of the astrologer.

Lilly studied thousands of horary charts, most of the time successfully giving correct answers for a wide range of questions from the location of missing fishes to the outcome of battles. Worked examples of horary charts are found in Volume 2 of *Christian Astrology*.

He then began to issue his prophetical almanacs and other works, which met with serious attention from some of the most prominent members of the Long Parliament. Lilly wrote a preface to Sir Christopher Heydons *An Astrological Discourse with Mathematical Demonstrations*, a defence of astrology written about 1608 which was first published posthumously, largely at the expense of Elias Ashmole.

After the Restoration he very quickly fell into disrepute. His sympathy with the parliament, which his predictions had generally shown, was not calculated to bring him into royal favour. He died in 1681. In 2003 a commemorative plaque was placed next to the disused Aldwych tube station on the Strand. Lilly lived close to this spot.

Richard James Morrison (15 June 1795 — 5 April 1874) was an English astrologer, commonly known by his pseudonym **Zadkiel**. Morrison served in the Royal Navy, but resigned with the rank of lieutenant in 1829. He then devoted himself to the study of astrology, and in 1831 issued *The Herald of Astrology*, subsequently known as *Zadkiel's Almanac*.

In this annual pamphlet Morrison, over the signature Zadkiel Tao-Sze, published predictions of the chief events of the coming year. In 1863 Morrison brought a libel action against Admiral Sir Edward Beicher, who had accused him of obtaining money by charlatanism in the form of crystal-gazing. He was awarded twenty shillings damages, but was deprived of his costs. Morrison died on 5 April 1874.

www.ingramcontent.com/pod-product-compliance
Lightning Source LLC
Chambersburg PA
CBHW021129230426
43667CB00005B/76